A Companion to *The Doctrine of the Hert*

'This book is a careful and ambitious attempt to cover the whole gamut of Latin and vernacular traditions of *The Doctrine of the Hert*. It deserves considerable credit as a pioneering work in its field which also manages to be a compendium of everything one needs to know about this text.' **Nicholas Watson, Harvard University**

The Doctrine of the Hert is the fifteenth-century English translation of *De doctrina cordis*, a thirteenth-century Latin treatise addressed to members of religious orders. The geographical and chronological reach of *De doctrina cordis*, and the popularity of its different vernacular versions, do much to enrich our understanding of the history and literature of spirituality and the devotional life of religious women.

This book consists of ten essays from an international group of scholars of medieval religion discussing the Middle English text alongside its Latin forebear and other European vernacular translations. University of Exeter Press's recently published critical edition of the Middle English version provides much-needed access to a text that has until lately largely escaped the attention of scholars. This *Companion* will illuminate the *Doctrine*'s significance, establish its place in the context of European vernacular theology, and serve as a foundation for future scholarship.

Denis Renevey is Chair of Medieval English Literature and Language at the University of Lausanne, Switzerland. He has published widely in the field of vernacular theology and female religious writings.

Christiania Whitehead is Associate Professor in Medieval English Literature at the University of Warwick. Her fields of interest lie in medieval allegory and female spirituality.

EXETER MEDIEVAL TEXTS AND STUDIES

Series Editors: Vincent Gillespie and Richard Dance

Founded by M. J. Swanton
and later co-edited by Marion Glasscoe

A Companion to *The Doctrine of the Hert*

The Middle English Translation and its Latin and European Contexts

edited by
Denis Renevey
and
Christiania Whitehead

UNIVERSITY
of
EXETER
PRESS

First published in 2010 by
University of Exeter Press
Reed Hall, Streatham Drive
Exeter EX4 4QR
UK
www.exeterpress.co.uk

British Library Cataloguing in Publication Data
A catalogue record for this book is available from the British Library.

ISBN 978 0 85989 821 8

Typeset in Adobe Garamond 11/13
by Carnegie Book Production, Lancaster

Printed in Great Britain
by Short Run Press Ltd, Exeter

Contents

Part III: European Vernacular Translations

Acknowledgements

We would like to thank Liz Herbert McAvoy, the organizer of the *Rhetoric of the Anchorhold* conference (Gregynog Hall, Newtown, Powys, July 2005), where several of these essays were initially presented. We would also like to mention the International Anchoritic Society, under whose aegis the conference took place, and the Centre for Research into Gender in Culture and Society, University of Wales, Swansea, who lent it their support.

Additionally, we would like to acknowledge the kindness of a number of individuals: Sonia Petisco Martínez (University de Las Palmas de Gran Canaria), for her detective work in sourcing and copying the early printed edition of the Spanish translation of *De doctrina cordis*: *Del enseñamiento del coraçon* (Salamanca, 1498); Marleen Cré (University of Antwerp), whose linguistic skills aided us in finding our way through the Belgian scholarship on *De doctrina*, and the staff of the Bodleian Library, Oxford, for their help in creating an electronic facsimile of the Naples, 1607 edition of *De doctrina*.

We would like to thank Anna Henderson, the commissioning editor, and Vincent Gillespie and Richard Dance, the series editors, at University of Exeter Press, for their support and guidance throughout this project. However, the last word should be reserved for our contributors. No editors could have had better ones, and we are indebted to them, both for the excellence of their research and for the good humour, patience and courtesy with which they have helped us to bring this project to fruition.

Notes on Editors and Contributors

Marleen Cré teaches at the Vrije Universiteit Brussel and is an associated researcher at the Ruusbroecgenootschap, University of Antwerp. She published *Vernacular Mysticism in the Chapterhouse: A Study of London, British Library, MS Additional 37790* in 2006. She has also published various articles on Julian of Norwich's Short Text, *A Vision Showed to a Devout Woman*, as well as on the translations into Middle English of John Ruusbroec's *Spiritual Espousals* and *Sparkling Stone*, and Marguerite Porete's *Mirror of Simple Souls*. She is currently working on the fifteenth-century reception of Walter Hilton's shorter works, and on the writings of Benet Canfield, Augustine Baker and Gertrude More.

Vincent Gillespie is J.R.R. Tolkien Professor of English Literature and Language at the University of Oxford, and a Fellow of Lady Margaret Hall. He works on catechetical, devotional and contemplative texts produced in England in the Middle Ages. He is also interested in medieval literary theory and the psychology of literary response. His current work examines the 'reformist orthodoxy' of the generations after Arundel's 1409 decrees.

Catherine Innes-Parker is Professor in the Department of English at the University of Prince Edward Island. Her research interests lie in vernacular theology in medieval England. Her current research includes the late-medieval vernacular translations of Bonaventure's *Lignum vitae*. She is also completing an edition and translation of the thirteenth-century *Wooing Group*.

Anthony John Lappin is Senior Lecturer in the School of Languages, Linguistics and Cultures at the University of Manchester, and has a particular interest in textual editing and Iberian ecclesiastical and religious history of the Middle Ages and the early modern period. He has published widely on such areas as Renaissance Portuguese, Hispano-Latin hagiography and Spanish Golden Age Drama. His most recent publication is a study of a thirteenth-century poet, *Gonzalo de Berceo: The Poet and his verses* (2008).

Anne Mouron is Director of Studies for English at St. Bede's Hall, a Catholic independent college in Oxford. Her interest focuses on late medieval religious texts in Latin and in the vernacular. She has published articles on Middle English devotional texts and is preparing an edition of *The Manere of Good*

Lyvyng, a unique rendition of the long pseudo-Bernardine text *De modo bene vivendi ad sororem*. She is also co-editor, with Christiania Whitehead and Denis Renevey, of the Middle English edition *The Doctrine of the Hert: A Critical Edition with Introduction and Commentary* (Exeter, 2010).

Nigel F. Palmer has held the position of Professor of German Medieval and Linguistic Studies at the University of Oxford and Fellow of St Edmund Hall, Oxford, since 1992, and is a Fellow of the British Academy. In 2007 he was awarded the Humboldt-Forschungspreis of the Alexander von Humboldt Foundation. His publications include *Zisterzienser und ihre Bücher* (1998) and *Bibelübersetzung und Heilsgeschichte. Studien zur Freiburger Perikopenhandschrift von 1462 und zu den deutschsprachigen Lektionaren des 15. Jahrhunderts* (2007).

Denis Renevey is Professor of Medieval Language and Literature in the Department of English at the University of Lausanne, Switzerland. He works in the field of vernacular theology. He has recently co-edited the Middle English edition *The Doctrine of the Hert: A Critical Edition with Introduction and Commentary* with Christiania Whitehead and Anne Mouron (Exeter 2010), and *Medieval Texts in Context* with Graham Caie (2008). His forthcoming publications include a chapter in the *Cambridge Companion to Medieval English Mysticism*, edited by Vincent Gillespie and Samuel Fanous.

Karl-Heinz Steinmetz is Assistant Professor of Theology of Spirituality at the Catholic Faculty of the University of Vienna, Austria. He has published on the theology of contemplation in the *Cloud of Unknowing* and on various medieval and contemporary devotional texts. He is currently working on late medieval texts, altar-pieces and music, especially in the context of the fifteenth-century Vienna School of devotional theology.

Annie Sutherland is a fellow in Old and Middle English at Somerville College, Oxford. She has recently published articles on *The Chastising of God's Children*, *The Cloud of Unknowing*, Julian of Norwich and Richard Rolle. As well as continuing to work and publish on Middle English mystical texts, she is researching and writing a book on vernacular translations of the Psalms in the English Middle Ages.

Christiania Whitehead is Associate Professor (Reader) in the Department of English and Comparative Literature, University of Warwick. She has published in the fields of medieval allegory, medieval translation and religious writing for women in Latin and the vernacular, and has recently completed essays on Chaucer and the Bible, and on the function of Julian of Norwich in late-twentieth-century spirituality. She is co-editor of the Middle English edition *The Doctrine of the Hert: A Critical Edition with Introduction and Commentary* (Exeter, 2010).

Abbreviations

CCC	*Cîteaux: Commentarii Cistercienses*
CCCM	*Corpus christianorum, Continuatio mediaevalis*
CCSL	*Corpus christianorum, Series latina*
CSS	Cistercian Studies Series
De doctrina	*De doctrina cordis.* Gerardus Leodiensis, *Speculum concionatorum ad illustrandum pectora auditorum, in septem libros distributum* (Naples, 1607). Oxford, Bodleian Library, 8° L 12 Th. BS

[This Naples 1607 edition is practically identical to the first printed edition of Paris, 1506 (Oxford, Bodleian Library, Vet. E1.f.1) which differs only in some divisions and chapter headings from one of the earliest manuscripts of *De doctrina*: Oxford, Bodleian Library, MS Lat. th. f. 6, s. xiii (last third).]

Candon, *Doctrine*	Sister M.P. Candon (ed.), '*The Doctrine of the Hert*, Edited from the Manuscripts with Introduction and Notes' (unpublished doctoral dissertation, Fordham University, 1963)
Doctrine of the Hert	C. Whitehead, D. Renevey and A. Mouron (eds), *The Doctrine of the Hert: A Critical Edition with Introduction and Commentary* (Exeter, 2010)
EETS	Early English Text Society
Hendrix, *Hugo I*	G. Hendrix, *Hugo de Sancto Caro's traktaat De doctrina cordis. Vol. 1: Handschriften, receptie, tekstgeschiedenis en authenticiteitskritiek*, Documenta Libraria 16/1 (Louvain, 1995)
Hendrix, *Hugo II*	G. Hendrix, *Hugo De Sancto Caro's traktaat De doctrina cordis. Vol. 2: Pragmatische editie van De bouc van der leeringhe van der herten naar handschrift Wenen, ÖNB, 15231*, Documenta Libraria 16/2 (Louvain, 1995)
PL	*Patrologia latina*, ed. J.-P. Migne, 221 vols (Paris, 1842–80)
OGE	*Ons geestelijk erf*
RTAM	*Recherches de théologie ancienne et médiévale*

Introduction

Denis Renevey and Christiania Whitehead

Although *De doctrina cordis* may not be the sole textual witness to a pan-European devotional phenomenon in late medieval Europe, its wide dissemination, in Latin and several vernacular languages, invites a serious and sustained study of the text and its contribution to medieval religious culture. This volume, which accompanies the edition of the Middle English version of *De doctrina*, aims to introduce readers to the Middle English version at the same time as providing, through the history of the dissemination of its different versions in Latin and vernacular languages, a broader view of the devotional landscape of late medieval Europe. *A Companion to The Doctrine of the Hert*'s aims are both modest and groundbreaking. They are modest in the sense that many of the contributions are a first foray into the complexities of the translation, compilation, dissemination and reading practices of this text in several of its vernacular versions. Apart from the Middle English and the Dutch versions, which have received a little attention recently, most of the other vernacular versions have been almost completely neglected, and the chapters offered in this book all show an awareness of the further research which the textual transmission of this text, in all its different garbs, still awaits. On the other hand, the *Companion* breaks new ground in the pan-European breadth of its perspective on *De doctrina*, and in the range of specializations that it mobilizes to achieve this breadth.

De doctrina cordis: text and context

The Latin *De doctrina cordis* circulated in more than 200 manuscripts in different formats, defined mainly according to the nature of the two specific prologues which introduce the text. The so-called IP- (long) and HV- (short) versions were named in this way by Guido Hendrix in relation to a detail in the content of the two prologues that demonstrates their sensitivity to their targeted audiences; the IP- version contains the phrase 'ignaros predicatores' (hence IP), whereas the HV- version replaces this criticism with a sentence beginning 'In hoc verbo' (hence HV), which places emphasis on the responsibility of the preacher to offer spiritual food to those who listen.[1] The number of Latin versions attests to the complexity of the dissemination of the content of this 'en mouvance' text, perhaps from the inception of its composition, and indicates its multi-purpose usage in its very early days.[2] The picture is further complicated by the number of different translated versions that appear in the vernaculars. Not only are there major differences in translation practices between, for example, the Dutch and the French versions of *De doctrina*, but some of the versions in the same vernacular seem to obey drastically opposed textual strategies. In the light of the paucity of evidence that we have (so far) for the readership of the various versions of the treatise, an assessment of the role played by the audience of these translations yields at best little, at worst no, information whatsoever.

If internal evidence filters only limited information about the readership of the various versions, there is even less to gather in the text about its author and, in the vernacular versions, about their translators or compilers.[3] The question of authorship addressed in Palmer's essay in this volume is likely to stir further discussions and possible disagreements. As new evidence regarding the identity of the author is unlikely to come out in the foreseeable future, this issue may remain unresolved, and the Dominican Hugh of St Cher and the Cistercian Gerard of Liège, the former favoured as author by Guido Hendrix, the latter by Palmer (and formerly Wilmart), may remain in competition as potential candidates for quite some time. What both proposals render implicit, however, is the fact that the text was

---

1 G. Hendrix, *Hugo de Sancto Caro's traktaat De doctrina cordis. Vol. 1: Handschriften, receptie, tekstgeschiedenis en authenticiteitskritiek*, Documenta Libraria 16/1 (Louvain, 1995), p. 149. Hereafter, Hendrix, *Hugo I*. For further information on this point, see the essay by Marleen Cré in this volume, pp. 209–11.

2 Ibid., pp. 177–89, discussed in further detail by Cré in this volume, pp. 208–13.

3 For a discussion of the translator of the Middle English text as a 'compiler', see Mouron's essay in this volume, pp. 105–6. See also D. Renevey and C. Whitehead '"Opyn þin hert as a boke": Translation Practice and Manuscript Circulation in *The Doctrine of the Hert*', in J. Jenkins and O. Bertrand (eds), *The Medieval Translator 10* (Turnhout, 2007), pp. 125–48.

written in Liège or in its environs sometime in the mid thirteenth century, in a place where, and at a time when, the *mulieres religiosae* phenomenon was reaching a peak and providing the religious authorities with food for thought. Another exceptional phenomenon in the history of the church took place at around the time and place of composition of *De doctrina*: the feast of Corpus Christi was first celebrated by Hugh of St Cher in the church of St Martin in Liège in 1251, several years after Juliana of Cornillon, followed by her disciple Eve of St Martin, had fought for its establishment.[4]

However tempting and convincing a contextualization of the treatise as an offshoot of eucharistic preoccupations with, and interests in, the feast of Corpus Christi may be, it is nevertheless also necessary to situate *De doctrina* and its vernacular versions within the larger perspective of Cistercian affective theology, thirteenth-century scholasticism and ongoing penitential and pastoral concerns. In this respect, *De doctrina* bears many resemblances to *Ancrene Wisse*, the religious treatise written after 1215 by a Dominican author to the attention of an initial audience of three anchoresses.[5] Rather than highlighting the anchoritic aspects of the treatise, recent scholarship places more emphasis on *Ancrene Wisse*'s penitential character, the impact of Parisian scholastic practice upon the structure of the work, and the reference to a wider audience made up of religious and lay people of both genders, for whom certain parts of the treatise are specifically designed. A consideration of its generic variety, specifically its generic resemblance to ascetic treatises, devotional prose, penitential writings, sermons and manuals of consolation and of the spiritual life, shows the range of possible influences upon the text and the uses to which it has been put.[6] Similarly,

4 For a groundbreaking account of the *mulieres religiosae* phenomenon in the Lower Countries, with special reference to the lives of anchoresses, see A.B. Mulder-Bakker, *Lives of the Anchoresses: The Rise of the Urban Recluse in Medieval Europe*, tr. M. Heerspink Scholz (Philadelphia, 2005). Much of this part of the introduction summarizes some of the points offered by Mulder-Bakker.

5 For a comparative study of the two texts, see D. Renevey, 'Figuring Household Space in *Ancrene Wisse* and *The Doctrine of the Hert*', in D. Spurr and C. Tschichold (eds), SPELL 17 (Tübingen, 2005), pp. 69–84.

6 See B. Millett, 'The Genre of *Ancrene Wisse*', in Y. Wada (ed.), *A Companion to the Ancrene Wisse* (Cambridge, 2003), pp. 29–44 (29); in the same volume, see also the chapter by A.S.G. Edwards, 'The Middle English Manuscripts and Early Readers of *Ancrene Wisse*', pp. 103–12; B. Millett, 'General Introduction', in *Ancrene Wisse: A Corrected Edition of the Text in Cambridge, Corpus Christi College, MS 402, with Variants from Other Manuscripts*, ed. by B. Millett, vol. 2, EETS 326 (2006), pp. ix–lvii; C. Gunn, *Ancrene Wisse: From Pastoral Literature to Vernacular Spirituality*, Religion and Culture in the Middle Ages (Cardiff, 2008).

as Whitehead points out in her chapter, the manuscript context of *De doctrina* reveals a close association with preaching handbooks and sermon series; it shows the text to have been used as a guide for novices, and to have served as a catechetical tool in its reduced format. In other manuscript contexts scribes also foreground its meditative and contemplative aspects. Whitehead's chapter convincingly suggests that the eclectic uses to which *De doctrina* was put are understood best if one considers it structurally as a 'mélange of small text units' whose assemblage can vary according to its specific function.[7] This evidence extends the point made by Hendrix, who shows Leiden, Bibliotheek der Rijksuniversiteit, MS BPL 2579 – which he claims to have autograph elements – to offer either the IP- or HV- prologue options, thus suggesting a variety of uses for the original Latin text.[8] The concept of 'mouvance' which has been used convincingly in relation to *Ancrene Wisse*, applies to *De doctrina* as well and is an integral part of the original version. The translations and adaptations of the text into several vernaculars represent only the most visible part of the 'mouvance' of this treatise.

Structurally, *De doctrina* is divided into seven books that each treat a different action of the heart – *praeparatio*, *custodia*, *apertio*, *stabilitas*, *datio*, *elevatio* and *scissio* – in association with one of the gifts of the Holy Spirit.[9] Although more unified in its overall reach than *Ancrene Wisse*, which is concerned with the outer as well as the inner aspects of the spiritual life,

---

7 See in this volume, C. Whitehead, '*De doctrina cordis*: catechesis or contemplation?', p. 70.

8 For a summary of Hendrix's view, see Cré's chapter, pp. 210–13.

9 G. Hendrix, *Hugo De Sancto Caro's traktaat De doctrina cordis. Vol. 2: Pragmatische editie van De bouc van der leeringhe van der herten naar handschrift Wenen, ÖNB, 15231*, Documenta Libraria 16/2 (Louvain, 1995), p. vii. Hereafter, Hendrix, *Hugo II*. The book titles in the Middle English version are: '*Capitulum primum*. How and in what wise a mynche shuld make redy here hert to God be þe yifte of drede. *Capitulum secundum*. How and in what wise a mynche shuld kepe here hert to God be the yifte of pite. *Capitulum tercium*. How and in what wise a mynche shuld opyn here hert to God be þe yifte of kunnynge. *Capitulum quartum*. How and in what wise a mynche shuld stable here hert to God be þe yifte of strengthe. *Capitulum quintum*. How and in what wise a mynche shuld ȝyve here hert to God bi þe yifte of counseile. *Capitulum sextum*. How and in what wise a mynche shuld lefte up here hert to God be þe yifte of undirstondyng. *Capitulum septimum*. How and in what wise a mynche shulde cutte here herte be the yifte of wisdom.' C. Whitehead, D. Renevey and A. Mouron (eds), *The Doctrine of the Hert: A Critical Edition with Introduction and Commentary* (Exeter, 2010), p. 4, ll. 41–54. Hereafter cited as *Doctrine of the Hert*.

each book addresses different levels of spiritual competence, suggesting that it could be read non-sequentially. While addressing a primary audience of male and female novices, *De doctrina*, like *Ancrene Wisse*, aims to reach beyond the convent: some of its parts respond to new demands which were formulated officially on the occasion of the 1215 Fourth Lateran Council. In fact, a reading of the treatise in the light of confessional and eucharistic preparation, for the attention of a mixed audience of female and male novices as well as putative beguines and anchoresses, at a time when enthusiasm for the feast of Corpus Christi was high, gives considerable coherence to both the structural pattern and content of the treatise. That a translation of the treatise in French exists perhaps as early as the thirteenth century, as attested by Oxford, Bodleian Library, MS Holkham Misc. 42, with some additions to the Latin indicating a knowledge of courtly hunting practices, speaks in favour of a possible extra-monastic audience soon after the composition of the treatise.[10] Even if the strong association of *De doctrina* with a monastic milieu is undeniable, nonetheless, several of the concerns expressed by the text have a universal appeal about which the author was certainly aware. The penitential material preparing the believer for confession in the first book would have appealed to both monastic and lay audiences. In addition, the moderately ambitious spiritual claims made in the final book of the treatise are sufficiently toned down to meet the needs of a wide range of individuals. In the Middle English version, which addresses an audience of nuns, the deliberate omission of some biblical quotations makes the translation even more accessible than its Latin original. More importantly, the milieu in which the Latin text was written and circulated, that is, the Liège area in the middle of the thirteenth century, was characterized by the rise of what Mulder-Bakker calls 'common' theology: a theology based on lived experience, but not devoid of sophisticated ideas which circulated orally between anchoresses, beguines and their spiritual male guardians. According to Mulder-Bakker, Hugh of St Cher and Gerard of Liège OP were among the scholastic theologians most favourable towards the common theology spread by anchoresses and beguines in the Liège area. Even if the author of *De doctrina* is neither Hugh nor Gerard OP, nonetheless, his knowledge of Hugh of St Cher's *Postillae* clearly demonstrates Hugh's impact upon the composition of the treatise. Moreover, that impact was not limited to his scholastic input, as reflected by the numerous borrowings of his *Postillae*, but also to his groundbreaking role in supporting the *mulieres*

10 See in this volume A.E. Mouron, 'The French Translations of *De doctrina cordis*', pp. 194–6.

religiosae movement in the Lower Countries, and in giving support to the common theology which they invented.[11] Incarnational ideas and devotions were central to Juliana of Cornillon's theology. The intellectual exchanges which such men as Hugh of St Cher, Gerard of Liège, James of Vitry and Thomas of Cantimpré, to mention just a few, shared with the Brabant-Liège women were, according to Mulder-Bakker, an incentive for the popularization of their ideas in the form of sermons and devotional tracts.[12] *De doctrina* reflects both the popularizing effect generated by the cross-fertilization of ideas between the reformers and the *mulieres religiosae*, and the incarnational dimension which they promulgated as part of their common theology.

Mulder-Bakker and Wogan-Browne argue for the increased importance of the household in medieval society at large from the eleventh century on, and for the ordering of many aspects of society, including religion, upon the model of the household.[13] Monastic houses, especially women's communities, resembled the characteristics of secular households in their architectural space and in the nature of their social structures. As Gillespie shows astutely in his chapter in this volume, and Renevey elsewhere, *De doctrina* constructs its pastoral theology via a series of linked images deploying the imaginary space of the household.[14] The reader's sense of interiority is constructed on the premise of an analogy with a household and its manifold activities, both within its own secluded space, and in relation to other exterior spaces. Household preparations for the welcoming of a noble guest provide the allegorical framework for much of book 1, which makes up half the length of the Latin and Middle English treatises. A central and riveting feature of this framework is the attention paid to culinary activities within the spacious kitchen of *De doctrina*'s figurative household. The negotiation of the exchange with Christ which the reader

11 Mulder-Bakker, *Lives of the Anchoresses*, pp. 16, 88–9.

12 Ibid., p. 101. Mulder-Bakker, following Bataillon and Bériou, attributes *De doctrina* to Gerard of Liège; see ibid., n. 47, p. 238.

13 A.B. Mulder-Bakker and J. Wogan-Browne, 'Introduction Part II: Medieval Households', in A.B. Mulder-Bakker and J. Wogan-Browne (eds), *Household, Women, and Christianities in Late Antiquity and the Middle Ages*, Medieval Women: Texts and Contexts 14 (Turnhout 2005), pp. 125–31; esp. p. 127.

14 V. Gillespie, 'Meat, Metaphor and Mysticism: Cooking the Books in *The Doctrine of the Hert*', pp. 131–58; D. Renevey, 'Household Chores in *The Doctrine of the Hert*: Affective Spirituality and Subjectivity', in C. Bęattie, A. Maslakovic and S. Rees Jones (eds), *The Medieval Household in Christian Europe c.850–c.1550: Managing Power, Wealth, and the Body* (Turnhout, 2003), pp. 167–87.

is invited to initiate is based on the former's greatest gift: the body and blood of Christ, offered symbolically to the disciples at the Last Supper and raised to sacramental status in the form of the eucharist. It is *this* gift, rather than the gift of the body of Christ on the cross, which marks *De doctrina* and gives it a somewhat bizarre tinge. For indeed, the serious reference to Christ's consumption of the reader's heart in this context is possible only if considered as a reflex action based upon the symbolically cannibalistic action of the consumption of the body and blood of Christ in the eucharist. The Middle English *Doctrine of the Hert*'s reverence for the sacrament of the eucharist is clearly indicated:

> Also, he hath yiven his blissid body in the sacrament of þe aughter for oure meete, as for þe most worthiest yifte þat ever he yaf to mankynde, as he seith himself: *Caro mea vere est cibus: et sanguis meus, vere est potus.* 'My flessh' he seith, 'is very gostly mete, and my blode is very gostly drynke.' This is an excellent shewyng of love to mankynde: it passith al his oþer yiftes. Thus shalt þou considere þe excellent benefices of the sacrament of the aughter.[15]

The complex articulation of the reader's relationship with Christ through cooking imagery follows consideration of the sacrament of the eucharist. It is interesting to note the attention given to this sacrament in *De doctrina* in the light of the moves to instigate the feast of Corpus Christi in Liège by Juliana of Cornillon, Eve of St Martin and Hugh of St Cher.[16] The times were ripe for the daring use of images of ingestion and consumption, and for the symbolic offer of the believer's cooked heart as a gesture of spiritual love.[17] It is within this daring and reformist context of interchange between lived experience and scholastic theology that *De doctrina* saw the light of day.

---

15 *Doctrine of the Hert*, p. 21, ll. 639–46.

16 See Mulder-Bakker, *Lives of the Anchoresses*, pp. 118–47.

17 The theme of the eaten heart is also found within secular love narrative. See, among other examples, Dante's *Vita nuova*, book 3, and *Le Roman du Castelain de Couci et de La Dame de Fayel*, a work written *c.*1300 in the Picard dialect (Hainaut area) localised in north-eastern France. For a general survey of the theme, with reference to the texts mentioned above, see http://www.brown.edu/Departments/Italian_Studies/dweb/themes/heart/heart.shtml (last accessed 12.10.09).

De doctrina cordis: the history of scholarship

The history of scholarly reference to *De doctrina cordis* from the Middle Ages to the present day can be quickly recounted. Palmer details the earliest known external reference to the treatise in the late-thirteenth-century bio-bibliographical *Catalogus virorum illustrium* (*c.*1270–72), where it is attributed to Gerard, a Dominican lector at Liège, and designated profitable reading for monks and nuns. This attribution is repeated in Johannes Trithemius's *Liber de scriptoribus ecclesiasticis* (1494), where the same Gerard is also credited with two sermon cycles, and in the prefaces to the two Neapolitan early-seventeenth-century editions of *De doctrina* (1605, 1607).[18] In 1639, Aubertus Miraeus linked *De doctrina* with another thirteenth-century text, *De remediis contra amorem illicitum*, a work previously ascribed to a Cistercian, Gerard of Liège, and suggested that the two might stem from the same author.[19] This tentative double ascription was repeated by some subsequent bibliographers (Johann Albert Fabricius, *Bibliotheca latinae media et infirmae aetatis* [1735]; Jean François Foppens, *Bibliotheca Belgica* [1737]), while others, most notably Quétif and Échard, in their *Scriptores ordinis Praedicatorum* (1719–23), retained Trithemius's single attribution to 'Frater Gerardus ordinis Predicatorum'.[20]

Little was added to these bibliographical references and even less attention given to the treatise until the early twentieth century, when *De doctrina* and its putative author, along with other closely linked texts, became the subjects of a searching investigation by the Benedictine scholar André Wilmart.[21] In addition to providing a list of the Latin manuscripts of *De doctrina*, assessing the scholastic method and literary quality of the text and passing comment upon the limits of its spiritual profundity – 'une analyse

---

18 N. Palmer, 'The Authorship of *De doctrina cordis*', pp. 19–39. See also A. Wilmart, 'Gérard de Liège. Un traité inédit de l'amour de Dieu', *Revue d'ascétique et de mystique*, 12 (1931), 349–430 (p. 353); Hendrix, *Hugo I*, p. 203.

19 Aubertus Miraeus, *Bibliotheca ecclesiastica* (Antwerp, 1639), pp. 172f. See Palmer, 'Authorship', pp. 31–2; Wilmart, 'Gérard', p. 353f; Sister M.P. Candon, '*The Doctrine of the Hert,* Edited from the Manuscripts with Introduction and Notes' (unpublished doctoral dissertation, Fordham University, 1963), p. xliv; Hendrix, *Hugo I*, p. 215.

20 Candon, *Doctrine*, pp. xliv–xlv; Palmer, 'Authorship', pp. 20–1.

21 Wilmart, 'Gérard', 349–430; A. Wilmart, 'Reg. lat. 71 (fol. 34–62). Les traités de Gérard de Liège sur l'amour illicite et sur l'amour de Dieu', in A. Wilmart, *Analecta Reginensia. Extraits des manuscrits de la Reine Christine conservés au Vatican*, Studi e Testi 59 (Vatican City, 1933), pp. 181–247.

morale, facile, et simple'[22] – Wilmart also explored Aubertus Miraeus' link between *De doctrina*, *De remediis contra amorem illicitum* and a third work, *Quinque incitamenta ad Deum amandum ardenter*. These explorations led him to conclude that the three works shared a single author, and to identify that author as a Cistercian, Gerard of Liège, drawing upon apparently personal references to the Cistercian vocation in *Quinque incitamenta*.

Apart from the rather transitory questioning of this attribution by Samuel Harrison Thomson on the basis of an early manuscript colophon naming one 'Guido cardinalis',[23] Wilmart's work upon *De doctrina* remained uncontested until the late 1970s,[24] when Guido Hendrix commenced what Palmer describes well as an 'exceptionally extensive and complex series of publications', commenting upon various Latin and Middle Dutch redactions of *De doctrina*. As Hendrix's investigations proceeded, he began to discover significant similarities between passages from *De doctrina* and Hugh of St Cher's *Postillae* on the Bible, the major Dominican Parisian academic enterprise of the 1230s; in 1980 these similarities led him to propose the reattribution of *De doctrina* to the Dominican cardinal Hugh of St Cher (d. 1263).[25] Hendrix's reattribution, which underpins his later series of editions of redactions and translations of *De doctrina*, has remained largely unquestioned for the last twenty-seven years. However, Nigel Palmer, in a groundbreaking essay in this volume, queries his conclusions. After a minute re-examination of Hendrix's arguments in the light of *De doctrina*'s manuscript colophons, its presence in bibliographical surveys and its relationship to adjacent spiritual works, he lends his voice to Wilmart's earlier conviction that evidence internal and external to the text points most strongly in the direction of *Cistercian* authorship, and opts for Gerard of Liège OCist, conceivably an abbot of the abbey of Val-Saint-Lambert, but certainly operative in the French-speaking region of the southern Low Countries.

---

22 Wilmart, 'Gérard', p. 364.

23 S.H. Thomson, *The Writings of Robert Grosseteste, Bishop of Lincoln, 1235–1253* (Cambridge, 1940), p. 249. The manuscript in question is Wrocław, Biblioteka Uniwersytecka, MS I.Q.108.

24 Wilmart's authorial conclusions and general view of the text were accepted by Sister M.P. Candon in her 1963 edition of the Middle English translation, Candon, *Doctrine*, pp. xxxii–l. Additionally, Palmer notes Kaeppeli's omission of Gerard of Liège OP as author of *De doctrina cordis* in his *Scriptores ordinis Praedicatorum medii aevi* (1970–93), 'Authorship', p. 21.

25 G. Hendrix, 'Les *Postillae* de Hugues de Saint-Cher et le traité *De doctrina cordis*', *RTAM*, 47 (1980), 114–30.

While Hendrix's attribution of *De doctrina* can no longer be accepted without question, this should not be allowed to detract from his other very considerable achievements in the field of *De doctrina* scholarship. In the course of uncovering and listing more than 200 manuscripts of Latin and vernacular versions of *De doctrina* (many more than the earlier manuscript lists of Wilmart and Thomson), he identified two main recensions of the text – the 'long' and 'short' versions noted earlier. This differentiation led him to publish a facsimile edition of the version of *De doctrina* contained in Leiden, Bibliotheek der Rijksuniversiteit, MS BPL 2579, on the basis that this early manuscript uniquely incorporates key elements of *both* recensions.[26] In the 1990s, Hendrix's continued belief in the significance of MS BPL 2579 also led him to publish a critical edition of the closely related Middle Dutch translation contained in Vienna, Österreichischen Nationalbibliothek, MS 15231.[27] The first volume of this two-volume monograph offers invaluable descriptions of all known manuscripts of *De doctrina*, together with extensive material upon the text's biblical, patristic and scholastic sources and theological content. More recently, Hendrix has published a critical edition of another Dutch prose translation of *De doctrina* (The Hague, Koninklijke Bibliotheek, MS 135 F 6), along with an edition of the related sermon series (Paris, Bibliothèque nationale, MS lat. 16483), which he also ascribes to Hugh of St Cher.[28]

Much of this material – in particular, the first volume of Hendrix's 1995 monograph – has proved seminal to the essays gathered in this volume. Hendrix has assembled the textual tools that have enabled many of our investigations. However, other than listing the known manuscripts of the various vernacular translations of *De doctrina* (and with the obvious exception of the Middle Dutch versions), Hendrix does very little with the vernacular aspect of *De doctrina*'s afterlife. His relative silence on

---

26 G. Hendrix, *Le manuscrit Leyde Bibliothèque de l'Université, BPL 2579, témoin principal des phases de rédaction du traité De doctrina cordis à attribuer au dominicain français Hugues de Saint-Cher (pseudo-Gérard de Liège)*, facsimile edn, De doctrina sive praeparatione cordis 1 (Ghent, 1980).

27 Hendrix, *Hugo II*.

28 G. Hendrix (ed.), *Hugo de Sancto Caro's traktaat De doctrina cordis. 3 Pragmatische editie van Dat Boec van der bereydinge des harten naar handschrift Den Haag, Koninklijke Bibliotheek, 135 F 6*, Documenta libraria 16/3 (Louvain, 2000); id. (ed.), *Hugo de Sancto Caro's traktaat De doctrina cordis. 4. De sermoenen in handschrift Parijs Bibliothèque Nationale, 16483*, Documenta libraria 16/4 (Louvain, 2000). Palmer agrees that *De doctrina* and the sermon series probably share a single author, but identifies that figure as Gerard of Liège OCist ('Authorship', pp. 28–31, 39).

this subject acts to licence many of the explorations undertaken here, which focus in some detail on the translation practices represented by the different vernacular versions, together with their new reading environments, purposes and circulations. In addition, Hendrix, for the main, writes as a textual historian and a theologian. His editions and commentaries pay little attention to the more literary aspects of *De doctrina* – a text charged with striking, outlandish figurative language – especially in the light of more contemporary, theorized modes of reading. Vincent Gillespie's essay in this volume makes good this omission, offering sophisticated readings that set the astonishing culinary and spatial allegories of the first book alongside the influential spatial categorizations of Henri Lefebvre.

De doctrina cordis: the vernacular versions

In addition to the evident popularity of the Latin *De doctrina cordis* within medieval, monastic Europe,[29] a popularity that has gone all but unnoticed by modern scholars of the period, we should not underestimate the spread and significance of *vernacular* versions of the text, nor the important information they can convey regarding differing practices of and attitudes towards translation in diverse language contexts. From the late fourteenth to the early sixteenth century, in line with a European-wide enterprise of religious translation to support monastic and ecclesial devotional education programmes, *De doctrina* was translated into six European vernaculars. We are currently aware of *four* extant manuscripts of a Middle English *Doctrine of the Hert*, the earliest dating from around the second quarter of the fifteenth century, descendants of a single act of translation; of *four* French manuscripts of *Le traitiers de la doctrine du cuer*, one considerably interpolated, offering at least two independent translations of the text;[30] of *four* Dutch manuscripts (*De bouc van der leeringhe van der herten*), offering translations of both the short and long recensions of the Latin text; of *seven* German manuscripts presenting either *capitula selecta* or complete translations in a variety of dialects; of *one* Italian manuscript; and, finally, of *nine* early printed texts of a very late-fifteenth-century Spanish translation

---

29 More than 200 manuscripts of *De doctrina* survive, provenanced in at least nine European countries.

30 Two of the French manuscripts (Oxford, Bodleian Library, MS Holkham Misc. 42, and Paris, Bibliothèque nationale, MS fr. 13272) have only come to light in the last few years and are not included in Hendrix's manuscript listings of 1995. Astonishingly, the Holkham translation may date from as early as the thirteenth century. See Mouron, 'French Translations', p. 188.

(*Del enseñamiento del coraçon*), representing four late-fifteenth-century and early-sixteenth-century editions.

Only the Middle English and Middle Dutch translations of *De doctrina* have been edited[31] and, apart from the interpretative and textual apparatuses surrounding these editions, none of the vernacular versions have received any critical attention in recent times. The essays upon the vernacular versions in this volume thus represent, in many instances, the first detailed explorations into manuscript relations, translational practice and reception, and the first attempts to place these translations within their distinct regional and national contexts of monastic and canonical reform, devotional pedagogy or ecclesial proscription.

Fifteenth-century currents of monastic reform in Germany, Austria and the Low Countries, in particular the reform spirituality of the Windesheim Chapter, form the context for detailed analyses of the German and Middle Dutch translations of *De doctrina* in the essays of Karl-Heinz Steinmetz and Marleen Cré. Steinmetz offers an informative overview of monastic reform objectives in the German-speaking lands of central Europe following the Councils of Constance (1414–17) and Basel (1431–49), and convincingly argues the case for *De doctrina*'s participation in this programme, noting the presence of Latin and vernacular *De doctrina* manuscripts in monasteries associated with the reform movement, and highlighting its position *within* these manuscripts alongside the works of notable German reform theologians. Cré, by contrast, offers a narrower, more detailed focus on a single manuscript: the Middle Dutch translation of the 'long' recension contained in Vienna, Österreichischen Nationalbibliothek, MS 15231, used by, and very possibly translated for, the Augustinian canonesses of the Abbey of St Trudo near Bruges. Cré paints a careful picture of St Trudo's relationship with the Windesheim Chapter (a group of reforming Augustinian priories inspired by the teachings of Jan van Ruusbroec) through the course of the fifteenth century, and elucidates the ways in which the spirituality of *De doctrina* works in sympathy with the devotional aims of the Windesheim reform. In addition, she offers us a method with which to gauge contemporary assessments of *De doctrina*'s spiritual pitch: it was given to the canonesses to read in its entirety within a reform milieu in which mystical and philosophical teachings, and the translations of such

31 The Middle English translation was critically edited as an unpublished doctoral dissertation by Sister Mary Patrick Candon in 1963. A new critical edition is published by the editors of this volume, along with Anne Mouron, in 2010. Hendrix's editions of two Middle Dutch manuscripts are detailed above in notes 9 and 28.

texts from Latin into Dutch, were expressly forbidden to nuns or sisters.[32] *De doctrina* plainly fell well outside this forbidden category.

While Steinmetz's and Cré's essays focus upon the reforming contexts of their respective translations, Anne Mouron's essay upon the French translations and Anthony Lappin's upon the Spanish text take a closer look at the *nature* of translation practice into the French and Spanish vernaculars – at the translator at work, as it were. After conducting a meticulous preliminary examination of the French manuscripts of *Le traitiers de la doctrine du cuer*,[33] Mouron assesses the comparative fidelity of both French translations to their Latin original and comments on marked divergences from the Middle English translator's practice. In France, as in Spain, and by contrast with Germany, the Netherlands and England, there is no evidence to suggest the vernacular text's direct use by women religious. It remains part of the holdings of male monastic libraries, and Mouron reflects upon this provenance, and upon the simultaneous presence of Latin and vernacular copies of *De doctrina* at the great Cistercian establishment of Clairvaux, by speculating that, following a downturn in monastic Latinity in the later years of the fifteenth century, some of the Clairvaux monks may have found the French translation an invaluable aid in achieving full comprehension of the heavily abbreviated Latin texts.

The Spanish translation likewise seems to have remained confined within traditional monastic circles: some indicators in the attribution and early print editions of the text may suggest a specifically *Franciscan* frame of reference. In addition, however, Anthony Lappin notes fascinating linguistic and bibliographical evidence suggesting the translation's possible associations with the Salamanca circle of Antonio Nebrija, the leading Spanish humanist of his day. Lappin also looks at length at the *processes* of this translation – again, at the translator at work: his preferences and practices – and notes the translator's lower educational expectations of his target audience (some parity here with the Clairvaux monks' need of a French reading aid?), and his desire to 'domesticate and modernize' the language of his translation to reflect the cultural and social milieu of late-fifteenth-century Spain.[34]

---

32 See Cré's essay in this volume, pp. 217–21.

33 With the exception of the extensively interpolated version contained in Paris, Bibliothèque nationale, MS fr. 13272. This is treated separately in a further essay by Anne Mouron, forthcoming in D. Renevey and C. Whitehead (eds), *The Medieval Translator/ Traduire au Moyen Age 12* (Turnhout, 2010).

34 A. Lappin, 'The Spanish Translation: *Del enseñamiento del coraçon*', p. 252.

The Doctrine of the Hert

The Middle English translation of *De doctrina* is obviously the main focus of this collection, and its exploration here, alongside its vernacular counterparts abroad, throws some particular features into relief. First, of all the vernacularizations of *De doctrina*, it is the only translation to lose the Latin prologue laying out the dual responsibilities of preachers and their audiences,[35] and to substitute a unique Middle English prologue directed towards 'unkunnyng … symple soules',[36] effectively exchanging the erudite, heavily scriptural approach of the original for a plainer, more devout, mode of address.[37] Mouron's essay on the Middle English *Doctrine of the Hert* makes a detailed comparison of these two prologues and explains their differences with reference to the translator's explicitly low educational expectations of his envisaged audience of religious sisters ('mynchen'). Our comparative perspective allows us to observe that vernacularizations of the text for female religious on the continent show no comparable 'simplification': rather, the scholastic method of frequent biblical and patristic citation is retained intact.

The wish to rework the prologue to address a non-*litteratus* audience also determines the translator's attitude to the body of the text. Mouron charts the very significant changes made: the startling omissions and abbreviations, and the reductions in biblical and patristic citation; she formulates a set of principles by which to account for the translator's decisions to omit material, and she observes that, given the extent and character of the changes made, the text barely fulfils the expectations of a translation any longer: we would do better to think of it as an adaptation.

Attention to the changes made by the 'compiler', with specific regard to the text's biblical voice, also determines Annie Sutherland's approach to the *Doctrine* in her essay '"Comfortable wordis" – the Role of the Bible in *The Doctrine of the Hert*'. Sutherland undertakes a searching examination of references to scripture throughout the Middle English text, and notes that while, for the most part, these references retain the Latin of their source text in common with other devotional vernacular writings of the period,

---

35 Palmer's and Mouron's essays (on the Middle English *Doctrine of the Hert*) in this volume offer detailed analyses of the Latin prologue: pp. 48–9; 99–104.

36 *Doctrine of the Hert*, p. 3, ll. 6, 10.

37 See also Vincent Gillespie's essay in this volume, pp. 137–40. A further detailed examination of the *Doctrine*'s new prologue in relation to other fifteenth-century Middle English prologues is provided in Renevey and Whitehead '"Opyn þin hert as a boke"', pp. 126–33.

nonetheless, via a series of small interventions and modifications, including the omissions and abridgements that Mouron charts more broadly, the compiler of the *Doctrine* succeeds in 'produc[ing] a biblical tone distinctive to his own narrative'.[38]

The clarity with which the Middle English *Doctrine* turns to address specifically *female* religious readers, and the devotional, non-academic reorientation of its contents, is supported by an investigation into the manuscript contexts in which it appears in England. Catherine Innes-Parker examines the *Doctrine*'s innovative relationship with two further anonymous epistolary texts addressed to nuns, *The Tree and xii Frutes of the Holy Goost*, in two of the four manuscripts in which it survives. Her readings in these later texts show how they could well have been paired with the *Doctrine* to form a structured reading programme for religious that emphasized the growth of the heart in devotion. Additionally, she comments that intertextual references in the *Tree* suggest that this 'reading threesome' could well have been intended to stand prior to subsequent, more complex meditations upon the passion.[39]

The Middle English *Doctrine* was clearly intended for female religious readers. Manuscript evidence of its use in the fifteenth century within the Franciscan convents of Bruisyard in East Anglia and St Botolph without Aldgate in London, correlates to some degree with the witness of Germany and the Netherlands, where there is also strong evidence for the vernacular *De doctrina*'s *direct* possession and use by female religious readers. However, this is not the end of the story. In England, there is also unique evidence for the *Doctrine*'s possession by a lay reader: one Margaret Purdans, a gentry widow of Norwich.[40] The easy traffic of anchoritic and conventual treatises between nuns and devout laywomen in fifteenth-century England has long been recognized and scrutinized.[41] However, a new and interesting perspective is afforded *not* by viewing the *Doctrine* against comparable Middle English translations – *The Chastising of God's Children*; the *Stimulus amoris* – but by viewing it in relation to its vernacular counterparts abroad. Framed in

---

38 Sutherland, '"Comfortable wordis"', p. 123.

39 C. Innes-Parker, 'The Middle English *Doctrine of the Hert* and its Manuscript Context', pp. 159–81.

40 See Renevey and Whitehead '"Opyn þin hert as a boke"', pp. 141–5.

41 Seminal treatments include F. Riddy, '"Women talking about the things of God": A Late Medieval Sub-Culture', in C.M. Meale (ed.), *Women and Literature in Britain 1150–1500* (Cambridge, 2nd edn 1996), pp. 104–27; M.C. Erler, *Women, Reading and Piety in Late Medieval England*, Cambridge Studies in Medieval Literature 46 (Cambridge, 2002).

this way, the effect is very different. Nowhere else in Europe is there any evidence for lay reading or access; nowhere else is the text simplified and amended to a degree that makes lay access practical or conceivable; nowhere else is the text pressed into such new and unprecedented uses. Placing this particular Middle English example by reference to its Latin and vernacular counterparts elsewhere, creates a strong case for arguing the *atypicality* of the English translation and its audience reception through the fifteenth century, and for reasserting the strength of local ecclesial circumstances – the vernacular enthusiasms of Wycliffism, the clamp-down of Arundel, the anxieties surrounding learning for the laity – as a means of accounting for its difference.

To conclude: this volume is a beginning and not an end. Much more remains to be done on practically every aspect touched on by these essays. Several of the vernacular translations still await critical editions; in nearly every case, we need to know more about the circumstances in which they were read and circulated. The question of the authorship of *De doctrina* will no doubt excite further discussion. The language and imagery of the text, and the extraordinary mental landscapes it creates, will repay further theorization and close reading. More remains to be said about the place of the Middle English *Doctrine* within its fifteenth-century devotional milieu. We still know insufficient about the Latin versions from which the vernacular translations were made. Our aim in this volume has been to introduce this undeservedly little-known text to a wider audience, and to demonstrate its importance within the broader field of late medieval European devotional theology. Our hope is that some of our readers may become sufficiently interested and involved to pick up where we have left off.

Part I

De doctrina cordis

I

The Authorship of *De doctrina cordis*

Nigel F. Palmer

Introduction

Does authorship matter? The old-fashioned view, that it does matter, was well expressed by Richard Sharpe in the opening words of his recent essay on an evidence-based approach to the way we refer to medieval texts: 'Everyone who studies a text needs to be able to place its composition in a context of time and place and audience. [...] Who wrote the text is often the fundamental clue to its understanding: knowledge of the author allows us to place the text in the intellectual milieu, perspective, and even personal aims and interests of its creator, and beyond that to read it in context.'[1]

The case under consideration provides ample material for reflection on most of the issues raised by Sharpe. About two-thirds of more than 200 manuscripts of the Latin treatise with the incipit 'Praeparate corda vestra', generally referred to today as *De doctrina cordis*, present it as an anonymous work. Nonetheless, there is a tradition going back to at least 1281, and probably earlier, according to which the author was a certain Gerard, Dominican lector at Liège, who then came to be known as Gerard of Liège (taking his name from his convent rather than from his place of origin, as was more usual). The name was carried forward by manuscript colophons and catalogues. Whereas in the *editio princeps* (Paris, 1506) the text is anonymous, the Naples editions of 1605 and 1607 reinstate the attribution to brother Gerardus Leodiensis OP.

The identification of the author as Gerard of Liège OP was maintained until the publication, in 1931, of the first major analysis of the literary

1 R. Sharpe, *Titulus: Identifying Medieval Latin Texts. An Evidence-Based Approach* (Turnhout, 2003), p. 21.

content of the text by André Wilmart, who suggested on the basis of internal evidence and an investigation of other texts attributed to Gerard of Liège that the author was most likely to be a Cistercian.[2] Further studies have been conducted by Guido Hendrix, who in his first publications went with the Gerardus Leodiensis OCist hypothesis, but then, in a series of articles and monographs beginning in 1980, put forward the view that the author of *De doctrina cordis* was the Paris master, Dominican provincial and later cardinal Hugh of St Cher (d. 1263).[3] In his later publications the attribution to Hugh of St Cher assumes the status of a fact. Whether this view has truly found general acceptance, on the basis of a consideration of the evidence, is hard to say. The Cistercian scholar Edmond Mikkers, who was in correspondence with Hendrix in the 1980s, excludes *De doctrina cordis* from his overview of Cistercian writing in the *Dictionnaire de spiritualité*.[4] The authoritative early-eighteenth-century handbook of Dominican writers

---

2 A. Wilmart, 'Gérard de Liège. Un traité inédit de l'amour de Dieu', *Revue d'ascétique et de mystique*, 12 (1931), 349–430, proposing Abbot Gerard (1206) of Val-Saint-Lambert on the outskirts of the city of Liège as the most likely candidate. In his later publication 'Reg. lat. 71 (fol. 34–62). Les traités de Gérard de Liège sur l'amour illicite et sur l'amour de Dieu', in *Analecta Reginensia. Extraits des manuscrits de la Reine Christine conservés au Vatican*, Studi e Testi 59 (Vatican City, 1933), pp. 181–247, he places the text later and identifies the author with the Cistercian abbot Gerard, abbot of Val-Saint-Lambert 1249–54 (p. 181). For this discussion see also J. Van Mierlo, 'Wanneer leefde Geraard van Luik?', *OGE*, 23 (1949), 409–12; S.G. Axters, 'Nederlandse mystiek in het buitenland. Van Rupert van Deutz tot Ruusbroec', *Verslagen en mededelingen van de Koninklijke Vlaamse Academie voor Taal- en Letterkunde* (nieuwe reeks) (1965), 163–325, here pp. 222–33 ('Gerard van Luik, O.Cist.'). Several handbook articles have adopted Wilmart's position regarding attribution and authorship: M. Standaert, 'Gérard de Liège, cistercien, 13e siècle', in *Dictionnaire de spiritualité*, vol. 6 (Paris, 1967), cols 276–9; É. Brouette et al., *Dictionnaire des auteurs cisterciens*, vol. 1 (Rochefort, 1975), cols 284f.; V. Honemann, 'Gerhard von Lüttich', in K. Ruh et al. (eds), *Die deutsche Literatur des Mittelalters. Verfasserlexikon*, 2nd edn, vol. 2 (Berlin/New York, 1980), cols 1233–5.

3 For a bibliography of Hendrix's publications relevant to *De doctrina cordis* see pp. 23–5 below. See also, for a review of Hendrix's research on this subject, A. Welkenhuysen, 'Een harts-tochtelijke queeste. Guido Hendrix en zijn *De doctrina cordis*', in L. Kenis & F. Gistelinck (eds), *Illi qui vitae lustra tredecim valens explevit. Bij de vijfenzestigste verjaardag van Guido Hendrix* (Louvain, 2003), pp. 7–13; 'Bibliografie van Guido Hendrix', ibid., pp. 33–55.

4 E. Mikkers, 'Robert de Molesmes (saint), fondateur de Cîteaux, vers 1028–1111. II. La spiritualité cistercienne', in *Dictionnaire de spiritualité*, vol. 13 (Paris, 1988), cols 738–814.

by Jacques Quétif and Jacques Échard had included a prominent article on F. Gerardus Leodiensis OP as author of *De doctrina cordis* and several other works, but he was not included by Thomas Kaeppeli in the *Scriptores ordinis Praedicatorum medii aevi*.[5] We may presume that this was on the basis of Wilmart's findings. Volume IV of the *Scriptores ordinis Praedicatorum* lists Hendrix's publications as addenda, under the name of Hugh of St Cher, but *De doctrina* is not assigned a number in the catalogue of Hugh's writings. There is no mention of *De doctrina* in the recent collection of studies on Hugh of St Cher assembled by Louis-Jacques Bataillon and others.[6]

Does it matter who was the author of *De doctrina cordis*? The following study, which takes the opposing views of Wilmart and Hendrix as its starting point, was undertaken with a view to understanding the literary and historical context in which *De doctrina* should be read, and in the end the significant question will prove to be one about audience as much as authorship. If Wilmart's hypothesis were to be correct it would be easy to understand the work, for reasons to which I shall return at the end, as a Cistercian contemplative treatise intended for monks and nuns of that order, and it would occupy a place in the Cistercian-orientated contemplative literature of the southern Low Countries, a body of texts embracing both contemplative treatises and the lives of holy women and men. If it were attributable to Hugh of St Cher then we would be faced with a very different perspective on the intellectual milieu in which the treatise originated, and it would be necessary to consider how the composition of such a work could fit into the career of a man who was a leading figure in the Dominican order at Paris and in Rome. The old view, that the author was a certain Gerard, Dominican lector of the convent at Liège, raises rather different questions about the relationship between the author and the audience of religious men and women for whom the treatise was composed.

The fundamental information on which a consideration of these questions must draw has been set out in the exceptionally extensive and

---

5 J. Quétif/J. Échard, *Scriptores ordinis Praedicatorum recensiti*, 2 vols in 4 (Paris, 1719–23), I, 248f.; T. Kaeppeli/[E. Panella], *Scriptores ordinis Praedicatorum medii aevi*, 4 vols (Rome, 1970–93). Cf. R. Aubert, 'Gérard de Liège, cistercien'; 'Gérard de Liège, dominicain', in A. Baudillart et al. (eds), *Dictionnaire d'histoire et de géographie ecclésiastique*, vol. 20 (Paris, 1984), cols 776f., who follows Wilmart in distinguishing the two figures, but notes Hendrix's position regarding the authorship of *De doctrina*.

6 Kaeppeli/Panella, *Scriptores ordinis Praedicatorum*, IV, 24; L.-J. Bataillon, G. Dahan, & P.-M. Gy (eds), *Hugues de Saint-Cher († 1263), bibliste et théologien*, Bibliothèque d'histoire culturelle du moyen âge 1 (Turnhout, 2004).

complex series of publications by Guido Hendrix alluded to above, which I shall be taking issue with and reinterpreting. His synthesis was set out in 1995 in a two-volume monograph, the first part of which is devoted to the manuscripts, textual history, authorship, and theological content of the Latin *De doctrina cordis*:

> *Hugo de Sancto Caro's traktaat De doctrina cordis. Vol. 1: Handschriften, receptie, tekstgeschiedenis en authenticiteitskritiek*, Documenta Libraria 16/1 (Louvain, 1995).[7]

The second part is a critical edition of the Dutch prose translation preserved in a Vienna manuscript from the abbey of St Trudo in Bruges, the special significance of which is that it relates so closely in its readings to the archetype of the whole Latin tradition, as represented by the Groenendaal manuscript L13, now in Leiden, as to have textual authority for the Latin text:

> *Hugo de Sancto Caro's traktaat De doctrina cordis. Vol. 2: Pragmatische editie van De bouc van der leeringhe van der herten naar handschrift Wenen, ÖNB, 15231, autograaf van de Middelnederlandse vertaler*, Documenta Libraria 16/2 (Louvain, 1995).

The planned critical edition of the Latin text has never appeared. A basis for citing a large portion of the text, however, if one accepts Hendrix's plausible analysis of the textual history, is provided in his partial facsimile of L13, which stands at the head of the textual tradition of both the long and short recensions and is either an autograph or in the hand of the primary redactor:

> *Le manuscrit Leyde Bibliothèque de l'Université, BPL 2579, témoin principal des phases de rédaction du traité De doctrina cordis à attribuer au dominicain français Hugues de Saint-Cher (pseudo-Gérard de Liège)*, facsimile edition with an introduction by Guido Hendrix, De doctrina sive praeparatione cordis 1 (Ghent, 1980).[8]

---

7 Cited henceforth as Hendrix, *Hugo I*. Reviewed by A. Derolez in *Ephemerides theologicae Lovanienses*, 74 (1998), 208f., who gives cautious approval to the 'original and unexpected answer' Hendrix provides to the authorship question.

8 See also Hendrix, 'Het Leidse handschrift' (1980), passim. He does not seem to have expressed a clear view on the identification of the hand responsible for the Leiden manuscript and its subsequent modifications. For full details of the articles cited here and in n. 9 see p. 24.

Several substantial sections of the planned critical edition have been published separately in journal articles and in the monograph of 1995, in some cases with an extensive and extremely informative commentary.[9] The 1995 edition of the medieval Dutch text identifies all Bible citations (with an index), and these identifications can be used in conjunction with the Latin text. Volume I of the 1995 publication contains a complete analysis of the sources of the Latin *De doctrina*, book by book, referring to the text by the line numbers of the medieval Dutch edition.[10] For want of any modern edition giving the complete Latin text, it is convenient to have recourse to one of the early printed editions, although very few copies of these have survived.[11]

For ease of reference I will provide here at the beginning a chronological list of twenty-two further publications by Hendrix relating to *De doctrina*, so that they can be referred to subsequently by short-title and date:

— 'Gerardus Leodiensis – *De doctrina cordis*', *CCC*, 27 (1976), 135–8.

— '*De doctrina cordis*. Manuscripts of Clairvaux and Cîteaux provenance', *CCC*, 28 (1977), 94–100.

— 'Handschriften en in handschrift bewaarde vertalingen van het aan Gerard van Luik toegeschreven traktaat *De doctrina cordis*. Een overzicht', *OGE*, 51 (1977), 146–68.

---

9 See in particular the critical edition of the two recensions of the prologue (distinguished as 'Ignaros praedicatores' and 'Hoc verbo') in Hendrix, 'Het Leidse handschrift' (1980), pp. 168–73, of 'De custodia linguae' (book 2, ch. 4) in Hendrix, 'De apercione' (1981), pp. 190–96, of 'De apertione cordis' and 'De impedimentis' (book 3, ch. 1) in ibid., pp. 183–90, of 'De stabilitate cordis' (book 4, complete) in Hendrix, *Hugo I*, pp. 372–403, and of 'De scissione cordis per amorem' (book 7, complete) in Hendrix, 'Postillae' (1980), pp. 118–29, repeated in Hendrix, *Hugo I*, pp. 414–28.

10 Hendrix, *Hugo I*, pp. 271–330.

11 For details see Hendrix, 'Drukgeschiedenis' (1978), passim; id., *Hugo I*, pp. 152–9. The Paris 1506 edition is known to exist in Avignon, Göttingen, Munich (Bayerische Staatsbibliothek), Oxford, Stuttgart, Wolfenbüttel and Xanten, the Paris 1517 edition in The Hague, Cologne (Universitätsbibliothek) and Seville, the Naples 1605 edition in Berlin (Staatsbibliothek zu Berlin – Preußischer Kulturbesitz), Vienna (Österreichische Nationalbibliothek) and the Vatican, the Naples 1607 reprint only in Oxford. For reading the text I have used Gerardus Leodiensis, *Speculum concionatorum ad illustrandum pectora auditorum, in septem libros distributum* [...] (Naples, 1607), Oxford, Bodleian Library, 8º L 12 Th. BS, which appears to offer a mixture of the long and short recensions identified by Hendrix. Hereafter cited as *De doctrina*.

— 'Deux textes d'attribution incertaine à saint Bonaventure, restitués à Gérard de Liège', *RTAM*, 45 (1978), 237–8.

— 'Drukgeschiedenis van het traktaat *De doctrina cordis*', *Archives et bibliothèques de Belgique/Archief- en bibliotheekwezen van België*, 49 (1978), 224–39.

— 'À la recherche de "frater Thomas de ordine fratrum heremitarum sancti Augustini"', *RTAM*, 46 (1979), 214–15.

— 'Handschriften van het traktaat *De doctrina cordis*. Aanvullende opsomming', *OGE*, 54 (1980), 39–42.

— 'Het Leidse handschrift BPL 2579 en de tekstoverlevering van het traktaat *De doctrina cordis*', *OGE*, 54 (1980), 158–81.

— 'Hugh of St. Cher O.P., Author of two texts attributed to the 13th-century Cistercian Gerard of Liège', *CCC*, 31 (1980), 343–56.

— 'Les *Postillae* de Hugues de Saint-Cher et le traité *De doctrina cordis*', *RTAM*, 47 (1980), 114–30.

— '*De apercione cordis*, *De impedimentis* and *De custodia linguae*. Three pseudo-Bernardine texts restored to their true author, Hugh of St. Cher', *RTAM*, 48 (1981), 172–97.

— 'Kleine queste naar de auteur van *De duodecim utilitatibus tribulationum*', *OGE*, 56 (1982), 109–24.

— 'Onderzoek naar het œuvre van "Gerardus Leodiensis"', *OGE*, 56 (1982), 300–341.

— 'Le *De doctrina cordis*, source directe du *Chastel perilleux*', *RTAM*, 50 (1983), 252–66.

— 'Onderzoek naar het œuvre van "Gerardus Leodiensis". Tweede deel', *OGE*, 58 (1984), 281–99.

— *Dat boec vander bereydinge des harten. Middelnederlandse vertaling van De praeparatione cordis (Hugo van Saint-Cher, pseudo-Gerard van Luik)*, ed. by M. De Cock and G. Hendrix, De doctrina sive praeparatione cordis 2 (Ghent, 1986).

— 'Luik, Gerard van, geestelijk schrijver', in *Nationaal Biografisch Woordenboek*, vol. 12 (Brussels, 1987), cols 437–42.

— *De lange redactie van De doctrina cordis (Hugo van Saint-Cher, pseudo-Gerard van Luik) in Middelnederlandse vertaling uitgegeven naar de handschriften Wenen, O.N.B., 15231 en Ser. nov. 12805*, De doctrina sive praeparatione cordis 3–4 (Ghent, 1987).

— 'Note relative aux manuscrits des traités *De doctrina cordis* et *De praeparatione cordis*', *RTAM*, 54 (1987), 255–6.

— 'De vertalingen van *De doctrina cordis* en *De praeparatione cordis* (Hugo van Saint-Cher, Pseudo-Gerardus Leodiensis)', in *Miscellanea Neerlandica. Opstellen voor Dr. Jan Deschamps ter gelegenheid van zijn zeventigste verjaardag* (Louvain, 1987), part 2, pp. 19–29.

— *Hugo de Sancto Caro's traktaat De doctrina cordis. Vol. 3: Pragmatische editie van Dat Boec van der bereydinge des harten naar handschrift Den Haag, Koninklijke Bibliotheek, 135 F 6*, ed. by G. Hendrix, Documenta libraria 16/3 (Louvain, 2000).

— *Hugo de Sancto Caro's traktaat De doctrina cordis. Vol. 4: De sermoenen in handschrift Parijs Bibliothèque Nationale, 16483*, ed. by G. Hendrix, Documenta libraria 16/4 (Louvain, 2000).

The *De doctrina cordis* attributed to Gerard of Liège

The earliest bibliographical work to mention a treatise on the seven dispositions of the heart with the incipit 'Praeparate corda vestra' is the *Catalogus virorum illustrium*, a bio-bibliographical catalogue that circulated in the Low Countries in the fourteenth and fifteenth centuries, covering some sixty authors from about 1050 to 1270 and plausibly dated by its most recent editor to *c.*1270–72.[12] Whereas in the lost manuscript used for the first printed edition of 1639 the author of the *Catalogus* was given rather implausibly as the Paris master Henry of Ghent (d. 1291), Franz Pelster argued for a monk of the Benedictine house of Affligem, near Aalst, north of Brussels (because of a cluster of Affligem authors cited in the last section). Hendrix argued that the prominence of Cistercian writers makes Cistercian authorship more likely. More recently this attribution too has been doubted.

[12] N. Häring, 'Der Literaturkatalog von Affligem', *Revue bénédictine*, 80 (1970), 64–96; for the date see pp. 72f. Cf. F. Pelster, 'Der Heinrich von Gent zugeschriebene *Catalogus virorum illustrium* und sein wirklicher Verfasser', *Historisches Jahrbuch*, 29 (1918), 253–68; G. Hendrix, 'Cistercian sympathies in the 14th-century *Catalogus virorum illustrium*', *CCC*, 27 (1976), 267–78; id., '"Der Literaturkatalog von Affligem". Some notes on a *Catalogus virorum illustrium*', in A. Raman & E. Manning (eds), *Miscellanea Martin Wittek. Album de codicologie et de paléographie offert Martin Wittek* (Louvain/Paris, 1993), pp. 181–8; E. Mantingh, *Een monnik met een rol. Willem van Affligem, het Kopenhaagse 'Leven van Lutgart' en de fictie van een meerdaagse voorlezing*, Diss. Utrecht (Hilversum, 2000), pp. 55f. (indicating that the *Catalogus* displays Carthusian rather than Cistercian sympathies).

Whoever the compiler of the catalogue may have been, his comments on the value of the texts listed to contemplative readers suggest that he had the interests of a monastic audience in mind, and that he therefore had first-hand knowledge of the milieu for which *De doctrina cordis* is likely to have been intended.

The author of the 'Praeparate corda vestra', which is said to be particularly good reading for 'religiosi' (monks and nuns), is identified in the *Catalogus* as brother Gerard, lector at the Dominican house of Liège:

> Frater GERARDUS ordinis Predicatorum, lector domus Leodiensis. Composuit tractatum religiosis ualde utilem sumpto themate ab illo loco libri Regum: Preparate corda uestra domino et cetera, septem dispositiones circa cor faciendas docens multaque ad edificationem pertinentia hinc inde de scripturis colligens.[13]

This statement regarding the authorship of *De doctrina* is corroborated by the earliest dated manuscript of the text from 1281, preserved in the Cistercian abbey of Kaisheim, north of Donauwörth, in the diocese of Augsburg: 'Incipit opus fratris gerhardi lectoris fratrum predicatorum leodiensium de cordis doctrina.'[14] Fifteen further attributions to brother Gerard have been assembled by Hendrix in his comprehensive analysis of the manuscript tradition, in which he lists and catalogues some 204 manuscripts all told.[15]

---

13 (Brother Gerard of the order of Preachers, lector of the monastery at Liège. He composed a treatise that is extremely valuable for monks and nuns based on that passage in the Book of Kings 'Prepare your hearts unto the Lord' etc., setting out seven different approaches to the subject of the heart and drawing together numerous edifying citations from different parts of the Scriptures.) Häring, 'Der Literaturkatalog', p. 94. Cf. Wilmart, 'Gérard', p. 353; Hendrix, *Hugo I*, p. 203.

14 (Here begins the work of brother Gerard, lector of the Friars Preacher at Liège, concerning the doctrine of the heart.) Munich, Bayerische Staatsbibliothek, Clm 7984 (= Hendrix M[1]), fol. 1v. Hendrix, *Hugo I*, pp. 65 and 200. The only manuscripts that can definitely be placed earlier are Leiden, Bibliotheek der Rijksuniversiteit, MS BPL 2579 and Paris, Bibliothèque nationale de France, MS lat. 15958 (presented to the Collegium Parisiense by Robert de Sorbonne 1274).

15 Hendrix, *Hugo I*, pp. 13–105. For discussion of the attributions to Gerard, see Hendrix, 'Onderzoek' (1982), pp. 305–13; repeated in id., *Hugo I*, pp. 200–208. Where library catalogues, such as that of the Cistercian abbey of Villers, give Gerard as the author the likelihood must always be borne in mind that the attribution derives from the bibliographical tradition, and not from an independent medieval source. For a reference to 'Giraldus' Leodiensis in a Metz manuscript destroyed in the Second World War, see ibid., p. 141.

For the moment it will suffice to note one attestation from the Carmelite convent in Mainz (first half of the fifteenth century) naming the author Gerard the Divine OP and indicating that he addressed his work to a nun – 'Incipit doctrina seu preparatio cordis. Hunc libellum composuit frater Gerhardus dictus divinus de ordine predicatorum cuidam religiose persone filie in christo ut patet in sequentibus'[16] – and a tradition attested already in the fourteenth century which states that, although he came to be known as Gerard of Liège because of his long association with the Dominican convent in that town, he originally hailed from Reims:

> Explicit liber de doctrina vel custodia cordis, ut fertur compositus a fratre Gerardo natione Remensi, sed Leodiensi dictus propter longam inhabitationem conventus fratrum ordinis predicatorum Leodiensium, magno et famoso predicatore temporibus suis.[17]

The attribution to Gerard, Dominican lector at Liège, was carried forward by the German Benedictine Johannes Trithemius, abbot of Sponheim in the central Rhineland, in his widely consulted bio-bibliographical surveys of Latin ecclesiastical writers (1494) and of notable German writers (1495),[18]

---

[16] (Here begins the doctrine or preparation of the heart. This little book was composed by brother Gerard, known as the Divine, of the order of Preachers for a certain nun, his daughter in Christ, as is evident from what follows.) Mainz, Stadtbibliothek, MS II 27, fol. 1r (= Hendrix M2). Hendrix, *Hugo I*, pp. 61 and 201 (adding 'multum dilecte' after 'christo'). A second manuscript with 'dictus divinus', Frankfurt, Stadt- und Universitätsbibliothek, MS Carm. 10, was thought by Hendrix, *Hugo I*, p. 207 to be a copy of that at Mainz. See also the attribution to 'Ioannes Divinus' in the library catalogue of the Cistercian abbey of Cambron in Hainaut, as noted by Wilmart, 'Gérard', p. 379; Hendrix, *Hugo I*, p. 113. See further pp. 38f. below.

[17] (Here ends the book about the doctrine or custody of the heart, said to have been composed by brother Gerard, who came from Reims, but took his name from Liège because of his long residence at the monastery of the Friars Preacher at Liège, in his day a great and famous preacher.) Charleville-Mézières, Bibliothèque municipale, MS 87, fol. 89v (= Hendrix C2, dated 1344, from the Carthusian monastery of Mont-Dieu in the Ardennes). Wilmart, 'Gérard', p. 355, n. 13 (no. 9); Hendrix, *Hugo I*, pp. 25f. and 201.

[18] Johannes Trithemius, *Liber de scriptoribus ecclesiasticis* (Basel: Johannes Amerbach, [after 28.VIII.] 1494), fol. 76v; id., *Cathalogus illustrium virorum Germaniam suis ingenijs et lucubrationibus omnifariam exornantium* (s.l. et a. [Mainz: Peter Friedberg, not before 14.VIII.1495]), fols 25v–26r. Cf. K. Arnold, *Johannes Trithemius (1462–1516)*, Quellen und Forschungen zur Geschichte des

and taken up again in the Naples editions of *De doctrina* in 1605 and 1607.

The attributions to brother Gerard demand our attention for two reasons: they are attested very early, already in the thirteenth century, and the author 'Frater Gerardus ordinis Predicatorum lector domus Leodiensis' is such a little-known figure that it is hard to see on what grounds his name might have been associated with the 'Praeparate corda vestra' text if he was not actually the author. Only one of the sixteen manuscripts naming Gerard fails to indicate that he was a Dominican.[19] That plausible candidates for the author get a mention in historical sources, in particular a Dominican lector attested at Liège in the second quarter of the thirteenth century, has long been recognized.[20] Other names which occur occasionally in scribal colophons as prospective authors of the work are Albert the Great, Anselm, Bernard of Clairvaux, Bonaventure, Conrad of Saxony, Robert Grosseteste, Guy of L'Aumône, Hugo (for whom see below), Thomas the Cistercian and 'frater Thomas de ordine fratrum heremitarum S. Augustini'.[21]

Further works attributable to Gerard of Liège

Gerard's name is not only associated with the treatise 'Praeparate corda vestra'. Trithemius, in his *Liber de scriptoribus ecclesiasticis*, includes an account of brother Gerard OP that is clearly based on the tradition of manuscript colophons we have already encountered, but in which he is

Bistums und Hochstifts Würzburg 23, 2nd revised edn (Würzburg, 1991), pp. 117–37. Hendrix in 'Onderzoek II' (1984), p. 283, and *Hugo I*, pp. 203f. and 214, confuses the *Catalogus* with the *Liber de scriptoribus ecclesiasticis*, citing the slightly differently worded text from the Kassel manuscript of the former under the title of the latter.

19 Cologne, Historisches Archiv der Stadt Köln, MS W* 151 (= Hendrix K2, early 14th century), fol. 1r: 'Opus fratris Gerhardi de remis quod vocatur preparate'. Hendrix, *Hugo I*, pp. 48 and 202.

20 Quétif/Échard, *Scriptores*, I, 248. Cf. in particular C. Renardy, *Le monde des maîtres universitaires du diocèse de Liège, 1140–1350. Recherches sur sa composition et ses activités*, Bibliothèque de la Faculté de Philosophie et Lettres de l'Université de Liège 227 (Paris, 1979), p. 385; id., *Les maîtres universitaires du diocèse de Liège. Répertoire biographique 1140–1350*, Bibliothèque de la Faculté de Philosophie et Lettres de l'Université de Liège 232 (Paris, 1981), pp. 234f.; Hendrix, 'Onderzoek' (1982), p. 316; id., *Hugo I*, pp. 195f.

21 Wilmart, 'Gérard', p. 358; Hendrix, 'Onderzoek' (1982), pp. 302–305; id., *Hugo I*, pp. 197–200.

presented as the author of several different texts. He names *De doctrina cordis*, a collection of sermons for the temporal and sanctoral cycles, and goes on to mention, in the last sentence, 'a number of other works which I have not seen':

> GErardus ordinis fratrum praedicatorum: natione teutonicus: lector conuentus Leodiensis: uir in diuinis scripturis studiosus et eruditus: et in sermonibus faciendis ad populum declamator egregius: ingenio clarus et scholastice comptus eloquio. Scripsit ualde utilem tractatum deuotis et religiosis personis: docens septem dispositiones circa cor faciendas: multaque ad aedificationem pertinentia: hinc inde de scripturis diuinis sagaciter colligens: quem praenotauit:
>
> De doctrina cordis: li. j Praeparate corda uestra.
>
> Sermones de tempore. li. j
>
> Sermones de sanctis: li. j
>
> Alia insuper quaedam edidit: quae ad noticiam meam non uenerunt.[22]

The statement in the *Catalogus illustrium virorum Germaniam exornantium* of 1495 is almost identical.

Whether Trithemius had in truth seen collections of sermons for the temporal and sanctoral cycles under Gerard's name we cannot know. That Gerard did indeed preach seems likely from the evidence of a thirteenth-century Paris manuscript from the Sorbonne which contains a collection of seventy sermons attributed in an added, but near-contemporary inscription ('dont le style décèle encore le XIIIe siècle': Wilmart / early fourteenth century: Hendrix) to Gerard of Liège: 'Sermones sunt hic fratris Gerardi.

---

22 (Gerard of the order of Friars Preacher, by origin a German, lector of the convent at Liège, noted for his learning and erudition in the Holy Scriptures, outstanding as a preacher of sermons to the people, clear of mind and scholarly in speech. He wrote an extremely useful treatise for the devout and for monks and nuns setting out seven approaches to the subject of the heart and drawing together with great wisdom numerous edifying citations from different parts of the Holy Scriptures, which we have seen:

On the doctrine of the heart: book i Prepare your hearts

Sermons for the year. book i

Sermons on the saints book i

In addition he produced some other writings which I have not been able to see.) Trithemius, *Liber de scriptoribus ecclesiasticis*, fol. 76v.

De Liege. Le Deuin'.[23] The existence of the Paris sermons was first signalled by Quétif in 1719. They received a brief discussion, principally as an example of Latin sermons with French inserts, by Albert Lecoy de la Marche. The sermons were described in detail by Johannes Baptist Schneyer, and they are now available in a diplomatic edition published in 2000 by Hendrix, who in 1995 expressed skepticism about the authorship of the sermons. The commentary volume to the edition is said to be in preparation.

Wilmart, in the only published analysis of the sermons, makes a strong case, both on stylistic grounds (including the use of French material) and on the basis of the heading, for Cistercian authorship and attribution to Gerard of Liège. Just what might be meant by 'authorship' in the context of such a collection of sermons, however, merits further discussion. Sermon 13 (Schneyer 13) on 'Oues mee uocem meam audiunt' (John 10:27) is the shorter version of the *Tractatus super septem verba dicta a Domino Jesu Christo pendente in cruce*, the longer version of which is attributed to Gerard of Liège in the manuscripts (see below). Sermon 61 (Schneyer 63) contains a heading 'Sermo in cena Domini fratris Gerardi de Liege' (fol. 94r), from which one might infer that the scribe or annotator attributed this sermon to Gerard, but not necessarily all the others. Similarly, the annotator attributes sermon 67 (Schneyer 69), which has the heading 'Sermo in cena Domini in capitulo Quintini' (St Quentin in Piccardy), to 'magist[er] Joann[es] de Abbevilla' (John Halgrin of Abbeville). Hendrix, in the brief preface to his edition, suggests further attributions: Odo of Chateauroux (sermon 43/Schneyer 45), Guiard of Laon (sermon 20/Schneyer 22 and probably sermon 10/Schneyer 10) and Gerard of Mailly (sermons 24/Schneyer 26, 53/Schneyer 55, 54/Schneyer 56, 59/Schneyer 61, probably also 67/Schneyer 69). To what extent the sermons for which no specific association with

---

23 Paris, Bibliothèque nationale de France, MS lat. 16483, fol. 3r. Wilmart, 'Gérard', pp. 378–84, here p. 378. See also Quétif/Échard, *Scriptores*, I, 249; A. Lecoy de la Marche, *La chaire française au moyen âge spécialement au XIIIe siècle d'après les manuscrits contemporains* (Paris, 3rd edn, 1886), pp. 125f.; J.B. Schneyer, *Repertorium der lateinischen Sermones des Mittelalters für die Zeit von 1150–1350 (Autoren: E–H)*, [vol. 2], Beiträge zur Geschichte der Philosophie und Theologie des Mittelalters: Texte und Untersuchungen 43/2 (Münster i.W., 1970), pp. 173–78; Hendrix, *Hugo I*, pp. 234–6, id., *Hugo* [...] *4. De sermoenen* (2000), pp. ix–xi. Lecoy de Marche and Schneyer make reference to a second Paris manuscript, lat. 14956, which according to Wilmart contains quite different texts that have nothing to do with the Gerard of Liège sermons. Schneyer also lists a third manuscript, lat. 13581, fols 3–31v, which Hauréau describes as containing the sermons of Hugh of St Cher.

Gerard can be demonstrated are his and to what extent he had a hand in the redaction of the compilation in MS lat. 16483 are still open questions and ones which it is premature to attempt to answer before the appearance of Hendrix's commentary volume. A particular feature of the sermons which must concern us here is the presence of explicit cross-references to the text of *De doctrina*, demonstrating that the manuscript was compiled in a milieu where not only 'brother Gerard of Liège the Divine' was known, but also where the principal text attributed to him was known and available for consultation. Hendrix drew attention in 1995 to passages in sermons 2 (Schneyer 2) and 62 (Schneyer 64) where the reader is invited to consult the 'liber de doctrina cordis' for additional information. Similarly, there is a reference in the sermon sketch no. 38 (Schneyer 40) to the passage in *De doctrina* which discusses the book of conscience, but here without explicit mention of the work's title.[24] These references provide strong support for the view that Gerard of Liège had a hand in the making of this compilation. They also provide strong supporting evidence for the close association of the name of Gerard of Liège with *De doctrina*.

A first suggestion as to what Trithemius might have meant by certain 'other works' by Gerard of Liège was provided by Valerius Andreas in his *Bibliotheca Belgica* of 1623. Andreas signals a Cistercian writer with this name as the author of *De remediis contra amorem illicitum*, which he knew from a manuscript at the Benedictine abbey of Saint-Bertin in Saint-Omer.[25] This reference was picked up by Aubertus Miraeus, in his *Bibliotheca ecclesiastica* of 1639, who suggested that *De remediis* might in fact be attributable not to the Cistercian Gerardus Leodicensis but to his Dominican namesake, the author of *De doctrina*. Miraeus's note on the writings of Gerard of Liège OP is an augmented restatement of the material compiled by Trithemius:

> GERARDVS ordinis Praedicatorum, Lector domus Leodiensis, composuit tractatum religiosis valde vtilem, sumpto themate ab illo loco libri Regum, Praeparate corda vestra Domino etc. septem dispositiones circa cor faciendas docens multaquae ad aedificationem pertinentia hinc inde de Scripturis colligens.
>
> Gerardus, *Leodicensis Lector seu Professor sacrarum litterarum apud collegas suos Dominicanos, circa annum millesimum trecentesimum floruit. Scripsit librum* De doctrina cordis; de Virtutibus; de Tempore et Sanctis.

---

24 See Hendrix, *Hugo I*, p. 235; id., *Hugo* [...] *4. De sermoenen* (2000), p. ix.

25 Valerius Andreas, *Bibliotheca Belgica* (Louvain, 1623), p. 315 (reading 'Ms Audomaropoli ad S. Martinum'). 'S. Martinum' is a misprint for 'S. Bertinum', corrected in the 1643 edition of the same work. Cf. Wilmart, 'Gérard', p. 384.

> *Extant hi libri mss. in Valle Viridi, et Louanij ad S. Martinum. Eiusdem Gerardi fortasse liber est* De remediis contra amorem illicitum; *quem nonnemo alteri* Gerardo Leodicensi, monacho ordinis Cisterciensis, *adscripsit.*[26]

The information compiled by Andreas and Miraeus was not without foundation. A thirteenth-century manuscript from the Cistercian abbey of Clairvaux contains two treatises on the subject of love, the first of which is introduced by a scribal heading naming 'brother Gerard of Liège', but with no indication of religious affiliation: 'Frater Gerardus de Leodio. Septem remedia contra amorem illicitum ualde utilia.'[27] The *Septem remedia contra amorem illicitum* (fols 183r–197r) is followed directly by a second text, the *Quinque incitamenta ad Deum amandum ardenter* (fols 197r–226v), and in the sixteenth-century library catalogue of Clairvaux these two texts are attributed to a single author, now unaccountably described as 'Germain' rather than Gerard: 'Germani de leodio de septem remediis contra amorem illicitum et incitamenta ad amorem dei et proximi.'[28] Certainly the two

---

[26] (Gerard of the order of Preachers, lector of the monastery at Liège, composed a treatise that is extremely valuable for monks and nuns based on that passage in the Book of Kings 'Prepare your hearts unto the Lord' etc., setting out seven approaches to the subject of the heart and drawing together numerous edifying citations from different parts of the Scriptures.

Gerard, lector at Liège or professor of the Holy Scriptures to his fellow Dominicans, lived around the year 1300. He wrote a book *On the Doctrine of the Heart*, also *On the Virtues*, a temporal cycle (of sermons) and a sanctoral cycle. Manuscripts of these works are to be found at Groenendaal and at Saint-Martin in Louvain. Perhaps the book *On the Remedies against Improper Love* is by the same Gerard, a work which some others have ascribed to Gerard of Liège, a monk of the Cistercian order.) Aubertus Miraeus, *Bibliotheca ecclesiastica sive nomenclatores VII. veteres* [...], vol. 1 (Antwerp, 1639), pp. 172f. (ch. 53). Cf. Wilmart, 'Gérard', pp. 353f.; Hendrix, *Hugo I*, p. 215.

[27] (Brother Gerard of Liège. *The Seven Remedies against Improper Love*. Extremely useful.) Troyes, Bibliothèque municipale, MS 1890, fol. 183r; cited by Wilmart, 'Gérard', p. 386.

[28] (Germain of Liège: *On the Seven Remedies against Improper Love* and the *Incitements to Love God and One's Neighbour.*) Hendrix, '*De doctrina cordis*: Manuscripts' (1977), p. 98; id., *Hugo I*, p. 220. Wilmart's article of 1931, for which see n. 2 above, contains a provisional, incomplete transcription of the texts from the Clairvaux manuscript. For a full critical edition, based on the same manuscript, see Wilmart, 'Reg. Lat. 71', pp. 183–205 (*Septem remedia*), 205–47 (*Quinque incitamenta*).

texts form a pair: the first is a warning to monks against the dangers of carnal love, while the second encourages them to devote themselves to the love of God. Wilmart, who published a critical edition of both the *Septem remedia* and the *Quinque incitamenta*, was able to identify a second manuscript with both works in the Vatican library, and a third manuscript, in Brussels, with just the *Quinque incitamenta*. Neither of the new textual witnesses contains an author attribution, but Wilmart was confident that the two treatises were the work of the same writer, the Cistercian Gerard of Liège, who was also author of *De doctrina*.[29]

The *Quinque incitamenta ad Deum amandum ardenter* contains good internal evidence of its author's religious affiliation. The third part of the treatise proposes four different ways to love God, the first of which is 'amor verecundus'. At the beginning of this section the author rehearses how the man who would lift up his heart to God will think back to what he promised at baptism, in particular at his second baptism when he took his religious vows. Speaking from the perspective of an inclusive 'we', in which he places himself and his audience together, he formulates the need to remember how what they promised on taking the vows of the Cistercian order has separated them from the world:

> Quam perfectionem nos omnes, qui ordinem Cisterciensium professi sumus, deuouimus, idest coram deo et sanctis eius promisimus, quod nos magis sancte, magis pure et deuote, et magis perfecte uiueremus in ordine quam aliqui in toto mundo qui simili uinculo non sunt astricti, et sine dubio illud quod uouimus oportebit nos reddere.[30]

The *Septem remedia* also contains mention of the Cistercian order, but not in such a way as to require that the author should be understood to be a Cistercian himself. As an exemplum to illustrate the justification of the

---

29 Wilmart, 'Reg. lat. 71', pp. 181f. Cf. Axters, 'Nederlandse mystiek', pp. 225 and 230, for the same view. For further discussion of the *Quinque incitamenta* see J. Reynaert, 'Hadewijch: mystic poetry and courtly love', in E. Kooper (ed.), *Medieval Dutch Literature in its European Context*, Cambridge Studies in Medieval Literature 21 (Cambridge, 1994), pp. 208–25, especially pp. 216–20.

30 (That is the perfection which all those of us who have made their profession in the Cistercian order vowed, that is we promised before God and his saints that we would live a life more holy, more pure and devout, and more perfect in the order than anyone in the world who is not tied by similar bonds. Undoubtedly we are obliged to honour what we vowed.) Wilmart, 'Reg. lat. 71', p. 212. Cf. id., 'Gérard', pp. 388f.

fourth 'remedium amoris', namely avoidance of the company of women, reference is made to a Cistercian monk who had lived in the order for fifty years and who at the age of eighty became infatuated in a woman, left his monastery and the order for the world and died.[31]

As preserved in the Troyes and Vatican manuscripts the two texts are placed together to form a thematically linked pair. The *Septem remedia* begins with a preface ('Cum omnis anime rationalis summum bonum sit amorem suum ab omni carnali et illicito amore retrahere …') setting out the scope of the work and the central hypothesis, namely that one should flee carnal love in order to adhere to God in perfect love. The seven 'remedies' are introduced by a heading which indicates that this section will be followed by a discussion of those things which can 'incite and compel' us to love God: 'Primo ponemus et dicemus septem remedia contra amorem illicitum, et postea, deo adiuuante, ponemus ea que nos incitare possunt et debent ad amorem diuinum' (Prol. 31–33).[32] The seven remedies are now presented in turn, each concluding with a formula indicating that 'sufficient' about this matter has now been said, for example 'Et hec de secundo remedio sufficiant' (II, 72).[33] The treatise ends with the author's apology for having had to omit much material from his account of the remedies, and a statement of intent that 'in the following work' he will investigate those things which can incite and enflame us with divine love. The material referred to as contained 'in sequenti opere' is clearly that which in the preface he said would be presented in a second section, 'postea':

> Sed propter fastidiosos et indeuotos lectores multum multa salubria et utilia omittimus et in sequenti opere uertamus nos ad inuestigandum et inquirendum ea que incitare et inflammare nos possunt et debent ad amorem diuinum. (Rem. VII, 167–70)[34]

---

31 Wilmart, 'Reg. lat. 71', p. 193. Cf. id., 'Gérard', p. 388.

32 (First we shall set out and describe seven remedies against improper love, and afterwards, God willing, we shall set out those things which can and must incite us to pursue the love of God.) Wilmart, 'Reg. Lat. 71', p. 184.

33 Ibid., p. 189. Cf. Wilmart, 'Gérard', p. 387 n. 103, pointing out how this use of common formulae links these two works to *De doctrina*: 'Cet example des plus matériels suffirait, me semble-t-il, prouver que les traités inédits sortent de la même fabrique que le *De doctrina cordis*'.

34 (But on account of certain hypercritical and impatient readers we have omitted many extremely beneficial and useful things, and in the work that follows we shall turn our attention to investigating and inquiring into those things which

What is promised in these concluding words is then fulfilled in the treatise that follows, the *Quinque incitamenta*, which begins with a short preface, picking up on the vocabulary we have already encountered:

> Cum ad amandum deum multa et mira incitamenta in sacra scriptura habeamus, et ad contempnendum et fugiendum omnem amorem illicitum multa habeamus uera et salubria hortamenta, stupendum, mirandum et ualde dolendum est quod ad illud quod corpus nostrum inquinat et destruit … tanto conamine rapimur. (Prol. 3–6)[35]

A first section sets out the five 'incitamenta', section two is a *quaestio* about the definition of love, section three explores the four ways of loving God, and a final section sets out five stages by which love of God increases. The formulaic expressions that are used to lead the reader through the numbered structures, particularly the concluding formulae that indicate that 'sufficient' has now been said, are the same as in the *Septem remedia*. For Wilmart the integration of the two texts into what he called a 'diptych', two separate parts with their own headings, the second of which assumes the status of a 'work', was an indication of common authorship. This conclusion was confirmed by the use of common formulaic expressions and by the frequent use of French words and phrases inserted into the Latin text, a feature which both these works share with *De doctrina* and the Paris sermons and which Wilmart considered sufficiently uncommon to be a distinctive feature.[36] The use of French expressions is a feature which varies in quantity, in the length of the individual items and in the type of material so presented from one work to another. It is particularly prominent in the *Quinque incitamenta*, where the author makes use of verses, a number of which can be attested in contemporary love songs. Nico van den Boogaard, who published a study of the lyric insertions, came to the conclusion that Gerard of Liège,

---

can incite us to, and indeed must inflame us in the pursuit of the love of God.) Ibid., p. 205

35 (Since many notable incitements to love God are to be found in the Holy Scriptures, along with many unquestionable and valuable exhortations to condemn and flee all improper love, it is astonishing, amazing and much to be deplored that we are seized with such eagerness … to do things that besmirch and destroy our bodies …) Ibid., p. 205

36 Wilmart, 'Gérard', pp. 372f. For a broader discussion of the phenomenon of French vernacular inserts in Latin sermons see M. Zink, *La prédication en langue romane avant 1300*, Nouvelle bibliothèque du moyen âge 4 (Paris, 1976), pp. 93–102.

in his *Quinque incitamenta*, shows a knowledge of just that part of the contemporary motet repertoire which can be shown, on the basis of the manuscript tradition, to have circulated in clerical circles.[37]

In the second part of his 1982/84 study of the oeuvre of Gerard of Liège Hendrix disputed Wilmart's suggestion that a number of stylistic traits of the *Septem remedia*, when taken together, indicate common authorship with the *Quinque incitamenta*, which, as we have seen, was clearly the work of a Cistercian. In particular, he had in mind the structural features that had been seen as linking the two works, the use of certain common formulaic expressions, and the use of French inserts.[38] He also challenged the association with *De doctrina*, suggesting that in fact we have here three works by three different authors. In essence, his argument is that although there are similarities in the use of imagery and allegory, in formulaic expressions and in the employment of French, there are too many differences in the detail of how these features are handled for attribution to a single author to be plausible. He argues that the attribution of the *Septem remedia* to 'Frater Gerardus de Leodio', although in the hand of the scribe who copied the text, was added later, and thus carries less weight, and that the *Septem remedia* and *Quinque incitamenta* are too different in their range of reference and in their literary quality to be the work of a single author. He explains the presentation of a bipartite structure in the prologue by the hypothesis that this material was added by a redactor to bind two originally quite distinct texts together. This is not the place to challenge the detail of this analysis, but three points must be made against it. The argument gives very little weight to the fact that a scribal attribution to a little-known author associates the *Quinque incitamenta* with another work with which, apparently by chance, it shares certain quite marked stylistic features in common. Secondly, the assertion that the joining-together of the two texts by internal structural markers could have arisen in the course of a process of redaction not evident in the manuscripts, in which the prologues were added, underestimates the complexity of the verbal links made between the two texts and their parts in the introductory and concluding sentences.

---

37 N. van den Boogaard, 'Les insertions en français dans un traité de Gérard de Liège', in *Marche romane. Mélanges de philologie et de littératures romanes offerts à Jeanne Wathelet-Willem* (Liège 1978), pp. 679–97. The French inserts in *De doctrina* have not been studied in detail; see for example the citation from a vernacular song in book 6, ch. 1 (*De doctrina*, p. 267, with a Latin text).

38 Hendrix, 'Onderzoek II' (1984). Cf. the restatements of this position, using the same arguments, in Hendrix, 'Luik, Gerard van' (1987), cols 440f., and Hendrix, *Hugo I*, pp. 213–28.

Thirdly, the statements about stylistic inconsistency are based on untestable assumptions about the differences that may exist between the literary compositions of a single author. It remains tantalizing that the Gerardus Leodiensis attested in the manuscript tradition of *De doctrina* is regularly said to be a Dominican, whereas the 'unattached' Gerardus de Leodio of the *Septem remedia* would appear, on the basis of internal evidence, to be identical with the Cistercian author of the *Quinque incitamenta*.

Two further works attributable to the author of *De doctrina cordis* need mention in order to complete the picture.[39] The first is *De duodecim utilitatibus tribulationum* (long version, inc. 'Da nobis domine auxilium de tribulatione [Ps. 107:13]. Tibi anime tribulate et temptate ...'), printed in the *Patrologia Latina* under the name of Peter of Blois.[40] No detailed study has as yet been made of the manuscripts, but it is not known to have been attributed by scribes to Gerard, and the original attribution was based on grounds no better than the fact that it is preserved alongside *De doctrina* in Vienna, Österreichische Nationalbibliothek, cod. 4316. Nonetheless, the detailed investigation published by Hendrix in 1982 drew attention not only to the use of French expressions in a manner similar to the Paris sermons, *De doctrina*, the *Septem remedia* and the *Quinque incitamenta*, but also to eleven textual parallels with the *Postillae* of Hugh of St Cher very similar to those observable in *De doctrina* (for which see below), as well as similar use of imagery and seven textual parallels with *De doctrina* itself.[41] One of the links with *De doctrina* is the French gloss 'gallice *a bone chiere*', which is common to these two texts and which I shall discuss further below. On the basis of this study, and in his summary article of 1987, Hendrix proposed

---

39 In addition to these, there are also several further titles which have at various times been proposed for attribution to Gerard of Liège, none of them based on adequate manuscript evidence. They will not concern us here. Cf. Quétif/Échard, *Scriptores*, I, 248f.; [P.-C.-F.] Daunou, in *Histoire littéraire de la France*, vol. 19 (Paris, 1895), pp. 130f.; Wilmart, 'Gérard', pp. 360–63; Axters, 'Nederlandse mystiek', pp. 231f.

40 *PL* 207, cols 989–1006 (with a variant incipit 'Ordo et modus docendi ...'). M.W. Bloomfield et al., *Incipits of Latin Works on the Virtues and Vices, 1100–1500 A.D.* (Cambridge, MA, 1979), no. 1302. Cf. [J.]B. Hauréau, *Notices et extraits de quelques manuscrits latins de la Bibliothèque nationale*, vol. 4 (Paris, 1892), pp. 125–8; A. Auer, *Leidenstheologie im Spätmittelalter*, Kirchengeschichtliche Quellen und Studien 2 (St. Ottilien, 1952), pp. 1–71, reprinting the text from Migne, pp. 1–18; A. Barratt, *The Book of Tribulation ed. from MS Bodley 423*, Middle English Texts 15 (Heidelberg, 1983), especially pp. 22–6 (with a list of Latin MSS, distinguishing the long and the short version); Hendrix, 'Luik, Gerard van' (1987), col. 441.

41 Hendrix, 'Kleine queste' (1982), passim.

attribution of *De duodecim tribulationibus* to the author of *De doctrina* (whom he argued was likely to be Hugh of St Cher). In later publications, however, he appears to have changed his mind, and in his monograph of 1995 the attribution is unaccountably rejected without further discussion.[42] Until such a time as convincing counter-arguments have been set out, the attribution of *De duodecim utilitatibus tribulationum* to the author of *De doctrina* must stand.

The *Tractatus super septem verba dicta a Domino Jesu Christo pendente in cruce* (inc.: 'Est tempus loquendi et tempus tacendi ...') is preserved in two manuscripts with the full version of the text, both with an attribution to Magister Gerardus built into the heading: 'Tractatus magistri Gerardi in divinitate super septem verba dicta a Domino Jesu Christo pendente in cruce.'[43] The designation 'magister ... in divinitate', which Tobias A. Kemper, in his recent analysis of the text, is surely mistaken in taking to be part of the title, seems to hark back to the tradition of the Dominican 'frater Gerhardus dictus divinus' which we encountered above, both in the transmission of *De doctrina* and in the Paris sermon manuscript, where he is given the epithet 'Le Devin'. For the editor of the *Septem verba*, Edmond Mikkers, there was little doubt that the author, whose association of Christ's Seven Words with seven localities within an enclosed monastery so clearly points to the viewpoint of a monastic author, was the Cistercian Gerard of Liège, albeit in his view more probably a simple monk than the abbot of Val-Saint-Lambert proposed by Wilmart. Hendrix's 1980 study of the text brought to light, as with *De duodecim utilitatibus tribulationum*, a considerable number of reminiscences of the *Postillae* of Hugh of St Cher, including a falsely attributed Bernard/Bede citation which is also used in a

42 Hendrix, *Hugo I*, pp. xxx, 229–32.

43 (A treatise by Gerard, master of divinity, on the seven words spoken by the Lord Jesus Christ as he hung on the cross.) E. Mikkers (ed.), 'Le traité de Gérard de Liège sur les Sept Paroles de Notre Seigneur en Croix', *Collectanea ordinis Cisterciensium reformatorum*, 12 (1950), 176–94, continued in 13 (1951), 18–29. The shorter version (inc.: 'Oues mee uocem meam audiunt ...') is published as 'sermo 13' in Hendrix, *Hugo* [...] *4. De sermoenen* (2000), pp. 71–9. See also Hendrix, 'Hugh of St. Cher' (1980), passim; id., *Hugo I*, pp. 232f.; T.A. Kemper, *Die Kreuzigung Christi. Motivgeschichtliche Studien zu lateinischen und deutschen Passionstraktaten des Spätmittelalters*, Münchener Texte und Untersuchungen zur deutschen Literatur des Mittelalters 131 (Tübingen, 2006), pp. 329–35, with a detailed textual analysis and reference to the previously unrecorded reception of the *Septem verba* in the German treatise *Vierzig Myrrhenbüschel vom Leiden Christi*.

similar context in *De doctrina*. In this case, therefore, scholarship is agreed that the *Septem verba* is the work of the writer who was also responsible for *De doctrina* and *De duodecim utilitatibus tribulationum*. All three works make use of French expressions embedded in the Latin text, they display internal links in their use of material associated with the *Postillae* of Hugh of St Cher, and *De doctrina* and the *Septem verba* have manuscript attributions to Gerardus. A significant difference of opinion remains, as we shall see, in the interpretation of the material these texts share with the *Postillae* and of the problem that, despite strong pointers to a monastic, most probably Cistercian authorial perspective, the author Gerardus is said in the manuscripts of *De doctrina* to have been a Dominican lector.

Whereas it may not be possible to say with complete certainty exactly when, by whom and where *De doctrina* was written, if it is set alongside the sermons, the *Septem remedia*, the *Quinque incitamenta*, *De duodecim utilitatibus tribulationum* and the *Septem verba*, all of which can be associated, directly or indirectly, with the name of a certain 'Gerard of Liège', a literary context can be established which places it at a very particular point in the development of thirteenth-century monastic literature. What weight, then, must be given to the counter-argument, which arises from the source investigations of Guido Hendrix, and to the association that he has demonstrated for all these works with the Dominican provincial and cardinal Hugh of St Cher? Before turning to these questions, it may be helpful to present in summary some of the salient points we have established so far:

- Attributions to Gerard of Liège are contained in manuscripts of *De doctrina cordis* (sixteen out of 204), the sermons (one), the *Septem remedia* (one of three) and the *Septem verba* (three).
- Gerard's added name 'dictus Divinus', attested in manuscripts of *De doctrina*, ties up with his designation as 'Le Devin' in the sermons and as 'magister … in divinitate' in the *Septem verba*, suggesting that this is a reference to an individual with a certain reputation, not just a name created by a stroke of the pen.
- Only the manuscripts of *De doctrina* and the *Catalogus virorum illustrium* specify that Gerard was a Dominican lector in Liège.
- The author of the *Quinque incitamenta* identifies himself and his audience, in the body of the text, as Cistercians.
- All the texts contain French insertions, ranging from individual words and short French expressions to longer sentences, proverbs and even citations from secular lyrics.

Hugh of St Cher

Here, too, we can begin with a question. Who was the author Hugh of St Cher? Of the man the handbooks tell us that he must have been born at Saint-Cher near Vienne, in the Dauphiné, in the last decade of the twelfth century; that he became a secular master in Paris, joined the Dominican order on 22 February 1225, rose to the position of provincial of the French province in 1227–30 (and again in 1236–44), prior of the Paris convent in 1230, vicar general in 1240–41; and that from 1244 until his death in 1263 he served as the first Dominican cardinal under Popes Alexander IV (1254–61) and Urban IV (1261–4).[44] His literary oeuvre, which Kaeppeli presents in a list of twelve items,[45] embraces some of the more usual writings that one might expect of a Paris master, such as his commentary on the Sentences and a widely read treatise on the mass, but also three quite exceptional works, the *Correctorium* of the Bible, the *Concordantiae* of the Bible, and his *Postillae* on the books of the Bible. These are not just the byproducts of a Paris master's duties in the university; rather, they formed part of a programme to shape the whole enterprise of Dominican teaching and study. As an enterprise they had some success, as is demonstrated by Patricia Stirnemann's recent list of 420 manuscripts of the *Postillae*.[46] In the scholarship of the last thirty years, following a lead given by Beryl Smalley, Hugh of St Cher has been seen not so much as a writer but as the project manager of the Paris enterprise during the years 1230–44. Robert Lerner's summary may be regarded as typical of the position maintained by the most recent scholarship:

> In reality the three vast projects that were completed in the Parisian Dominican convent of St. Jacques in the 1230s – the concordance of the scriptures, the *correctorium*, and the *Postills* – despite their nominal attribution to Hugh of St. Cher were produced by a team of energetic

---

44 É. Mangenot, 'Hugues de Saint-Cher', *Dictionnaire de théologie catholique*, vol. 7 (Paris, 1921), cols 221–39; Kaeppeli/Panella, *Scriptores ordinis Praedicatorum*, II, 269–81; R. Aubert, 'Hugues de Saint-Cher', in A. Baudillart et al. (eds), *Dictionnaire d'histoire et de géographie ecclésiastique*, vol. 25 (Paris, 1995), col. 287; J. Verger, 'Hugues de Saint-Cher dans le contexte universitaire parisien', in Bataillon et al. (eds), *Hugues de Saint-Cher*, pp. 13–28. Cf. Hendrix, *Hugo I*, pp. xiii–xix.

45 Kaeppeli/Panella, *Scriptores ordinis Praedicatorum*, nos 1983–94.

46 P. Stirnemann, 'Les manuscrits de la *Postille*', in Bataillon et al. (eds), *Hugues de Saint-Cher*, pp. 31–42.

> young friars under Hugh's direction. Not only is it inconceivable that a single individual could have accomplished such a vast amount of work by himself while also attending to weighty academic, homiletic, and administrative responsibilities, but the *Postills* contain within them different opinions that attest multiple authorship.[47]

The *Postillae* amounted to a project more like building a ship than composing a monograph, and the interplay of authority, authorship and the preparation of manuscripts must have been a process so complex that the resulting work cannot be thought of as a book written by Hugh of St Cher in the normal sense. This is the context in which the problematic proposal to attribute *De doctrina cordis* and related writings to Hugh of St Cher must be seen.

Of the texts discussed above only *De doctrina* is ever ascribed to Hugh (of St Cher) in the manuscripts. Hendrix has drawn attention to six such attributions, one of which makes it quite clear which Hugo is intended: 'Et sic est finis istius tractatuli de doctrina cordis. Item. Causa efficiens huius libri dicitur fuisse Hugo cardinalis.'[48] Four manuscripts simply record the name of Hugo as author in the incipit formula or colophon: 'Explicit Hugo' (Liège, Bibliothèque du Grand Séminaire, MS 6 N 20, fol. 143r; Hendrix L[15]); 'Explicit opusculum fratris Hugonis de preparacione cordis' (Kraków, Biblioteka Jagiellońska, MS 1382, fol. 74v; Hendrix K[10]); 'Incipit prologus Hugonis de preparacione cordis et est liber spiritualis'/

---

47 R. Lerner, 'The vocation of the Friars Preacher: Hugh of St. Cher between Peter the Chanter and Albert the Great', in Bataillon et al. (eds), *Hugues de Saint-Cher*, pp. 216–31, here p. 215. Cf. B. Smalley, *The Study of the Bible in the Middle Ages* (Oxford, 3rd edn, 1983), pp. 270–75, and *The Gospels in the Schools c.1100–c.1280* (London, 1985), pp. 125–43, who describes Hugh of St Cher's role in the production of the *Postillae* in similar terms.

48 (And this is the end of this little treatise concerning the doctrine of the heart. Furthermore, the efficient cause behind this book is said to have been Cardinal Hugh.) Berlin, Staatsbibliothek zu Berlin – Preußischer Kulturbesitz, Ms. theol. fol. 327 (= Hendrix B[16]), from Liesborn OSB; cited from Hendrix, 'Onderzoek' (1982), p. 321; id., *Hugo I*, p. 19. The manuscripts with attributions to 'Hugo' have been set out by Hendrix several times: 'Hugh of St. Cher' (1980), p. 355; 'De apercione' (1981), pp. 196–9; 'Onderzoek' (1982), pp. 320f. (incorrect shelfmark for the Prague MS., p. 340). See also the entry for 'Hugo de doctrina' in the medieval catalogue of St. Ägidien in Nuremberg: Hendrix, 'Hugh of St. Cher' (1980), p. 355; id., *Hugo I*, p. 127. Unaccountably, the Liège manuscript is no longer listed in the catalogue of *De doctrina* manuscripts in Hendrix, *Hugo I*, where the siglum L[15] has been reassigned (p. 51).

'Liber Hugonis' (Prague, Národní knihovna České republiky, MS XI–I. A.14, fol. 66r/v; Hendrix P2); 'Incipit prologus in librum Hugonis de preparatione cordis'/'Incipit liber hugonis de preparacione cordis' (Würzburg, Universitätsbibliothek, M.ch.f.229, fols 2ra/vb; Hendrix W4). The sixth manuscript offers the reader alternative authors: 'Hugonis vel Anshelmi episcopi Liber de doctrina cordis' (Munich, Bayerische Staatsbibliothek, Clm 18647, fol. 160r; Hendrix M12). It has been stressed by Hendrix that the attributions to Hugo, unlike those to Gerard of Liège, are to be found in manuscripts of both the short and long recensions of the text, which lends them greater authority. This evaluation of their distribution is dependent upon the questionable assumption that such attributions are only passed down by vertical descent in the copying tradition.

It should also be pointed out that only one of the six manuscript attributions makes it explicit which 'Hugo' is intended, and even here the scribe covers himself with 'dicitur fuisse'. Certainly it is the case that Hugh of St Cher is frequently identified simply as 'Hugo' rather than as 'Hugo Cardinalis' in colophons.[49] Nonetheless, the writer most commonly intended when the name 'Hugo' is attached to a medieval text is Hugh of St Victor, and it is not at all clear that the scribes of the other five manuscripts were really intending an attribution to Hugh of St Cher. This argument acquires additional weight if one considers Hugh of St Victor's penchant for allegory and figurative language and his place in the literary history of devotional treatises for a monastic audience.

Whereas the manuscript attributions are of considerable importance, a second argument adduced for the authorship of Hugh of St Cher is more problematic. Two works by the author whom we are seeking contain a French gloss which Hendrix interprets as a reference by the author to his own name. The first example is contained in *De doctrina*, book 7 ('De scissione cordis'): 'Bonus vultus istius amici consolatio spiritualis est et multum perdit qui bonum vultum, gallice *bone chiere*, amici sui perdit.'[50] A similar gloss occurs at the beginning of *De duodecim utilitatibus tribulationum*: 'non solum pacienter, sed et hylariter, gallice *a bone chiere*,

---

49 This observation is based on no more than a spot-check in those manuscript catalogues, rather few in number, which report precisely on the manuscript headings and colophons of well-known works such as the *Postillae*.

50 (The look of approval on the face of one's beloved signifies spiritual consolation, and whoever loses the approval of their beloved, in French *bone chiere*, has lost a good deal.) Hendrix, 'Postillae' (1980), p. 124, ll. 229–31; id., *Hugo I*, p. 422, ll. 20–22; id., *Manuscrit Leyde Bibliothèque de l'Université*, p. 158, ll. 7–9; *De doctrina*, p. 286.

eas sustineas et ediscas consolari interius.'[51] The parallel has some weight as an argument for common authorship, but given the lack of parallels for such a practice it is most implausible that a figure such as Hugh of St Cher might have 'hidden' his own name in the text in this way.

The strength of Hendrix's argument lies in the combination of the external evidence of author attributions in the colophons and internal evidence assembled on the basis of a comparison of *De doctrina* with the *Postillae* of Hugh of St Cher. The main evidence for the association of *De doctrina* with the *Postillae* is set out in a series of articles from the early 1980s, which present a detailed analysis of the textual parallels.[52] A summary of the position reached, as set out in 1982 (and repeated in 1995), indicates that the parallels are not restricted to certain parts of Hugh of St Cher's oeuvre, but extend through six of the seven volumes of the 1621 edition.[53] Whereas the demonstration of the existence of significant parallels is mostly conducted on the basis of an analysis of the prologue, book 3, chapter 1, and book 7 of the *De doctrina cordis*, this is backed up further by the detailed book-by-book analysis of sources, including numerous shared citations from patristic authorities, in the 1995 monograph.[54] The parallels can be divided up into explanations of individual words, images (allegories), and longer passages where there is verbatim correspondence between the two texts. That borrowing in some form or other has occurred is undeniable, and the numerous rather trivial parallels of wording and imagery provide a context for those which are more extensive, and make it seem most unlikely that the correspondences

---

51 (You will not only bear them (your tribulations) patiently, but happily, in French *a bone chiere*, and you will learn to be consoled inwardly.) Hendrix, 'Postillae' (1980), pp. 129f.; id., 'Kleine queste' (1980), pp. 122–4; id., 'Luik, Gerard van' (1987), col. 441. The citation is from Paris, Bibliothèque nationale de France, MS lat. 14955, also attested in Munich, Bayerische Staatsbibliothek, Clm 6977 ('gallice *o bone chere*'), which differ from the extremely unreliable text printed by Migne. Both manuscripts are cited by Auer, *Leidenstheologie*, p. 29; cf. Hauréau, *Notices et extraits*, IV, 126.

52 Hendrix, 'Het Leidse handschrift' (1980), pp. 173f. (analysis of the prologue); id., 'Hugh of St. Cher' (1980), pp. 352–4 ('quinque casus in quibus non obligatur aliquis ad corripiendum alium', from the end of book 5 = *De doctrina*, pp. 185f.); id., 'Postillae' (1980), pp. 116–29 (book 7, 'De scissione'); id., 'De apercione' (1981), passim (book 3, ch. 1).

53 Hendrix, 'Onderzoek' (1982), pp. 317–21, 335–8; id., *Hugo I*, pp. 263–70; with parallel texts of the allegorical interpretations of 'aquila', 'baculus', and 'aves'.

54 Hendrix, *Hugo I*, pp. 271–330. See in particular the review of citations from Ps.-Chrysostomus, *Opus imperfectum in Matthaeum*, pp. 259–61.

are to be explained by a common source. Very few parallels are to be found in book 4 ('De stabilitate') and none in book 5 ('De datione').[55] This distribution pattern is further evidence that the correspondences are not due to chance. In themselves, though, as Hendrix concedes, the numerous parallels provide no clear indications as to the direction of borrowing. He is aware that Hugh had a reputation for being a writer from whom others borrowed, as is stated in the words 'De eius tractatibus, libris et postillis postmodum multi hauserunt' of the *Commendatio virorum magnorum ordinis sancti Dominici predicatorum, qui scripserunt multa utilia in Ecclesia* published by Albert Auer.[56] The reasons given for rejecting the obvious conclusion, that the author of *De doctrina* drew on the widely copied *Postillae*, are circumstantial and essentially speculative. He argues that a Dominican writer (if one follows the attribution to Gerardus Leodiensis OP) would have wished to provide named attributions to Hugh of St Cher in his work, in order to add the name of this contemporary Dominican to the panoply of authorities from the Bible and the church fathers through to Bernard and Gilbert of Hoyland, who are cited by name. His second point is that the *De doctrina* author's familiarity with the *Postillae*, the way he 'instinctively knows where to look for something', speaks for a single individual as author rather than the consultation of the *Postillae* by a later writer.[57] But how much weight can these arguments be allowed to carry?

If we approach the question from a different angle, namely what is known about Hugh of St Cher as a writer, then an explanation for the textual correspondences between *De doctrina* and the *Postillae* based on common authorship seems quite simply implausible. If the *Postillae* were a collaborative enterprise undertaken by the friars of Saint-Jacques under the leadership of Hugh of St Cher, what does it mean to say that the author of *De doctrina* knew 'instinctively where to look for' the material he needed? And was 'Hugo' an authority to be cited, where individual formulations from the *Postillae* were taken over, in the same way as Augustine, Bernard

---

55 Hendrix, *Hugo I*, pp. 263, 408. Hendrix considers the possibility that the two parts of book 5 were originally autonomous texts and the work of a different author or authors. He describes his analysis of the passages about beards and about the exchange of hearts, in the context of Hugh of St Cher's writing, as a 'rescue attempt'.

56 A. Auer, *Ein neu aufgefundener Katalog der Dominikaner Schriftsteller*, Dissertationes historicae 2 (Paris, 1933), p. 105; cited by Hendrix, *Hugo I*, pp. 210 and 268.

57 Hendrix, 'Onderzoek' (1982), p. 320; id., *Hugo I*, p. 268f.

or Bede? Certainly the attributions to 'Hugo' in the manuscript tradition are to be taken seriously, but this is just one of a dozen attributions of *De doctrina* to famous men, and the only special factor which attaches to it is the fact that more textual parallels exist to the *Postillae* than to any other single source text. These parallels are much more easily to be interpreted as evidence of a writer who had studied in Paris, whose reading of the Bible was deeply indebted to the school of biblical exegesis established by the great Dominican teacher and who drew on a manuscript copy of the *Postillae* in the course of his own pastoral duties (for example in preaching or the instruction of novices).[58] Quantitatively the large number of textual parallels is the equivalent, in terms of the internalization of Hugh of St Cher's teaching, to the phenomenon of a manuscript tradition of 420 manuscripts of the *Postillae*.

If it could be established that Hugh of St Cher were in truth the most likely author of *De doctrina cordis*, then the question would arise as to how the composition of such a work, in conjunction with the other writings that appear to be by the same author, could be accommodated into what we know of his career. Hendrix's answer to this is clear. From 1251 to 1253 the newly appointed cardinal was papal legate in the German lands, and assumed responsibility for the *cura monialium*, a task to which the content of *De doctrina* would seem relevant. On the basis of this assumption he suggests 1251–3 as the *terminus post quem* for the composition of the work.[59] Such a dating would sit comfortably alongside what we know of the manuscript circulation of the work, if we can entertain a gap of some twenty years before there is datable codicological evidence, but the case for Hugh of St Cher as the writer is simply so weak that it is not appropriate to factor in details of his career in considering the date to be assigned to the work.

58 See the formulation of this position by L.-J. Bataillon/N. Bériou, '"G. de Mailly" de l'ordre des Frères prècheurs', *Archivum fratrum Praedicatorum*, 61 (1991), 5–88, here pp. 21f., quoted with approval by A.B. Mulder-Bakker, *Lives of the Anchoresses. The Rise of the Urban Recluse in Medieval Europe* (Philadelphia, Pa., 2005), p. 89 with n. 47 (p. 238). Cf. Hendrix, *Hugo I*, p. 264.

59 Hendrix, 'De apercione' (1981), p. 197. Even before this period, in his capacity as French Dominican provincial, Hugh was expected to visit the Dominican convents in the area under his jurisdiction; cf. Mulder-Bakker, *Lives of the Anchoresses*, p. 89.

Gerardus Leodiensis OP and Gerardus Leodiensis OCist

Some time around the year 1210 Juliana, a young member of the lay community at Cornillon, a leprosorium on the outskirts of Liège, repeatedly experienced a vision of the fractured moon: 'Apparuit inquam ei luna in suo splendore, cum aliquantula tamen sui sperici corporis fractione'.[60] In response to her prayers Christ reveals to her that the moon stands for the Church, whereas the fracture indicates the failure to celebrate a certain feast on which he places great value, namely Corpus Christi. Juliana is instructed to devote herself to the institution of this feast. But in her modesty and weakness she feels herself to be incapable and unworthy of taking the necessary action, and she protests. Not until some twenty years or more have passed does she finally give in to Christ's will. She goes to John of Lausanne, canon of St Martin's in Liège, tells her story, and asks him to submit the content of her vision to the judgement of suitable ecclesiastical authorities, which he then proceeds to do. First of all he seeks the advice of the former Paris master James of Troyes (Jacques Pantaleon), archdeacon of Liège cathedral, later to become Pope Urban IV. Then brother Hugh (of St Cher), the French Dominican provincial, is approached, along with Guiard, bishop of Cambrai and formerly a canon of Notre-Dame, who are described as the two great shining lights of the contemporary church. The latter is Guiard of Laon, who is known in literary studies as the author of the *Sermo domini Wiardi de duodecim fructibus sacramenti*, also preserved in a reputedly authorial French recension known as *Des xii preus que li sacremens fait*.[61] This is the earliest recorded text on the Twelve Fruits of the Sacrament. Four further persons are now consulted, the chancellor

---

60 (Indeed the moon appeared to her in its splendor, and yet with a small crack in its spherical form.) This quotation and what follows are from the *Vita venerabilis virginis Christi Juliane de Corelion*, ed. by J.-P. Delville, in *Fête-Dieu (1246–1996). 2. Vie de Sainte Julienne de Cornillon*, Université Catholique de Louvain. Publications de l'Institut d'Études Médiévales: textes, études, congrès 19/2 (Louvain-la-Neuve, 1999), II, 6 (p. 120).

61 For the Latin text see A. Ampe, 'Een oud Florilegium Eucharisticum in een veertiende-eeuws handschrift', *OGE*, 31 (1957), 301–24, 32 (1958), 56–90, 38 (1964), 23–55, here vol. 31, pp. 308–24. For the French text see P.C. Boeren, *La vie et les oeuvres de Guiard de Laon 1170 env. – 1248* (The Hague, 1956), pp. 310–19. Cf. K. Ruh, 'Guiard von Laon', in K. Ruh et al. (eds) *Die deutsche Literatur des Mittelalters. Verfasserlexikon*, 2nd edn, vol. 3 (Berlin/New York, 1981), cols 295–9; W. Scheepsma, *De Limburgse sermoenen (ca. 1300). De oudste preken in het Nederlands,* Nederlandse literatuur en cultuur in de Middeleeuwen 26 (Amsterdam, 2006), pp. 131–8.

of the University of Paris[62] and three Dominican lectors – 'necnon et Egidio, Ioanni et Gerardo, lectoribus fratrum predicatorum Leodiensium' – and, in addition, many other distinguished people.[63]

Of the three Dominican lectors who are here named, Giles (Aegidius) may well not otherwise be recorded, John is probably John of Villers, attested 1256, and Gerard is probably the lector named in the colophons of *De doctrina* manuscripts. The exact date of these events is not known, but the consultations are estimated to have taken place at some point in the 1230s or 40s. The editor of the *Vita*, Jean-Pierre Delville, followed Christine Renardy in preferring a date some time around 1246, whereas Anneke Mulder-Bakker has recently argued for *c.*1235, before the death of Philip the Chancellor (d. 1236).[64] The six judges give consideration to Juliana's message, approve its content and declare that the Corpus Christi feast should be instituted. In due course this is done, and chapter II, 14 of the *Vita* describes how in 1251 Hugh of St Cher, in his capacity as cardinal and legate to the German lands, comes to Liège and confirms the introduction of the office for Corpus Christi, causing a great stir by his decision to perform the first celebration of the office in the church of Saint-Martin-en-Mont himself.

The life of Juliana of Cornillon has often been cited in the scholarship on *De doctrina* for its attestation of the Dominican lector Gerard.[65] But it has not previously been remarked that the passage brings together two of the principal candidates for the authorship of this text as members of the commission that was asked to pronounce on Juliana's visions. Nor has it

---

62 Delville, *Fête-Dieu*, vol. 2, p. 131 n. 186, suggests that this was Odo of Châteauroux (1238–44), thereby implying a date earlier in the 1240s. Odo was followed by Petrus Parvus (1244–*c.*1246) and Galterus (1246–9); see *Chartularium Universitatis Parisiensis*, vol. 1, ed. by H.S. Denifle and A. Chatelain (Paris, 1889), pp. xix–xx. Mulder-Bakker, however, is confident in identifying the chancellor mentioned here as Philip the Chancellor (1236); *Lives of the Anchoresses*, p. 89.

63 (and also Giles, John and Gerard, lectors of the Dominican friars at Liège.) *Vita Juliane de Corelion*, II, 7 (Delville, *Fête-Dieu*, vol. 2, p. 130). For the identification of the three Dominican lectors see Delville's footnote 187 (p. 131), with references. I am doubtful, for reasons of chronology, about his proposed identification of Giles as the preacher against the beguines in Paris in 1273. The unique manuscript of the *Vita* contains a long-since-recognized copying error, 'Renardo' for 'Gerardo'.

64 Renardy, *Le monde des maîtres*, p. 385; Mulder-Bakker, *Lives of the Anchoresses*, pp. 89f.

65 Quétif/Échard, *Scriptores*, I, 249; Daunou, *Histoire littéraire*, XIX, 130f.; Wilmart, 'Gérard', pp. 350f.; Axters, 'Nederlandse mystiek', p. 223; Hendrix, *Hugo I*, p. 195.

been noted how it documents that close relationship between the interests of religious women and leading figures of the Paris-educated intelligentsia which also finds expression in the incorporation of so much material from the Paris lecture courses, as represented by the *Postillae* of Hugh of St Cher, into a treatise which is evidently aimed at a monastic and at least to some extent female audience.

If we are to reject the attribution of *De doctrina cordis* to Hugh of St Cher, while at the same time recognizing the impact, and indeed direct influence of his teaching on the doctrine and methods of exposition which the work embodies, then who was the author? The figure identified in the manuscript tradition is Gerard, Dominican lector at Liège, who can be attested in historical sources for the period 1246–72.[66] We have seen from the manuscript colophons that he was known under the name of 'Gerardus dictus divinus', an attribution which carries a certain weight because of the parallel designations in the Paris sermon manuscript and the *Septem verba*, and that he was known at the time as a 'great and famous preacher'.[67] These scraps of information, even if they cannot be tested, are in line with what we can infer about the lector Gerard who served alongside Hugh of St Cher and Guiard of Laon as an assessor of the visions of Juliana of Cornillon, the choice of whom for such a task presupposes that he was considered a theologian of some distinction.

The prologue to *De doctrina* begins with an injunction to the recipients of the teaching contained in the text, 'Preparate corda vestra domino' (1 Sam. 7:3),[68] only to move immediately to the perspective of the preachers, addressing those entrusted with pastoral care: 'Loquimini ad cor Iherusalem' – 'Speak ye to the heart of Jerusalem' (Isa. 40:2). This is an admonition to preachers and teachers to ensure that they transmit the divine message in such a way that it touches the hearts of the listeners. The rest of the prologue sets out how the listener needs to be truly receptive, which involves ensuring that it is the divine teachings and not the filthy water of profane tales that flow into the chamber of the heart. The double perspective of the prologue stresses both the responsibilities of

66 This is the second Gerard of Liège listed by Renardy, *Les maîtres universitaires*, pp. 234f., whom she calls 'Maître Gérard de Reims'. He undertook various missions on behalf of Bishop Robert of Thourotte and Peter, cardinal-bishop of Albano and apostolic legate. He is attested as lector in theology at Liège on 10 December 1253. In 1250 and 1272 he is attested in Paris.

67 See p. 27 above.

68 Cited from the IP (= 'Ignaros Predicatores') recension, ed. Hendrix, 'Het Leidse handschrift' (1980), pp. 168–72.

the 'predicatores' and that of their charges. It ensures that the 'doctrine of the heart', although centrally concerned with the cultivation of the inner religious life, is to be read in the context of the interchange of pastoral care, which makes demands on both parties. The theme of pastoral care is strongly evident in book 1, the first section of which is concerned with preparation for confession.

The special interests required of the reader, which the author takes for granted, are those of the members of an enclosed monastic community.[69] Despite occasional asides to priests in charge,[70] the principal addressees of the treatise are to be thought of as members of a religious community, referred to by expressions such as 'religiosi' (p. 11), 'claustralis' (p. 30) and 'anima claustralis' (p. 88). Their world is the monastery ('Vnde contingit aliquando in claustro …', p. 67). Life is seen as strictly divided between the cloister and the world outside, as is evident from the criticism of go-betweens: 'Et tales sunt quasi homines *de terre de marche* habentes habitum claustralem, animum vero secularem' (p. 68).[71] The section about spiritual marriage in book 1 reminds the readers of their monastic vows of obedience and 'stabilitas loci' (p. 110). Reference is made to the reader's abbot (p. 36), where Dominicans would have had a prior, to the reader's male 'brethren' (p. 69), and a section of book 5 is devoted to an allegory of male tonsure, in particular the shaving of beards (pp. 250f.). The 'claustralis anima' wears a (monk's) 'cucullа' (p. 109). Where the reader is addressed as 'carissima' (e.g. pp. 264, 267, 268, 269), this can be read as referring to the 'anima carissima' and thus neutral in terms of gender. There are passages, however, which make explicit reference to the affairs of women, such as the criticism of nuns who smarten themselves up when they are called to the 'locutorium' (p. 92) and of those who weigh up the nun's dowry when she enters a convent (p. 96), and the address to a female novice entering the 'school of love' (p. 106). In particular, the allegory of the 'chapter of the heart' is presided over by an abbess (and not, as in a Dominican nunnery, by a prioress), and the author castigates those monks and nuns who fail to attend: 'Vae monacho siue moniali nunquam istud capitulum

---

69 See the material collected by Wilmart, 'Gérard', pp. 373–7, and his judgement: 'Ceci nous éloigne fort, évidemment, du ministère, soit doctrinal soit apostolique, des frères Prècheurs' (pp. 373f.).

70 E.g. book 2, ch. 7 (*De doctrina*, p. 189): 'Mitte ergo o praelate exemplo Domini, iram tuam, dum excessus corripis aliorum …' (repeated in book 5, ch. 2, p. 253). Page numbers in the text all refer to the 1607 edition of *De doctrina*.

71 (And such people are like frontiermen, wearing the monastic habit, but with a worldly mentality.)

intranti' (p. 27).[72] When, in book 4, the theme of compassion with Christ is introduced, both sexes are envisaged: 'quod fit fratri vel sorori' (p. 225), and there are other passages which deliberately allow for male and female readers: 'Sic tu, si vere Christi membrum es, si frater tuus aut soror te laeserit vel offenderit, non vindictam quaeras, sed patienter feras' (p. 226).[73] The implicit audience is thus one of monks and nuns living in enclosed monastic communities, and it seems likely, in view of the author's care to include women readers, that he has these particularly in mind.

One or two passages allow some further definition of this monastic audience. On one occasion lay brothers who wear the 'capa Benedicti' on their backs are mentioned (p. 141). Wilmart noted that the mention of the 'constitutiones et statuta ordinis' imposed by abbots (p. 198) has 'une forte saveur cistercienne'.[74] That the audience is to be thought of as following the Benedictine Rule, probably as monks and nuns of the Cistercian order, is further suggested by the division of the day into 'tempus laboris' and 'tempus orationis et lectionis' (p. 141), and by mention of the distinctive Cistercian ideal of 'vnanimitas et vniformitas quae inter Religiosos esse debet' (p. 132).[75]

The evidence assembled suggests a primary audience of enclosed monks and nuns, probably Cistercians, and in particular Cistercian nuns. This does not in itself pose a problem for the hypothesis, which we are for the moment considering, namely that the author might be identified as 'frater Gerardus ordinis Predicatorum lector domus Leodiensis'. In the mid thirteenth century the whole issue of the *cura monialium* by the male religious orders had become acute. On 26 September 1252 Innocent IV, under pressure, issued a bull releasing the Dominican order from almost all responsibility for nuns. But this was followed by a rearguard action, in which the papal legate Hugh of St Cher played a major part, by which the nun's privileges were largely restored.[76] In the Cistercian order the situation was not dissimilar in that conflicts are discernible from the 1220s onwards

---

72 (Woe on the monk or nun who never goes to the chapterhouse.)

73 (If you are truly a limb of Christ and your brother or sister wounds you or offends you, then you too will not seek reprisal, but will suffer patiently.)

74 Wilmart, 'Gérard', p. 375, n. 64. See also the mention of 'consuetudines ordinis tui' (p. 227).

75 (the unanimity and uniformity which ought to exist among monks and nuns.)

76 For a recent statement on the position in the mid-century see S. Tugwell, 'Were the Magdalen nuns really turned into Dominicans in 1287?', *Archivum fratrum Praedicatorum*, 76 (2006), 39–77, here pp. 43f.

between the General Chapter on the one hand, which regularly formulated a defensive position restricting the order's obligations towards nuns, and the popes, bishops and individual laymen on the other, who pressed, for a variety of reasons, for the foundation of Cistercian nunneries or for the incorporation of women living according to the *ordo Cisterciensium* into the order. The relevant statutes were incorporated into the 1237 version of the *Libellus definitionum* of the Cistercian order (under the heading 'de monialibus ordinis non sociandis'), and again in 1257, which retained the potentially negative and restrictive attitude towards nunneries.[77] If we are dealing here with a work written for Cistercian nuns then, although the convent will have had a strong attachment to a father abbot, we may not suppose that the *cura monialium*, and in particular confession, will have been exercised directly by Cistercians. Evidence for Cistercian monks undertaking the duty of confessor to nuns is extremely sparse in the thirteenth century, and in most cases the confessors will have been secular priests who had been granted the authority to hear confession by the legally responsible Cistercian father abbot.[78] There is no sense, then, in which a Dominican who addressed a pastoral work of this kind to Benedictine or Cistercian nuns would have been assuming a role which was the prerogative of the Cistercians. Whatever order the author belonged to, he was demonstrating a strong commitment to the women's cause by according them the prominence that he does in *De doctrina*.

The problem with attributing *De doctrina cordis* to a Dominican lector, as suggested by the scribal colophons and headings, is that there is good evidence that the same author was also responsible for the *Quinque incitamenta ad Deum amandum ardenter*, whose author places himself explicitly in a group of 'nos omnes, qui ordinem Cisterciensium professi

---

77 Cf. F.J. Felten, 'Zisterzienserinnen in Deutschland. Beobachtungen und Überlegungen zu Ausbreitung und Ordenszugehörigkeit', in *Unanimité et diversité cisterciennes. Filiations – réseaux – relectures du XIIe au XVIIe siècle. Actes du quatrième colloque international du CERCOR* (Saint-Étienne, 2000), pp. 345–400; id., 'Der Zisterzienserorden und die Frauen', in H. Schwillus and A. Hölscher (eds), *Weltverachtung und Dynamik*, Studien zur Geschichte, Kunst und Kultur der Zisterzienser 10 (Berlin, 2000), pp. 34–135, esp. 69–106.

78 For details of the legislation see G. Ahlers, *Weibliches Zisterziensertum im Mittelalter und seine Klöster in Niedersachsen*, Studien zur Geschichte, Kunst und Kultur der Zisterzienser 13 (Berlin, 2002), pp. 79–90. For the role of non-Cistercians in the *cura monialium* in this period see in particular Felten, 'Zisterzienserorden', pp. 37, 75f. (with the example of the appointment of a 'Franciscan or Dominican' as confessor at Tiefenthal, near Mainz, in 1246/47).

sumus'.[79] Wilmart could explain the conflicting evidence only as the result of a mistake that occurred at some point early on in the tradition, perhaps influenced by the prominence of the role of 'predicatores' in the prologue.[80]

The internal evidence that the writer of the *Quinque incitamenta* was a Cistercian would seem to be incontrovertible. The case for attributing *De doctrina* to a Cistercian author rests in part on the internal evidence of the exclusively monastic, 'cloistered' perspective maintained throughout. Equally important, however, is the argument that *Quinque incitamenta* and *De doctrina* are to be attributed to the same author. For this there is a combination of both internal and external evidence. The internal evidence, on which we cannot place too great demands, amounts, as we have seen, to similarity in style, expository method and the use of French insertions. The comparison is difficult because of the distinctive agenda that drives the *Quinque incitamenta*, namely to set out a religious 'reinterpretation' of courtly love in terms of the love of God, a concern that we cannot expect to be replicated in other works by the author. Nonetheless, Mikkers describes the *Quinque incitamenta* as 'un développement définitif des derniers livres de la *Doctrina*'.[81] The external evidence for common authorship is more substantial, because the *Quinque incitamenta* is preserved as the second section of a two-part treatise, the first part of which (the *Septem remedia*) points forward explicitly to the second and is introduced by a heading naming Gerard of Liège as the author. Gerard of Liège is the name to which *De doctrina* is attached in sixteen manuscripts. Hendrix disposes of the coincidence of attribution to Gerard in manuscripts of both *De doctrina* and the *Septem remedia*/*Quinque incitamenta* by arguing that the *Septem remedia* and the *Quinque incitamenta* are not the work of a single author, but rather originally autonomous works that were only later joined together by a redactor. This argument is too speculative to be given much weight when we are assessing the primary evidence for authorship.

Both works, the *Quinque incitamenta* and *De doctrina*, demonstrate a Cistercian orientation and would appear to have been written with Cistercian readers in mind, althought by no means exclusively for these. There is therefore internal evidence to underpin the external evidence of the common authorial name 'Gerardus Leodiensis', but it stands in conflict with the attribution to a Dominican lector. We are faced with a choice.

---

79 (all those of us who have made their profession in the Cistercian order.)

80 Wilmart, 'Gérard', p. 304, n. 27; id., 'Reg. lat. 71', p. 181 ('une confusion très ancienne').

81 Mikkers, 'Le traité de Gerard de Liège', p. 177.

One option is to suppose that, by coincidence, there were two writers who went by the same name, a Dominican and a Cistercian. In this case we can safely attribute *De doctrina* to a Dominican lector in Liège writing for Cistercian men and women. The similarities of style between the two writers must be explained by the fact that they were addressing the same audience at about the same moment in time. A second possibility is that the name of a Dominican lector, who wrote *De doctrina* for a Cistercian audience, was transferred to a pair of genuinely Cistercian texts, the *Septem remedia*/*Quinque incitamenta*, in error. A third possibility is that a Cistercian writer, Gerard of Liège, came to be confused, in the early years of the manuscript tradition, with a well-known figure who lived for many years in the Dominican convent at Liège, with the result that sixteen manuscripts of *De doctrina* and the *Catalogus virorum illustrium* have inherited a false attribution. The first of these options allows too much scope to coincidence. With the second option the motivation for the transfer of the name of a Dominican author to Cistercian writings is weak. It should further be noted that the name Gerard of Liège is ill-matched to a friar of the convent in that city, as is apparent from the fact that the scribe of the Mont-Dieu manuscript C^2 found it necessary to provide an explanation for it (see above, p. 27). The most likely solution, which is the position favoured by Wilmart, is that we are dealing with a Cistercian writer, Gerard of Liège, whose name came to be confused with that of brother Gerard, lector of the Dominican convent in Liège, an individual who on account of his preaching, pastoral duties and contacts with the local ecclesiastical hierarchy may have been rather better known to the early scribes than the Cistercian author.

If the author of *De doctrina cordis* was indeed a Cistercian and also the author of the other texts attributed in the manuscripts to Gerardus Leodiensis or Gerardus de Leodio, then he was also a man of learning with some knowledge of the world, who probably passed through the schools before taking his vows of profession in the order. That such a career was possible is demonstrated by the case of Guy of L'Aumône, a Paris master who became abbot of Petit Cîteaux (fl. 1254/56, d. 1272).[82] Another comparable figure, but with an even more substantial literary oeuvre, is John of Limoges (fl. *c.*1246–74), who proceeded from being a secular master to vows as a Cistercian in Clairvaux.[83] For an understanding

---

82 Cf. P. Michaud-Quantin, 'Guy de l'Aumône, premier maître cistercien de l'université de Paris', *Analecta sacri ordinis Cisterciensis*, 15 (1959), 149–219.

83 G. Raciti, 'Jean de Limoges', in *Dictionnaire de spiritualité*, vol. 8 (Paris, 1974), cols 614–18. John of Limoges is the author of the *Religionis elucidarium*, which Quétif/Échard, *Scriptores*, I, 249 suggest might be attributed to Gerard of Liège.

of *De doctrina*, however, it is the 'Cistercian' audience that matters rather than the identity of the author. A historical interpretation of the work, as a contemplative treatise directed at an audience of both monks and nuns at once, placing them on the same level, needs to be set in the context of the contemporary discussion of whether the nuns should truly be allowed to be full members of the Cistercian community.[84] The value which the author places on the cultivation of the inner life of the heart, in which nuns participate as much as monks, presupposes a 'progressive view' on the *Frauenfrage*, and it is in the Brabant-Liège region, where Gerard appears to have been active, that such a progressive view is attested by the flourishing of hagiographical/biographical writings celebrating the lives of holy women, both laywomen (beguines) and Cistercian nuns, in the first half of the thirteenth century. The case of the Corpus Christi feast, promoted by Juliana of Cornillon and Eve of St Martin, for which Juliana composed the Latin office, illustrates how devout women, in a situation of conflict, could succeed in their aims by enlisting the support of the ecclesiastical hierarchy – men such as Hugh of St Cher and Guiard of Laon. Both the Dominicans of Liège and the Cistercian abbey of Villers were quick to take up the feast of Corpus Christi after it was instituted by Hugh of St Cher in 1251.[85] To see the writings of Gerard of Liège in this regional context, informed by developments in both the Dominican and Cistercian orders in which Hugh of St Cher played an important part, is not to seek a rapprochement with Hendrix, but rather to show the links that clearly existed between the intellectual world of the schools and the promotion of new forms of contemplative literature in a monastic culture which by the mid thirteenth century was coming to be dominated by the needs of women.

Wilmart sought the author of *De doctrina cordis* in the abbey of Val-Saint-Lambert in Liège, where he was able to point to an Abbot Gerard in the mid century.[86] The main point of reference for the Cistercian literary culture of the southern Low Countries in this period, however, was surely not Val-Saint-Lambert, but rather the abbey of Villers-en-Brabant, which

---

84 For the issue of nuns living as members of the *ordo Cisterciensis*, but not more formally attached to the order, and the intricate and disputed questions relating to *incorporatio* and *commissio* see Felten, 'Zisterzienserorden', especially pp. 40–42; Tugwell, 'Magdalen nuns', pp. 45–8 (with particular reference to Dominican nuns).

85 J. Cottiaux, 'L'office liégeois de la Fête-Dieu. Sa valeur et son destin', *Revue d'histoire ecclésiastique*, 58 (1963), 5–81, 405–59, here pp. 424–9.

86 See n. 2 above.

was a centre of hagiography, male and female, and also saw the production of the *Flores paradisi* and the 'pseudo-Bernardine' prayers of Abbot Arnulph of Louvain (1240–48).[87] It is in this milieu, from which Val-Saint-Lambert need not be excluded, that we can find the most plausible home for the remarkable oeuvre of Gerard of Liège. Four works are firmly associated with his name by scribal attributions in the manuscripts – the Paris sermon collection, *De doctrina cordis*, the *Septem remedia contra amorem illicitum* (paired with the *Quinque incitamenta ad Deum amandum ardenter*) and the *Tractatus super septem verba dicta a Domino Jesu Christo pendente in cruce*. To these may be added, with a fair degree of certainty, *De duodecim utilitatibus tribulationum*. Taken together this amounts to a very considerable body of contemplative literature in Latin directed not just at monks but also at enclosed men and women that needs to be set alongside those other literary productions of the French-speaking region between Nivelles and Liège, just south of the language border, that have attracted so much more attention in modern scholarship. The author appears to have been a Cistercian, Gerard of Liège, whose learning was strongly indebted to the more recent developments in the Paris schools under Hugh of St Cher. His work is notable for the use he makes of distinctive figural language and allegorical representations drawn from Bible exegesis, such as was expounded in the schools, but refunctionalized in the context of monastic meditation. With this penchant for allegory he stands in a tradition of monastic writing which was developed particularly by the Victorines, above all by Hugh of St Victor, in the twelfth century. Gerard seems to have adapted this tradition to the contemplative needs of a new monastic audience, perhaps in response to the thirteenth-century *Frauenbewegung*, and this may explain why we see him again and again as one of the first exponents of themes that were to have a major impact on late medieval devotion: the seven words spoken by Christ on the cross, the exchange of hearts between the holy woman and Christ, the meditational allegory of the cloister, the seven gifts of the

---

87 T. Falmagne, *Un texte en contexte. Les* Flores paradisi *et le milieu culturel de Villers-en-Brabant dans la première moitié du 13ᵉ siècle*, Instrumenta patristica et mediaevalia 39 (Turnhout, 2001), pp. 27–72; B. Newman, 'Preface. Goswin of Villers and the visionary network', in *Send me God. The Lives of Ida the Compassionate of Nivelles, Nun of La Ramée, Arnulf, Lay Brother of Villers, and Abundus, Monks of Villers, by Goswin of Bossut*, tr. and intro. M. Cawley, with a preface by B. Newman, Medieval Women: Texts and Contexts 6 (Turnhout, 2003), pp. xxix–xlix, with a detailed bibliography. See also S. Roisin, 'L'efflorescence cistercienne et le courant féminin de piété au XIIIe siècle', *Revue d'histoire ecclésiastique*, 39 (1943), 342–78.

Holy Spirit, the house of conscience, the seven signs of ecstatic love, courtly profane love as an expression of the love of God. His principal work was *De doctrina cordis*, and it was this treatise which seems to have caught the imagination of readers, as is documented by its widespread reception not only in Latin but also in vernacular languages.

2

De doctrina cordis: Catechesis or Contemplation?

Christiania Whitehead

In important work upon the Latin *De doctrina cordis* in the 1980s and 1990s, Hendrix identified two distinct versions of the text – a long and a short, characterized by differing prologues (the HV and IP), which Marleen Cré discusses in greater detail in her essay in this volume. It has since proved convenient to utilize these distinctions as primary categories in discussions focused upon the text. However, these categories by no means offer complete or even adequate insight into the many different textual manifestations of *De doctrina* that survive in Latin manuscripts; on the contrary, they have the often uncomfortable side-effect of tending to marginalize other more 'incomplete' or less amenable versions, such as summaries and resumés, chapter excerpts and significantly reordered renditions of the treatise. This essay will conduct a short examination of *De doctrina* in its Latin manuscript contexts in order to establish the most prevalent modes of perception of the text and patterns of use. Working against the grain of current emphases, it will demonstrate the key importance of individual 'incomplete' or summary versions in obtaining an understanding of perception and use; by the same token, it will challenge the current priority given to a 'two version' account of the text. The last portion of the essay will extend the knowledge derived from the present studies of *De doctrina*'s vernacular manuscript contexts in this volume to offer an overview of the ways in which the text was reformulated, used and circulated in the French, German, Dutch, English and Spanish vernacular versions of the fifteenth and early sixteenth centuries.

Four categories of perception and use

A survey of the ways in which *De doctrina cordis* is recorded and embedded within the 200 or so Latin manuscripts in which it survives[1] suggests that it is possible to detect four main categories of perception and use. First, an examination of contexts reveals that the text was perceived to have close generic affinities with the medieval homily. A selection of manuscript examples illustrate this. In Freiburg im Breisgau, Universitätbibliothek, MS 111 (a manuscript originating from the Dominican friary at Freiburg), a summary version of *De doctrina* is placed amid a long list of sermons for various church feasts and occasions. Basel, Öffentl. Bibliothek der Universität, MS B.X.4, another Dominican manuscript, places 'select chapters' from *De doctrina* alongside sermons. Lilienfeld, Stiftsbibliothek, O.C.S.O., MS 136 juxtaposes a summary version of the text with *Sermons de tempore et de sanctis*.[2] The fourteenth-century library catalogue of the Yorkshire Cistercian Abbey of Meaux includes a manuscript, now unfortunately lost, containing a *Liber de doctrina cordis*, together with a Lenten sermon, a Bernardine sermon on the nativity of Mary and further *Sermones multi*.[3] Oxford, Bodleian Library, MS Laud Misc. 208, which originates from the Carthusian house of Mainz in southern Germany, contains a two-folio summary of *De doctrina*, identified by the scribe as a 'sermo fratris Alberti' (fol. 32r), following on from and in the same hand as a series of sermons and tracts on confession, sin and penitence.[4] There are many additional examples.

Further internal evidence supports this association with preaching. The Latin prologue to *De doctrina* is largely occupied with expounding the exemplary relationship between a preacher and his listeners.[5] A preacher ('predicator') should take care not to irritate his listeners, nor to give undue

---

1 These manuscripts are listed, with notes on their contents, in G. Hendrix, *Hugo de Sancto Caro's traktaat De doctrina cordis. Vol. 1: Handschriften, receptie, tekstgeschiedenis en authenticiteitskritiek*, Documenta Libraria 16/1 (Louvain, 1995), pp. 7–105. Henceforth cited as Hendrix, *Hugo I*.

2 Hendrix, *Hugo I*, pp. 36, 16, 53.

3 D.N. Bell (ed.), *The Libraries of the Cistercians, Gilbertines and Premonstratensians*, Corpus of British Medieval Library Catalogues 3 (London, 1992), p. 76, Z14 Meaux, item 305.

4 H.O. Coxe (ed.), *Bodleian Library, Quarto Catalogues II. Laudian Manuscripts* (Oxford, 1973), cols 180–1. Hendrix, *Hugo I*, p. 71.

5 This prologue is analysed in further detail in Anne Mouron's essay upon the Middle English translation of *De doctrina* in this volume.

attention to the arrangement of his words. Rather, he should 'Loquimini ad cor … verbum diligenter exponere, vt vinum spiritualis intelligentiae vsque in cellarium cordis fluat.'[6] In turn, the recipient should take care not to turn his or her hearing aside 'a cellario … id est, diuina doctrina … ad aquam turbidam, et immundam fabulationum saecularium.'[7] Towards the end of the prologue, the impersonality of this discussion is exchanged for a first-person pronoun: 'Vt ergo ad cor tuum loquar'.[8] By the evidence of this opening, both the nature of the communication envisaged throughout the text and the credentials of its author appear entirely homiletic. The author opens by representing himself as a preacher, and proceeds to prepare his recipient for the doctrine to come via advice on the dual responsibilities of preachers and their audiences.

To what degree is this initial implication of genre borne out by the text which follows? Does *De doctrina* read like a sermon series? Does it bear any relation to the shape or expository method of a thirteenth-century homily? At first glance, the correlation does not seem obvious. It is hard to imagine how the text, in its entirety, could have been partitioned to form a viable sequence of oral talks. Nonetheless, we should not ignore its broad organization around the seven gifts of the Holy Spirit. These gifts were used on a number of occasions to structure material designed for preaching, as in Étienne de Bourbon's *Tractatus de diversis materiis praedicabilibus*, an early *exemplum* collection, written around 1260.[9] Neither should we

---

6 All Latin quotations are taken from the 1607 printed edition of *De doctrina cordis* (Gerardus Leodiensis, *Speculum concionatorum ad illustrandum pectora auditorum, in septem libros distributum* (Naples, 1607), Oxford, Bodleian Library, 8o L 12 Th. BS), which has been checked for identity against the Paris first printed edition of 1506, and against a late-thirteenth-century manuscript, Oxford, Bodleian Library, MS Lat. th. f. 6. It is hereafter referred to as *De doctrina*. *De doctrina*, pp. 1–2 (Speak to the heart … set[ting] forth these words carefully, so that the wine of spiritual knowledge may flow into the cellar of the heart), tr. Anne Mouron.

7 *De doctrina*, p. 2 (From the cellar … that is, divine doctrine … to the muddy and impure water of worldly conversation.)

8 *De doctrina*, p. 4 (Therefore, that I may speak to your heart.)

9 It also seems salient to quote from Richard Wetheringsett's *Summa*, '*Qui bene presunt*' regarding the essential contents of elementary preaching: 'Maxime vero ad fidem et ad mores pertinentia et frequentius predicanda sunt: simbolum fidei, duodecim articulos fidei continens; oratio dominica, vii habens petitiones; dona dei generalia et specialia, specialiter vii dona spiritus que enumerat Ysas. 30: 9, que sunt sapientia, intellectus, consilium et fortitudo, scientia et pietas et timor.' London, British Library, MS Royal 4 B.VIII, fol. 222r. (Indeed, [these things] are of greatest relevance to faith and practice, and should be often preached on:

disregard the extraordinary flexibility of *De doctrina*, both in terms of its arrangement of material and its size. Commencing each chapter with an Old Testament 'proof text', defining an action or condition of the heart, it then typically opens out into examples and further sub-definitions that could have been elaborated or retracted at will. From the manuscript examples adduced above, it seems clear that when *De doctrina* is placed alongside other sermons, it most often appears in such a retracted or summary form. We can interpret the import of this summary form by referring to David D'Avray, who has done some of the most extensive contemporary research into mendicant sermons. D'Avray notes that it was common for sermons to become boiled down to simple summaries or schemas in the course of their transmission;[10] it would then have been left up to the individual preacher to elaborate imaginatively upon, or perhaps even to vernacularize, this Latin summary containing a basic structure of ideas.[11]

It is also possible to place this interpretation of the summary versions of *De doctrina* in the context of its close working relationship with the *Postillae* of Hugh of St Cher: namely, the use it makes of a number of lengthy passages from the *Postillae*.[12] Second Master of the Dominican Order, Hugh would have been closely concerned with encouraging preaching, overseeing the provision of preaching materials and analysing the components of effective preaching and exemplary reception. Thus it comes as no surprise that his major work of the 1230s, his *Postillae* upon the whole Bible updating the theological thought of the *Glossa ordinaria*, includes an innovative emphasis upon preaching in several of its commentaries.[13] Judging by thematic notes

the Creed, containing the twelve articles of faith: the Lord's prayer, having seven petitions; the general and particular gifts of God, in particular the seven gifts of the Spirit listed in Isa. 30:9, which are wisdom, understanding, good counsel and courage, knowledge and piety and fear [of God].) I am grateful to Rev. Dr Ruth Tuschling for assistance with this and all following translations.

10 D.L. D'Avray, *The Preaching of the Friars* (Oxford, 1985), pp. 102–4.

11 D'Avray writes that, although preaching to women religious frequently took place in the vernacular, sermons were generally written down in Latin since they could then be transferred relatively easily between different language areas. Ibid., pp. 93–5.

12 G. Hendrix, 'Les *Postillae* de Hugues de Saint-Cher et le traité *De doctrina cordis*', *RTAM*, 47 (1980), 114–30. Hendrix's realization that *De doctrina* drew heavily upon the *Postillae*, proved central to his 1980s' attribution of *De doctrina*'s authorship to Hugh of St Cher.

13 R.E. Lerner, 'Poverty, Preaching and Eschatology in the Revelation Commentaries of Hugh of St Cher', in K. Walsh and D. Wood (eds), *The Bible in the Medieval World* (Oxford, 1985), pp. 157–91. For further discussion of the

in the text margins in several of the extant manuscripts, it also seems to have functioned as a homiletic reference work, signalling the presence of embedded moral topics and interpretations that could be extracted and utilized by preachers. Given the speaker and recipient identifications of *De doctrina*'s Prologue, it would seem that the author of *De doctrina* may well have viewed the character of the *Postillae*, and his extractions from it, in a very similar light.

In addition to *De doctrina*'s affinities with Hugh's *Postillae*, it also appears to share a close relationship with the collection of seventy sermons preserved in Paris, Bibliothèque nationale, MS lat. 16483, where two of the sermons explicitly refer their readers to a 'liber de doctrina cordis' as a source of supplementary information.[14] If, as André Wilmart, Guido Hendrix and Nigel Palmer have all independently argued, the Paris sermons and *De doctrina* share a common author, this again acts to support the *De doctrina*'s author's active involvement with preaching, and suggests that the summary versions of the treatise may well have been intended to assist regular preachers preparing sermons for delivery to congregations of male or female religious.[15]

The second major way in which *De doctrina cordis* was perceived and used, on the evidence of its manuscript contexts, has points of contact with its homiletic perception, but for the sake of clarity will be treated separately. Perhaps not at all surprisingly, *De doctrina* appears in a number of manuscript contexts that suggest that it was perceived, in some environments at least, as a treatise of guidance upon the religious life, or

---

Postillae as a corporate Dominican enterprise, see Nigel Palmer's essay in this volume, pp. 40–1.

14 Hendrix, *Hugo I*, p. 235; id. (ed.), *Hugo de Sancto Caro's traktaat De doctrina cordis. 4. De sermoenen in handschrift Parijs Bibliothèque Nationale, 16483*, Documenta libraria 16/4 (Louvain, 2000). As his title would suggest, Hendrix attributes these sermons to Hugh of St Cher, along with *De doctrina* itself. André Wilmart ('Gérard de Liège. Un traité inédit de l'amour de Dieu', *Revue d'ascétique et de mystique*, 12 (1931), 349–430) and Nigel Palmer, in this volume, accept the near-contemporary manuscript attribution of the sermons to Gerard of Liège, and argue for Gerard's likely authorship of both the sermons and *De doctrina*.

15 Accepting Hendrix's attribution of the text to Hugh of St Cher, Denis Renevey argues that Hugh's support of beguine communities in Liège and Aarschot may be indicative of further intended female communities of reception. D. Renevey, 'Household Chores in *The Doctrine of the Hert*: Affective Spirituality and Subjectivity', in C. Beattie, A. Maslakovic and S. Rees Jones (eds), *The Medieval Household in Christian Europe c.850–c.1550* (Turnhout, 2003), pp. 167–85 (167–8).

for religious novices. Thus, in Cambrai, Bibliothèque municipale, MS 838, it is copied alongside Johannes de Hagen's *Tractatus de diversis gravaminibus religiosorum*, Guilliaume Lugdunensis's *Super professione monachorum* and the *Tractatus magistri Theodorici de peculio seu proprietate monachorum*. In Wiesbaden, Hessische Landesbibliothek, MS 17, it is aligned with tracts attributed to Jacobus Carthusiensis entitled *De temptatione noviciorum* and *Tractatus de progressu religiosorum*. In Cambridge, Peterhouse College, MS 203, it is followed by Smaragdus's *Diadema monachorum*, by homilies by Basil of Caesarea and Eusebius designed for monks and by Macarius's *Liber ad monachos*.[16] And in Trier, Stadtbibliothek, MS 745, it is described by the scribe as a 'tractata in libro noviciorum religiosorum nuncupato praeparatio cordis'.[17] Elsewhere, it is possible to see a travelling association with David of Augsburg's *Formula novitiorum* and Hugh of St Victor's *De institutione novitiorum*, two works immediately concerned with the practicalities of the religious novitiate, although the manuscript contexts in these last two instances are sometimes more eclectic.[18]

As stated above, it is not at all surprising to see *De doctrina* linked so closely with texts explicating the religious novitiate. A long section in the first book of the treatise describes three types of spiritual matrimony, linking the novitiate with the first, and commenting upon it in some detail:

> Haec autem, quae de matrimonio incoepto, confirmato, et consummato diximus, signanter Dominus, Ieremiae 2. loquens animae claustrali, exprimit dicens: Recordarus sum tui, miserans adolescentiam tuam, et charitatem desponsationis tuae, quando secuta es me in deserto. Quod dicit: Miserans adolescentiam tuam, hoc pertinet ad nouitias, quae incoeperunt matrimonium cum Christo … De primo notandum, quod miseratur Dominus adolescentulis suis, id est, nouitiabus, quae in tenera aetate propter verba labiorum eius, vias duras, scilicet labores

---

16 M.R. James, *A Descriptive Catalogue of the Manuscripts in the Library of Peterhouse* (Cambridge, 1899), pp. 238–42.

17 (A treatise in the book of religious novices named the preparation of the heart.) These manuscripts are listed, with notes on their contents, in Hendrix, *Hugo I*, pp. 23–4, 102, 24–5, 90.

18 See, for example, Fritzlar, Dombibliothek, MS 38, and Mainz, Stadtbibliothek, MS I 48, where *De doctrina* travels with David of Augsburg's *Formula novitiorum* (Hendrix, *Hugo I*, pp. 36, 58–9). Also, Uppsala, Universitetsbibliothek, MS C 631 (ibid., pp. 92–3), and the non-extant MS from Meaux Abbey in Yorkshire (Bell, *Libraries of the Cistercians*, p. 76, item 305), in which *De doctrina* travels with Hugh of St Victor's *De institutione novitiorum*, among others.

> ordinis difficiles sunt aggressae ... Unde o Nouitia, scito te positam esse ad scholas amoris, et si in illo statu diligere illum cui desponsata es, non addiscas; vix postea in amoris arte proficere poteris. Haec est facilis lectio, Dilectio lectio saepius recitanda est, de qua sponsus tuus in cathedra Crucis scholas tenuit, vbi mortuus est prae amore. Tace ergo o Nouitia, et sede.[19]

As can be seen from the second-person pronouns in this passage, and from the direct form of address – 'o Nouitia' – the author appears directly to identify the intended recipient of his words as a religious novice. Nonetheless, since *De doctrina* is nothing if not multidexterous, in address as well as in form and purpose, it is important to specify that there are also many passages directed unambiguously towards 'sovereynes' or superiors within the religious life. An especially extended passage occurs in book 2, instructing the superior on how to administer correction to more junior religious in his or her care.[20] And so, the perception of *De doctrina* as a treatise aligned with the formation of novices is two-edged. On the one hand, it addresses novices directly with advice pertinent to their status and inexperience. On the other, it contains sections designed for superiors or for novice masters or mistresses, offering instruction on the spiritual formation and disciplining of those within their care. Flexibly, it lays itself out to accommodate a spectrum of different readerships.

The third category of perception and use again contains points in common with the two previous discussions. *De doctrina cordis* is found on occasion in what is probably best described as a catechetical setting, among tightly numerically-ordered treatises which reproduce the catechetical basics of the faith. Oxford, Bodleian Library, MS Laud Misc. 530 offers a

---

19 *De doctrina*, pp. 105–6 (These things, which we said above concerning the beginning, confirmation and consummation of marriage, the Lord clearly expresses in Jeremiah 2 (speaking to the enclosed soul), when he says, 'I remembered you, taking pity on your youthfulness ...' His words 'taking pity on your youthfulness' pertain to novices, who have begun their marriage with Christ ... First one must note that the Lord takes pity on his young people, that is, novices, who at a tender age, because of the words of his lips, have set out on a hard path, that is, the difficult labours of their order ... Hence, O Novice, know that you are placed in the school of love, and if you do not learn, in that state, to love him to whom you are betrothed, you will scarcely be able to make progress in the art of love later on. This is an easy lesson: Love must often be recited as a lesson, about which your bridegroom lectured from the chair of the Cross, on which he died for love. Be silent therefore, O Novice, and sit.)

20 'Quae sunt attendenda in correctione alterius', ibid., pp. 187–90.

particularly useful example of this kind of setting. A thirteenth-century manuscript originating from the important Charterhouse at Mainz,[21] it holds the following contents:

fol. 1	Guillaume de Peraldus, *Summa de virtutibus*
fol. 224	*Summa de vitiis et virtutibus*
fol. 227	*De doctrina cordis*
fol. 232	*De comparatione x. plagarum Egypti ad x. praecepta*
fol. 233	*De ordine petitionum Pater Noster*
fol. 234	*Auctoritates Patrum de diversis*[22]

In other words, in this particular manuscript setting, *De doctrina* is found embedded alongside 'vices and virtues' literature, a numerically-structured comparison between the ten plagues of Egypt and the ten commandments, and a similarly numericized short treatise on the seven petitions of the Lord's Prayer. It is also worth noting that these treatises all run on from each other, in a single hand, almost without pause. Of greatest note, however, is the way in which *De doctrina* is 'boiled down' within this manuscript. Despite only covering five folios, the text as it stands manages to encompass all seven books. Each of these books is identified by its habitual heading: 'De apertione cordis', 'De datione cordis' and so on, and each commences longhand, as it were, reproducing in full the initial sentences and images. However, following this initial adhesion to the complete text, each book then becomes increasingly abbreviated, reducing its contents down to a list of systematically numbered points. So, for example, after discursive openings, book 2 reduces to a list of the ten follies of spiritual battle; book 3 becomes bullet points upon the seven impediments to opening the book of the conscience; book 6 is cut back to four reasons for lifting up one's heart, and book 7 confines itself to brief headings upon the seven signs of amorous love. This method of labelled, numbered points continues seamlessly into the next treatise upon the plagues of Egypt, and into the one following, upon the Lord's Prayer.

What conclusions can be derived from this? It is clear that MS Laud Misc. 530 animates *De doctrina* within a distinctly catechetical setting. It

---

21 The Mainz Charterhouse seems to have shown a particular interest in *De doctrina*. At least six extant manuscripts housed within its medieval library contain versions of the text (Hendrix, *Hugo I*, pp. 58–61, 71–2).

22 Coxe, *Laudian Manuscripts*, cols 386–7.

is included alongside simple texts, organized around numbered points, that would have been of relevance to professional religious consigned to provide instruction in the basics of the faith – the seven vices and virtues, the seven gifts of the Holy Spirit, the Ten Commandments, the seven petitions of the Lord's Prayer. Of especial interest, however, is the way in which the overriding allegorical scheme of *De doctrina* – the seven main actions of the heart, whereby it is prepared, guarded, opened, and so on – seems conceivably to have been viewed as a numerical scheme with *equivalent* didactic authority and utility to the Ten Commandments or the seven petitions of the Lord's Prayer. Or, to put it in other words, the organization and function of the manuscript make it appear just as central to basic doctrine to commit to memory the seven actions of the heart as to memorize the seven petitions of the Lord's Prayer. If this holds true on any substantial scale (additional manuscript trials must be made), the implications would seem far-reaching. Most notably, the purposes to which *De doctrina* is put in this manuscript would appear to indicate the existence of a breadth of catechetical material in some quarters, in the late thirteenth and fourteenth centuries, well beyond the assumptions of contemporary scholarship – and of a devotional milieu in which the seven actions of the heart had currency as a familiar and fundamental catechetical tool.

In this context, before moving on to the fourth category of perception, it also seems pertinent to make a brief comment on *De doctrina cordis*'s close association, in England at least, with two further, even less well-known, Latin treatises: the *De lingua* and *De oculo morali* of pseudo-Grosseteste.[23] *De doctrina* travels adjacent to *De lingua* in five Latin manuscripts of medieval English provenance: Durham, The Dean and Chapter Library, MSS B.III.18 and B.III.19; Cambridge, University Library, MS Ff. 3.24; Oxford, University College, MS D62–63, and the lost Syon Library, MS O.7;[24] in addition, three of these manuscripts – Durham, MSS B.III.18 and B.III.19, and Univ. Coll. MS 62–63 – also contain versions of *De oculo morali*. These juxtapositions are, in themselves, thought-provoking

[23] *De lingua* is nowadays attributed tentatively to John of Wales, while *De oculo morali* is thought probably to be by Peter of Limoges (d. 1306). S.H. Thomson, *The Writings of Robert Grosseteste, Bishop of Lincoln, 1235–1253* (Cambridge, 1940), notes British MSS of *De lingua*, pp. 252–3, and British MSS of *De oculo*, pp. 256–7.

[24] V. Gillespie (ed.), *Syon Abbey, with the Libraries of the Carthusians*, ed. A.I. Doyle, Corpus of British Medieval Library Catalogues 9 (London, 2001), p. 306. The Syon library catalogue attributes *De doctrina* to John of Wales (Franciscan, active 1260–80), while the Cambridge MS attributes it to Robert Grosseteste.

and suggestive. *De doctrina* is drawn into the fold of Oxford Franciscan scholarship and aligned closely with works of an erudite, even scientific, flavour. The links would repay further investigation. However, in keeping with the present focus upon catechetical remodellings of *De doctrina*, I would like to single out the idiosyncratic example of Oxford, Univ. Coll. MS D 62–63. In this manuscript, intriguingly, *De doctrina* appears to have been merged with *De lingua* (an annotation in the manuscript, repeated nearly verbatim in the library catalogue, describes the text as 'Extractum Lincolniensis de lingua et corde' [fol. 1r]),[25] and then reordered into a long alphabetical list of spiritual topics with paragraphs of brief comment beneath each. So, for example, opening headings include 'Amicum' and 'Amor', followed slightly later by 'Bello spirituali' and 'Blaspheme', and later still by 'Caritas' and 'Confessio'. Particularly recognizable snippets from *De doctrina* include 'Cor eleuandum est racione' (fols 19rb–20ra), 'Hec sunt de corde' (fols 60rb–62ra), and 'Remedia septem sunt' (fol. 53va). While not strictly catechetical, it would appear that the cutting and splicing of *De doctrina* along these lines enables it to fulfil a relatively similar purpose. Its alphabetical reordering effectively transforms it into a versatile spiritual reference work, supplying quickly accessible definitions and explications of Love, Blasphemy, Spiritual warfare and so on, that could easily have been put to the use of catechetical instruction or culled by a preacher to flesh out the bones of a skimpy monastic sermon.

Up until now, I have stressed the points of contact between the modes of perception and use of *De doctrina* under review. A manuscript resumé might well simultaneously offer themes and structures for preachers, generate some tools for catechetical instruction, and even, in its spelling out of simple material, be of use in the formation of the novitiate. By contrast, my fourth and final category of perception and use constitutes a marked departure from all that has gone before. There are a sizeable number of Latin manuscript survivals in which *De doctrina cordis* is embedded with sophisticated affective and devotional texts, and a number in which it sits alongside texts best categorized as mystical or contemplative. Mainz, Stadtbibliothek, MS I 48 (once again a product of the influential Charterhouse at Mainz) places an extract from *De doctrina* amid Hugh of Balma's *De triplici via ad Deum* and Richard of St Victor's *Benjamin minor*, *Ex contemplatione* and *De quattuor gradibus violentae caritatis*. Graz, Universitätsbibliothek, MS 577 insets a summary alongside Bonaventure's *Lignum vitae* and *De triplici via*, Hugh of St Victor's *De arrha animae* and

[25] H.O. Coxe, *Catalogus codicum MSS qui in collegiis aulisque Oxoniensibus hodie adservantur*, Pars. 1 (Oxford, 1852), p. 19.

Richard of St Victor's *De gradibus caritatis*. Berlin, Staatsbibliothek zu Berlin – Preußischer Kulturbesitz, Ms. lat. oct. 272 (from the Charterhouse of St Barbara in Cologne) consists of an extract from *De doctrina* and Hugh of Balma's *De triplici via ad Deum*. Munich, Bayerische Staatsbibliothek, Clm 21232 places *De doctrina* among texts by Hugh and Richard of St Victor, Hugh of Folieto and Bonaventure.[26] Finally, and of particular interest in this context, Oxford, Bodleian Library, MS Laud Misc. 479[27] contains, in a single scribal hand, a *Tractatus de septem gradibus contemplationis*; a significantly reordered version of *De doctrina*, commencing with its final chapter; running straight on, a text describing itself as Richard of St Victor's *De contemplatione* (perhaps the *Benjamin major* or *minor*); Richard's *De gradibus caritatis*; and some excerpts from Gregory the Great's commentary on Ezechiel, itself an exegesis with strongly contemplative overtones. Once again, it is possible to adduce further examples.

The majority of manuscripts cited above offer a summary or excerpt from *De doctrina*. Significantly, this excerpt is practically always the last book of *De doctrina*, 'De scissione cordis', in which the heart is finally severed definitively from earthly ties following the earlier stages of preparation, stabilization and so on, and drawn up into an ecstatic love alienating the lover from his or herself through absorption into their beloved:

> Hunc gustum expertus erat Augustinus in libro Confessionum dicens: Aliquando introducis me, o bone Iesu, in affectum multum inusitatum introrsum, nescio in quam dulcedinem, quae si perficiatur in me, nescio quid erit, quod in vita ista non erit. Sed recido in ijs aerumnosis ponderibus, et solutus resorbeor, et multum fleo. Hic esse volo, sed non valeo, ibi valeo, sed non volo, miser vtrobique. Attende charissima Augustinum introductum in affectum inusitatum, et introrsum … Iste autem affectus multus, et inusitatus comparatur amori ecstatico, qui amare per amores vulgariter appellatur. Ecstaticus enim ab ecstasi: vnde amor ecstaticus dicitur, qui mentem alienat, qui non sinit cor aliud cogitare, nisi circa rem dilectam. Sumitur tamen amor ecstaticus in bono, aliquando secundum quod de eo loquitur Dionysius, qui appellat amorem ecstaticum illum amorem, qui totaliter transfert amantem in vsum, et profectum amati. Tali amore (sicut idem dicit) nos Deus dilexit, se totum in vsum nostrum, et profectum totaliter transferens, dicens

---

26 These manuscripts are listed, with brief notes on their contents, in Hendrix, *Hugo I*, pp. 58–9, 39–40, 20, 68.

27 Ibid., pp. 71–2. Once again, this manuscript originates from the Charterhouse of Mainz. See also, Coxe, *Laudian Manuscripts*, cols 346–47.

> de tali amore: Est amor ecstaticus, qui non sinit suos esse amantes, sed amatorum.[28]

Much of the remainder of the chapter is spent identifying and expounding the seven external signs of ecstatic love via an extended analogy with the external signs of earthly courtly love.

The inference to be drawn from the manuscript evidence is unambiguous. The compilers of these manuscripts clearly viewed the seventh book of *De doctrina* as a contemplative tract of the same calibre and mystical type as the writings of the Victorines, Bonaventure and Hugh of Balma. They perceived it as a relatively self-contained piece of writing, adequate to stand alone without the preparatory support of the preceding chapters. They envisaged it as suitable reading matter for those practising an advanced monastic spirituality. And, indeed, the preponderance of manuscripts from German Charterhouses suggests that 'De scissione' was judged especially compatible with Carthusian spiritual reading tastes. All these outcomes significantly complicate our perception of a text that the opening part of this essay identified as homiletic, didactic and relatively elementary. They also serve to undermine the judgement of the text's previous Middle English editor, Sr. Mary Candon, who tends to denigrate the text as mundane and workaday, opining that *De doctrina* belongs:

> to that genre of religious writing which centers its attention on the practical side of attaining perfection rather than on the analysis of

---

28 *De doctrina*, pp. 278–9 (Augustine experienced this taste in his book of Confessions, saying: at one time you lead me, O good Jesus, into great and extraordinary interior emotion, into I know not what sweetness, which, if it is perfected in me, I do not know what it will be, because it will not be in this life. But I fall back into those weary weights, and am dissolved and swallowed up again, and weep greatly. I want to be here, but am not strong enough; there I am strong enough, but I do not want to be there, and am wretched in both. Pay attention, beloved, to Augustine, led into unusual and interior emotion … That great and unusual emotion may be compared to ecstatic love, which is called in the vulgar tongue 'loving through loves'. 'Ecstatic' comes from 'ecstasy': love is called ecstatic, because it draws the mind away, because it does not permit the heart to dwell on anything else but the beloved object. Ecstatic love can be taken to be a good thing, at least according to what Dionysius says of it, who calls that love ecstatic love which entirely makes over the lover to the use and profit of the beloved. As the same Dionysius says, God loved us with such a love, handing himself over entirely to our use and profit. He says of such a love: ecstatic love is love that does not permit lovers to belong to themselves, but to the beloved.)

> the advanced stages of perfection … this is not the writing of one of the great mystics of the Church. It has very little in common with the advanced stages of the spiritual life as described by a John of the Cross or a Catherine of Siena.[29]

My remarks so far have centered on those manuscripts where the extracted seventh book of *De doctrina* is placed adjacent to other contemplative texts. MS Laud Misc. 479 presents a rather different case. Here, as mentioned earlier, the manuscript does in fact incorporate the bulk of *De doctrina*, but in a significantly reordered version, so that the text *begins* – running straight on from the *Septem gradibus contemplationis* – with its most contemplative section, the 'De scissione cordis'. The majority of the other books then follow in what appears to be a random collation, titled in accordance with the more numerous chapter headings that occur in many Latin manuscripts.[30] Rather than enumerating these individual headings at length, it is possible to extrapolate a broad progression through discrete text units, from 'De datione cordis' and 'De elevatione cordis', to 'De preparatione cordis' and 'De custodia cordis', these last two being significantly entertwined (the allegory of the furnished house of the heart [book 1] is followed by advice on the custody of the tongue [mid book 2], and on the need to closely guard the castle of the heart [book 2 – opening]. This is followed in turn by a brief section from the close of book 1: 'De dulcedine divine eloquii').

The version of *De doctrina* found in MS Laud Misc. 479 defies all of the established modes for categorizing the text. It is not a 'long' nor a 'short' version; neither is it a straightforward text skeleton or an excerpt. Arranged in a section order that prioritizes its contemplative content (in a nod to its textual neighbours), and then traces an idiosyncratic course through assorted text units from the preceding chapters, the Laud *De doctrina* violates our most intrinsic expectations of textual integrity and chronology.

---

29 Sister M.P. Candon (ed.), '*The Doctrine of the Hert*, Edited from the Manuscripts with Introduction and Notes' (unpublished doctoral dissertation, Fordham University, 1963), pp. xli, xxxix. Hereafter cited as Candon, *Doctrine*.

30 A number of Latin manuscripts (Oxford, Bodleian Library, MS Lat. th. f. 6 is a useful and early example) ignore the seven-book layout, dividing the subject matter of *De doctrina* into two main books, the first containing fifty and the second twenty-seven short chapters. These chapter divisions are retained by the early printed editions of *De doctrina*: the Paris edition of 1506, and the Naples edition of 1607, although in both these instances, these smaller, more numerous chapters are reassessed as subdivisions of seven overarching books that reflect the more familiar divisioning of material.

That does *not* mean it should be placed out of sight in favour of 'complete' versions of the text, along with reduced versions more easily amenable to categorization and analysis. On the contrary, the uncomfortable witness of the Laud *De doctrina* and others like it requires that we relinquish our presuppositions and attempt instead to encounter the text on something like its own terms: as a sizeable mélange of small text units – the ten 'Stultitiae imprudentium in bello spirituali'; 'De articulis fidei'; 'De custodia linguae'; 'De ornamento argenteo diuini eloquii'; 'De signis amoris', etc. – that can either be utilized independently, shepherded into the standard seven-book format or assembled in any variety of other orders to support a range of contextual and didactic purposes.

A group of manuscripts of select text units from *De doctrina*, identified by Hendrix in the early 1980s, tells a very similar story.[31] These extracts – 'De apercione cordis', 'De impedimentis' and 'De custodia linguae' – drawn from the opening and continuation of book 3 and the middle of book 2,[32] occur in Frankfurt, Stadt- und Universitätsbibliothek, MS Lat. qu. 6; Würzburg, Universitätsbibliothek, M.ch.f.219; Salzburg, Bibliothek Erzabtei St Peter, MSS a.III.30, b.III10, and a.VII.18; Vienna, Österr. Nationalbibliothek, MS 1052, and Berlin, Staatsbibliothek zu Berlin – Preußischer Kulturbesitz, Ms. theol. lat. qu. 172, where they are attributed to St Bernard of Clairvaux; and in Basel, Öffentl. Bibliothek der Universität, MS B.X.6, and Mainz, Stadtbibliothek, MSS I 311 and I 317, where they are attributed to Albertus Magnus.[33] In other words, they seem to have circulated largely within a southern German/west Austrian milieu.[34] Unlike the more mystical excerpts detailed above, these text units, examining the opening of the heart through confession, the obstacles to true confession and the guarding of the tongue in communal communication, seem best suited to poorly educated monastic brothers or to the religious novitiate, exploring

---

31 G. Hendrix, '*De apercione cordis*, *De impedimentis* and *De custodia linguae*: 3 Pseudo-Bernardine Texts restored to their true author, Hugh of St. Cher', *RTAM*, 48 (1981), 172–97.

32 In *De doctrina*, these extracts commence on pp. 191, 195 and 175 respectively.

33 Further detail upon these manuscripts is given in Hendrix, '*De apercione cordis*', pp. 173–80.

34 Three extant manuscripts: Klosterneuburg, Stift Augustinerchorherren, MS 363; Munich, Bayerische Staatsbibliothek, Cgm 447; Eichstätt, Kloster St. Walburg, MS Cod. Germ. 7, contain translations of these extracts into the German vernacular. See Hendrix, '*De apercione cordis*', pp. 177–8, and Karl-Heinz Steinmetz's valuable essay in this volume, tracing the connections of these translations with the fifteenth-century monastic reform movement.

as they do the external, sacramental and catechetical aspects of the faith.[35] Normally, such deductions about readership gleaned from text content and manuscript surround necessarily remain implicit and conjectural. However, on this occasion, in Salzburg, Bibliothek Erzabtei St. Peter, MS a.III.30, we are lucky enough to receive *explicit* information from the librarian of St Peter's Benedictine Abbey in the form of a preface to the extracts, presenting his perception of their audience and specific didactic function.

> Oculus non saciatur visu nec auris auditu intelligendo novitatibus anime edificationis, ut inquid prudentissimus Salamon sancti inspiratus flamine. Ideo licet habeantur multa volumina in theologia in librariis, tamen quedam sunt nimis longa et dispendiosa et quedam difficiliora quam simplicium fratrum religiosorum capacitas potest intelligere. Ideo proposui revendo in Christo patri et domino petro abbati Sancti petri in civitate archiepiscopali Salczburgensi et suo conventui conplacere cum paucis devotissimis beati bernardi flosculis de rectificatione conscientie et pugna contra peccatum et de vii impedimentis legendi in libro conscientie illo sacro tempore pascali.[36]

This overlooked preface sheds fascinating light on a fifteenth-century Benedictine librarian's perception of these text units from *De doctrina*. First, he links them to Bernardine spirituality and labels them 'devotissimis … flosculis' (very devout little flowers); that is, he categorizes them as devotional material, suited to affective and meditative reception. Of the four categories of modes of perception and use listed above, this designation

---

35 That said, at least two of these manuscripts (Mainz, MSS I 311 and I 317) copy these extracts alongside much more advanced spiritual material: the *Itinerarium mentis in dominum* and *Lignum vitae* of St Bonaventure (Hendrix, *Hugo I*, pp. 60–61).

36 The Latin preface is reproduced from Hendrix, '*De apercione cordis*', p. 175 (The eye is not satisfied with seeing nor the ear with hearing new knowledge to edify the soul, as the most prudent Solomon says, inspired by the holy spirit. Thus, although there are many volumes of theology in the libraries, some are too long and prolix and some are too difficult for the abilities of simple monks to understand. Thus I intend to please the reverand father in Christ and lord abbot Peter, of Saint Peter in the archepiscopal city of Salzburg and his community, with a very few devout little flowers of blessed Bernard about the rectifying of the conscience, and the war against sin, and of the seven impediments to reading in the book of the conscience, this holy Easter tide.) In the manuscripts in which they occur, the three extracts tend to travel beneath the title: *De rectificatione conscientie et pugna contra peccatum et de vii impedimentis legendi in libro conscientie.*

probably shares most in common with the fourth category of devotional and contemplative writing. Second, he explicitly opposes these extracts to the 'multa volumina in theologia in librariis ... nimis longa et dispendiosa et quedam difficiliora'. These extracts are *not* testing theology; they are not long, prolix or intellectually difficult. Instead, they are appropriately tailored to the intellectual capacity of 'simplicium fratrum religiosorum'. So, despite the relative erudition and theological sophistication of *De doctrina* when read in its entirety, here, reduced to 'capitula selecta', it is seen to work on a different level entirely. Shades here, then, of the second category of modes of perception and use – a sense that the religious instruction contained is fundamentally elementary, best suited to brothers of limited learning and intellect or to those newly initiated into the religious life. Third, the extracts are linked with a specific season in the liturgical calendar. They are designated appropriate reading for the run-up to Easter. In other words, they are envisaged supporting a programme of individual penitence and self-examination, an emphasis certainly in keeping with their discussion of the pitfalls of communication, and of the best means of preparation for the act of confession which can now be identified (in this context at least) as Easter confession. Fourth, the librarian of St Peter's Abbey unambiguously envisages a *male* religious readership – 'fratrum religiosorum' – a point to which I shall return in my closing discussion of vernacular readership. Another manuscript or, in this case, group of manuscripts, that sheds doubt on conventional procedures for categorizing *De doctrina*, then, and underscores the wisdom of viewing it as a sequence of variably chosen and ordered small text units. In addition, the tendency of these particular 'capitula selecta' to be put to uses that are simultaneously devotional and affective, pedagogically elementary and season-specific (somewhat like a set of sermons guiding its recipients through Lent) demonstrates in no uncertain terms the limitations surrounding the imposition of any single critical model of function and reception.

Changed patterns of use in vernacular translations

In the previous section we reviewed the protean character of the Latin *De doctrina cordis* and its ability to reissue itself in formats suitable to both catechesis and contemplation, the formation of the novitiate or the requirements of a homilist. It is now necessary to enquire whether any or all of these versatile dispositions remain to the fore in the fifteenth century, when the text undergoes translation into a range of European vernaculars.

Hendrix's valuable lists of the extant vernacular translations of *De doctrina* have since been supplemented, both in number and depth of understanding, by the scholars contributing essays to the final section of this volume.[37] The present project – to discern some overarching modes of perception and patterns of use in the vernacular, thus relies very heavily upon their researches into individual vernacular contexts and is deeply indebted to their expertise and rigour. The current picture, it would then appear, is as follows. We are aware of four extant manuscripts of a Middle English *De doctrina*, descendants of a single act of translation;[38] of four manuscripts of a French *De doctrina*, one considerably interpolated, offering at least two independent translations; of four Dutch manuscripts; of six German manuscripts, encompassing partial and complete translations of the text; and of nine early printed texts of a Spanish translation, representing four sixteenth-century editions.[39]

While it is nigh-on impossible to observe any schemes of use and textual understanding that hold true for *all* these vernacular witnesses, some general trends are nonetheless perceptible. First, in the Netherlands and Germany, Dutch and German versions of *De doctrina* are placed in textual and institutional locations that suggest their association with fifteenth-century programmes of monastic and canonical reform. In German manuscripts, partial and complete translations of *De doctrina* are copied alongside writings by reform-theologians such as Johannes Tauler, Ludolf of Saxony, Johannes Nider, Meister Eckhart and Heinrich Suso, and these manuscripts utilized in religious houses associated with the reform movement.[40] In the Netherlands, one of the Middle Dutch manuscripts of *De doctrina* is owned by an abbey of Augustinian canonesses associated (via the Groenendaal Augustinian priory) with the reform spirituality of

---

37 Vernacular translations mingle with Latin copies in Hendrix's list of extant mansucripts: Hendrix, *Hugo I*, pp. 7–105.

38 C. Whitehead, D. Renevey and A. Mouron (eds), *The Doctrine of the Hert: A Critical Edition with Introduction and Commentary* (Exeter, 2010).

39 The editions in question are the Salamanca edition of 1498; the Toledo first edition of 1510; a Toledo second edition of 1525, and a Baeza edition of 1551. For more details on the manuscripts and early printed texts of all these vernacular versions please see the relevant essays in the final section of this volume.

40 Relevant manuscripts include Berlin, Staatsbibliothek zu Berlin – Preußischer Kulturbesitz, MS Germ. qu. 1130; Munich, Bayer. Staatsbibliothek, Cgm 447; Eichstätt, Kloster St. Walburg, Cod. Germ. 7; Solothurn, Zentralbibliothek, MS S 353. For a more detailed consideration of these manuscripts and their role in fifteenth-century German monastic reform, see the essay by Karl-Heinz Steinmetz in this volume.

the Windesheim Chapter.[41] The association of these vernacular versions of *De doctrina* with north European reform spirituality indicate strongly that it was primarily viewed as a *devotional* treatise, of moral and educational value. Nonetheless, we should be cautious of assuming that this devotional categorization necessarily shades into the kind of contemplative expectation implicit in various of the Latin manuscripts.[42] Rather, Marleen Cré notes cogently that the canonesses of St Trudo were allowed access to a *full* text of *De doctrina* in Middle Dutch in a reform milieu that increasingly forbade nuns from meddling with writings of a mystical or revelatory character.[43]

Devotional content remains an expectation in the translations of *De doctrina* circulating in Spain and England in the fifteenth and sixteenth centuries. In Spain, the second, third and fourth printings of the Spanish translation all attribute *De doctrina* to St Bonaventure, the notable Franciscan church doctor and devotional author (*Doctrina cordis de sant buena ventura en romance*).[44] In England, in two out of the four extant manuscripts, the Middle English *Doctrine of the Hert* travels with an anonymous spiritual treatise, *The Tree and xii frutes of the Holy Goost*,[45] which is unquestionably devotional in tone and also contains long passages of nigh-on contemplative sophistication.[46] Additionally, it is the case that in the one testamentary

---

41 The manuscript in question: Vienna, Österr. Nationalbibliothek, MS 15231, was owned by the Augustinian canonesses of St Trudo, near Bruges. Houses forming or associated with the Windesheim Chapter became the chief monastic representatives of the *Devotio Moderna*. For a more detailed account of the history of this manuscript and its links with Dutch reform spirituality, see the essay by Marleen Cré in this volume.

42 See pp. 66–8 above.

43 See the chapter by Marleen Cré in this volume, pp. 216–17.

44 See the essay by Anthony Lappin in this volume, p. 238.

45 *A Deuout Treatyse Called the Tree & xii Frutes of the Holy Goost*, ed. by J.J. Vaissier (Groningen, 1960). The manuscripts in question: Durham, University Library, MS Cosin V.III.24, and Cambridge, Fitzwilliam Museum, MS McClean 132.

46 One thinks, in particular, of the exposition of the tree (signifying the soul) growing high through 'devout contemplation of heaven' in Part I of the treatise. This exposition includes participatory dramatic meditations on the passion and nativity, and explicit hyperlinks to Victorine texts on non-vocal meditative prayer. Contemplative spirituality is also implied in the rather rhapsodic expositions of the fruit of charity and joy at the beginning of Part II. A third manuscript of the *Tree and xii Frutes*, along with one of the surviving copies of its first printing in the early sixteenth century, were owned by the Bridgettine nuns of Syon, renowned for their studiousness and sophisticated spiritual reading tastes. *De doctrina*'s association

record we possess detailing vernacular lay ownership, the Middle English *Doctrine* is bequeathed by a gentry widow, Margaret Purdans, along with two other relatively 'advanced' spiritual texts: 'an English book of St Bridget' and 'a book called Hylton'.[47] Margaret is known to have had connections with recluses and contemplatives in and around her home's locality in Norwich.[48] While it is always dangerous to conclude too much from simple physical proximities, it would nonetheless seem in this instance that a woman who was interested in the contemplative vocation and read texts of some contemplative and revelatory sophistication also found spiritual value in the contents of the Middle English *Doctrine*.

Alongside the fairly consistent devotional categorization of the vernacular *De doctrina*, which ranges, however, from the vehemently non-mystical in Middle Dutch religious circles to the potentially contemplative in Middle English, it is also possible to detect other patterns of changed use and perception in vernacular contexts. It is clear, for example, that in certain vernaculars *De doctrina* is brought into much closer first-hand contact with *female* religious readers. In Germany, England and the Netherlands vernacular manuscripts are housed in women's convents for direct private or communal reading,[49] rather than, as is almost entirely the case with

---

with the *Tree and xii Frutes*, the presence of Latin *De doctrina* manuscripts at Syon, and the interest in *De doctrina* shown by the Carthusian order, make it tempting to suggest that the Middle English *Doctrine* may well have been known at, or possibly even generated from, Syon or Sheen, its Carthusian partner institution.

[47] The full will is quoted in H. Harrod, 'Extracts from Early Wills in the Norwich Registries', *Norfolk and Norwich Archeological Society*, 4 (1855), 335–6.

[48] M. Erler, *Women, Reading and Piety in Late Medieval England* (Cambridge, 2002), pp. 68–84; D. Renevey and C. Whitehead, '"Opyn þin hert as a boke": Translation Practice and Manuscript Circulation in *The Doctrine of the Hert*', in J. Jenkins and O. Bertrand (eds), *The Medieval Translator 10* (Turnhout, 2007), pp. 125–48 (142).

[49] In Germany, Solothurn, MS S 353 was owned, in the late fifteenth century, by the Dominican sisters of St Maria Magdalena an den Steinen in Basel, and in the sixteenth century by the Cistercian nuns of Olsberg in the Basel diocese; Eichstätt, Cod. Germ. 7 was owned by the Benedictine nuns of St Walburg, Eichstätt. In the Netherlands, Cologne, Diözesanbibliothek, MS 248 was owned by the Augustinian canonesses of the Jerusalem convent at Venraai; Vienna, Österr. Nationalbibliothek, MS 15231, by the Augustinian canonesses of St Trudo, Bruges, and Vienna, Österr. Nationalbibliothek, MS Ser. nov. 12805, by the Carmelite nuns of Syon in Bruges. In England, Cambridge, Trinity College, MS B.14.15 was owned by the Franciscan convent of St Botolph without Aldgate, London. In addition, a lost manuscript was bequeathed by the gentry widow, Margaret

the Latin manuscripts, remaining the possession of monasteries and friaries, where they would perhaps have been used indirectly to determine the content and structure of sermons to neighbouring convents. In other words, it is possible to detect a shift away from the dominantly public and homiletic perception of the Latin text towards an environment of vernacular reception in which *De doctrina* was utilized more individually and intimately as a aid to private devotional encounter. The address to a religious sister, 'charissima', repeated unambiguously throughout complete texts of the Latin *De doctrina*, although generally erased from summaries, extracts and 'capitula selecta', thus becomes markedly less mediated. As opposed to texts addressing the religious sister via the intermediary of a male preacher – a mediation open to varying degrees of rewriting, exposition, abridgement or suppression – the religious sister gains a freedom of hermeneutic response via her own direct engagement with the words on the page.[50]

This is not to say that the vernacular versions of *De doctrina* housed in conventual libraries necessarily offer a transparent rendition of the thought and expression of the Latin 'original', questionable as that concept may be. Rather, on occasion, the mediating role of the preacher is simply assumed by the translator. In vernacular versions in German and Middle Dutch, surprisingly,[51] nuns are given access to the unexpurgated text, complete with a demanding array of references to the Church Fathers, classical writers and points of church doctrine.[52] Much is obviously expected of them. In the Middle English translation, by contrast, the anonymous translator expects, or feels it necessary to construct, a far more 'symple' and 'unkunnyng' female religious reader.[53] Reducing the translation to less than a third of its

Purdans, to the East Anglian Franciscan convent of Bruisyard. It is also worth noting the increased specificity surrounding the reader's gender in the Middle English translation: the recipient is designated a 'mynche' (nun), and repeatedly addressed as 'sistir'.

50 In an unpublished talk delivered at the University of Bangor, Wales, in March 2006, I discuss the way in which devotional images of the 'House of the Heart' produced by the Benedictine nuns of St Walburg, Eichstätt, may represent a series of daring and unconventional hermeneutic responses to passages from the German translation of *De doctrina*. For reproductions and analysis of these images, see also J. Hamburger, *Nuns as Artists: The Visual Culture of a Medieval Convent* (Berkeley, CA, 1997), pp. 137–75.

51 Marleen Cré notes the phenomenon as 'remarkable' in her essay in this volume.

52 I refer in particular here to Solothurn, MS S 353, and Vienna, Österr. Nationalbibliothek, MS 15231.

53 *Doctrine of the Hert*, p. 3, ll. 6, 10.

Latin length, he carefully hones the treatise so as to minimize its intellectual demands, erasing all classical references, severely curbing citations of the Fathers and omitting passages of abstract theological discussion.[54] Without advancing too far down avenues of speculation tangential to the main concerns of this essay, it would appear that the extra layer of adaptation, reduction and simplification that the Middle English translator seems to have felt it necessary to add may well have arisen from the restrictions placed upon the production of religious writing in fifteenth-century England, in the aftermath of Archbishop Arundel's censorious Constitutions of 1409.[55]

Vernacular versions of *De doctrina* were used directly by convents of female religious in the Netherlands, Germany and England, and, in some instances, copied specifically for them. However, there are as many examples where the opposite is true – where vernacular versions of the text seem to hold to the functions and orbit of their Latin precursors, and to remain housed within the libraries of male monastic establishments, conceivably for consultation by novices or younger monks at a period, in the late fifteenth and sixteenth centuries, when monastic Latinity was not always to be as readily relied upon. The one extant early printed edition of the Spanish translation of *De doctrina* to carry some indicators of provenance – the second edition published in Toledo in 1510 – seems to have been used in this way in the third quarter of the sixteenth century.[56] Similarly, the Troyes manuscript of the French translation (again, the only one of the extant French translations to carry any clues as to provenance) is known to have been housed in the Cistercian monastic library at Clairvaux in the late fifteenth and early sixteenth centuries, alongside a number of copies of the Latin text.[57]

Of course, we should not be surprised that, in parallel with its expanded usage by female religious, vernacular versions of *De doctrina* continued to be utilized much as they always had been – as versatile manuals for vernacular

---

54 A more detailed analysis of the Middle English translator's method is given in Renevey and Whitehead, '"Opyn þin hert as a boke"', pp. 134–8, and in Anne Mouron's essay in this volume.

55 The classic article upon this subject is N. Watson, 'Censorship and Cultural Change in Late-Medieval England: Vernacular Theology, the Oxford Translation Debate, and Arundel's Constitutions of 1409', *Speculum*, 70 (1995), 822–64.

56 For a detailed analysis, see Anthony Lappin's essay in this volume.

57 Hendrix, *Hugo I*, pp. 90–92. See also A. Vernet, *La bibliothèque de l'abbaye de Clairvaux du XIIe au XVIIIe siecles* (Paris, 1979), p. 224. Mouron speculates cogently that the French translation may have been designed to assist the Clairvaux monks in reading and comprehending the Latin text.

preaching, as guides to novices and as textbooks of devotion specifically geared toward a monastic clientale. Just as the address 'charissima' and the occasional allegorical episode worked specifically for female identification seem not to have bothered the Latin text's male readers, so too vernacular versions of the text appear to have found favour fairly impartially with both male and female religious readers. At times, gendered pronouns are suppressed or swopped in the course of making or copying the translation;[58] in other instances, in vernacular summaries and 'capitula selecta', indications of reading gender tend in any case to disappear.[59]

So, a continued inclusiveness of application is not surprising. What is perhaps more singular is the lack of evidence for *lay* possession of any translation of *De doctrina*, in any vernacular, with the single English exception of the Norwich gentry widow Margaret Purdans. I have commented elsewhere on the ways in which Margaret Purdans might have applied passages from the Middle English *Doctrine* to her lay spiritual routine; I have also pointed out the not inconsiderable portions of *De doctrina* that seem completely unamenable to meaningful lay usage.[60] The research carried out for this volume on the fate of the other vernacular versions in mainland Europe allows us to frame the example of Purdans within new and significant contexts. These vernacular contexts indicate, in so far as we can tell, that Purdans seems utterly alone in her lay access to this text. One possible explanation for this singularity may stem from the extra liberties taken with the text by its Middle English translator; the loss of the erudition and scholastic density retained within the other continental translations may have assisted in bringing the *Doctrine* within the spiritual orbit of a laywoman. Alternately, it may be possible to view Purdans' interest

58 Mouron describes how references to a female reader are suppressed or exchanged for references to a male reader in Troyes, Bibliothèque municipale, MS 1384 (pp. 199–200). Similarily, in one of the Middle English manuscripts, Durham, University Library, MS Cosin V.III.24, female third-person pronouns are frequently replaced by masculine pronouns or by gender-inclusive phrases: 'religious *man or* woman' (*Doctrine of the Hert*, p. 54, l. 265, [see Textual Variants] my italics), suggesting, despite the bias towards female religious use in England in general, that this particular copy was prepared for an English monastic house.

59 Vernacular translations of *De doctrina* consist largely of complete versions rather than of extracts or summaries. However, several manuscripts of 'capitula selecta': namely, 'apertio cordis', 'custodia linguae' and 'impedimenta', exist in German translation. See my discussion above, and also Karl-Heinz Steinmetz's essay in this volume.

60 Renevey and Whitehead, '"Opyn þin hert as a boke"', pp. 143–5.

in the *Doctrine* as part of a wider late medieval English phenomenon in which devout laypersons turned, albeit with some difficulty, to monastic productions to compensate for the dearth of non-elementary lay spiritual guidance created in the wake of Arundel's Constitutions.

Finally, a few comments are required upon the degree of interest manifested in the vernacular *De doctrina* by the different religious orders, giving some sense of how precisely its spiritual instruction was held to tally with the ideals of various enclosed regimes. At first glance the distribution of manuscript provenances between the different orders seems wholly random – vernacular copies are held by Benedictines, by Dominicans, by Augustinian canons, by Franciscans, by Carmelites, by Cistercians – a testament to the truism that works of monastic spirituality frequently transcend the distinctions of individual regimes. However, on closer investigation, some clearer patterns of association begin to stand out. In the Netherlands, in Germany and also, possibly, in France, the vernacular *De doctrina* appears to have held special interest for Augustinian houses and, to a lesser extent, Dominican priories, associated with fifteenth-century currents of reform.[61] In Spain and England, the text seems to have become linked with Franciscan spiritual practice. In Spain, second and subsequent prints of the vernacular text are attributed to St Bonaventure, the thirteenth-century Franciscan church doctor.[62] In England, the Middle English *Doctrine* appears twice in the possession of Franciscan convents (Bruisyard in Suffolk and St Botolph without Aldgate in London), one of approximately thirteen English books known to have been housed in English Franciscan convent libraries, and the only book, apart from Walter

---

61 In the Netherlands, vernacular versions of *De doctrina* are owned by the Augustinian canonesses of Jerusalem at Venraai, and St Trudo at Bruges (the second clearly linked to the Windesheim reform). In German-speaking lands, vernacular versions are owned by the reforming Augustinian houses of Klosterneuberg and Rebdorf, and by the reforming Dominican convent of St Maria Magdalena near Basel (see the essays by Cré and Steinmetz in this volume). In France, unfortunately, we lack the signs of ownership that would enable us to associate extant manuscripts of the translations to any specific foundation. Nonetheless, Mouron argues cogently in her essay in this volume that the emphasis placed upon St Augustine as a patristic source, in Douai, Bibliothèque municipale, MS 514, may suggest an Augustinian or Dominican origin for this manuscript (pp. 198–9).

62 Anthony Lappin's valuable essay in this volume considers this point in more detail; it also discusses the implications of the Franciscan imagery found upon the printer's shield in the Salamanca first edition of 1498 (pp. 261–2).

Hilton and two variant formulations of *The Book of Vices and Virtues*, to appear twice.[63]

Once again, it is important to stress that the manuscript evidence remains very partial. Nonetheless, as far as we can tell from the observations cited above, the spiritual guidance and perception of community life promulgated by *De doctrina* seem to have found particular favour with mendicant regimes – Dominican and Franciscan – and with Augustinian houses. Neither should come as a particular surprise. The extended discussion of godly preaching and its exemplary reception in the Prologue to *De doctrina* immediately brings the treatise into sympathy with the homiletic fervour of the mendicant orders, while the content chimes well with their continuing emphasis upon the importance of devotional and catechetical education. From the inception of canonical houses in the eleventh and twelfth centuries, canonical spiritual writing tends to stress the responsibility of members of an enclosed community to edify and educate one another through behaviour, example and speech. Caroline Walker Bynum writes that:

> Behind the explicit exhortations to educate *verbo et exemplo* found in many canonical commentaries lies the assumption that an individual living a cloistered life is responsible in whatever he says or does not only for the state of his own soul but also for the progress of his neighbour.[64]

A compatible emphasis appears repeatedly in *De doctrina*: in the concern with how unguarded speech will impact upon the spiritual development of others, and in the attention given to the necessity of mutual charitable correction within the cloister.[65] It also appears to provide a more specific example, in the clear sense given in the initial allegory of the cloister as God's kitchen, that the nuns uphold one another – the strong carrying the

63 D.N. Bell, *What Nuns Read: Books and Libraries in Medieval English Nunneries*, Cistercian Studies Series 158 (Kalamazoo, 1995), pp. 121–2, 134–5, 149–52; Erler, *Women, Reading and Piety*, pp. 140–41, 145–6. For an informative account of the strong literary culture centred upon the Franciscan convent of St Botolph without Aldgate, see C.M. Meale and J. Boffey, 'Gentlewomen's Reading', in L. Hellinga and J.B. Trapp (eds), *The Cambridge History of the Book in Britain, vol. III. 1400–1557* (Cambridge, 1999), pp. 526–40 (531–4).

64 C.W. Bynum, *Jesus as Mother: Studies in the Spirituality of the High Middle Ages* (Berkeley, CA, 1982), p. 40. An extended discussion of the distinctiveness of canonical spirituality is offered at pp. 22–58.

65 *De doctrina*, book 2.

weak – in preparing themselves for consumption by Christ. I quote using the vivid idiom of the Middle English translation of this passage:

> The[r]for sister, suffre þe fatnes, the wiche is charite of thi sistren, to drepe intoo þin hert, considering the gret devocioun, þe meknes, þe pacience, and the obedience of hem: how mekly and how gladly þey obeye.
>
> Of such take ensample, and not of hem þat with angwisse bere the crosse of obedience with Symon, þat of everything the wiche is put to þeyme of here sovereynes wil dispute and make questiouns. A lene hen is not wont to be rosted with another lene hen, but with a fatte hen. Right so do thou in thi rostyng; take noon ensample of hem þat lakken devocioun, meknes, and paciens, but of hem þat ben replete with devocioun and charite.[66]

Conclusion

From the evidence of manuscript contexts, and by paying due attention to 'incomplete' versions such as summaries and excerpts, it is possible to create a detailed picture of the ways in which the Latin *De doctrina cordis* was perceived and utilized from the thirteenth to the fifteenth centuries. In particular, it is possible to discern four main categories of perception and use. It was closely associated with medieval preaching handbooks and sermon series; it was envisaged as a guide for novices; it was reduced into a catechetical format; and it was also, on occasion, extracted in such as a way as to foreground its meditative and contemplative potential. Inherent in the identification of these categories is the sense that we would do as well to revise our preconception of *De doctrina* as a unitary text ordered upon linear principles; a truer picture is obtained by responding to it as a sizeable mélange of small text units that can be assembled in a variety of sequences.

An analysis of the vernacular versions of *De doctrina* vis-à-vis their manuscript context and provenance (where known) allows us to extend these conclusions a little further. In a majority of instances it would seem that it is the devotional, morally educational potential of *De doctrina* that is brought to the fore, in particular within the context of North European monastic reform movements. In translation, copies of *De doctrina* find their way directly into a number of female religious houses for private and communal

66 *Doctrine of the Hert*, p. 24, ll. 737–47.

reading. Nonetheless, the text also continues to be utilized by male religious, although very rarely by lay readers. In so far as it is possible to detect any order-specific partiality for the translated *De doctrina*, it would seem that the text finds greatest favour and accords best with the educational aspirations and communal ideals of the mendicant and canonical orders. A comparative evaluation of the different vernacular versions as regards their faithfulness or otherwise to the Latin original, their textual travelling companions and the circumstances in which they were read perhaps succeeds in highlighting to a greater extent than has previously been acknowledged the marked singularity of the Middle English translation.

Part II

The Doctrine of the Hert

3

The Doctrine of the Hert: A Middle English Translation of *De doctrina cordis*

Anne Elisabeth Mouron

Introduction

John Trevisa, in an epistle to Thomas, Lord of Berkley, says the following about his translation of Higden's *Polychronicon*:

> For to make this translacioun cleer and pleyne to be knowe and understonde, in somme place Y shal sette worde for worde, and actif for actif, and passif for passif, arewe right as thei stondeth, without chaunging of the ordre of wordes. But in somme place Y mot chaunge the rewe and the ordre of wordes, and sett the actif for the passif, and ayenward. And in somme place Y mot sett a resoun for a worde and telle what it meneth. But for alle siche chaunging, the menyng shal stonde and nought be ychaunged.[1]

Translating in this way, i.e. keeping the 'menyng' of the original text but allowing grammatical adjustments due to the new linguistic medium, is how we understand the concept of translation today. However, this is not the only way the Middle Ages understood it. In the 'proheme of Þe boke þat is clepid þe Mirroure of þe blissed lyffe of oure lorde Jesu cryste', Nicholas Love gives quite a different assessment of his translation:

1 John Trevisa, 'Epistle', in J. Wogan-Browne, et al. (eds), *The Idea of the Vernacular. An Anthology of Middle English Literary Theory 1280–1520* (Exeter, 1999), pp. 134–5.

> Wherfore at þe instance & þe prayer of some deuoute soules ... is þis drawynge oute of þe forseide boke of cristes lyfe wryten in englysche with more putte to in certeyn partes & [also] wiþdrawyng of diuerse auctoritis [and] maters as it semeth to þe wryter hereof moste spedefull & edifyng to hem þat bene [of] symple vndirstondyng.[2]

So, if John Trevisa's purpose is clarity of understanding, Nicholas Love's is spiritual edification, and it seems that the latter intention justifies a much more interventionistic attitude by the translator. Additions to and omissions from the original text are therefore silently included. The extent of these changes will determine whether one should today endorse the vernacular work as a translation or rather as an adaptation of the original Latin work.

Unlike Nicholas Love's translation, the name and identity of the translator of the Middle English version of *De doctrina cordis* has not come down to us, but his intentions have survived in a different Prologue to the text, which will be examined in greater detail later in this essay. For the moment, it is sufficient to look at how he explains his intentions:

> Many, I wote wel, þer ben that speken to the body ouȝtward, but few to the hert inward of symple soules, and that is pite.
>
> I, þerfore, oon of thoo whiche oure lord hath clepid to his servise in religioun, alþogh I be no trew servaunt of his, have compilid this tretice that is clepid 'the doctrine of the herte', to the worship of God principally, and to edificacioun of symple soules, wherein is comprehendid an informacioun of hertis.[3]

This declaration of intent suggests two observations. Firstly, there is no acknowledgment of the text being a translation from the Latin.[4] In this excerpt, as throughout the prologue, the translator systematically refers to

---

2 Nicholas Love, *The Mirror of the Blessed Life of Jesus Christ*, ed. by M.G. Sargent (Exeter, 2004), p. 10.

3 *Doctrine of the Hert*, p. 3, ll. 17–24.

4 There seem to be just two places where the Middle English text specifically refers to the Latin. Firstly, while discussing the 'ellevenþ arayment' given by God, i.e. a crown, one reads: 'This crowne is clepid in Latyn *auriola*', *Doctrine of the Hert*, p. 45, ll. 1534–5. Secondly, in its examination of the second article of the Creed, the text says: 'In Latine we sey þus: *Et in Jhesum Cristum, filium ...*', *Doctrine of the Hert*, p. 69, l. 48. In neither case, though, has the reference to the Latin anything to do with the fact that the *Doctrine* is a translation.

the text as 'this tretice'. Secondly, and perhaps even more so than Nicholas Love's, the translator's purpose is moral and spiritual. It seems to be his concern for the overly materialistic approach of the 'symple soules' that has prompted his 'compil[ing]' of the text. Thus what comes first is not 'to make this translacioun cleer and pleyne to be knowe and understonde', but the 'worship of God' and the 'edificacioun of symple soules'. Is, then, the translator here stating principles of translation akin to Nicholas Love's?

Assessing Sister Candon's account of the translation

In the introduction to her unpublished 1963 doctoral edition of *The Doctrine of the Hert*, Sister Candon examines the translating process at work in the Middle English *Doctrine*. She gives the following overall observation:

> A comparison of the Latin and English versions of the *Doctrine* makes it very clear that the English is not a recension or a paraphrase but a translation. *So closely does the English follow the Latin* that one seems safe in conjecturing that if the translator had worked on a gem of Latin literature he would have produced a gem in the English.[5]

After decades of scholarship on such medieval works as the *Ancrene Wisse*, Sister Candon's somewhat negative comment upon *De doctrina* (in Latin or in the vernacular) may no longer be shared, but what about her claim of a close translation? Has the translator followed John Trevisa's method after all?

The first thing Sister Candon notes in a more detailed analysis of the work of the translator is that the Middle English text has been considerably abridged: 'The typewritten manuscript of the Latin covers 262 pages, that of the English 156'.[6] Candon explains that these omissions do not appear to be random, but to follow some kind of method:

> It would seem that there are discernible three general rules by which the translator rejected material. First, in a series of explanatory material he seems to have chosen the first items and discarded the last. Second, he has avoided the mention of profane authors and of material not directly

5 Sister M.P. Candon (ed.), '*The Doctrine of the Hert*, Edited from the Manuscripts, with Introduction and Notes' (unpublished doctoral dissertation, Fordham University, 1963), p. lxv, my italics. Henceforth cited as Candon, *Doctrine*.

6 Ibid., p. lx.

> connected with the spiritual life. Third, he seems to have omitted many passages which for want of a better word I shall call virile.[7]

Candon illustrates her first rule of omission with an example taken from book 2, or 'How and in what wise a mynche shuld kepe here hert to God be the yifte of pite'.[8] Using the familiar metaphor of the heart as a castle, the text advises the sister how to guard it and defend it from enemy attacks. In so doing, it looks at 'many gret folyes wher þorogh soules ben overcome in here gostly batayle.'[9] The Latin text gives ten 'stultitiae imprudentium in bello spirituali',[10] but the Middle English omits the last five. The first five are:

> On is of such þat wil not do on here armoure unto þe tyme þei ben hurt and woundid …
>
> The secunde foly is of hem þat don on such armoure þe wiche is to hevy for hem, and so ben overthrow in here owne harneyce and encombred …
>
> The þrid foly is of such, whan þey shuld goo to batayle and fight, þan þei caste away here armour …
>
> The fourth foly is of hem þat wil not distroye here enemyes al þe while þei be litelle, but suffre hem to grow and wex myghti in age, and þan it is hard to overcome hem …
>
> The fifthe foly is of hem þat wil not withstonde here enemyes at þe narew yates of þe cite where þei myght sone overcome hem …[11]

And the next five are:

> Sexta stultitia est illorum, qui contra suos pugnant, et hostes suos non cognoscentes, eos amicos reputant …
>
> Septima stultitia est eorum, qui de prope volunt pugnare cum hoste …

---

7 Ibid., pp. lx–lxi.

8 *Doctrine of the Hert*, p. 4, ll. 43–4.

9 Ibid., p. 51, ll. 149–50.

10 Gerardus Leodiensis, *Speculum concionatorum ad illustrandum pectora auditorum, in septem libros distributum* (Naples, 1607), Oxford, Bodleian Library, 8º L 12 Th. BS, p. 165, henceforth referred to as *De doctrina*. (Follies of ignorant men in spiritual warfare.) All translations are my own.

11 *Doctrine of the Hert*, p. 51, ll. 152–3, 162–4, 170–1, p. 52, ll. 192–4, 199–200.

> Octaua sultitia est eorum, qui hostem fugiendo euadere, et euitare volunt, quando fugientes magis insequitur, et persequitur …
>
> Nona stultitia est eorum, qui cum esset pugnandum contrarijs, pugnant similibus, vt odio contra odium, … cum potius amore contra odium pugnandum esset …
>
> Decima stultitia est eorum, qui laborant in impugnatione hostium; cum honorabilius possent vincere quiescendo, quasi, 'sans cop ferir' …[12]

When one examines all ten 'folyes', it is not obvious why the translator stops at the fifth, for all of the subsequent 'folyes' offer valuable advice for the religious. Candon explains it thus: 'In comparing the two versions one almost gets the idea of a man, who, when he has reached the point of satiety, simply stops.'[13] Such explanation, though, is more modern than medieval, for texts of the late Middle Ages abound with such lists. To mention but one example, in book 4, or 'Temptations', of the *Ancrene Wisse*, for instance, one finds a list of nine 'comforts';[14] the text then lists remedies against temptations, the third of which is faith. Faith is then itself divided into 'hu alle þe seouene deadliche sunnen muhen beon afleiet þurh treowe bileaue',[15] of which the consideration of anger has nine examples of 'hu god is anrednesse of luue; ⁊ annesse of heorte.'[16] It seems that the author of the *Ancrene Wisse* knows that he is stretching his list within lists, for he

---

12 *De doctrina*, pp. 170–74. (The sixth folly is of those who fight against themselves and, not recognizing their enemies, consider them as friends … The seventh folly is of those who want to fight their enemy from too close a quarter … The eighth folly is of those who want to get away and to escape the enemy by fleeing, when he so much the more follows and pursues the fugitives. The ninth folly is of those who, when one should fight contraries, fight likenesses, such as hatred with hatred … when one must rather fight against hatred with love … The tenth folly is of those who labour in the attack of the enemies, when they could prevail more honourably by keeping quiet, as if 'sans cop ferir' …)

13 Candon, *Doctrine*, p. lxi.

14 *The English Text of the Ancrene Riwle: Ancrene Wisse, Edited from MS. Corpus Christi College, Cambridge, 402*, ed. by J.R.R. Tolkien, EETS 249 (1962), pp. 117–23.

15 Ibid., p. 127 (how all the Seven Deadly Sins can be put to flight through true faith.) This and following translations are taken from A. Savage and N. Watson (eds and trs), *Anchoritic Spirituality: Ancrene Wisse and Associated Works*, Classics of Western Spirituality (New York, 1991), p. 138. Henceforth, *Ancrene Wisse.*

16 Ibid., p. 128 (how good are constancy of love and oneness of heart), *Ancrene Wisse*, p. 139.

says: 'Þe Seoueðe forbisne is þis ȝef ȝe riht telleð. Dust ⁊ greot as ȝe seoð. for hit is isundret ⁊ nan ne halt to oþer; a lutel windes puf to driueð hit al to nawt.'[17]

Not only does the translator of *De doctrina* arbitrarily omit the last five 'folyes', but his account of the first five does not strictly render the Latin either.[18] Indeed, a close comparison of both passages in Latin and in Middle English shows that the translator's intervention is much more drastic than Candon allows one to believe. A look at the rendering of the first three 'folyes' will suffice here. The Middle English first folly involves omissions, additions and variants. First of all, the Middle English passage, like the text as a whole, is considerably shorter than the Latin. All the biblical quotations have been omitted,[19] as have most of the images which portray the fight against vices as an actual battle: 'imprudentes in bello spirituali' is now 'soules';[20] 'ante pugnam' is 'unto þe tyme';[21] 'cum gladio linguae nequam fuerint vulnerati'[22] completely disappears from the Middle English, and so on. The advice to the reader has been reduced and simplified: for example, 'Praeparatio ista est cogitatio de modo resistendi tentationi, quod faciendum est antequam impugnet tentatio' is now more vague: 'be wel war of þis foly'.[23] Specific vices and virtues are passed over: 'Semper debes cum armis incedere: vt dicenti tibi conuitium, statim clypeum patientiae et taciturnitatis opponas, voluptati disciplinam, vanitati paupertatis amorem obijcias, vt non feriaris ad nudum'[24] has been

17 Ibid., p. 129 (The seventh example, if you are counting properly, is this. A little puff of wind drives dust and grit all to nothing), *Ancrene Wisse*, p. 140.

18 In the Middle English translation, the order of the fourth and fifth follies are reversed from the Latin order, *Doctrine of the Hert*, p. 52, n. 27.

19 The description of the first folly in the Latin *De doctrina* includes the following Biblical quotations: Eph. 6:13; Job 40:27, Ecclus. 4:34. References to Latin biblical quotations are to the Vulgate. Translations into English are usually from the King James Bible. When these differ too widely from the Latin or when they are from biblical books not included in the King James Bible, quotations from the Jerusalem Bible are also offered.

20 *De doctrina*, p. 165 (the man imprudent in spiritual war); *Doctrine of the Hert*, p. 51, l. 149.

21 *De doctrina*, p. 165 (before the fight); *Doctrine of the Hert*, p. 51, l. 152.

22 *De doctrina*, p. 165 (when they have been wounded by the sword of the tongue.)

23 *De doctrina*, p. 165 (This preparation [i.e. against temptation] is to consider the way in which to resist temptation, which should be done before the temptation assails you); *Doctrine of the Hert*, p. 51, l. 156.

24 *De doctrina*, p. 165 (You must always march with your weapons: as their

rephrased as 'go alway armyd with þe armour of paciens and þe scheld of meknes, þat whan þi gostly batayle begynneþ þou mow withstonde þin enemy, þe fende, and alle his lymes.'[25] The mention and example of the Passion is gone – 'Dominus quasi pugnator in pugna passionis locutus est, pauca, et multa, et grauia tolerauit'[26] – as is the reference to women as gossips who cannot suffer much:

> Alioquin pugnant sicut mulieres, quae multum possunt loqui, et pauca facere, vel sufferre. Pugna enim mulierum contentio est, quae fortes sunt in lingua, infirmae in manibus, sicut dicit Chrysostomus. Ita, qui multa docent, et pauca operantur, pugnam exercent mulierum.[27]

In the first Middle English folly, the translator sees the addressee as assisting him in his task: 'be the grace of God and þi devoute prayeris, summe [i.e. follies] I shal reherse.'[28] He also inserts a reference to the religious life: 'So don many in religioun'.[29] He then adds the word 'gostly' twice, so that, in the Middle English, 'gostly' is repeated three times within a few lines: 'gostly batayle', 'gostly batayle', 'þin [gostly] enemyes'.[30]

Candon states in her notes that 'in the elucidation of the first folly in the Latin St John Chrysostom is quoted on the inadvisability of fighting as women who are strong in words but weak in deeds. The omission indicates a certain tact in the translator.'[31] But, as can be seen from the above, the changes introduced by the translator are in fact much more significant than Candon's comments would imply.

---

clamour reaches your ears, you should immediately set against them the shield of patience and of taciturnity, you should oppose discipline to sensual pleasure, and love of poverty to vanity, so that you may not be struck on bare flesh.)

25 *Doctrine of the Hert*, p. 51, ll. 156–9.

26 *De doctrina*, p. 166 (Our Lord, just as a fighter, spoke few words in the battle of his Passion, and endured much and severe [pain].)

27 Ibid., p. 166 (Otherwise, they fight like women, who can talk a lot, and do or suffer only a little. Indeed such fighting is a dispute of women, who are strong in their tongue, weak in their hands, as St John Chrysostom says. Thus those who teach a lot, and work only a little, practice the fighting of women.)

28 *Doctrine of the Hert*, p. 51, ll. 150–1.

29 Ibid., p. 51, l. 153.

30 Ibid., p. 51, ll. 150, 157, 160. The third 'gostly' appears only in two of the four manuscripts of the Middle English *Doctrine*: Oxford, Bodleian Library, MS Laud Misc. 330, and Cambridge, Trinity College, MS B.14.15.

31 Candon, *Doctrine*, p. 187, n. 84/13.

The second folly is about the same length in both Middle English and Latin, but there is again much variation in the treatment of the text. For instance, 'Sicut animae nouitiae, quae a principio antequam paulatim se assueuerint ieiuniorum, et vigiliarum ponderibus, plus debito se grauant, in tantum, vt post amissionem virium, eis onerosa, imo *odiosa poenitentia reddatur*'[32] has been rendered as: 'as don many new fervent soules þat, in þe begynnyng of here conversioun, þei take so moche upon hem undiscretly of over moche fastyng and wakyng, þat *þei lese here gostly myghtes for to pray devoutly*.'[33] Here the Middle English does not merely simplify what is said, but changes it from a difficulty to perform penance to a difficulty to pray.

The same reworking continues in the third folly. The Middle English, for instance, omits the quotation 'Vnde dictum est in Boetio primo de Consolatione Philosophiae. Talia tibi contuleramus arma, quae nisi prior abiecisses, inuicta te firmitate tuerentur',[34] and, later, the observation 'Dum enim ibi audis quosdam bestiarum dentibus dilaceratos, alios igne crematos, quosdam in eculeo extensos sub diuersis Imperatoribus'[35] has been toned down to 'þou mayst here how summe were scorgid, and summe brennyd, and summe tormentid with diverse tormentis.'[36] None of these changes are mentioned in Candon's notes. However, the omission of Boethius can be seen as an illustration of the second rule described by Candon: that is, the omission of profane authors in the Middle English text; and the less violent description of the saints' torments can illustrate the third rule: that is, the omission of 'virile' or 'more violent' passages.[37] Apart from illustrating Candon's three rules of omission, the analysis of the 'folyes' also demonstrates an essential point, in that the translator still alters the

---

32 *De doctrina*, p. 166, my italics (As novice souls, who from the beginning, before they may gradually accustom themselves to the weight of fasts and vigils, burden themselves with a greater obligation, to such a degree, that after the loss of their strength, *penance may be made burdensome, indeed hateful to them*.)

33 *Doctrine of the Hert*, p. 51, ll. 164–7, my italics.

34 *De doctrina*, p. 167 (Hence it is said in Boethius's first Book of *The Consolation of Philosophy*: we gave you such arms which, if you had not thrown them down, would have protected you with invincible strength.) See Boethius, *Philosophiae consolatio*, ed. by L. Bieler, *CCSL* 94 (Turnhout, 1984), Book 1, p. 4.

35 *De Doctrina*, pp. 167–8 (Indeed in that place you hear that some were torn to pieces by the teeth of beasts, others were burned by fire, some were stretched out on wooden racks under various emperors.)

36 *Doctrine of the Hert*, p. 51, ll. 183–5.

37 Candon, *Doctrine*, p. lxii.

text considerably, even when Latin and Middle English share the same material.

If the translator's omissions are drastic, the same cannot be claimed about his additions and variants. Candon says: 'The few brief additions (usually little more than a phrase or a clause) in the English have practically nothing to do with the content but rather are inserted either in place of omitted material or for the sake of clarity.'[38] For example, in the third folly already mentioned, 'Cum insurgit carnis tentatio, statim vigorem mentis amittunt. Hoc est, arma in bello proijcere'[39] becomes in the translation 'whan þei ben sterid with flesshly temptaciouns, þei put away here gostly strength in prayer and discrete *fastyng and wakyng*.'[40] This change is quite interesting, for it shows that the translator is not bound by the sentence as a unit, but pays attention to the greater picture. For the insertion about 'fastyng and wakyng' should remind the reader of what was said in the second folly – that is, 'þei take so moche upon hem undiscretly of over moche *fastyng and wakyng*, þat þei lese here gostly myghtes for to pray devoutly.'[41] This passage is not specifically mentioned in Candon's notes.

However, in a separate section of her introduction, 'The Original Prose',[42] Candon comes back to the translator's additions. After noting how little additional material there is, apart from the prologue – which we shall look at next – she then remarks:

> Much of the rest of the original prose is in one or two sentences at the beginning of a chapter to link the gift of the Holy Ghost with the instruction, as in the fourth chapter (116/8–9): 'We must haue nedis þe ȝift of gostly strength for þat is necessarie to þe stabilyng of our vndirstondyng.'[43]

Further additions can also be noted, especially at the end of a section where wording may be replaced or altered. For instance, the second folly that we have discussed ends in the Latin with a biblical quotation: 'Quod significatum est in Dauid, qui arma Saulis proiecit, quia nimis erant

38 Ibid., p. lx.

39 *De doctrina*, p. 167 (When the temptation of the flesh arises, immediately they loose their mind's vigour. That is to say, they throw down their weapons in the battle.)

40 *Doctrine of the Hert*, p. 51, ll. 174–6, my italics.

41 Ibid., p. 51, ll. 165–7, my italics.

42 Candon, *Doctrine*, pp. lxxvii–lxxx.

43 Ibid., p. lxxviii.

ponderosa, nec sic armatus poterat incedere: vt dicitur. I Regum 17.'[44] The Middle English has instead an appeal to the addressee: 'Therfor sister, lete discrecioun, þe chyveteyn of þi gostly batayle, teche þe to be armyd, and not undescrecioun.'[45] Candon observes in her notes: 'This sentence is substituted for a brief account in the Latin of David's being weighed down by Saul's armor.'[46] The examination of omissions and of additions in the Middle English, then, suggests that *The Doctrine of the Hert* is a translation in Nicholas Love's sense of the word.

Candon's above-mentioned observation that 'so closely does the English follow the Latin'[47] implies that, apart from her three rules of omissions and quite scarce and limited additions, the Middle English text basically follows the Latin. In her 'Notes' to the text, Candon indeed gives some account of the lengthier passages omitted by the translator by briefly summarizing what is left out. But, more often than not, one has no real sense of why there is an omission and whether this means a few words or several pages. Consider, for instance, Candon's two contiguous notes 38/15 and 39/2:

> 38/15.[48] At this point in the Latin there is further development of the theme of charity symbolized by fat or grease which prevents burning, mention of the three children in the fiery furnace, and a reminder that Our Lord has commanded us to take up His burden whi[ch] is sweet and light.
>
> 39/2. In the Latin there is a separate section on the consideration of the Passion. It is an extension of the idea of placing a vessel to gather the blood of the Crucified Christ as a means of preserving charity. There is a reference also to the sacrifice of the Old Law which prefigured Christ's sacrifice of Himself.[49]

---

44 *De doctrina*, p. 166 (Which [i.e. penance becoming hateful, see n. 32 above] is signified by David who threw down Saul's weapons, because they were too heavy and with such armour on, he could not move forward, as it is said in 1 Sam. 17:39). Note that Vulgate, 1–2 Regum, corresponds to 1–2 Sam., King James Bible.

45 *Doctrine of the Hert*, p. 51, ll. 168–9. As the content and tone of the substituted sentence in the Middle English are so totally different from the Latin, I do not regard this sentence as a variant, but as an omission of the biblical verse followed by an addition.

46 Candon, *Doctrine*, p. 187, n. 84/20–22.

47 Ibid., p. lxv.

48 Actually, it should say 38/16.

49 Candon, *Doctrine*, pp. 171–2.

Omissions here do not appear to be explained by Candon's three rules and, in mentioning a 'separate section' in note 39/2, she seems to say that the omission referred to in note 38/16 is a small one.[50] The omitted Latin passage in note 38/16 begins:

> In huius signum praeceptum est in lege, Leuit. 3 et 7. quod adeps adoleretur in omni sacrificio. Quid per adipem, qui est pinguedo interior, nisi charitas intelligitur? Vnde tria fiebant in lege circa sacrificia, quae ad tria praecedentia referuntur, vt dicitur Leuit. 1 et 2. Primo, pellis extrahebatur ab animali; secundo membra super ignem in altari ponebantur; tertio adeps fundebatur super sacrificium in altari. Pellis extractio (vt dictum est) pertinet ad temporalium possessionum renuntiationem. Ignis appositio ad tribulationum tolerantiam. Adeps ad charitatem. Haec tria in tribus pueris reperimus positis in fornace, Daniel. 3. Primo, spoliati fuerunt dignitate, et primitia, quam habebant in curia Regis Babylonis: secundo positi fuerunt in fornace ignis: tertio Angelus Domini descendit in fornacem, et fecit medium fornacis, quasi ventum roris flantem, ita, vt omnino non laeserit eos ignis, neque contristaretur. Quid per Angelum fornacem mitigantem intelligitur, nisi charitas, omnem tentationis, et tribulationis adustionem temperans, et in dulcedinem vertens? in tantum vt sicut illos fornax nec laesit, nec contristauit; ita te, si charitatem tecum in fornace tribulationis habueris, laedere non poterunt quaecunque genera grauaminum. Nulla enim (dicit Gregorius) nocebit aduersitas, si nulla dominetur iniquitas. Attende, quod non dicit Gregorius in collecta: Si nulla sit iniquitas, sed dicit, si nulla dominetur iniquitas. In multis enim iniquitas esse dicitur, vt in illis, qui motus ad peccatum habent, sed in illis tantummodo dominatur, qui peccato mortali consentiunt. Secundum hunc modum dicit Apostolus ad Rom. 6. Non regnet peccatum in vestro mortali corpore. Tunc peccatum regnat in homine, quando dominatur homini per consensum, quod petit amoueri a se Psalmista, dicens: Non dominetur mei omnis iniustitia . Et si enim peccatum senseris, tu tamen non consenseris, nulla nocebit tibi aduersitas, eo quod nulla dominetur iniquitas.[51]

---

[50] It must be emphasized that in the absence of a modern and easily available edition of the Latin, it is quite difficult to give a succinct and comprehensive account of the omitted passages in the Middle English. All things considered, Candon's notes are more than adequate for her edition. The following analysis, therefore, should in no way be regarded as a criticism of what she set out to achieve.

[51] *De doctrina*, pp. 70–72. For the translation of this passage, see Appendix A.

And the entire omission is approximately twice this length. Without going into any details of the contents of this extended omission, the tone of the text in the Latin is immediately different. The use of biblical and patristic quotations is much more akin to the intellectual style of writers such as St Bernard than to the more 'populist' vernacular translations as found in Nicholas Love's *Mirror*. The Latin then continues with a new section entitled: 'Quod pellis extractio, coctio, et pinguedo fuerunt in Christo passo',[52] of which the intervening lines of the Middle English are an abbreviated summary. Here is the Middle English:

> Thes þre were wel founde in oure lord whan he suffred his passioun. He was flayn whan his cloþis were take from hym and was put naked upon þe crosse. He was rostid upon þe spite of þe crosse be þe Jues, þe wiche were his kokis, in gret tribulacioun. But he was not brennyd because þe þrid wantid not, þe wiche was þe fatnes of charite that flowid oute be þe fyve gret holis of his body.
>
> What was ellis þe blood flowyng oute of his woundis, but þe holy anoynement of charite? Good sister, put undir þe panne of thin hert and gadre inow of þis precious oynement, and þan schalt þou lakke no lardir in tyme of tribulacioun.[53]

This passage reads in the original:

> Haec tria, videlicet, pellis extractionem, coctionem, et pinguedinem in Christo tuo reperies, vt scias, secundum quod tibi superius dictum est de auctoritate Salomonis Prouerb. 23. Quoniam talia oportet te praeparare, vt ipse tibi, et tu ei facias. Primo ergo Domino tuo Christo, quasi pellis amota fuit, cum nudus fuit positus in cruce tanquam in hastili. Vnde Iudaei coqui fuerunt ipsius pretiosissimi, et delicatissimi cibi; non ipsis, quia inde non gustauerunt; sed tibi ibi igne tribulationis coctus est et exustus. Vnde significatur per piscem assum in Euangelio Ioannis 21. Nam piscis assus, Christus passus, significatur etiam per fabrum illum, de quo dicitur Ecclesiastici 38. Vapor ignis vret carnes eius. Per vaporem ignis vehementia tribulationis [significatur], quae carnes Christi tui exustas reddidit, non combustas. Non combustas dico, eo quod ibi non defuit tertium, scilicet pinguedo charitatis, quae per quinque foramina de suo corpore defluxit. Quid enim aliud fuit sanguis de latere, et

52 Ibid., p. 74 (That the removal of the skin, its cooking and its fat took place in the suffering Christ.)

53 *Doctrine of the Hert*, p. 25, ll. 768–77.

> vulneribus manuum, et pedum defluens, nisi quod pinguedo charitatis ad nos peruenerit? Fac ergo de corde tuo (charissima) patellam ad tam pretiosum liquorem recipiendum, ne decidat in terram, quod ipse Dominus tuus petit ne fiat, dicens Iob 16. Terra ne operias sanguinem meum. Tunc terra sanguine Christi operitur, quando beneficium passionis Christi a cordis memoria defluit, et amor terrenorum eidem praeponitur. Pinguedinem velles colligere vnius anseris, vel gallinae, quare ergo, a tam precioso liquore colligendo cor tuum subtrahis?[54]

Although this somewhat reduced Middle English version of this passage refers to Christ being 'flayn', 'rostid' and 'brennyd', a threefold process which the text (in Latin and Middle English) has explored for some time, the Middle English version of this reduced section has been severed from its immediate context. For, with the lengthy omission noted above, this reduced passage has lost the important typological example of Daniel and the three youths, which is explicitly seen as an anticipation of Christ's own example. This missing link is here made all the more obvious with the omission in the reduced Middle English passage of the reference to 'roasted fish' and the blacksmith of Ecclus. 8:29. Such changes intrinsically affect the reading and understanding of this section of the text which, in the Middle English, has not only been reduced in size, but more importantly in its range.

At this point the Latin continues with the separate section mentioned by Candon in note 39/2 above:

> **De praemeditatione passionis Christi.**
> Suppone ergo patellam cordis tui, passioni Christi, eius charitatem, patientiam, obedientiam, et passionem recolendo, vt in eam pinguedo ista defluat; vt quae in sanguine tuo coqui non potes, in pinguedine domini tui coquaris, et conseruata remaneas a combustione. O quantum esuriebat te Deus tuus, qui de intimis suis traxit pinguedinem, vt te [lardaret] cibum sibi delicatum! Si ergo ignis cuiusque tribulationis cordi tuo adhibetur, recurre ad pinguedinem charitatis Dei tui, quae praecipue in sua passione apparuit, eam meditando, ruminando quantum videlicet dilexit te, quanta fecit, quanta sustinuit pro te … In camino ergo paupertatis, et tribulationis posita, dic Christo tuo: Defluat Domine, defluat in cor meum charitatis tuae pinguedo, sanguis inquam tuus: beneficia passionis tuae recolendo, vt in tuo sanguine frigi queam, quae non sum proprio sanguine saginata, in tantum vt dolores

54 *De doctrina*, pp. 74–5. For a translation of this passage, see Appendix B.

> meos, tua dilectione impinguata non sentiam, vt tui memoria omnium angustiarum mearum sensus, et memoriam deleat, et abstergat. Quis me consolabitur, quod te non vidi cruce suspensum, plagis liuidum, pallidum morte, quia non sum Crucifixo compassa, obsecuta mortuo; vt saltem lacrymis meis loca illa vulnerum delinirem? Vide, reuertendo ad propositum, quanta tibi Deus tuus praeparauit, vt eidem talia studeas praeparare, spoliationem paupertatis, coctionem tribulationis, et pinguedinem charitatis.[55]

It may not be surprising that the translator does not translate the reference to Lev. 3, which alludes to the lengthy passage he did not translate earlier, as pointed out in Candon, note 38/16. However, it is not so obvious why he fails to translate the rest of this section. Indeed, the intellectual tenor of the previously omitted passage is much less prominent in this latter section. Instead, a more mystical tone seems to have been preferred, emphasizing the relationship between the reader and God, as he/she is made to address Christ directly. It would appear, therefore, if this conclusion could be extended to the whole of the Middle English translation, that the translator has not only left out the overly intellectual contents of the Latin, but also that he has moderated its more mystical tone.[56] As a matter of fact a comparison of both prologues, Latin and Middle English, suggests that this double move was very much the intention of the translator.

In her defence, Candon states that 'there is no claim in this study for an exhaustive, conclusive analysis of the methods of translation',[57] but a greater appreciation of the translation process is essential. The above lengthy passage is just one example, but one among many. Such drastic changes, though, are not without their effect on the text as a whole. Hence it could be argued that, although the essential message of the Latin has been preserved in the Middle English *Doctrine*, a substantial part of its meaning has been left out. Such a method of translation is definitely more akin to Nicholas Love's than to John Trevisa's. As a brief examination of the Latin and Middle English prologues of the text shows next, the method espoused here by the translator is perhaps already indicative of some differences between the Latin and the Middle English.

---

55 Ibid., pp. 75–6. For a translation of this passage, see Appendix C.

56 For similar conclusions with regard to the context in which the Middle Dutch translation was read, see Marleen Cré's essay in this volume.

57 Candon, *Doctrine*, p. lxxiv.

The prologues[58]

The sheer number of Latin manuscripts of *De doctrina cordis*, as well as the absence of a modern critical edition of the Latin text, make it hard to ascertain the original readership of the text. There is no doubt, however, that the Middle English translation is aimed at a different audience, as a comparison of the Latin and vernacular prologues clearly demonstrates.[59]

As Candon notes, the Middle English prologue is not a translation of the Latin:

> The English introduction is almost completely different from that of the Latin text which is copiously sprinkled with Biblical quotations. In it there is an admonition to turn aside from fables to hear the truth and a reminder that the *De doctrina cordis* was written 'ut non aures tuas tantum mulceat sed potius cor tuum pungat'. There is no list of chapter headings as there is in the English, only the statement that the work is divided into seven tracts.[60]

Indeed, the Latin prologue counts eleven scriptural quotations, all of which, with the exception of 2 Tim. 4:4, are from the Old Testament.[61] In comparison, the Middle English prologue has only three biblical quotations.[62] True, the Latin prologue is almost twice as long – over 700 words, whereas the Middle English contains about 450 – but even with the length of the respective prologues taken into account, the biblical input of the Middle English has been greatly reduced. This reduction, and the fact

---

58 The analysis below does not take into account the fact that there are two different versions of the Latin prologue, described by Hendrix as HV- and IP-prologues. See G. Hendrix, *Hugo De Sancto Caro's traktaat De doctrina cordis. Vol. 1: Handschriften, receptie, tekstgeschiedenis en authenticiteitskritiek*, Documenta Libraria 16/1 (Louvain, 1995), pp. 165–9. Only the HV-prologue is considered here, which is the version in the Naples, 1607 edition of *De doctrina*. However, what follows holds true of both, if one agrees that the IP-prologue addresses similar issues but from a more negative point of view. For further detail on the differences between the two prologues, see Marleen Cré's essay in this volume, p. 210.

59 In the following analysis, only the first part of the prologue will be considered. It does not include the explanation of the work's division into seven books which forms the prologue's second part.

60 Candon, *Doctrine*, p. 157, n. 1–3.

61 Not to mention two from St Augustine and one each from St Gilbert and from Seneca.

62 And one from St Augustine and one from St Gregory.

that the Middle English translates or glosses the Latin quotations, suggest a non-*litteratus* audience.

Both prologues begin with a scriptural quotation in Latin, but, significantly, not the same one. Whereas the Latin begins 'Praeparate corda vestra Domino',[63] the Middle English has instead '*Intelligite, insipientes in populo; et stulti, aliquando sapite*',[64] which hints at a lack of understanding in its audience. This is confirmed by the comment 'Myght not wel thees wordes be undirstonde of suche that ben *unkunnyng in religioun* …',[65] and the Middle English prologue repeatedly refers to '*symple soules*'.[66] At no time does the Latin clearly indicate who its audience is. The Middle English not only specifies that it is written for 'symple soules', but also adds a list of contents which directly refers to the intended audience, i.e. nuns: '*Capitulum primum*. How and in what wise *a mynche* shuld make redy here hert to God be þe yifte of drede.'[67] All four Middle English manuscripts are intended for a female audience.

A comparison of the structure of the two prologues also shows the greater intellectual sophistication that was expected from the reader of the original Latin. The Middle English prologue is divided into three sections, each of which has one of the three biblical quotations previously mentioned. The first section, beginning with '*Intelligite* …' (Ps. 93:8) identifies the audience, i.e. simple souls. The second section, with Isa. 40:2: '*Loquimini ad cor Jerusalem*',[68] first explains the moral meaning of 'Jerusalem', here given as 'symple chosyn soules',[69] and then provides the usual kind of material to be found in prologues: the work's title, 'this tretice that is clepid "the doctrine of the herte"';[70] some information about the author, 'I, þerfore, oon of thoo whiche oure lord hath clepid to his servise in religioun';[71] some description

---

63 *De doctrina*, p. 1, 1 Sam. 7:3 (Prepare your hearts unto the Lord.)

64 *Doctrine of the Hert*, p. 3, l. 1, Ps. 93: 8, Vulgate (Understand, ye brutish among the people: and ye fools, when will ye be wise?), Ps. 94:8, King James Bible. The numbering of Psalms is different in the Vulgate and the King James Bible.

65 *Doctrine of the Hert*, p. 3, ll. 5–6, my italics.

66 Ibid., p. 3, ll. 10, 15, 18–19, 23, my italics.

67 Ibid., p. 4, ll. 41–2, my italics. This is further made obvious by frequent remarks in the text proper: 'Loo, sister' (ibid., p. 5, l. 25); 'Sister' (ibid., p. 6, l. 47); 'Now sister' (ibid., p. 49, l. 107), which are not in the Latin.

68 Isa. 40:2 (Speak to the heart of Jerusalem), Jerusalem Bible.

69 *Doctrine of the Hert*, p. 3, ll. 13–14. According to 'The First Prologue of Nicholas of Lyra to the *Postilla litteralis*', Jerusalem 'in its moral sense … refers to the faithful soul', quoted in D. Turner, *Eros and Allegory*, CSS 156 (Kalamazoo, 1995), p. 384.

70 *Doctrine of the Hert*, p. 3, l. 22.

71 Ibid., p. 3, ll. 20–1.

of his intentions – he has written the text 'to the worship of God principally, and to edificacioun of symple soules';[72] and some details about the contents and the number of chapters, 'wherein is comprehendid an informacioun of hertis dividid into seven chapitres, in the whiche thei mow … come to sadnes of good lyvyng.'[73] Finally, the third section, making use of 1 John 2:27, '*Unccio eius docet nos de omnibus*',[74] considers how the text should be read: 'In this wise, þerfor, shuld this tretice be rad or herd … namly, þer the hertis be clene that redith it or herith it.'[75]

The Latin prologue can also be divided into three parts, each one of which gives a different explanation of Isa. 40:2, 'Loquimini ad cor Jerusalem', but in the Latin it is not the word 'Jerusalem' which is glossed but 'Loquimini'. In each section, moreover, two points of view are considered: that of the preacher and that of the audience. The first part describes the preacher's task as explaining the word of God to his audience, and the audience's duty as listening to the word of God thus exposed to them. The second part tells the preacher how to fulfil his task, i.e. by 'verbi dulcedine amicos multiplic[ando] non exasperan[do] auditores.'[76] As for the audience, they must 'amplect[i]' and not 'repelle[re]' the 'verbum doctrinae cordis'.[77] And the third part advises the preacher to use simple words rather than to hide the meaning of his words behind rhetorical flourishes, and thus to talk to his audience's heart rather than merely to their ears. The audience's responsibility is to listen and 'attende[re] doctrinam cordis [eorum] propositam'.[78] All of this is well illustrated by numerous biblical and patristic quotations, as has been noted above. Setting out the preacher's task in the Latin prologue seems to suggest that the text may have been originally aimed at a male audience,[79] while the inclusion of the audience's duties intimates that, already in the Latin, *De doctrina* was not restricted to its primary audience.

---

72 Ibid., p. 3, ll. 22–3.

73 Ibid., p. 3, ll. 23–6.

74 (The same anointing teacheth you of all things.) Note that the Vulgate reads 'vos', not 'nos'.

75 *Doctrine of the Hert*, p. 3, ll. 31–3. In this case, the biblical quotation follows the explanation of the paragraph's theme.

76 *De doctrina*, pp. 2–3 (Multiply[ing] friends with the sweetness of words, not irritating his listeners.)

77 Ibid., p. 3 ('Embrace' and not 'repel' the 'words of the doctrine of the heart'.)

78 Ibid., p. 4 (Pay attention to the doctrine offered to [their] heart.)

79 For additional discussion of *De doctrina*'s envisaged audience, see Nigel Palmer's essay in this volume, pp. 49–51.

Unlike other devotional treatises, such as Aelred of Rievaulx's *De institutione inclusarum* or the pseudo-Bernard *Liber de modo bene vivendi*, the Latin prologue of *De doctrina* does not claim that the work was written in response to someone's request. In the Latin prologue the double emphasis on the preacher and his audience, as well as the absence of any biographical detail about the author, may have appeared confusing to the translator, who then decided to rewrite the prologue in an unambiguous and perhaps more conventional way. In doing this, as well as in omitting most of the biblical quotations, the translator appears to have impoverished the prologue. There is no reason, for instance, to believe that an accurate translation of the Latin prologue would have been beyond the grasp of the original audience of the *Ancrene Wisse*.

There is also a difference of tone between the Latin and Middle English prologues, which may indicate that less was expected of the vernacular audience. Although the Latin prologue does not mention Christ's 'spouses', as the Middle English prologue does at one point, nonetheless the tone of the Latin prologue is definitely more mystical, that of the Middle English more devotional. Neither prologue has any direct quotation from the Song of Songs, but the Latin is suffused with vocabulary and imagery which can be traced back to it. For example, the comment 'Sunt enim verba Dei, quasi vuae, multa faecunditate repletae: vnde oportet vuam exprimere, quod est, verbum diligenter exponere, vt vinum spiritualis intelligentiae vsque in cellarium cordis fluat'[80] is reminiscent of Song of Songs 2:4: 'Introduxit me in cellam vinariam.'[81] The adjective 'Vinarius' actually occurs in the very next sentence of the prologue: 'Auris enim bona, torcular est (vt dicit Augustinus) *vinaria* verborum retinens, et vinum spiritualis

80 *De doctrina*, pp. 1–2 (Indeed, the words of God are like grapes filled by great fecundity. Hence it is necessary to squeeze out the grapes, that is, to set forth these words carefully, that the wine of spiritual knowledge may flow into the cellar of the heart.)

81 (He brought me to the banqueting house.) Note also Alan of Lille's comments on this verse: 'Eleganter autem nomine cellae vel cellarii significatur proprietas coeli; quia (ut praemittamus allusionem vocabuli) sicut in cellario reponuntur vina quae hominem satiant, inebriant, a curis saecularibus alienant … Vel per cellaria intelligitur repositio thesaurorum sapientiae et scientiae Dei', Alan of Lille, *Elucidatio in Cantica*, *PL* 210, col. 56B–C (The word 'cells' or 'cellars' is just the right word for it signifies what belongs to the 'celestial'. For bearing in mind the overtones of the word, the wines which fill and inebriate and release the mind from the cares of the world are stored in cellars … Or else, we can take the word 'cellars' to mean the storehouse of the treasures of the wisdom and the knowledge of God), translated in Turner, *Eros and Allegory*, pp. 299–300.

intelligentiae vsque ad cellarium cordis transmittens.'[82] The text continues thus: 'Quotiens ergo tibi praedicatur, totiens vinum spirituale ad cordis tui cellarium, ad te potandum, ad te inebriandum transmittitur',[83] which may echo words from Song of Songs 5:1: 'Bibi vinum meum ... bibite; et inebriamini.'[84] There is not even a hint of such imagery in the Middle English prologue. It may be that the translator preferred not to mention 'drunkeness', fearing that his audience might not be able to differentiate between the literal and allegorical meaning of 'inebriare'. The fact that the Middle English prologue refers to those who 'ben unkunnyng in religioun, the whiche also nowadayes ben moche unstable in theire lyvyng, folowyng rather the ensample of seculer folk than the ensample of sad goostly religious folk'[85] suggests that the translator believed that his vernacular audience needed some reforming.

A comparison of the Latin and Middle English prologues suggests that the original Latin audience may have shared more of the author's intellectual sophistication[86] as well as the habit of continual reading and meditation on the Scriptures. And so they would have expected and enjoyed the numerous biblical quotations, not to mention a reference to Seneca: 'Oratio, quae veritati dat operam, incomposita debet esse, et simplex.'[87] The translator

---

82 *De doctrina*, p. 2, my italics (The good ear is indeed a wine-press [as St Augustine says] keeping the wine-flasks of words, and transferring the wine of spiritual knowledge into the cellar of the heart.)

83 Ibid., p. 2 (Therefore, as many times as it is preached to you, so often spiritual wine is transferred to the cellar of your heart for you to drink [and] for you to be drunk.)

84 (I have drunk my wine ... drink, yea, drink abundantly.) Note that the literal translation of 'inebriamini', is 'get drunk'.

85 *Doctrine of the Hert*, p. 3, ll. 6–9.

86 Imagery inspired by the Song of Songs is certainly used by other Latin writers. A certain Gilbert (perhaps Gilbert of Stanford or Gilbert of Hoyland) wrote: 'Nosti enim quod sacrae verba Scripturae, cum semel et bis vindemiata sunt, ac si gravida sacris iterum soleant influere sensibus et quasi prius tacta non essent, ubertem et inebriantem effundant expressa liquorem, Prol. in Matt.', quoted in H. de Lubac, *Medieval Exegesis. Volume 1: The Four Senses of Scripture*, tr. M. Sebank (Edinburgh, 1998), p. 330, n. 74. (For you know that the words of Sacred Scripture, when they have been gleaned for a first and second vintage, can be squeezed so as to yield a rich and intoxicating liquid, as if it were usual for them, laden with sacred meanings as they are, to flow again even as if they had never been touched in the first place), translated in de Lubac, *Medieval Exegesis*, p. 79.

87 *De doctrina*, p. 3 (A speech which gives attention to the truth must be

omitted Seneca's words, having recognized that his audience belonged to a different world; however, he endorsed Seneca's advice, and managed in his Prologue to retain the essence of the original in a simplified form, as Candon herself remarked: '[he] matched the style of the *Doctrina* itself. In this brief space he has quotations from Saints Austin, Gregory, John and the prophet Isaias. The purpose for his writing, to inform the hearts of the religious, is set forth clearly.'[88] Thus, an examination of both Latin and Middle English prologues forcibly identifies the Middle English *Doctrine of the Hert* as an adaptation of the text for a less intellectual and non-*litteratus* audience, a conclusion which is borne out by a look at the provenance of the four surviving manuscripts of the *Doctrine*.[89]

The Doctrine of the Hert, however, is not the only Middle English translation of a Latin devotional text for religious women.[90] The pseudo-Bernard *Liber de modo bene vivendi ad sororem* was also translated into Middle English under the title *The Manere of Good Lyvyng*,[91] and both late medieval translations were unmistakably aimed at religious women. A detailed comparison of the *Liber* and its Middle English translation shows that the latter has also been adapted to a less sophisticated and non-*litteratus* audience.[92] Like the *Doctrine*, variants, additions and omissions are frequent, but on a much smaller scale. In the *Manere*, it is not a question of paragraphs or pages, but rather of words or clauses. To take but one typical example of omission in the *Manere*, consider the following passage of the *Liber*:

---

unstudied and simple.) See Seneca, *Ad Lucilium epistulae morales*, ed. and tr. R.M. Gummere, Loeb Library, 3 vols (London, 1953), vol. 1, epistle 40, p. 264.

88 Candon, *Doctrine*, p. lxxviii.

89 See D. Renevey and C. Whitehead, '"Opyn þin hert as a boke": Translation Practice and Manuscript Circulation in *The Doctrine of the Hert*', in J. Jenkins and O. Bertrand (eds), *The Medieval Translator 10* (Turnhout, 2007), pp. 125–48; and Catherine Innes-Parker's essay in this volume.

90 Aelred of Rievaulx's *De institutione inclusarum* is another example of a Latin text translated into the vernacular. However, as there are two different translations of this text into Middle English, it is not discussed here. For the Middle English translations of Aelred's text, see *Aelred of Rievaulx's De institutione inclusarum: Two English Versions*, ed. by J. Ayto and A. Barratt, EETS 287 (1984).

91 Oxford, Bodleian Library, MS Laud Misc. 517. The present writer is preparing an edition of the text, to be published by Brepols.

92 In *The Manere of Good Lyvyng*, most biblical quotations are only given in their Middle English translations (i.e. the Latin is not quoted first). For an assessment of the *Manere* as a translation, see A. Mouron, '*The Manere of Good Lyvyng*: the Manner of a Good Translator?', *Medium Aevum*, 78 (2009), 300–22.

> Debemus Deum diligere ex tota corde, id est ex toto intellectu, et ex tota anima, et ex tota voluntate, et ex tota mente, et ex tota memoria: ut omnem intellectum et omnes cogitationes nostras, et omnem vitam nostram ad eum dirigamus, a quo omnia bona habemus; *ut nulla pars vitae nostrae otiosa relinquatur, sed quidquid in animam venerit, illuc dirigatur, ubi impetus dilectionis currit.*[93]

It is rendered in the *Manere* as:

> We ouȝt to love God with a perfite undirstandyng, a perfite soule, a perfite wyll, a perfite mynde and with a perfite memorye, so þat we doo referre all our knoulege and all our thouȝtis and all our good lyfe unto hym, of whom we have all goodnes.[94]

The highlighted clause in the Latin has been left out but, by comparison with the *Doctrine*, the omission is quite insignificant and does not affect the overall meaning, tone or register of the passage. The *Liber*, which is described in its Epilogue as 'verba sanctae admonitionis',[95] is clearly also intended to the 'edificacioun' of its reader. Nevertheless, in the *Manere*, the translator has adopted John Trevisa's method of translation rather than Nicholas Love's.

It would appear, therefore, that the translator of *The Doctrine of the Hert* had a choice. Indeed, a new medium, a new audience and a desire for edification do not in themselves require the drastic changes he introduced in the *Doctrine*. Translations of *De doctrina* in other European vernaculars make this quite clear.[96] In the case of the *Doctrine*, then, it would be much more accurate to speak of an adaptation of the Latin rather than of a translation. After all, and unlike Nicholas Love's work, which, incidentally,

---

93 Pseudo-Bernard, *Liber de modo bene vivendi ad sororem*, *PL* 184, cols 1206D–1207A, my italics. ('We ought to loue God with our whole heart, that is with our whole soule, and with our whole will, and with our whole mind, and with our whole memorie: to the end that we direct all our vnderstanding, and all our thoughts, and all our life to him from whome we haue all good things: or let euerie thing that commeth into our mind be directed to that streame, where the force of loue doth runne', St Bernard, *A Rule of Good Life*, tr. A. Batt (Doway, 1633; repr. Menston, 1971), p. 32).

94 MS Laud Misc. 517, fol. 14r.

95 *Liber de modo bene vivendi*, *PL* 184, col. 1305B (words of holy admonition.)

96 See, in particular, Anne Mouron's essay on French translations of *De doctrina*, and Anthony Lappin's essay on the Spanish translation, in this volume.

could probably also be regarded as an adaptation,[97] the *Doctrine* does not claim that it was translated from the Latin. On the contrary, as has been shown above, the translator (for want of a better word) most emphatically says that he '*compilid* this tretice that is clepid "the doctrine of the herte"'.[98]

Although any scholarly approach to a compilation should attempt to identify as many sources as possible, the compilation itself should also be judged on its own merits. This is most probably how the original audience approached *The Doctrine of the Hert*, and it is how it should be appraised today.

Appendices

A. Omitted Latin passage

In token of this, it was ordered in the Law (Lev. 3 and 7) that fat should be burnt in every sacrifice. What is understood by the fat, which is interior fatness, if not charity? Hence in the Law three things were done in sacrifices, which are referred to in these three things previously mentioned, as it is said in Lev. 1 and 2. First, the skin was removed from the animal; secondly, its limbs were placed on the fire on the altar; thirdly the fat was poured out on the sacrifice on the altar. Removing the skin (as it is said) concerns the renunciation of temporal possessions. The placing the limbs on the fire concerns the endurance of tribulations. The libation of fat relates to charity.

These three things we find in the three youths placed in the furnace (Dan. 3). Firstly they were deprived of their dignity and their lordship ['primitia'], which they had in the court of the King of Babylon; secondly they were placed in a furnace of fire; thirdly the Angel of the Lord came down in the furnace, and made in the middle of the furnace a blowing wind of moisture as it were, so that the fire could not at all harm them or make them sad. What is understood by the Angel appeasing the furnace, if not charity, which controls the burning pain of all temptations and tribulations and turns it into sweetness? To such a degree that, as the furnace neither harmed them nor made them sad, thus, if you have with you charity in the furnace of tribulation, no kinds of incommodities whatsoever will be able to harm you. Indeed (as Gregory says) no adversity will injure you, if no wickedness has dominion over you.

---

97 Love, *Mirror*, p. xviii.

98 *Doctrine of the Hert*, p. 3, ll. 21–2, my italics.

Notice that Gregory does not say in his argument:[99] if there is no wickedness, but he says, if no wickedness has dominion over you. Indeed wickedness is said to be in many, as in those who have an impulse to sin, but it has dominion only over those who consent to deadly sin. According to this manner, the Apostle says in Rom. 6:12: 'Let no sin, therefore, reign in your mortal body.' Then sin reigns in a man, when it has dominion over a man through his agreement to it, which the Psalmist asks to be removed from himself, saying: 'let not any iniquity have dominion over me.'[100] And indeed, if you perceive sin, but you yourself do not consent to it, no adversity will harm you, in that no wickedness may have dominion over you.

B. That the flaying of the skin, its cooking and its fatness were found in the crucified Christ.[101]

These three things, that is to say, the flaying of the skin, its cooking and fatness, you will find them in your Christ, that you may know, according to what is told you above about Solomon's authority in Prov. 23:1.[102] Since you need to prepare such things, as he himself does it for you, do it yourself for him. First, then, just as the skin was removed from the Lord, your Christ was put on the cross when naked as on a spit. Whence the Jews acted as cooks for this most precious and delicate food, not for themselves, because they did not partake of it, but for you it was cooked and burned there, in the fire of tribulation. This is shown, therefore, by the roasted fish in John 21:9. For the roasted fish is Christ crucified. This is also indicated by the blacksmith, of whom it is said in Ecclus. 38:29: 'the breath of the fire scorches his skin.' By the 'breath of the fire', is signified the intensity of the tribulation, which burned but did not consume your Christ's flesh. I say not consumed, because there the third was not lacking, that is to say the fatness of charity, which oozed out from his body by five holes. Indeed, what else was the blood oozing out from his side and from the wounds of his hands and his feet, if not the fatness of charity which reached us? Therefore, dearest, make of your heart a dish to receive this liquid so precious, lest it fall off on the ground, which your Lord himself asks not to happen, as Job

---

[99] Latin: 'in collecta', possibly for 'in collectione'?

[100] Ps. 118:133.

[101] The Latin word 'passus' means 'extended' and 'suffering', from two different Latin verbs; both actually apply to Christ.

[102] '*Cum sederis ad mensam principis, diligenter attende que sunt posita ante faciem tuam. Et scito quia talia te oportet preparare.* "Whan þou art set" he seith, "at þe kynges table, take hede what is set afore the.' See *Doctrine of the Hert*, p. 20, ll. 573–6.

16:19 says: 'O earth, cover not thou my blood.' The earth then is covered by the blood of Christ, when the benefit of Christ's passion oozes out from the heart's memory, and the love of earthly things is preferred to it. If you wanted to collect the fat of a goose or a hen, why, then, do you draw away your heart from collecting a liquid so precious?

C. Of the premeditation of Christ's Passion.

Place the dish of your heart, then, under the Passion of Christ by reflecting upon his charity, his patience, his obedience and his Passion, that this fatness oozes out into that dish, that you who cannot be cooked in your own blood, may be cooked in your Lord's fat, and may remain safe from burning. O how much your God hungers for you, who draws out fat from his heart, that he may lard you and make you into delicate food for himself! If, then, the fire of this tribulation is applied to your heart, resort to the fatness of your God's charity, which manifests itself especially in his Passion, meditating on it and ruminating how much he clearly loves you, how many things he did, how many he endured for you … Then, when you are placed in the furnace of poverty and tribulation, say to your Christ: Ooze out, Lord, let the fatness of your charity which is your blood ooze out into my heart, in that reflecting on the benefits of your Passion, I may be able to be roasted in your blood, I who was not fattened by my own blood, so that made fat by your love I may not feel my pains so much, and that the memory of you may destroy and wipe off the feeling and the memory of all my distresses. Who will comfort me, that I did not see you hung up on the cross, a leaden hue from your wounds, and sallow through death, because I did not suffer with the Crucified, I did not submit to the dead one, that at least I may assuage the places of your wounds with my tears? See, by returning to our theme, how many things your God has prepared for you, that you may take pains to prepare such things for him, that is the stripping of poverty, the roasting of tribulation and the fatness of charity.

4

'Comfortable Wordis' – The Role of the Bible in *The Doctrine of the Hert*[1]

Annie Sutherland

In the 1548 Book of Common Prayer, we read: 'Hear what comfortable words our Saviour Christ saith unto all that truly turn to him.'[2] Following the Confession and prefacing the administering of the sacrament of Holy Communion, these 'comfortable words' take the form of quotations from Matthew 11:28 ('Come unto me, all you that labour, and are burdened, and I will refresh you'), John 3:16 ('For God so loved the world, as to give his only begotten Son; that whosoever believeth in him, may not perish, but may have life everlasting'), 1 Timothy 1:15 ('A faithful saying, and worthy of all acceptation, that Christ Jesus came into this world to save sinners, of whom I am the chief') and 1 John 2:1 ('But if any man sin, we have an advocate with the Father, Jesus Christ the just: And he is the propitiation for our sins'). In this liturgical context, the obvious meaning of 'comfortable' is 'comforting' or 'consoling'.[3] Yet these 'comfortable words' are not simply consoling, they are also spiritually invigorating, emphasizing the reality

---

1 In keeping with general practice in this volume, all *Doctrine of the Hert* quotations are taken from C. Whitehead, D. Renevey and A. Mouron (eds), *The Doctrine of the Hert: A Critical Edition with Introduction and Commentary* (Exeter, 2010). Hereafter cited as *Doctrine of the Hert*. Throughout the chapter, numeration refers to page and line of this edition. All vernacular biblical quotations are taken from *The Holy Bible: Douay Version Translated from the Latin Vulgate*.

2 *The Book of Common Prayer* (Cambridge, 1922), p. 252.

3 See OED A. *adj*. I. With active sense. 5.a. Affording mental or spiritual delight or enjoyment; pleasant, enjoyable. *Obs*. 6. Affording or conveying consolation; comforting, consolatory: of persons (*obs*.) or things (*arch*.).

of human sin, the necessity of human belief and the promise of divine forgiveness. Comfort, it seems, is found in being challenged as well as in being consoled.[4]

We find an emphasis on spiritually efficacious language as both consoling and sustaining in the thirteenth-century Latin treatise *De doctrina cordis*.[5] Towards the end of *De doctrina*'s prologue, we read of the anonymous author's desire that his own teaching ('doctrina mea') and, more importantly, that of Christ ('imo potius Christi') might sustain ('nutriat') and console ('consoletur') his audience so that not only are ears soothed, but hearts pierced: 'vt non aures tantum tuas mulceat, sed potius cor tuum pungat'.[6] Indeed, words that *comfort* are explicitly equated, in this Latin text, with words that feed. The author states: 'Per manna, quod habebat omnem saporis suauitatem, spiritualis consolatio, (iuxta verbum Bernardi) intelligitur: Dilecta est diuina consolatio …'[7] And while manna represents spiritual nutrition, 'farina Aegypti' (Egyptian flour) represents nothing more than 'verba inutilia, leuia, et mundana' (useless, trifling and mundane words).

The early-fifteenth-century Middle English version of *De doctrina* does not adopt these specific references to nutrition and consolation, but it does persist in a similar emphasis on words that both comfort and sustain. For example, in book 1's chapter on 'gostly matrimony' ('spiritualis matrimonium'), both Latin and English treatises quote from Jeremiah 2:2: 'Go, and cry in the ears of Jerusalem, saying: Thus saith the Lord: I have remembered thee, pitying thy soul, pitying thy youth, and the love of thy espousals, when thou followedst me in the desert, in a land that is not sown.' The English text follows the Latin in applying the words directly to those in the religious life:

---

4 See OED A. *adj.* I. With active sense, 1.a. Strengthening or supporting (morally or spiritually); encouraging, inspiriting, reassuring, cheering. *Obs.* or *arch.*

5 In keeping with general practice in this volume, all references to *De doctrina cordis* are to the printed Naples 1607 edition (Oxford, Bodleian Library, 8º L 12 Th. BS). Hereafter cited as *De doctrina*. Throughout the chapter, numeration refers to page numbers in this edition. It is recognised that the comparison of a fifteenth-century English translation with a seventeenth-century edition is potentially problematic, but investigation has revealed that the Latin text contained in the printed edition does not differ substantially from that contained in earlier Latin manuscripts (e.g. Oxford, Bodleian Library, MS Lat. th. f. 6).

6 *De doctrina*, p. 4.

7 Ibid., p. 13 (By manna, which has all sweetness of taste, the consolation of the spirit is understood (according to the words of Bernard): Dear is divine consolation …) For the Bernardine reference, see *In Psalmum XC, Qui Habitat*, Sermo 4, *PL* 183, col. 0194B.

> Therfor, sister, yif þou be a novice, þenk þat þi weddyng is begunne betwene þe and þi love, Jhesu. Yif þou be professid, þenke þat it is confermyd. And whan þou hast tastid þes swetnes of oure lord, þenke that thi weddyng in perseveraunce of þe cloyster in maner is made perfight. Of þees þre gostly weddyngis spekith oure lord be Jeromy, þe prophete, to every clene soule þe wiche is entred into religion, thus: *Recordatus sum tui, miserans adolescenciam tuam, et caritatem disponsacionis tue, quia secuta es me in deserto.*[8]

But, in an addition to the Latin text, the English compiler goes on to emphasise the hortatory value of these words by exclaiming: 'Good sister, take hertly heede to þees *comfortable wordis*. For þer þat oure lord seith þat he þenketh merciably upon thi tendre age, undirstond that he menyth al þe while þou art a novice, for so longe þou art but tendre of age in religioun.'[9] A further aside on the 'comfortable' nature of biblical words is found later in the first book of the *Doctrine* when, having borrowed a *catena* of three 'swete' New Testament quotations from the Latin *De doctrina*, concluding with Luke 23:43: 'O wher, also, was a swetter word þan þat, þe wiche was seyde to þe trew þef, hongyng on þe right side of þe crosse: *Hodie mecum eris in paradiso.* "Today" he seyde, "þou shalt be with me in paradise"',[10] the English compiler again adds to his Latin source by asking: 'Were not þis, trowist þou, a *comfortable word* to a repentaunt synner, whan he shal passe out of þis world?'[11]

So, both Latin and English texts emphasize the consolatory and strengthening force of divinely inspired language. And in recognition of the unique significance of such language, both liken God's Word to the sweet sound emitted by chiming silver. Yet both also warn us that the uniquely sweet sound of God's Word can be discerned only by those who are 'devoutly disposid' ('bene dispositi'): 'Like as silver yiveth a swete sowne among al oþer maner of metallis, right so, þe wordis of oure lord sownyth more swetly in þe eere of a clene soule þat is devoutly disposid for

8 *Doctrine of the Hert*, p. 31, ll. 1014–21.

9 Ibid., p. 31, ll. 1025–28, my italics. I refer to the English 'compiler' in keeping with his own characterisation of himself in the prologue: 'I, þerfore, oon of thoo whiche oure lord hath clepid to his servise in religioun, alþogh I be no trew servaunt of his, have compilid this tretice that is clepid 'the doctrine of the herte …' Ibid., p. 3, ll. 20–22.

10 Ibid., p. 46, ll. 1583–85.

11 Ibid., p. 46, ll. 1586–87, my italics. For the first two quotations in this 'comfortable' *catena*, see John 8:11 and Luke 7:50.

to undirstond hem, þan þe wordis of any oþer creatures.'[12] This sense of what is comprehensible and appropriate to different audiences at different stages of spiritual development characterizes both Latin and English texts, and is reflected upon most explicitly in their final chapter.[13] Here, in an exploration of what it means to be a 'gostly lover' of God, the *Doctrine* points out that those advanced in the spiritual life often speak a language which is comprehensible to only 'such þat ben gostly loveris, as þei ben.'[14] *De doctrina* characterizes this language as 'defectiua' (grammatically imperfect) and, in illustrating it, both Latin and English texts quote Song of Songs 2:16a: 'Dilectus meus mihi et ego illi'.[15] Such language, they both argue, is immediately comprehensible to the true 'gostly lover' who 'bene nouit intelligere amoris linguagium' (knows well how to understand the language of love).[16] Indeed, for such as this it requires no explanatory glossing ('apud dilectum non est necessaria ista suppletio' [among the beloved that expansion is not necessary]):[17] 'it nedith never for to be expounnyd to a lovyng soule, for þe schortest sentence of love is opyn inow to here.'[18] It is, however, nonsensical to those who are not true 'gostly lovers' since it does not explain *what* my lover is to me, nor *what* I am to my lover: 'But þes wordis were more openly declared, it semyth right unperfit, for she tellith not what here love is to here, ne what she is to here love' ('Hic supplendum est, non enim determinauit ista, quis sibi sit dilectus, vel quæ ipsa sit dilecto').[19] That neither the author of the Latin nor the compiler of the English necessarily regard their audience to be sophisticated 'gostly lovers' is brought home to us by the fact that they both offer three explanatory glosses on Song of Songs 2:16. Borrowing directly from the Latin, this is how the English compiler puts it:

---

12 Ibid., p. 46, ll. 1569–72. For the Latin inspiration behind this passage, see *De doctrina*, p. 153. The Latin also contains a biblical quotation at this point (Ecclus. 40:21: 'The flute and the psaltery make a sweet melody, but a pleasant tongue is above them both.'). For the biblical background to God's Word as silver, see Ps. 11:7.

13 For an exploration of the relationship between literary competence and spiritual maturity, see D. Renevey, *Language, Self and Love: Hermeneutics in the Writings of Richard Rolle and the Commentaries on the Song of Songs* (Cardiff, 2001).

14 *Doctrine of the Hert*, p. 87, ll. 81–2.

15 (My beloved to me and I to him.)

16 *De doctrina*, p. 281.

17 Ibid., p. 281.

18 *Doctrine of the Hert*, p. 87, ll. 99–101.

19 *Doctrine of the Hert*, p. 87, ll. 85–87; *De doctrina*, p. 280.

> But like as Aaron spake for Moyses, so must gostly resoun speke for oure affeccioun, and fulfille þe unperfit wordis of a loving soule and sey þus: 'My love to me is able, and bi his mercy I am made to him able.' Or þus: 'Like as my love to me is mede and reward of al my labouris … right so, I am þe reste of his laboure … Or þus: 'My love to me lived and for me died, so schal I live to him and for him shal I digh.'[20]

According to the texts' own logic, such glossing would not be required by the more spiritually advanced.[21]

However, despite registering the possibility of 'gostly' inexperience in their audience, both Latin and English texts are resolute throughout in addressing themselves to the 'gostly' 'inward' man, to 'the chamber of the heart' as discussed in Catherine Innes-Parker's essay in this volume. In particular, both adopt the motif of the interior heart as locus of understanding. Indeed, the prologue to *De doctrina* opens in biblically inspired reflection on the heart: 'Praeparate corda vestra Domino: Verba sunt Samuelis, 1. Reg. 7. Loquitur Dominus prædicatoribus per Isai. 40. dicens: Loquimini ad cor Ierusalem.'[22] And this is a biblically driven motif which is echoed in a later section of the prologue to the English *Doctrine*: 'Suche symple soules it is charite to enforme, namly seth oure lord yivyth us in charge, seiyng be the

---

20 *Doctrine of the Hert*, p. 87, ll. 87–96. For the equivalent material in *De doctrina*, see pp. 280–81. *De doctrina* contains further expansions and biblical citations omitted from the English.

21 It is noteworthy that the *Doctrine* departs from its source in labelling S. of S. 2:16a as an utterance appropriate to those who have entered into 'perfight matrymony' with Christ (p. 35, l. 1157) (i.e., to those whose soul 'is knet and coupled unseparatly to þi spouse, Jhesu, bi perseveraunce, abidyng in the observaunce of the cloyster in maner tastyng of swetnes of joye.' *Doctrine of the Hert*, p. 31, ll. 1010–13). This would seem to confirm the English compiler's particular understanding of S. of S. 2:16 as a keynote text, fully comprehensible only to those advanced in the 'gostly' life. At the equivalent moment, *De doctrina* quotes from S. of S. 7:10 and 5:10.

22 *De doctrina*, p. 1 (Prepare your hearts for the Lord: The words are those of Samuel, 1 Kings 7. The Lord speaks to preachers through Isaiah 40, saying: Speak to the heart of Jerusalem.) Biblical references are to 1 Kgs. 7:3 ('… turn to the Lord with all your heart …') and to Isa. 40:2 ('Speak ye to the heart of Jerusalem …'). It is important to note that the specific reference to biblical chapter and verse is a particular feature of the 1607 printed edition of *De doctrina*. Some other manuscript versions of the treatise limit themselves to a reference to biblical book. See, for example, the equivalent moment in Oxford, Bodleian Library, MS Lat. th. f. 6, which reads 'v[er]ba s[un]t samuel[is] in libro regu[m]' (fol. 1r).

prophete Ysaye thus: *Loquimini ad cor Jerusalem*. That is, "spekith to the hert of Jerusalem".'[23] But despite echoing *De doctrina*'s quotation from Isaiah, the English prologue actually begins differently, with a Vulgate quotation from Psalm 93:8: '*Intelligite, insipientes in populo; et stulti, aliquando sapite*.'[24] This is followed by a vernacular reference to Augustine:

> As Seynt Austyn seyth, thes wordis ben undirstonde in this wise: 'ye that ben unkunnyng in the nombre of Goddis peuple *inwardly* undirstondith, and ye that ben unavisid, yif ye have grace of any gostly kunnyng, sumtyme savorith sadly in *hert*.'[25]

and then by a concluding rhetorical rumination:

> Myght not wel thees wordes be undirstonde of suche that ben unkunnyng in religioun, the whiche also nowadayes ben moche unstable in theire lyvyng, folowyng rather the ensample of seculer folk than the ensample of sad goostly religious folk? I trowe yis.[26]

It seems that this introductory material is unique to the English text and although it shares *De doctrina*'s focus on the heart as locus of inward understanding, it also anticipates the vernacular compilation's very particular awareness of its audience's situation and capabilities, and its specific emphasis on the importance of 'hertly redyng'.[27]

Departing from its Latin source, the English text is explicit in addressing

---

23 *Doctrine of the Hert*, p. 3, ll. 10–12. The quotation from 1 Kgs. 7:3 also appears, in a different location, in the *Doctrine* (see p. 5, ll. 3–5), and is repeated in the same place in *De doctrina* (p. 4).

24 *Doctrine of the Hert*, p. 3, l. 1 (Understand, ye senseless among the people: and, you fools, be wise at last.) This Psalm quotation does not appear in *De doctrina* at the corresponding point. (Vulgate Psalm numeration is adopted throughout this chapter).

25 Ibid., p. 3, ll. 1–5, my italics. Similar material (which refers to Augustine) is found in Peter Lombard's *Commentarium in psalmos*, *PL* 191, col. 0868 B–C. I am indebted to Anne Hudson for this reference.

26 Ibid., p. 3, ll. 5–9.

27 Ibid., p. 3, l. 30. Echoing the prologue's emphasis on reading with the heart, the English text also instructs its audience to understand 'gostly and not flesshly' (p. 28, l. 887). This is an addition to *De doctrina* and recalls, of course, the similar interpretative anxiety voiced repeatedly in *The Cloud of Unknowing*. See *The Cloud of Unknowing and the Book of Privy Counselling*, ed. by P. Hodgson, EETS OS 218 (1944).

itself to an audience of female religious; references to 'my dere sister' and to 'mynchen' abound throughout the treatise and, in an addition to *De doctrina*, the compiler registers that among his audience literary abilities will vary:

> With þis silver [i.e. the Word of God], sister, þou art wel arayed, whan þou occupiest þe in heryng of þe blissid wordis of oure lord, wheþer it be in redyng or heryng of devout tretises, or ellis in heryng of devout sermonys, or swete communicacioun sewyng to vertu.[28]

The particular audience awareness that characterizes the *Doctrine* results in certain changes being made to the Latin original, of which the most obvious is, of course, the translation of the treatise into English.[29]

Yet while *De doctrina* undergoes almost wholesale vernacularization in the course of its adaptation for an English audience, one significant element of the treatise retains its Latinity – namely, its biblical voice. Like the vast majority of Christian devotional writing of the Middle Ages, *De doctrina* is organized around biblical quotation and supporting patristic allusion; indeed, such biblical and patristic reference provides the very foundation on which the treatise constructs itself. As one might expect, a proportion of this reference material is imported into the English text. Yet while the *Doctrine* vernacularizes entirely all patristic references borrowed from its Latin source, it remains resolute in providing its audience with the Vulgate text of the scriptures.[30] Only having made such provision does it then furnish us with vernacular translation, which ranges from the quite close and literal – '*Fuerunt michi lacrime mee panes die ac nocte.* "My teeres" he seith, "han be to me loves both day and nyght"'[31] – to the rather more expansive:

---

28 Ibid., p. 46, ll. 1590–93.

29 Indeed, as explored in other essays in this *Companion*, *De doctrina* was translated into several European vernaculars in the Middle Ages.

30 The *Doctrine* compiler is not unusual in vernacularising his patristic references while retaining Latinate biblical quotation. Such, for example, is Walter Hilton's general practice in *The Scale of Perfection*. See also the anonymous fifteenth-century religious dialogue, *Dives and Pauper*.

31 *Doctrine of the Hert*, p. 81, ll. 57–8. Some exceptions to this rigorous biblical Latinity can be found in the English text. See, for example, the treatment of Heb. 12:6 ('For whom the Lord loveth, he chastiseth; and he scourgeth every son whom he receiveth.') The text is rendered thus in *De doctrina*: 'quia, Ipse est (vt dicit Apostolus ad Hebræ. 12) qui flagellat omnem filium, quem recepit' (p. 27). However, the English *Doctrine* simply provides a vernacularisation: 'for he it is,

> Of þis corrupt blood desired þe prophete to be delyvered, whan he seyde thus: *Libera me de sanguinibus, Deus, Deus salutis mee*. That is: 'lord God, my lord Jhesu, þou that lovest þe helþe of my soule, delyvere me I beseche þe, from the corrupt blood of synne.'[32]

The *Doctrine* is not unusual in displaying such overt reliance on the Vulgate text of the bible.[33] Neither is it alone in accompanying the Latin with vernacular translation; such, for example, is Walter Hilton's practice in *The Scale of Perfection*, the *Cloud* author's practice in *The Book of Privy Counselling* and Richard Rolle's practice in at least some of his English writings. Indeed, the *Doctrine*'s biblical tone and emphasis are in keeping with the general tenor of late medieval devotional writing which is characterized by its extensive and particular reliance on the authority of the Old Testament Psalms and the New Testament gospels and epistles.[34] It is the biblical voice of the *Doctrine* which this chapter is now going to explore.

Almost without exception the *Doctrine*'s biblical quotations are lifted from the Latin *De doctrina* (an obvious exception is the Psalm quotation

---

as holy writ seith, that blameth and chastiseth every child that he resceyveth' (p. 14, ll. 360–1). See also the treatment of 2 Chr. 11b (*Doctrine of the Hert*, p. 16, ll. 416–18; cf. *De doctrina*, p. 39); treatment of Heb. 1:14 (*Doctrine of the Hert*, p. 21, ll. 621–22; cf. *De doctrina*, p. 63), and the treatment of Prov. 11:1 (*Doctrine of the Hert*, p. 62, ll. 113–14; *De doctrina*, p. 198) (the Latin text locates this quotation to 'Proverb 11. 16 et 20'). On such occasions, the English compiler is aware of the biblical origins of his words (confirmed by references to 'holy writ', 'as Abya seyde', 'as Seint Poule seiþ', 'as Salomon seyth') but it seems that he has slipped into unconscious 'translation mode' as it were.

32 *Doctrine of the Hert*, p. 7, ll. 96–100. For these Psalm quotations, see Ps. 41:4 and Ps. 50:16 (both are borrowed from *De doctrina*). For an unusual example of the English compiler vernacularising a biblical text before translating, see 'Than be reson, "þer þi tresor is, þer shuld þin hert be": *Ubi est thesaurus tuus, ibi et cor tuum erit*' (*Doctrine of the Hert*, p. 83, ll. 126–27). The quotation is from Matt. 6:21 and is borrowed from *De doctrina*.

33 It is arguable that such sustained and overt reliance on the Vulgate as the Word of God is a product of a post-Arundelian devotional climate, anxious to foreground its awareness of Latin as the authoritative language of divine revelation.

34 Drawing on its Latin source, the English *Doctrine*'s reliance on Old Testament sapiential literature is perhaps rather more extensive than that of other contemporary Middle English devotional writing.

discussed above, with which the English prologue opens).[35] The primary purpose of such biblical referencing, in both *De doctrina* and the *Doctrine*, is to confer 'comfortable' divine authority on the devotional narrative. But the repeated device of quotation also operates on a literary level, providing the narrative with a framework around which to organize itself. In particular, both Latin and English texts base each of their seven chapters on a particular biblical theme, introduced by seven quotations made at the outset of book 1.[36] So, for example, both include a quotation from Proverbs 4:23 at the beginning of book 2 –

> Aftir this longe chapitre, þe wiche techith a mynche to make redy here hert, I purpose, be the grace of God, to declare how she shuld also kep here hert, aftir þe biddyng of Salomon where he seith þus: *Omni custodia serva cor tuum*. 'Kepe wel þin hert' he seith, 'with al maner of bisynesse.'[37]

– although the English departs from the Latin in concluding the book with a repetition of the same quote.[38] Similarly, both base book 3 around the themes of 2 Machabees 1:4: 'May he open your heart in his law, and in his commandments, and send you peace', although the English repositions the quotation somewhat earlier in the book and repeats it.[39] Book 4, on

---

35 For other biblical citations apparently original to the English *Doctrine* see, for example, John 13:13 (p. 21, ll. 631–3). Of course, such apparent differences may well be attributable to the fact that the English compiler was working from an earlier version of *De doctrina* which did contain these quotations. The sheer extent of the compiler's biblical indebtedness to its source text is highlighted by comparison with, for example, the roughly contemporary compilation *The Chastising of God's Children*. The anonymous author of this text is somewhat more adventurous in supplementing the biblical references of his sources with some of his own. See *The Chastising of God's Children and the Treatise of Perfection of the Sons of God*, ed. by J. Bazire and E. Colledge (Oxford, 1957).

36 1 Kgs. 7:3; Prov. 4:23; 2 Macc. 1:4; Heb. 13:9; Ecclus. 39:6; Lam. 3:41 and Joel 2:13.

37 *Doctrine of the Hert*, p. 47, ll. 1–5. The *Doctrine* abbreviates *De doctrina*'s biblical reference, which reads: 'Omni custodia serua cor tuum, quia ex ipso vita procedit' (p. 155). As already noted, this Proverbs text is also quoted at the beginning of *De doctrina*'s prologue.

38 Ibid., p. 58, ll. 441–2.

39 For the quotations in the *Doctrine*, see ibid., p. 60, ll. 52–6 and p. 65, ll. 227–31. For *De doctrina*, see p. 203. Book 3's first biblical reference, in both the Latin and the English treatises, is to Ezek. 2:9: 'And I looked, and behold, a hand was sent to

the subject of maintaining stability of heart, is introduced and concluded in both treatises by the same quotation from Hebrews 13:9: 'Off stabilnes of hert, Seynt Poule seithe in þis wise: *Optimum est gracia stabiliri cor.* "The best þing þat is" he seithe, "for to stabil þe hert is grace"',[40] and although the *Doctrine*'s book 5 introductory quotation from Ecclesiasticus 39:6 –

> The fifthe chapitre techeth for to yive oure hertis like as Salomon seith in commendacioun of rightwis soules, þus: *Justus cor suum tradet ad vigilandum diliculo ad Dominum, qui fecit illum.* 'The rightwisman' he seith, 'shal yive his hert for to wake to oure lord in þe erly mornyng.'[41]

– does not appear at the same point in the Latin text, both cite this text (fifth in the series of seven) in their introduction to the themes of the treatise at the outset of book 1. Finally, in both treatises, book 6 contains an early reference to Lamentations 3:41: 'Let us lift up our hearts with our hands to the Lord in the heavens',[42] and a quotation from Joel 2:13 is found at the beginning of book 7 in both treatises: 'And rend your hearts, and not your garments, and turn to the Lord your God: for he is gracious and merciful, patient and rich in mercy, and ready to repent of the evil.'[43]

---

me, wherein was a book rolled up: and he spread it before me, and it was written within and without: and there were written in it lamentations, and canticles, and woe' (see *Doctrine of the Hert*, p. 59, l. 25– p. 60, l. 26; *De doctrina*, p. 192).

[40] *Doctrine of the Hert*, p. 68, ll. 1–3. For the corresponding quotation in *De doctrina*, see p. 212. For the use of this quotation at the close of book 4, see *Doctrine of the Hert*, p. 76, ll. 311–13 and *De doctrina*, p. 244.

[41] Ibid., p. 77, ll. 1–5. In the *Doctrine*, book 5 closes in vernacular allusion to this Ecclus. text: 'But now, peraventure, þou woldist wete what þis gray mornyng shuld be þat I spake of in þe begynnyng of þis chapitre, wher I seyde a rightwis man shuld yive his hert for to wake to oure lord in þe erly mornyng' (*Doctrine of the Hert*, p. 79, ll. 87–90).

[42] See *Doctrine of the Hert*, p. 80, ll. 15–17 and *De doctrina*, p. 255. Although the Latin text begins book 6 with this quotation (p. 255), the English begins with a quotation from Wisd. 5:16: 'In commendacioun of such þat han here hert lift up to God bi holy meditaciouns, Salomon seith þus: *Cogitacio eorum apud Altissimum.* "The þoughtes of devought folk ben in almyghty God" he seith' (p. 80, ll. 4–7) and follows this with a quotation and translation of Ecclus. 6:37: '*Habe cogitatum tuum in preceptis Altissimi, et in mandatis eius assiduus esto*' (p. 80, ll. 9–10). *De doctrina* does contain these quotations, but positions them slightly later in the book (p. 256).

[43] Both the Latin (p. 276) and the English (p. 85, l. 4) quote only the initial phrase 'Scindite corda vestra.'

Yet although the English compiler quarries his source for biblical authorities, he is not enslaved entirely to *De doctrina*. Specifically, he has a keen sense of the dramatic for which he is not indebted to the Latin text; where the much lengthier *De doctrina* often meanders somewhat through countless biblical quotations, the English *Doctrine* tends to deploy quotation in a rather more succinct, even punchy, manner. To take just one instance of this, book 3 of the *Doctrine* (borrowing from the Latin) deals with the seven 'lettyngis' (impediments) which can prevent us from opening our hearts to God. In keeping with their general practice, both treatises bolster this narrative with biblical citation, yet while the Latin text's quotation is extensive, the English compiler pares down his source's extravagance. For example, inspired by the Latin, the English *Doctrine* labels the fifth impediment as the 'quenching of a good purpose conceyvid in þe hert.'[44] Both then quote from 1 Thessalonians 5:19: 'Therfor, sister, kepe þi first devout purpose of religious lyvyng and quenche it not, as Seynt Poule seith: *Spiritum nolite extinguere.* "Quenche not" he seith, "þi religious purpose".'[45] With this terse and relevant quotation, the English compiler concludes the material on the fifth impediment, proceeding immediately to the sixth. The author of *De doctrina*, by contrast, picks up on the theme of 'conception' and continues with a further quotation from Isaiah 37:3: 'Venerunt filii vsque ad partum, et non erat virtus pariendi',[46] and from Matthew 24:19: 'Væ prægnantibus, et nutritientibus in illis diebus'[47] before proceeding to discussion of the sixth impediment. While these quotations are woven efficiently into the Latin prose, they explore an illustrative theme of pregnancy and childbirth omitted from the English text. Furthermore, one might argue that they are not as immediately or obviously pertinent to the theme of 'quenching' as is the 1 Thessalonians quotation, and that, in omitting them, the English compiler is displaying an acute awareness of literary impact.[48]

Indeed, omission and abbreviation are the defining characteristics of the *Doctrine*'s response to *De doctrina*'s biblical voice – as they are of the

---

44 *Doctrine of the Hert*, p. 63, ll. 149–50.

45 Ibid., p. 63, ll. 162–4. For the same quotation in *De doctrina*, see p. 200.

46 *De doctrina*, p. 201. See Isa. 37:3: 'For the children are come to the birth, and there is not strength to bring forth.'

47 Ibid., p. 201. See Matt. 24:19: 'And woe to them that are with child, and that give suck in those days.'

48 Of course, out of sensitivity to his audience of celibate female religious, the compiler might have deleted inappropriate references to pregnancy and childbirth.

vernacular treatise's treatment of its Latin source as a whole. At the most basic level, the English compiler abbreviates individual quotations; so, for example, while *De doctrina* quotes thus from 1 Corinthians 9:20–22 in illustrating the behaviour of the ideal religious superior –

> Sic indutus erat Apostolus, qui omnibus se conformabat dicens: 1. ad Corinth. 9. Factus Iudæis tanquam Iudæus: ijs, qui sine lege erant, tanquam sine lege essem. Et post multa talia concludit: Omnia omnibus factus sum, vt omnes saluos facerem.[49]

– the English treatise abbreviates considerably, quoting from only 9:22b: 'A sovereyne shuld sey and be as Seynt Poule seith: *Omnia omnibus factus sum*. "I hamme made al þing" he seith, "to al folk".'[50] And the English compiler can be seen to take his abridging tendencies much further than this. Indeed, although his text is peppered heavily with biblical quotation and allusion, he deletes the majority of *De doctrina*'s abundant scriptural citations. In particular, he truncates *De doctrina*'s extended *catenae* of biblical quotation. Such, for example, is the case with book 1's lengthy exploration of Christ as a guest in the 'house' of the human heart. Introducing the theme thus in the Latin treatise –

> Præpara ergo cor tuum, tanquam domum ad magnum hospitem Christum Dominum tuuum recipiendum. Ipse enim tanquam vir vagus super terram, et declinans ad manendum; vt dicitur Ieremiæ 14. Cuius delitiæ sunt esse cum filijs hominum, sicut dicit Salomon, Prouerb. 8. Qui in tuo negotio tantum laborauit, vt in hospitio cordis tui lassatus, et vulneratus requiescere quærat, dicens per Isaiam cap 28. Hæc requies mea, reficite lassum.[51]

---

49 *De doctrina*, p. 129 (Thus the Apostle was clothed, who conformed himself to all, saying: 1 Cor. 9. To the Jews I became as if I were a Jew: to those who were without a law, I became as if I were without a law. And after many such things, he concluded: I was made all things to all men, that I might save some.) Of course, *De doctrina*'s quotation is itself an abbreviation of 1 Cor. 9:20–22.

50 *Doctrine of the Hert*, p. 39, ll. 1298–1300. For other examples of such biblical abbreviations, cf. 2 Macc. 1:4 in *De doctrina* (p. 4) with the corresponding section in the *Doctrine of the Hert* (p. 5, l. 10); cf. also Prov. 4:23 in *De doctrina* (p. 155) with the corresponding section in the *Doctrine of the Hert* (p. 47, ll. 3–4).

51 *De doctrina*, p. 6 (Therefore prepare your heart, just as a house is made ready to receive a worthy guest, Jesus Christ. For he is just like a man wandering over the earth, avoiding the obligation to remain; as is said in Jeremiah 14. Whose delights were to be with the sons of men, just as Solomon said, Proverbs 8. Who

– the author can be seen to rely upon three Old Testament texts in his portrayal of Christ as the wanderer seeking rest in the human heart.[52] While the English compiler picks up on this theme of the exhausted saviour in search of rest, he adds to his source an affective link with Christ's sacrifice on the cross – 'oure lord Jhesu Crist ... sekith amonges his childryn a restyng place, the whiche to here helth hath tendirly yivyn his herte blode'[53] – and borrows only the last of *De doctrina*'s three quotations:

> That he was wery for laboure in his passioun the prophete Ysaie berith witnes, where oure lord be the same prophete saith thus to clene hertis: *Hec requies mea. Reficite lassum.* 'This is my restyng place' he seith, 'refresshith me þat am wery.'[54]

Proceeding from these initial quotations, *De doctrina* goes on to quote from Isa. 43:24 –

> Ergo Christum tuum refice, vt in te locum refectionis, et quietis inueniat; qui in te, et a te causas laboris accepit. Laborem mihi præbuisti in iniquitatibus tuis, dicit ipse per lsaiam cap. 43. Quis pugilem suum de victoria redeuntem gloriosum, aspersum sanguine, liuidum, consossum, vulneratum in domo sua gratanter non reciperet? item, cum honore non occurreret?[55]

---

on your behalf laboured so much that, exhausted and wounded, he strives to rest in the guest room of your heart, saying through Isaiah chapter 28. This is my rest, refresh the tired.)

52 For the biblical origins of the 'vir vagus', see Jer. 14:9a: 'Why wilt thou be as a wandering man ('velut vir vagus'), as a mighty man that cannot save?'; for second reference, see Prov. 8:31b: '... my delights were to be with the children of men', and for third, see Isa. 28:12a: 'To whom he said: This is my rest, refresh the weary ...'

53 *Doctrine of the Hert*, p. 6, ll. 41–3.

54 Ibid., p. 6, ll. 44–7. The reference to 'clene hertis' is also an addition to *De doctrina* and is in keeping with the English compiler's particular emphasis on 'hertly redyng'.

55 *De doctrina*, p. 6 (Therefore repair your Christ, so that in you he may find a place of restoration and peace; who for you and from you undertook responsibility for this work. You were the cause of my labour with your iniquities, he says himself through Isaiah 43. Who would not receive joyfully into his home a fighter returning glorious from his victory, sprinkled, bruised, stabbed, wounded?) See Isa. 43:24b: '... But thou hast made me to serve with thy sins, thou hast wearied me with thy iniquities.'

– and follows this with an allusion to Hebrews 2:16: 'Huius gratiæ ciues Angelici non immemores, quos etiam non apprehendit, sicut dicit Apostolus ad Hebræ. 2.'[56] The treatise then returns to Isaiah – 'Id est, quorum naturam non assumpsit: cum gloria ascendenti occurrerunt, dicentes in Isaia cap. 63. Quis est iste, qui venit de Edom, tinctis vestibus de Bosra, iste formosus in stola sua, gradiens in multitudine fortitudinis suæ?'[57] – before the introduction is concluded with an echo of Matthew 25:43: 'Væ ergo tibi, si ipse possit improperare illud Euangelij Matthæi 25. Hospes sui, et non collegistis me.'[58] Again, however, the English compiler abbreviates his source at this point, submerging the themes of the first two biblical citations within his own vernacular prose:

> We ben cause of his grete laboure and werinesse, þat was woundid to the dethe for oure wikkidnesse … And what is he that wil not meete with such a glorious championn comyng home to his hous, seth it so is that angelis of heven, whos kynde he toke not upon hym but only the kynde of man …[59]

He does go on to provide us with the Vulgate text of the last two quotations[60] but again, he departs from the rather more theologically austere *De doctrina* by punctuating them with an affective, Christocentric appeal to his audience:

> yif angelis shewid suche reverence to him in his Assencioun, whom he bought not with his blood as he dede mankynde, whi shuld not we than mete him in þe way and receyve hym with reverence, comyng to oure hertis axing rest aftir his werynesse?[61]

---

56 *De doctrina*, p. 6 (Of whose grace the angelic citizens are not heedless, of whom he did not even lay hold, just as the Apostle says in Hebrews 2). See Heb. 2:16: 'For nowhere doth he take hold of the angels: but of the seed of Abraham he taketh hold.'

57 Ibid., pp. 6–7 (They, whose nature he did not assume: they ran to meet him ascending with glory, saying, in Isaish 63. Who is this that cometh from Edom, with dyed garments from Bosra, this beautiful one in his robe, walking in the greatness of his strength.) See Isa. 63:1a.

58 Ibid., p. 7 (Therefore, woe to you, if he is able to reproach you according to the Gospel of Matthew 25: I was a visitor and you did not welcome me.) See Matt. 25:43a: 'I was a stranger, and you took me not in.'

59 *Doctrine of the Hert*, p. 6, ll. 50–1, 55–8.

60 Ibid., p. 6, ll. 60–3 and p. 7, ll. 69–70.

61 *Doctrine of the Hert*, p. 6, l. 64–p. 7, l. 68. For another example of the *Doctrine*'s

Vernacular embroiderings such as this highlight the fact that although the *Doctrine*'s biblical voice is characterized primarily by its omission and abbreviation of 'comfortable words' found in *De doctrina*, its method is not unimaginative. Indeed, in the process of abridging his source the English compiler produces a biblical tone distinctive to his own narrative. As stated earlier in this chapter, the *Doctrine*'s scriptural voice is characterized overwhelmingly by its Latinity. However, on occasions we find that biblical language borrowed from *De doctrina* has been incorporated silently into the vernacular narrative; such, for example, was the case with the two submerged borrowings from Isaiah 43:24 and Hebrews 2:16 outlined above. Indeed, while *De doctrina* is careful in registering its scriptural sources, this tacit incorporation of biblical language into authorial narrative is unique to the English text and lends it an informality of tone less apparent in the Latin treatise.[62] A notable example of this is found in book 5's examination of obedience, wherein both treatises argue that one's obedience to a religious superior should recall Christ's obedience to his Father. In affirming this principle, the *Doctrine* reads:

> For, like as Crist Jhesu, dyghing on þe crosse, offred to his fadir of heven his spirit, whan he seyde: 'Into þine hondes, fadir, I yeld my spirit'; so shuldist þou do, beyng dede to þe world in þe crosse of religioun, yeld þi wyl bi trewþe into þe hondes of þi sovereyne in Godis name.[63]

Although the narrative obviously borrows from Luke 23:46 ('And Jesus

truncated *catenae*, see Prov. 4:23 (p. 51, ll. 147–8) and cf. the corresponding section in *De doctrina* which quotes from Nahum 3:13, 1 Cor. 13:11, Prov. 1:22, Prov. 4:23, Prov. 24:6, Eccles. 9:18 and Baruch 3:28 (pp. 163–5).

62 Again, comparison with the roughly contemporary devotional compilation, *The Chastising of God's Children* is instructive at this point. Where the *Doctrine* compiler is happy to tacitly incorporate biblical material into vernacular narrative, the anonymous *Chastising* compiler is more eager to differentiate biblical text from authorial voice. See *The Chastising of God's Children*, ed. by Bazire and Colledge.

63 *Doctrine of the Hert*, p. 78, ll. 46–50. Such unsignposted incorporation of Christ's voice into an affectively nuanced vernacular is reminiscent of Nicholas Love's practice in *The Mirror of the Blessed Life of Jesus Christ*. See Nicholas Love, *The Mirror of the Blessed Life of Jesus Christ*, ed. by M.G. Sargent (Exeter, 2004), especially *Capitulum xl Die Veneris*, pp. 159–88. It also recalls contemporary devotional lyrics in which Christ is presented as speaking to us from his position of torment on the cross. See, for example, R.T. Davies (ed.), *Medieval English Lyrics* (London, 1963), no. 41, p. 116; no. 102, pp. 197–8; no. 106, pp. 202–3; no. 110, pp. 207–8 etc.

crying out with a loud voice, said: Father, into thy hands I commend my spirit. And saying this, he gave up the ghost.') the compiler has buried the biblical debt within his own vernacular prose. In so doing, he creates an uninterrupted narrative that does not recall the equivalent moment in *De doctrina*, which contains a clear acknowledgement of its gospel source:

> Cor tuum o claustralis dedisti, quando voluntatem, et sensum tuum proprium in Prælati tui manu reliquisti, ad similitudinem Christi, ex obedientia in cruce morientis, et dicentis; Lucæ 23. Pater in manus tuas commendo spiritum meum.[64]

That the creation of such uninterrupted narrative is a conscious decision on the part of the English compiler is verified by his unsignposted vernacularization of other *De doctrina* biblical citations. For example, in book 1's exploration of the sacrament of the altar, he borrows a *catena* of three biblical allusions from the Latin treatise (John 6: 51, Exodus 12: 15, Wisdom 16: 20). The scriptural origin of each of these allusions is foregrounded in *De doctrina*, but the *Doctrine* ignores this, creating instead a sustained vernacular narrative:

> Therfor, take hede what is y-set afore þe for to be receyved into þi soule, for it is hevenly liflode, þe wiche come down from heven. It is also an undefoulid lamb þat must be etyn and receyvid with soure letuse of contricioun. It is also hevenly manna, þe wich hath þe tast of al maner of swetnes.[65]

However, despite such examples of unsignposted biblical borrowing, the *Doctrine* compiler is, in general, careful to alert his audience to his scriptural

---

64 *De doctrina*, pp. 248–9 (You gave your heart to the cloister, according to your will, and you abandoned your own thought into the hand of your sovereign, in the likeness of Christ, dying out of obedience on the cross, and saying; Luke 23. Father into your hands I commend my spirit.) As pointed out in n. 22, the precise reference to biblical chapter and verse is a particular characteristic of the 1607 edition of *De doctrina*. Other manuscripts tend to content themselves with a reference to biblical book.

65 *Doctrine of the Hert*, p. 20, ll. 578–82. For the corresponding material in *De doctrina*, see p. 57, although note that *De doctrina* supplements these three biblical citations with several others. For a further instance of the *Doctrine* submerging biblical references see, for example, *De doctrina*'s quotation from Rev. 3:1 (p. 219), rendered thus in the *Doctrine*: 'Þey han a name þat þey lyve, and ben dede.' (p. 71, ll. 119–20).

debts, and central to the English treatise's distinctive biblical tone is its manner of citing these debts. When reading *De doctrina*, one is referred consistently to biblical book but the English compiler often does away with such precise referencing, tending to favour a more generalized allusion to 'holy writ'. So, for example, while *De doctrina* locates its quotation from Hebrews 12:6 thus: 'quia, Ipse est (*vt dicit Apostolus ad Hebræ. 12*) qui flagellat omnem filium, quem recepit.'[66] the *Doctrine* reads: 'for he it is, *as holy writ seith*, that blameth and chastiseth every child that he resceyveth.'[67] And where *De doctrina* locates its quotation from Proverbs 17:17 thus: 'Omne enim tempore diligit, qui amicus est, *Prouerb 17*',[68] the *Doctrine* reads simply: '... *as holy writ seyth*: *Omni tempore diligit qui semel amicus est*. "He lovyth ever" *he seyth*, "þat is ones trewly made a frende."'[69]

The awkward movement from '*holy writ* seyth' to '*he* seyth' in the above citation of Proverbs highlights a further distinctive feature of the vernacular treatise's biblical voice; where *De doctrina* refers only rarely to the human author of any biblical text, the *Doctrine* is more resolute in naming names, often preferring the human to the textual.[70] Thus, while the quotation from Isaiah 40:2 ('loquimini ad cor Jerusalem') in the prologue to *De doctrina* is located thus: 'Loquitur Dominus prædicatoribus *per Isai. 40.* dicens: Loquimini ad cor Ierusalem',[71] the *Doctrine* contains no reference to book or chapter, instead naming divine inspiration and human author: 'Suche symple soules it is charite to enforme, namly seth *oure lord yivyth us in charge, seiyng be the prophete Ysaye thus*: *Loquimini ad cor Jerusalem*.'[72] This

---

66 *De doctrina*, p. 27, my italics.

67 *Doctrine of the Hert*, p. 14, ll. 360–1, my italics. As pointed out in n. 31, this is one of the occasions on which the *Doctrine* provides us with a solely vernacular biblical authority.

68 *De doctrina*, pp. 211–12, my italics.

69 *Doctrine of the Hert*, p. 67, ll. 326–8, my italics. For other examples of the *Doctrine* replacing *De doctrina*'s precise biblical references with allusions to 'holy writ', cf. 2 Kgs. 4 in book 1 of *De doctrina* (p. 51) with the *Doctrine* (p. 19, ll. 537–9); cf. Lev. 21:13–14 in book 1 of *De doctrina* (p. 85) with the *Doctrine* (p. 28, ll. 881–4); cf. 1 Kgs. 11 in book 2 of *De doctrina* (pp. 160–61) with the *Doctrine* (p. 48, ll. 65–6); cf. Gen. 4 in book 4 of *De doctrina* (p. 230) with the *Doctrine* (p. 74, l. 206); cf. Exod. 14 in book 7 of *De doctrina* (p. 280) with the *Doctrine* (p. 88, l. 107).

70 For exploration of the late medieval movement of *auctoritas* from 'the divine realm to the human' see A.J. Minnis, *Medieval Theory of Authorship: Scholastic Literary Attitudes in the Later Middle Ages* (Aldershot, 1984).

71 *De doctrina*, p. 1, my italics.

72 *Doctrine of the Hert*, p. 3, ll. 10–12, my italics. For other examples of the *Doctrine*'s 'personalising' tendency, cf. *De doctrina*'s 1 Kgs. 7:3 (p. 4) with the

personalizing trend is apparent throughout the *Doctrine* but is perhaps most obvious in its adaptations of *De doctrina*'s numerous Psalm quotations.[73] While the Latin text tends to refer to individual Psalms by means of number, the English compiler invokes David as supposed author, presenting him more obviously and consistently as a figure whose voice and actions we are called upon to emulate. For example, in encouraging us to purify our hearts by means of confession, *De doctrina* cites the second half of Psalm 76:7 ('And I meditated in the night with my own heart: and I was exercised and I swept my spirit.'): 'Munda ergo cor tuum confessione peccati, velut quadam scopa, conscientiæ tuæ tabernaculum purgando: vt possis dicere illud Psalmi 76. Exercitabar, et scopebam spiritum meum.'[74] The *Doctrine* also quotes from this Psalm, but its method of so doing personalizes David as author, foregrounding him as an exemplary model for the audience to imitate:

> But first, or thow go to confessioun, thow must serche thi conscience bi bisy examynacioun and aftirward swepe it bi diew confessioun. Thus dede Davith, the prophete, whan he seide: *Excercitabar et scopebam spiritum meum*. 'I' he seyde, 'with bisy inquisicioun serchid my consciens and afterward swept it be confessioun.'[75]

Looking at book 6's exploration of the heart lifted up to God, we see that both treatises quote for a second time from the same verse of the Psalter and, again, the different imperatives governing the two are made obvious. While *De doctrina* expresses a desire for its audience and the Psalm text to 'agree' or 'meet' in their articulation of meditative experience – 'Eleuetur ergo cordis tui meditatio, vt a corde ad carnem non defluat; imo in corde,

---

Doctrine (p. 5, ll. 3–5); *De doctrina*'s Isa. 28:12 (p. 6) with the *Doctrine* (p. 6, ll. 44–7); *De doctrina*'s Ecclus. 1:27 (p. 7) with the *Doctrine* (p. 7, ll. 74–6); *De doctrina*'s Ps. 75:3 (p. 17) with the *Doctrine* (p. 9, ll. 157–9); *De doctrina*'s S. of S. 4:4 (p. 167) with the *Doctrine* (p. 51, ll. 178–9); *De doctrina*'s Rev. 5:9 (p. 195) with the *Doctrine* (p. 60, ll. 46–50); *De doctrina*'s Wisd. 5:16 (p. 256) with the *Doctrine* (p. 80, l. 6).

73 The *Doctrine* compiler may well have dispensed with precise biblical references in the expectation that his audience would not have had access to a bible or would not have been able to read Latin. If this were the case, referring them to book and chapter would not have been of any practical use in enabling them to verify references for themselves.

74 *De doctrina*, p. 7 (Therefore sweep your heart of sin in confession, just as you would with a broom, having cleaned the tabernacle of your conscience: so that you are able to speak Psalm 76. I was exercised and I swept my spirit.)

75 *Doctrine of the Hert*, p. 7, ll. 81–5.

et cum corde stet, et maneat, *vt tibi conueniat illud Psal. 76.* Meditatus sum nocte cum corde meo: et exercitabar, et scopebam spiritum meum'[76] – the English treatise is more explicit in presenting David's voice as the ideal which the audience should hope to echo in its own spiritual life, drawing on *De doctrina*'s technique in first introducing this verse:

> Therfor, sister, put away such lusty þoughtes and lifte up þin hert in holy þoughtes, þat it falle not fro þe hert to þe flessh, but þat it abyde in þe hert with þe herte, *þat þou mow sey as Davyth seyth*: *Meditatus sum cum corde meo*. 'I have beþought me with myn hert.'[77]

By means of such characterizations of the bible as a 'script' which we can use to narrate our own life and spiritual experience, the *Doctrine* emphasizes more consistently than *De doctrina* that as well as speaking *to* us in an instructive or hortatory manner, the bible also speaks *with* us.[78]

Indeed, throughout the *Doctrine* we have a vivid of a sense of the bible as spoken word, primarily of the supposed human author but also as the personal utterance of the divine. Thus, rather than citing chapter and verse, the compiler introduces quotations from John 13:13 and 13:15 as the direct speech of Christ:

> … for *he seith hymself*: *Vos vocatis me Magister et Domine, bene dicitis: sum etenim*. 'Ye clepe me mayster and lord' *he seith*, 'ye say wel I am so.' Also … *he seith himself*: *Exemplum dedi vobis, ut quemadmodum ego feci, ita et vos faciatis*. 'I have yiven yow ensample that right as I have don, do ye.'[79]

It is a paradox of the *Doctrine* that although its biblical quotations are predominantly Latin (meaning that its non-Latinate audience sees the scriptures only when refracted through the lens of the compiler's

---

76 *De doctrina*, p. 257, my italics (Therefore the meditation of your heart should be raised up, so that it does not descend from the heart to the flesh; indeed, it should stand firm and remain in and with the heart, so that Psalm 76 may be appropriate to you. And I meditated in the night with my own heart: and I was exercised and I swept my spirit.)

77 *Doctrine of the Hert*, p. 81, ll. 43–6, my italics.

78 On occasion, the *Doctrine* compiler does mention biblical book rather than human author. See, for example, his reference to 'the boke of Machabeorum' (*Doctrine of the Hert*, p. 5, l. 9).

79 *Doctrine of the Hert*, p. 21, ll. 631–6, my italics. For the corresponding section in *De doctrina*, see pp. 63–4.

interpretative translations) the treatise's informal allusions to the bible by means of human author or as direct speech create an impression of God's Word as an accessible entity. Furthermore, although the compiler (as 'narrator') inevitably presents himself as possessing privileged insight into the bible, the wisdom of which he imparts to his audience, he is also notably careful to position himself with his audience as a co-recipient of divine wisdom.[80] Thus, for example, in their first chapter, both treatises quote from Matthew 25:43 ('I was a stranger, and you took me not in: naked, and you covered me not: sick and in prison, and you did not visit me'). But while *De doctrina* introduces its quotation with an accusatory address to its audience: '*Væ ergo tibi*, si ipse possit improperare illud Euangelij Matthæi 25. Hospes sui, et non collegistis me',[81] the English *Doctrine* replaces the accusatory 'tibi' with the inclusive 'we', indicating the compiler's awareness that he, as much as his audience, needs to prepare his heart for Christ: '*I drede but yif we receyve hym he wil another tyme shame us and seye*: *Hospes fui, et non collegistis me.* "I come to yow as a gest" he wil sey, "and ye wold not receyve me".'[82] Such inclusive awareness of himself and his audience as the joint beneficiaries of biblical wisdom is characteristic of the compiler's particular awareness of his readership and certainly marks him out as a more reassuring, or conventionally comforting, figure than the author of the Latin, whose particular brand of comfort is often of the challenging variety.

As indicated at the outset of this chapter, both *De doctrina* and the *Doctrine* present the Song of Songs as the most demanding of biblical books, accessible only to competent 'gostly loveris'. Further, by offering explanatory glossing of this demanding Old Testament book in their seventh book, both treatises suggest that their intended audiences are not

---

80 For examples of the compiler's self-presentation as privileged communicator of biblical wisdom, see his many references to himself as having read the scriptures: 'So I rede in the Boke of Kynges ...' (p. 10, ll. 195–6. cf. 4 Kgs. 5:2); 'as I fynde write thus ...' (p. 48, l. 50. cf. 1 Sam. 4:8); 'þe seven claspis þe wiche were schewid to Seynt John in the Apocalips where I rede þus ...' (p. 61, ll. 68–9. cf. Rev. 6). In fact, all of these biblical citations are borrowed from *De doctrina*.

81 *De doctrina*, p. 7, my italics (Therefore woe to you if he is able to reproach you with the gospel of Matthew 25. I was a stranger and you took me not in.)

82 *Doctrine of the Hert*, p. 7, ll. 68–70, my italics. For further evidence of the English compiler's inclusive language, see 'We rede in holy writ ...' (p. 20, l. 584); see also 'A, sister, now be we unkynde, þat wil not folow oure lord be good lyvyng into heven, whom oure lord sought and folowid into helle' (p. 71, ll. 101–3), and cf. the corresponding section in *De doctrina* (p. 218).

necessarily advanced in the 'gostly' life.[83] Despite this, however, *De doctrina* does cite the authority of the Song of Songs on occasion. For example, in book 1's exploration of the sacrament of the altar (discussed above), the Latin treatise argues that while manna (i.e., the sacrament) hardens in the destructive heat of fire, it melts in the productive heat of the sun (i.e., in the warmth of divine 'caritas'). Drawing on the authority of Song of Songs 5:6 ('I opened the bolt of my door to my beloved: but he had turned aside and was gone. My soul melted when he spoke …'), the text proceeds: 'Vt talis anima corpore Christi sic recepto possit dicere illud Cant. 5. Anima mea liquefacta est, vt dilectus meus loquutus est.'[84] The English treatise follows an identical line of reasoning at this point, arguing that upon receipt of the sacrament 'a soule þat hath þe heete of þe sonne, þe wiche is charite … meltith al in teris', while 'a soule þat is encombrid with þe heete of flesshly lust … wexith obstinate.'[85] However, although the compiler suggests that the charitable soul will dissolve into tears 'bi swetnesse of love',[86] he avoids anchoring such terminology in the Song of Songs, and makes no explicit allusion to the amorous language of this challenging text.

Providing more evidence of the English compiler's acute awareness of the suitability of the material with which he is presenting his inexperienced audience, Anne Mouron's essay in this volume notes that the prologue to the English treatise deletes the Song of Songs-inspired vocabulary and imagery found at the equivalent point in *De doctrina*. Further, book 3 witnesses him again deleting the richly erotic language of the Song of Songs. In its exploration of the heart opened to God, the third book of *De doctrina* boasts an extended rumination drawing on Revelation 3:20 ('Behold, I stand at the door and knock') and inspired by Song of Songs 5:2 ('Open to me, my sister, my love, my dove, my undefiled').[87] But the English treatise erases this language of love, opting only for the rather more prosaic Revelation quotation in demonstrating how 'oure lord knokkiþ at þe dore of oure hertis for to be lete in.'[88] A notable exclusion of eroticism is also found in

---

83 It should be noted, however, that the final chapter's preoccupation with the challenging language of the Song of Songs corroborates Catherine Innes-Parker's observation (in this volume) that the *Doctrine* compiler expects spiritual progress in its readers.

84 *De doctrina*, p. 59 (So that such a soul having thus received the body of Christ is able to say Cant. 5. My soul melted when my beloved spoke.)

85 *Doctrine of the Hert*, p. 20, ll. 600–1, 603–4.

86 Ibid., p. 20, l. 609.

87 *De doctrina*, p. 204.

88 *Doctrine of the Hert*, p. 65, ll. 243–4.

the *Doctrine*'s final book, which (as has been remarked) draws upon the Song of Songs in exploring the seven symptoms of love. Borrowing from *De doctrina*, the English treatise identifies the fifth symptom as an 'unordinat pous' ('pulsus inordinatus') and quotes from Psalm 83:3.[89] But while *De doctrina* refers us to the second chapter of Song of Songs and continues in rumination on the 'affectiones' as symbolized by the 'vbera sponsæ', the English treatise omits any such language.[90]

For the vast majority of the *Doctrine*, the compiler's omission of biblical material does not appear to be motivated by anything other than a desire for brevity. Indeed, that he and the author of *De doctrina* do not differ fundamentally in their biblical understanding is emphasized by the fact that the English compiler tends to follow (while simplifying) the exegetical readings of the Latin text. His omission of quotations from the Song of Songs, however, does seem to be governed by different factors. Uncomfortable with intensely erotic language and imagery, the compiler of the English *Doctrine* remains acutely aware of his audience and its vulnerabilities and capabilities in the matter of 'hertly redyng'. Not wanting to challenge his addressees beyond their 'gostly' capacities, he omits biblical language which they might perceive to be 'unperfit and defectif'[91] and retains those 'comfortable wordis' whose challenge is of a manageable intensity.

---

89 'My heart and my flesh crieth out for the living God.' For the corresponding material in *De doctrina*, see p. 291.

90 The relevant references to 'vbera' actually occur in S. of S. 4:5, 7:3 and 8:10. Note that the *Doctrine*'s deletion of Song of Songs material is not wholesale; it does retain some quotations found in *De doctrina*. See, for example, the partial quotation of S. of S. 5:1 (*Doctrine of the Hert*, p. 13, ll. 332–4; *De doctrina*, p. 38); S. of S. 4:4b (*Doctrine of the Hert*, p. 51, ll. 178–9; *De doctrina*, p. 167); the partial quotation of S. of S. 2:14 (*Doctrine of the Hert*, p. 89, ll. 168–70; *De doctrina*, p. 288); none of these quotations contains markedly erotic language or imagery. See also S. of S. 2:16a (*Doctrine of the Hert*, p. 35, ll. 1169–71) which replaces *De doctrina*'s quotations from S. of S. 7:10 and 5:10 (discussed in n. 21).

91 *Doctrine of the Hert*, p. 87, ll. 83–4.

5

Meat, Metaphor and Mysticism: Cooking the Books in *The Doctrine of the Hert*

Vincent Gillespie

> All great simple images reveal a psychic state. The house even more than the landscape is a 'psychic state', and even when reproduced as it appears from the outside, it bespeaks intimacy (Gaston Bachelard).[1]

A major rhetorical concern of much anchoritic literature is the cramming of infinite imaginative riches into the little rooms of an anchorhold or reclusory. The metaphorical empowerment of those who lead lives of reclusion from the world is both a convenient didactic enrichment of the limited space they occupy and the creation of a series of parallel imaginative landscapes layered onto their actual locus to endow them with a set of resources that are necessary both for their psychological well-being and for their long-term spiritual development.[2] Monks and nuns, encouraged to follow the example of Mary at the Annunciation, are invited to enter

---

1 G. Bachelard, *The Poetics of Space*, tr. M. Jolas (Boston, 1994), p. 72. This essay began as a plenary lecture to the *Rhetoric of the Anchorhold* conference of the International Anchoritic Society in July 2005. I am indebted to the editors of this volume for that invitation and for the opportunity to develop my thinking at greater length here.

2 For a recent discussion see E. Robertson, '"This Living Hand": Thirteenth-Century Female Literacy, Materialist Immanence, and the Reader of the *Ancrene Wisse*', *Speculum*, 78 (2003), 1–36, and the useful references included there; P. Dailey, 'Questions of Dwelling in Anglo-Saxon Poetry and Medieval Mysticism: Inhabiting Landscape, Body and Mind', in R. Copeland, D. Lawton and W. Scase (eds), *New Medieval Literatures* 8 (Turnhout, 2006), pp. 175–214.

into their *cubicula* – whether real or imaginary – and to turn them into magical spaces filled with allegorical edifices, mental paradigms, mystical metaphors and symbolic resonances. The world may be charged with the grandeur of God, but an enclosed religious has to work within a restricted compass to enact and explore the grandeur encoded by the divine author into his epic creation. The restriction of actual space must be compensated for by the development of skills in navigating and inhabiting the limitless landscapes of God's goodness and mercy. The largest and most limitless of those spaces is that which lies within the human heart.[3]

The Doctrine of the Hert, reworked in the first half of the fifteenth century from a highly clericalized Latin guide to interior landscapes from the thirteenth century, is an interesting example of how clerical translators rose to the challenge of blending the didactic and devotional strands of eremitical and monial literature into a form capable of responding to and resisting the diverse interpretative strategies that vernacular readers (both clerical and non-clerical) brought to such texts. The Latin text, *De doctrina cordis*, variously attributed to the thirteenth-century Cistercian Gerard of Liège and the Dominican Hugh of St Cher (d. 1263), is a witness to the concern of thirteenth-century schoolmen to provide pastoral resources suitable for the changing institutional and catechetic circumstances of the period.[4] The new pastoral theology of the university schools encouraged the application of the latest advances in theological and scriptural learning (such as the *Postillae* of Hugh of St Cher) for the benefit of those charged with the *cura animarum* either of the burgeoning numbers and types of religious women or of the lay people whose individualized catechization was supposedly a new priority for the universal church.[5] *De doctrina* was originally written as a teaching aid for priests charged with the pastoral

3 See the recent discussion in E. Jager, *The Book of the Heart* (Chicago, 2000); J.F. Hamburger, *Nuns as Artists: The Visual Culture of a Medieval Convent* (Berkeley, CA, 1997), esp. ch. 4: 'The House of the Heart', pp. 137–75.

4 For a new assessment of the authorship issue, and a critical account of the earlier scholarship, see the essay in this volume by Nigel F. Palmer.

5 On the developments in thirteenth-century pastoral theology, see F.D. Logan, *A History of the Church in the Middle Ages* (London, 2002); J. Goering, *William de Montibus (c. 1140–1213): The Schools and the Literature of Pastoral Care* (Toronto, 1992); M. Gibbs and J. Lang, *Bishops and Reform 1215–1272, with Special Reference to the Lateran Council of 1215* (London, 1934); W.A. Pantin, *The English Church in the Fourteenth Century* (Cambridge, 1955), pp. 189–243; L.E. Boyle, 'The Fourth Lateran Council and Manuals of Popular Theology', in T.J. Heffernan (ed.), *The Popular Literature of Medieval England* (Knoxville, 1985), pp. 30–60.

care of religious women (either nuns or beguines). Its clear and schematic presentation of moral psychology and its pragmatic and accessible blend of scriptural and patristic authorities clearly caught the imagination (or served the didactic purposes) of its clerical users, and the work enjoyed an extensive pan-European circulation in various recensions and, eventually, translations. Its Middle English version survives in four copies dating from around the second quarter of the fifteenth century onwards.[6] Manuscript and testamentary evidence shows that it was owned and read in fifteenth-century England by nuns and laywomen, as well as by male clerics. Margaret Yaxley, a Franciscan nun from Bruisyard in Suffolk, had a copy bequeathed by her lay sister-in-law Margaret Purdans, part of the mercantile elite of Norwich.[7] Another copy was owned by the minoresses at St Botolph without Aldgate in London.[8] A further copy was in the ownership of John Waynfleet, dean of Chichester, who died in 1481.[9]

Because of its temporal popularity and geographical reach, *De doctrina* offers a valuable example of the ways in which authors of texts of religious guidance for those in enclosed or conventual communities may have used the imagery and the imaginary of space.[10] Henri Lefebvre has commented

---

6 Oxford, Bodleian Library, MS Laud Misc. 330; Durham, University Library, MS Cosin V.III.24; Cambridge, Trinity College, MS B.14.15; Cambridge, Fitzwilliam Museum, MS McClean 132.

7 For a full discussion of Margaret Purdans, see M.C. Erler, *Women, Reading, and Piety in Late Medieval England* (Cambridge, 2002), pp. 68–84. The Durham copy comes from Suffolk, but has not been positively identified as the copy left by Purdans to Bruisyard.

8 The Trinity Cambridge copy has a lengthy colophon describing how the Minoress 'Cristyne sent nicolas … dowghtyr of nicolas seint Nicolas squier' left the book at her death in March 1455 for the use of officers of the abbey. The book was later owned and heavily annotated by Stephen Batman, who gave it the title 'The doctrine of the harte': see M.B. Parkes, 'Stephen Batman's Manuscripts', in M. Kanno et al. (eds) *Medieval Heritage: Essays in Honour of Tadahiro Ikegami* (Tokyo, 1997), pp. 125–56, esp. pp. 133 and 143.

9 The Durham copy has 'Amen Quod Iohannes Waynfleet' at the top of fol. iia. He was a brother to the famous Bishop of Winchester, William Waynfleet.

10 The subject of the representation of space in medieval literature has been receiving increased attention in recent years. My own thinking on this issue has been particularly influenced by M. de Certeau, *The Practice of Everyday Life*, tr. S. Rendall (London, 1984); C. Cannon, *The Grounds of English Literature* (Oxford, 2004), esp. pp. 139–71; D. Vance Smith, *Arts of Possession: The Middle English Household Imaginary*, Medieval Cultures 33 (Minneapolis, 2003); and, most profoundly, by H. Lefebvre, *The Production of Space*, tr. D. Nicholson-Smith

that every space, real or imaginary, can be decoded and encoded with significance (p. 150). With its allegories and metaphors of household tasks such as cleaning, cooking and bed-making, the first section of the Middle English version, which deals with the preparation of the heart to receive God, raises in particularly interesting ways some of the issues concerning the handling of space and imaginative landscape in eremitical and monial texts translated into Middle English.[11]

Lefebvre distinguishes three strands in his thinking about space: real space as it is lived in (*spatial practice*), real space as it is conceived of and interpreted (*representations of space*), and imaginary space as it is perceived and explored in the mind (*representational space*). First, there is *spatial practice*, which represents the way that a society deciphers and grants significance to its own actual spaces and what is performed in them. Lefebvre argues that 'a spatial code is not simply a means of reading or interpreting space; rather it is a means of living in that space: of understanding it and of producing it' (p. 47). It is an essential part of the legibility of daily life in religious communities as in secular households. In monastic terms, this spatial practice is reflected in the architecture of monastic buildings. The hierarchy of spaces contained within them, such as the sanctuary of the church, or the enclosure of the monks and nuns, or of the function-specific spaces like the cloister or chapter house which become embodiments of aspects of the lived rule under which the community operates. But para-monastic texts seek to describe a spatial practice that is often uneasily poised between the practice of the secular household and that of the monastery. Here spatial practice is articulated by the rules concerning access to and furnishing of the hermitage or

(Oxford, 1991), first published in 1974. (References to Lefebvre will henceforth be parenthetic in the main text.) I am grateful to Dr Laura Varnam of University College, Oxford, for stimulating discussions on the subject of sacred space.

11 For a valuable recent overview of this subject see C. Batt, D. Renevey and C. Whitehead, 'Domesticity and Medieval Devotional Literature', *Leeds Studies in English*, 36 (2005), 195–250, especially Renevey's discussion: 'Figuring Household Space in *Ancrene Wisse* and *The Doctrine of the Hert*' (pp. 198–214), and his previous explorations of the theme listed in his notes there; S. Salih, 'At Home; out of the House', in C. Dinshaw and D. Wallace (eds), *The Cambridge Companion to Medieval Women's Writing* (Cambridge, 2003), pp. 124–40; and C. Cannon, 'Enclosure', pp. 109–23 in the same volume. See also the essays in A. Mulder-Bakker and J. Wogan-Browne (eds), *Household, Women and Christianities in Late Antiquity and the Middle Ages*, Medieval Women: Text and Contexts 14 (Turnhout, 2006).

anchorhold. It was precisely the liminality of such para-monastic forms of living that later allowed them to be the avatars of a new lay spirituality aspiring to inhabit the theology of the mixed life, and that illustrated the ways in which spatial practice could be transferred from the concrete and particular to the abstract and imaginative realm of allegoresis. 'Ancre ant huses leafdi ah muchel to beon bitweonen' ('There ought to be a great difference between an anchoress and the lady of a house') says the *Ancrene Wisse*, whose outer rule in parts 1 and 8 defines the custom and practice of anchoritic living and encodes the conventions, taboos and disciplines that regulate physical living in the anchorhold.[12] While seeking to instil and enforce a monastic or para-monastic spatial code, many texts of this kind, including *De doctrina*, rely heavily on the narrative energy and normative trajectory of secular domestic and household imagery to power their spiritual allegories.

Lefebvre's second strand is what he calls *representations of space* (the way that actual space and real places are conceptualized and conceived). In religious terms, this is close to the allegorizations of church buildings and ornaments such as are found in Durandus' *Rationale divinorum officiorum* or Edmund of Abingdon's hugely influential *Speculum ecclesiae*, where every element of the church and its decoration and vestments can be charged with determinate meaning, and where the priest vesting for mass can configure himself as a warrior donning his armour for spiritual battle.[13] The choreography of liturgical observance, the symbolic performance of ritual in and around the sacralized spaces of the edifice, the hierarchy of holiness enacted in the physical layout of the abbey church or the separation of nave and chancel in a parish church: such representations of space assert, inform, produce and impose the social understanding of the space. Sacrilege and trespass are a violation of socially produced and policed understandings of such spaces, and their punishment by excommunication

---

12 *Ancrene Wisse: A Corrected Edition of the Text in Cambridge, Corpus Christi College, MS 402, with Variants from Other Manuscripts*, ed. by B. Millett, 2 vols, EETS OS 325 (2005) and 326 (2006), vol. 1, p. 29. Translation by H. White, *Ancrene Wisse: Guide for Anchoresses* (Harmondsworth, 1993), p. 37.

13 C. Whitehead, *Castles of the Mind: A Study of Medieval Architectural Allegory* (Cardiff, 2003) traces the pervasive presence of allegorical edifices in religious writing from the earliest periods of Christian history onwards. See also M. Carruthers, 'The Poet as Master Builder: Composition and Locational Memory in the Middle Ages', *New Literary History*, 24 (1993), 881–904. The foundational study on this subject was R.D. Cornelius, *The Figurative Castle: A Study of the Medieval Allegory of the Edifice* (Bryn Mawr, 1930).

or public penance visibly excludes or humiliates the offender as a means of repairing and reinforcing the damaged spatial codes and the violated social conventions. Lefebvre says that 'representations of space have a practical impact, in that they intervene in and modify spatial textures' (p. 42). Initially such representations of space and place worked with and required the kind of spatial literacy that was restricted to male clerics who perforce quickly learned the disciplines of communal life and the boundaries of communal space.

> Representations of space are shot though with a knowledge (*savoir*), that is a mixture of understanding (*connaisance*) and ideology, which is always reflective and in process of change. Such representations are thus objective, though subject to change. (p. 41)

For hermits, anchorites and beguines, however, this representation of sacral space is perhaps less clearly defined. Canon law legislated for monastic and other ecclesiastical spaces, but because of the late growth and often liminal existence of para-monastic communities they have much less explicit legislation, and therefore less inherited expertise in handling representations of space.[14] Hermits and anchorites have to know *how* to play this representational game without the benefits of communal tradition and without the guidance and example of novice masters and senior brethren: it requires a kind of idiolectal literary competence of the sort that we can see the author of the *Ancrene Wisse* or *Sawles Warde* teaching. Once learned it can be applied elsewhere. Texts of para-monastic spirituality, whether anchoritic or lay, have to generate in their reading or listening audience a distinctive *savoir* and *connaisance* in handling of representations of space. The various subsequent revisions to the *Ancrene Wisse* seek to inflect that literary competence for their own needs and conditions, from the small unified group of the original form of the text, through the larger and more spatially scattered (but imaginatively unified) group envisaged in the Corpus version, to the more amorphous and probably lay later audience of the *Pepys Rule* (where every man can be an anchorite inside the anchorhold of his own body) and the *Symple Tretis*.[15] Works like *What the Church Betokeneth*, a

---

14 For discussion, see E. Robertson, *Early English Devotional Prose and the Female Audience* (Knoxville, TE, 1990); S. Thompson, *Women Religious: The Founding of English Nunneries after the Norman Conquest* (Oxford, 1991); J. Wogan-Browne, *Saints' Lives and Women's Literary Culture: Virginity and its Authorizations* (Oxford, 2001).

15 For a snapshot of current scholarship on this subject, see the various

fifteenth-century vernacular epitome of Durandus and Edmund included as a supplementary text in the English vernacular version of the *Legenda aurea*, made such spatial representations available to a new kind of (often lay) reader.[16] In lay contexts, texts like *þe Holy Boke Gracia Dei* or the Latin *Instructions for a Devout and Literate Layman* teach their audience how to reconfigure or reconceptualize secular spaces (like the family meal table) and to sacralize aspects of secular social practice (how to pray as you walk down the street).[17] Such texts played a role in developing and enforcing spatial awareness as an important part of the evolving and developing *mythos* of medieval Christian practice for an ever-widening circle of monial and eventually lay readers.

This is relevant to the transmission and reception of a text like *The Doctrine of the Hert*, and the ways in which it remodels in its vernacular instantiation the representations of space in the Latin original. The probably original Latin prologue (IP- 'Ignaros predicatores') begins with a hard-hitting double exhortation which reflects thirteenth-century pastoral idealisms (later somewhat watered down in its criticism of priestly failings).[18] It addresses in Latin those priests who will eventually deliver

discussions in Y. Wada (ed.), *A Companion to the Ancrene Wisse* (Cambridge, 2003), especially the chapters by C. Innes-Parker, C. von Nolcken and N. Watson.

16 *Supplementary Lives in Some Manuscripts of the Gilte Legende*, ed. by R. Hamer and V. Russell, EETS OS 315 (2000), pp. 85–128. These additional lives and texts form part of the English bishops' fifteenth-century attempt to rekindle and reinforce traditional loyalties to the institutional church in the aftermath of Lollardy and the Great Schism.

17 W.A. Pantin, 'Instructions for a Devout and Literate Layman', in J.J.G. Alexander and M.T. Gibson (eds), *Medieval Learning and Literature: Essays Presented to Richard William Hunt* (Oxford, 1976), pp. 398–422; *Richard Rolle and þe Holy Boke Gratia Dei: An Edition with Commentary*, ed. by M.L. Arntz, Elizabethan and Renaissance Studies 92:2 (Salzburg, 1981); C.A.J. Armstrong, 'The Piety of Cicely, Duchess of York: A Study in Late Mediaeval Culture', now repr. in *England, France and Burgundy in the Fifteenth Century* (London, 1983), pp. 135–56.

18 Both recensions of the prologue are edited by G. Hendrix, 'Het Leidse handschrift BPL 2579 en de tekstoverlevering van het traktaat *De doctrina cordis*', *OGE*, 54 (1980), 158–81. I have also consulted the copy in Oxford, Bodleian Library, MS Lat. th. f. 6; and *Le manuscrit Leyde Bibliothèque de l'Université, BPL 2579, témoin principal des phases de rédaction du traité De doctrina cordis à attribuer au dominicain français Hugues de Saint-Cher (pseudo-Gérard de Liège)*, facsimile edn with an intro. by G. Hendrix, De doctrina sive praeparatione cordis 1 (Ghent, 1980).

the allegory that follows to their spiritual charges, probably in the local vernaculars. The opening exhoration 'Preparate corde vestra domino' (Prepare your hearts for the Lord)[19] is addressed to the eventual readers or hearers of the text. But the second, 'Loquimini ad cor Ierusalem' (Speak to the heart of Jerusalem and call to her, for her evil is come to an end and her iniquity forgiven),[20] is an urgent exhortation to the priests who will deliver the teaching of the text. This quotation, subjected to a triple exposition which takes up the bulk of the prologue, is presented as an urgent call to reformation, a voice of one calling out against those preachers who are ignorant of the virtues of sacred scripture and fail to 'frangere et exponere' (to break and expound) the words of scripture so that they are able to enter into the hearts of those listening.[21] Preachers have a responsibility to expound the gospel so that it can flow into the cellars of the hearts of those listening through the wine press of their ears, a process described by Augustine as 'vinaria verborum retinens et vinum spiritualis intelligentie ad cellarum cordis transmittens' (retaining them in wine flasks of words and transmitting the spiritual understanding of the wine into the cellar of the soul). The priest is warned against excessive rhetoric and verbal ornamentation in preaching practice, and the prologue stresses the dangers of vainglory in over-intellectualized and self-regarding clerical display: such rhetorical and intellectual display speaks only to the ears and not to the heart. The probably original Latin prologue, therefore, carefully controls access to the spaces of its text through an intellectual antechamber that stresses and reinforces the centrality of clerical teaching authority and the intellectual and institutional subsidiarity of its hearers. The target audience are configured as wine cellars to be filled, perhaps even flooded, with spiritual wine that will be poured out for them by the priests who control access to the text and to what flows from it. The primary responsibility of the (implied female) inscribed audience is to be obedient and attentive recipients of clerical wisdom: 'audi filia et vide et inclina aurem tuam [Ps. 44:11], attende doctrinam cordis tui propositam.'[22]

The translator's prologue to the Middle English version (which is one of the most significant additions made by the translator) sets up a very different textual representation of the work by locating it in a different

---

19 1 Sam. 7:3.

20 Isa. 40:2.

21 The other recension of the prologue (HV- 'In hoc verbo'), also found in the early printed texts, modifies and moderates the criticisms made of negligent and vainglorious priests.

22 This phrase is in both recensions of the prologue.

cultural, ecclesiastical and political landscape. The whole tone of the prologue is less magisterial, less clerical and less certain, more willing to acknowledge the relativity and provisionality of authority:[23]

> *Intelligite, insipientes in populo; et stulti, aliquando sapite.* As Seynt Austyn seyth, thes wordis ben undirstonde in this wise: 'ye that been unkunnyng in the nombre of goddis peuple inwardly undirstondith, and ye that ben unavisid, yif ye have grace of any gostly kunnyng, sumtyme savorith sadly in hert.' Myght not wel thees wordes be undirstonde of suche that ben unkunnyng in religioun, the whiche also nowadayes ben moche unstable in theire lyvyng, folowyng rather the ensample of seculer folk than the ensample of sad goostly religious folk? I trowe yis.[24]

The Latin prologue, talking over the heads of the intended audience to berate failing preachers, configures that audience as wine cellars to be stocked or flooded. But the Middle English text, starting from Psalm 93's call to understanding ('Understand, ye senseless among the people: and, you fools, be wise at last'), is glossed by the translator as offering the possibility of empowering the ignorant and foolish, and as recognizing that even the 'unkunnyng' and 'unavisid' among the people may 'sumtyme savorith sadly in hert' 'yif ye have grace of any gostly kunnyng'. So while not exactly flattering the inscribed audience, the vernacular translator allows for the possibility of spiritual growth and emancipation. Moreover, the recognition that many in religion are themselves 'unkunnyng' and 'unstable' and follow the example of secular folk rather than religious folk further destabilizes both the text and its audience, allowing it to appeal both to those in religion who want to do better and to those in secular estate who want to act like those in religion. And the surviving manuscripts testify that it was precisely these twin audiences to which the Middle English text appealed. There are instructions to a 'gostly sister' and to 'mynchen', and vocative addresses such as 'Loo, sister', which suggest an initial target audience of nuns. This probably reflects the original target audience of the Latin. But

---

23 In Lefebvre's terms, the Middle English prologue displays precisely that knowledge (*savoir*) of its own textual moment that is 'a mixture of understanding (*connaisance*) and ideology, which is always reflective and in process of change' (p. 41).

24 C. Whitehead, D. Renevey and A. Mouron (eds), *The Doctrine of the Hert: A Critical Edition with Introduction and Commentary* (Exeter, 2010), p. 3, ll. 1–9. Hereafter cited as *Doctrine of the Hert.*

the *Doctrine* follows the practice of many vernacular translations of this period in implicitly recognizing the likelihood that a text of this kind would achieve an audience in female textual communities that straddled both sides of the nunnery walls (a clericalized address to 'sisters' need not, after all, be limited to nuns).[25] In fact the translator explicitly reconfigures and expands his textual space by refusing to align his text with those that offer only an external rule of life: 'Many, I wote wel, þer ben that speken to the body ouȝtward, but few to the hert inward of symple soules, and that is pite.'[26]

The text is targeted at the 'edificacioun of symple soules',[27] without specifying their affiliation or status. There are similarities with the contrast between the *Ancrene Wisse*'s outer rule, which is only a textual envelope that represents and polices the spatial practice of the anchorites, and which delimits the inner spiritual spaces where the imaginative drama of the text will be performed, and the inner rule, which deals with governance of the heart and is applicable to all well-intentioned religious souls. 'þe utter riwle, þet is lute strengðe of, for-hwon þet te inre beo wel iset' ('The outer rule … is of little significance provided the inner rule is well kept'), says the *Ancrene Wisse*.[28] So it proved in the later *mouvance* of that text to address the needs and competencies of wider audiences. By the fifteenth century, the audience for such 'hertly redyng'[29] was rarely restricted to professed religious.[30]

'The hert inward': this space within is Lefebvre's final and most

---

25 For a discussion of this typical broadening of the target audience in such fifteenth-century Middle English religious texts, see V. Gillespie, 'Vernacular Books of Religion,' in J. Griffiths and D. Pearsall (eds), *Book Production and Publishing in Britain 1375–1475*, Cambridge Studies in Publishing and Printing History (Cambridge, 1989), pp. 317–44; 'Anonymous Devotional Writings', in A.S.G. Edwards (ed.), *A Companion to Middle English Prose* (Cambridge, 2004), pp. 127–49; 'Religious Writing', in R. Ellis (ed.), *The Oxford History of Literary Translation in English, vol. 1: 700–1550* (Oxford, 2008), pp. 234–83.

26 *Doctrine of the Hert*, p. 3, ll. 17–19.

27 Ibid., p. 3, l. 23.

28 *Ancrene Wisse*, ed. by Millett, part 8, vol. 1, p. 161; *Ancrene Wisse*, tr. White, p. 196. This phrase occurs in one of the revisions to the original text incorporated into MS Corpus 402.

29 *Doctrine of the Hert*, p. 3, l. 30.

30 See the essays in C.M. Meale (ed.), *Women and Literature in Britain 1150–1500* (Cambridge, 2nd edn, 1996), and the discussion in V. Gillespie, 'Vernacular Theology', in P. Strohm (ed.), *Middle English: Oxford Twenty-First Century Approaches to Literature* (Oxford, 2007), pp. 401–20.

interesting category, which he calls *representational space. Representational space* is 'space as directly lived through its associated images and symbols' (p. 39). As he says in a passage with curious resonance to the text under discussion here: 'the heart as *lived* is strangely different from the heart as *thought* and *perceived*' (p. 40). Lefebvre calls it 'the dominated – and hence passively experienced – space which the imagination seeks to change and appropriate. It overlays physical space, making symbolic use of its objects' (p. 39). By means of metaphor and metonymy, these representational spaces 'erect a mental and social architecture above spontaneous life' (p. 140). The codes for reading and understanding representational or imaginative space can be used to enforce and develop conformity and obedience to certain social (or in religious texts, spiritual) norms of behaviour and interpretation.

In conventional theological terms, this imaginative space is the place of exegesis, the layering and projection of meanings onto texts and contexts so as to make them resonate with the same frequency and on the same wavelength as the universal church's understanding of its mission and identity as articulated through its *magisterium* or teaching authority. The symbolic space of scriptural exegesis is therefore both liberating to inhabit and also tightly policed by the forces of orthodoxy and the 'deposit' of faith: consider the battle between orthodoxy and the Lollards about what constitutes the literal sense of scripture. Religious allegory is often used to layer certain privileged interpretations over scriptural texts. These usually reflect settled institutional ideologies that may tend to the repressive and the limiting, seeking to enforce orthodoxies of the mind as well as of behaviour. 'Symbols', says Lefebvre, 'always imply an emotional involvement, an affective charge … which is so to speak deposited at a particular place and thereafter "represented" for the benefit of everyone elsewhere' (p. 141). Mental space is every bit as sociologically and culturally determined as physical space, and it too is shaped by a process of production, of inculturation, of what those engaged in the present-day training of priests still call 'formation'. In many religious contexts, this exercise of control, domination and power is highly gendered. Just as religious and para-monastic women before the fifteenth century are often seen to be infantilized and controlled by their perceived need for certain kinds of spiritual direction, so lay spirituality, drawing heavily on vernacular materials produced for such religious women, often suffers at the hands of texts that seek to gender and infantilize the lay reader.

Parts 2 to 7 of the *Ancrene Wisse* serve as a training ground in exegetical gestures and interpretative appropriation of symbolic spaces of gradually increasing complexity leading up to the virtuoso interpretations of the challenging allegories of part 6. In one way this is an empowerment of the anchoresses: it gives them mental tools to generate and inhabit imaginative spaces spun from the limited scriptural and patristic resources at their disposal, and, more interestingly, also spun from the motifs of romance and chivalry (such as the besieged woman trope) that probably hark back to their former textual competencies in lay society. As Vance Smith comments, 'the household romance is profoundly concerned with the delimitation and management of a particular locus.'[31] But such imaginative space can be subject to cultural policing: 'In addition to being a means of production it is also a means of control, and hence of domination, of power', Lefebvre argues (p. 26). This kind of abstract space transforms the body by transporting it outside itself. Lefebvre calls this play of abstraction the 'space of castration':

> The space of a metaphorization whereby the image of the woman supplants the woman herself, whereby her body is fragmented, desire shattered, and life explodes into a thousand pieces. Over abstract space reigns phallic solitude and the self-destruction of desire. (p. 309)

Lefebvre writes well about the way that this fragmentation results in the body being 'pulverised' in a process that 'serves to fragment desire and doom it to anxious frustration, to the non-satisfaction of local needs' (p. 310). While the kinds of sublimation and liberation this involves are much desired and aspired to in contemplative theory and practice, they can also have other potentially less desirable sociological impacts and effects. 'Let your spirit be manly even though your gender is womanly' says Osbert of Clare (d. *c.*1170) in his letter to the nun Adelidis of Barking.[32] We can see the controlling and 'castrating' effect of this attitude in Osbert's use of the Judith story, whose various narrative locations are often employed as abstract representational spaces in anchoritic writing, and whose muscular and masculine heroism is a spiritual paradigm of the ways in which 'over abstract space reigns phallic solitude and the self-destruction of desire':

> Anyone who had applied his mind to meditation on this will be able to heal his mind of the wounds of perverse love; and while he savours

---

31 Vance Smith, *Arts of Possession*, p. 81. Future references will be given parenthetically in the text.

32 Osbert of Clare, 'Letter 42: to Adelidis, Abbess of Barking', tr. in V. Morton with J. Wogan-Browne, *Guidance for Women in Twelfth-Century Convents*, The Library of Medieval Women (Cambridge, 2003), p. 40.

> the delight of so much sweetness he will empty himself of the relish of illicit love ... You must, then, go secretly into the chamber of your soul and take on the nature of Judith, so that you may seize the sword and, with Holofernes lying dead, you may free the Jewish town from danger. For in the days of her widowhood Judith was in the habit of praying to the Lord; Valerian found Cecilia too, praying in her chamber, in the presence of an angel. In this way the Hebrews are 'transients' since they sought no abiding city in this world. Thus indeed those sanctified souls whom you lead cross over every day to the feast of the eternal king so that they may enjoy the repast of the heavenly banquet. They have turned away from pleasure in the victuals of the Assyrians and the pollution of their voluptuous sauces ... You must faithfully imitate Judith and you must imprint her appearance on your eyes in a spiritual manner.[33]

Lefebvre writes of a 'world of signs':

> Where the Ego no longer relates to its own nature, to the material world, or even to the 'thingness' of things (commodities), but only to things bound to their signs and indeed ousted and supplanted by them. The sign-bearing 'I' no longer deals with anything but other bearers of signs. (p. 311)

This place and this space is one towards which much contemplative writing seems to be gesturing. This is indeed Augustine's region of dissimilitude, Plotinus's holy of holies and the *Cloud*'s mid-space between forgetting and unknowing:

> This world of images and signs, this tombstone of the world ('Mundus est immundus' [the world is unclean]) is situated at the edges of what exists, between the shadows and the light, between the conceived (abstraction) and the perceived (the readable/visible). Between the real and the unreal. Always at the interstices, in the cracks. Between directly lived experience and thought. And (a familiar paradox) between life and death – presents itself as a transparent (and hence pure) world, and

---

33 Osbert of Clare, 'Letter 42', tr. Morton, *Guidance for Women*, pp. 31–2, 35. The Judith story is referred to in the *Ancrene Wisse*, and is a commonplace in Latin letters of spiritual guidance to enclosed women in the early Middle Ages. For an overview of the tradition, see M. Stocker, *Judith: Sexual Warrior* (New Haven, 1998).

> as reassuring on the grounds that it ensures concordance between the mental and the social, space and time, outside and inside, and needs and desire. (p. 389)

'Always at the interstices, in the cracks.' This familiar liminality, this imaginative threshold, is precisely the space where anchorites, recluses, hermits, beguines (and later aspirant lay people) often placed themselves, on the cusp of the monastic and secular worlds, dead and alive, neither fish nor fowl.[34] It is a version of the same liminality that in the fourteenth century fuels the development of a lay version of the theology of the mixed life, and that fuels the passover of anchoritic and monial literature into lay circulation.[35]

But the threshold is a powerfully productive imaginative space. Its representations can be labile and glitteringly multi-faceted. Because, in practice, *representational spaces* in religious contexts often have the potential to free themselves from many of the constraints placed on them by the *magisterium* and by tradition.[36] This is fundamental to the anxiety shown by the institutional church at the efflorescence of female visionary activity in the later Middle Ages, even though much of its expression remains close to the praxis and the iconography of conventional church teaching, configured according to traditional symbolism of sacred spaces and places. But although always already historicized, religious texts are also always subject to imaginative and social *mouvance*. New audiences read in new ways. New social and textual competencies generate new interpretations of old texts. 'Space is social morphology … it is to lived experience what form itself is to the living organism, and just as bound up with function and structure' (Lefebvre, p. 94). But those codes are dialectal, produced as 'part of a practical relationship, as part of an interaction between "subjects" and their space and surroundings' (p. 18). They therefore change and develop over time, just as texts and their readers change in different recensions and

34 C. Holdsworth, 'Hermits and the Power of the Frontier', in K. Bates et al. (eds), *Saints and Saints' Lives: Essays in Honour of D. H. Farmer, Reading Medieval Studies*, 16 (1990), 55–76; Cannon, *Grounds*, pp. 139–71.

35 The standard modern discussion of this trend is F.J. Steele, *Towards a Spirituality for Lay-Folk: The Active Life in Middle English Religious Literature from the Thirteenth Century to the Fifteenth* (Salzburg, 1995).

36 'Representational spaces … need obey no rules of consistency or cohesiveness. Redolent with imaginary and symbolic elements, they have their source in history – in the history of a people as well as in the history of each individual belonging to that people', Lefebvre, p. 41.

different cultural circumstances. A text written in Latin for priests to use when teaching nuns is later read in English by nuns in London, or nuns and laywomen in East Anglia, or by the dean of a great English cathedral in Sussex. Every hearing or reading potentially creates idiolectal interpretations of the text because every hearer or listener brings to it a slightly different imaginative and cultural archive. Once liberated or empowered, the imagination will play with representational spaces in unpredictable ways. 'Metaphor and metonymy do not naturalize the spatial realm, they also tend to make it evaporate – to dissolve it in a luminous (optical and geometrical) transparency' (Lefebvre, pp. 139–40). As Bachelard says, 'through dreams, the various dwelling places of our lives co-penetrate and retain the treasure of former days.'[37]

The worlds of metaphor and mythography are very close to each other. When texts of interior religion came to be produced or adapted for laymen they often borrowed as their dominant spatial allegory the structure and architecture of a monastic community (as in *The Abbey of the Holy Ghost*, *The Book to a Mother*, *The Pricking of Love*, *Fervor amoris* and *Gracia Dei*).[38] *The Eight Ghostly Dwelling Places* illustrates how compactly the idea can be deployed:

> Blessid is at religioun of whiche þe temple is holynes, þe scole sooþnes, and þe cloister stilnes, þe chapilte of equite, þe dortoir of chastite, and þe fermary pitee, þe fraitir sobirnes and þe hostrie largenes and charite. þerfore who þat haþ þese viij placis goostly in his soule and outward in hise werkis, his religioun is perfiȝt.[39]

By contrast, nuns, anchorites and contemplatives often get given domestic, household or courtly models upon which to hang their symbolic allegory: making beds, cleaning houses, childcare, herring scales, dripping eaves, besieged castles, jousts of love, and so on.[40] The key point of all these

---

37 Bachelard, *Poetics of Space*, p. 5.

38 The anti-clerical satire, 'Why I can't be a nun' is a dystopian example of this displaced allegory at work: *Six Ecclesiastical Satires*, ed. by J.M. Dean, TEAMS (Kalamazoo, MI, 1991), pp. 227–42.

39 J.W. Conlee (ed.), '*The Abbey of the Holy Ghost* and *The Eight Ghostly Dwelling Places* of Huntington Library HM 744', *Medium Aevum*, 44 (1975), 137–44.

40 For a similar observation, see N. Rice, 'Spiritual Ambition and the Translation of the Cloister: *The Abbey and Charter of the Holy Ghost*', *Viator*, 33 (2002), 222–60. On this text, see also L. Carruthers, 'In Pursuit of Holiness Outside the Cloister: Religion of the Heart in *The Abbey of the Holy Ghost*', in B.M. Kienzle

representational spaces is almost certainly the *alterity* of the social model provided for each group. The 'production of space', according to Lefebvre, can be seen as a 'a tool of thought and of action' (p. 26), but the generated metaphorical space is perhaps stronger and more vivid when already subject to an *a priori* process of defamiliarization and alienation, so that the core process of metaphorization is enacted on a vehicle that is always already absent. So in the case of the domestic allegories found in texts of this kind, their authors may be working with what Vance Smith has described as 'the association of the household with a mythic, feminized past that is irrevocably gone' (p. 62). For anchoresses and nuns that mythic feminized secular and/or courtly household is indeed irrevocably gone, but perhaps exercises a potent hold over their personal imaginary, a grip that needs to be engaged with and imaginatively focused if the desired transparency of representational and spiritual space is to be achieved.

Vance Smith observes that:

> Freud's recognition that the self is like a house rests on the emergence of the house as a powerful symbol of bourgeois identity, as a place of retreat, privacy, interiority and (in every sense of the word) appropriation, a place where the surplus of labor could be gathered, where property was established, where propriety was observed, where *le propre* (the self) itself resided. (p. 44)

While one might wonder how true this was in most medieval households, where private space would often have been at a premium (think of Margery Kempe's home life), it might very well have been true of the spatial practice of medieval religious houses, where, despite living in community, spiritual privacy and a sense of selfhood and propriety are woven into the spatial practice of daily living.[41] In using household imagery, religious texts explore an imaginative and representational space where the propriety of the new spatial practice of the anchorhold, beguinage or nunnery might be configured onto and by means of a sense of self generated by an old spatial practice of the secular household, and where selfhood, propriety and virginity (*propreté*) could cluster together in a playful association requiring and enforcing metaphorization and abstraction.

(ed.), *Models of Holiness in Medieval Sermons*, Textes et Études du Moyen Âge 5 (Louvain-La-Neuve, 1996), pp. 211–27. Robertson ('"This Living Hand"', p. 3) talks of the 'quotidian psychological realism' exploited in the *Ancrene Wisse*.

41 See the recent discussion in D. Webb, *Solitude: The Medieval Discovery of Personal Space* (London, 2007).

Vance Smith argues that 'The function of household law is to manage surplus, the thing that exceeds the law of household economy, to keep it from emerging destructively within the household' (p. 46). The alienating appropriation of household imagery in religious texts may be a way of dealing with a symbolic surplus, with secular imagery that needs to be controlled and focused into a more metaphorical and therefore liminal framework. Roberta Gilchrist has noted that 'within the community or household, arrangement for the acquisition, storage, preparation and consumption of food are essential in establishing gendered relationships.'[42] But in an all-female monastic or para-monastic community, such gendered relationships are subjected to spatial and imaginative re-orientation when the only substantial male figure is the absent bridegroom Christ (figured by the chaplain). Food imagery resonates, therefore, in different ways. Erich Jager's study of monastic and monial imagery observes that the labour imagery associated with monks is related to writing and book-making, while that typically associated with nuns is linked to nurturing: gardening, cooking, cleaning, embroidery.[43] Alterity and defamiliarization are part of the intended effect of these homely household images. Despite being functions that nuns might have undertaken in their daily work in the cloister, their primary iconic signification gestures towards the secular and courtly context of romance narrative, and of their own early lives. As Vance Smith puts it in relation to the Freudian notion of the *unheimlich*: 'In one sense the *unheimlich* is the *heimlich*, the other is always projected on to the memory of the home' (p. 44). Home is where we start from. Gaston Bachelard powerfully expresses the imaginative hold of these household images:

> The house we were born in has engraved within us the hierarchy of the various functions of inhabiting. We are the diagram of the functions of inhabiting that particular house, and all other houses are but variations on a fundamental theme. The word habit is too worn a word to express this passionate liaison of our bodies, which do not forget, with an unforgettable house.[44]

---

[42] R. Gilchrist, *Gender and Archaeology: Contesting the Past* (London, 1999), p. 45. This study has much to offer students of medieval religious space imagery.

[43] Jager, *Book of the Heart*, pp. 51–5, 101–2. Jager briefly discusses the Latin *De doctrina cordis* on pp. 58–60.

[44] Bachelard, *Poetics of Space*, p. 15. On Pierre Bourdieu's concept of *habitus* in this connection, see Gilchrist, *Gender and Archaeology*, pp. 81ff., and her *Gender and Material Culture: The Archaeology of Religious Women* (London, 1994), pp. 17ff.

In an attempt to break the habit of secular thought, and to instil the *habitus* of spiritual thinking, manipulation of this domestic imagery may represent an unconsciously 'castrating' gesture on the part of the male authors of texts for religious women: 'The space of a metaphorization whereby the image of the woman supplants the woman herself, whereby her body is fragmented, desire shattered, and life explodes into a thousand pieces' (Lefebvre, p. 309). The *Ancrene Wisse* warns: 'Ne makie þe nana gestnunges … Ha nis nawt husewif, ah is a chirch-ancre' ('Do not give any feasts … She is not a housewife but a church anchoress').[45] 'Mundus est immundus': the world is unclean.

Homely and domestic images often crop up in the most unlikely places in these texts, with a shock of unlikeliness as much as of recognition, and with little sign that they are effaced or being rendered transparent. There are familiar examples of this *imaginaire* in Julian of Norwich's account of the bleeding head of Christ:

> The plentuoushede is lyke to the droppes of water that falle of the evesyng of an howse after a grete shower of reyne, that falle so thycke that no man may nomber them with no bodely wyt. And for the roundnesse they were lyke to the scale of heryng in the spredyng of the forhede. Thes thre thynges cam to my mynde in the tyme: pelettes for the roundhede in the comyng ouȝte of the blode, the scale of heryng for the roundhede in the spredyng, the droppes of the evesyng of a howse for the plentuoushede vnnumerable. Thys shewyng was quyck and lyuely and hidows and dredfulle and swete and louely; and of all the syght that I saw this was most comfort to me, that oure good lorde, that is so reverent and dredfulle, is so homely and so curteyse, and this most fulfyllyd me with lykyng and syckernes in soule.[46]

The images, and Julian's ambiguous emotional response to them, suggest an urge to 'domesticate' the horror, but also to imbue the domestic and

45 *Ancrene Wisse*, ed. by Millett, Part 8, vol. 1, p. 156; *Ancrene Wisse*, tr. White, p. 192.

46 *A Book of Showings to the Anchoress Julian of Norwich*, ed. by E. Colledge and J. Walsh, Studies and Texts 35 (Toronto 1978), rev. 1, ch. 7, vol. 2, pp. 312–13. For discussion of Julian's use of domestic imagery, see V. Gillespie, 'Strange Images of Death: The Passion in Later Medieval English Devotional and Mystical Writing', *Analecta Cartusiana*, 117 (1987), 110–59; V. Gillespie and M. Ross, 'The Apophatic Image: The Poetics of Effacement in Julian of Norwich', in M. Glasscoe (ed.), *The Medieval Mystical Tradition in England*, V (Cambridge, 1992), pp. 53–77.

'homely' with the force and horror of the original image and the substance of its subsequent significations – to charge it, in other words, with a paradoxical symbolic surplus that makes the familiar and the homely resonate in new and unsettling ways. As Julian says herself: 'This bodely exsample was shewde so hygh that thys mannes hart myght be rauyssched and almost foryet hym selfe for ioy of thys grette homelynesse.'[47]

The shock of the familiar can have defamiliarizing effects. In the Latin didactic moral treatise known as *Postquam* patience is described as a frying pan, poised on the flames of tribulation and hardship.[48] Similar examples are found in *A Revelation of Purgatory* (describing a fifteenth-century nun's visions of the afterlife):

> and onone a deuele tuke hir and threwe hir in to the medill fyre, þare me thought he had belowes in his hande and he blewe faste and me thoghte scho lay and fryed in þe fyre als it had ben fysche in hate oyle. And þane me thoughte he toke hir vpe agayne and led hir thurgh-owte alle þat medill fyre and euer als scho went þe blaknes of hir felle awaye as it had bene talowe of a candill whene it dropes for hete; and by þat scho come to þe end of þat grete fyre, me thoghte scho wexe alle rede and wele-coloured als it had bene blode-rede flesche.[49]

And also, more allegorically, in *The Pricking of Love*:

> This ȝifte of pite wondirli fryȝeth a mannys herte. and tendrith hit al-so; for a man hath soche loue to þe blod of crist. þat wenne he seeth goddis lawe broken and cristes blood despised … his herte þenne sorweth and brenyth and pynefully gronyth as hit were þrist in a friynge panne; hym þinketh þat he may not suffer cristes blod so be despised. And al-so wenne he seeth his broder lyue wel. And serue god in all virtues; and in mekenesse. þenne tendrith his herte and melteth in-to gladnesse.

---

47 *Book of Showings*, ed. by Colledge and Walsh, rev. 1, ch. 7, vol. 2, p. 314.

48 'Item [paciencia] est frixorium in quo uruntur electi ut leuiores fiant et Deo delectabiliores' (Moreover patience is a frying pan in which the elect are burned so that they may become lighter and more pleasing to God), *Summa Virtutum de Remediis Anime*, ed. by S. Wenzel, The Chaucer Library (Athens, GA, 1984), pp. 166–7.

49 *A Revelation of Purgatory* (Thornton MS), in C. Horstmann (ed.), *Yorkshire Writers: Richard Rolle of Hampole and His Followers*, 2 vols (London, 1895–6), vol. 1, p. 389.

> Als-so ihesu crist hym-self in his passioun fulfilled þese dedis of mercy. For to ȝyue vs ensaunple. he ȝaf his owne fleshe baken. With þe feer of brennande loue on þe auter off þe crosse; for to fede vs þat were storuen for hunger. And he ȝaf vs drynke of his owne precious blood.[50]

(The Eucharistic imagery here is worth recalling when considering the similar lexis and imagery in *The Doctrine of the Hert*.) In such images it is hard to see which way the symbolic knap is brushed; is this the domestic gesturing to the ineffable or the mystical engaging with the domestic? Such ambivalence is in the essential nature of metaphor. There is always likely to be an over-inscribed surplus of meaning in such imagery. Magisterial exegesis, such as that found in the Latin *De doctrina*, is designed to harness and control that imaginative surplus, but the imaginative power of personal allegoresis is hard to limit. Even the translator of the Middle English version seems to have struggled to keep his imagination in check as he engaged with the Latin text.

In the first part of the Middle English *Doctrine* such homely, household images are the main structuring devices for an allegory on preparing the heart to receive God: the preparation of the house for an honoured guest; the preparation of food; and the preparation of the bed chamber and spouse. The play of images in the second of these (cooking the banquet) is particularly rich and strange in the light of what we have already said. Using the story of the devout woman who supplied the prophet Elisha with a house equipped with a bed, table, stool and candlestick, the author spins out a domestic allegory whose social and cultural determination leads to a fetishizing of the imagery of a secular household. The swept house, the made bed, the enclosed garden and the besieged noblewoman all come and go as routine gestures towards the conventional taxonomy of imagery in texts of this kind. But while the Latin text surrounds the allegory with scriptural and patristic citations, squeezing the life out of the allegory and leaving it as a clearly subsidiary vehicle for a rather mechanistic exposition of ascetic doctrine, the Middle English text explores the same imagery from a less magisterial and therefore less secure vantage point. Because many of the scriptural proof texts and patristic authorities are omitted from the Middle English translation, and many of the mechanical unravellings of the allegory are elided together, the literal force of the domestic story asserts itself with greater force and exercises more concentrated and sustained imaginative power. The lexical choices of the translator place the spatial allegory

---

50 *The Prickynge of Love*, ed. by H. Kane, Salzburg Studies in English Literature, Elizabethan and Renaissance Studies 92:10 (Salzburg, 1983), pp. 49–50, 65.

tantalizingly on the threshold between spiritual allegory and romance narrative, and unleash powerful and sometimes contradictory imaginative forces into his text.

When *De doctrina* explores issues of food and cooking the writing becomes denser and more complex in its symbolic play, and particularly so in the vernacular version.[51] That the culinary structures envisaged in the Middle English relate to a lay household rather than a religious one is suggested by one slight but significant difference in the translation from the Latin:

> Latin: Cum enim claustrum intrasti, cor tuum posuisiti in coquina ... Et sicut coquina non debet esse sine igne, sic claustrum Domini non est sine tribulatione.[52]

> Middle English: Sister, whan þou entrest first þe cloyster of þi religioun þou puttist þin hert into Godis kychyn, þer for to be rostid in þe fire of tribulacioun. For right as a lordis kychyn shuld not be withoute fire, right so shuld not a cloyster be withoute tribulacioun.[53]

Whereas the Latin source refers to 'claustrum Domini' (the Lord's cloister), the lordly possessive is transferred in the Middle English from the cloister to the kitchen, turning it at a stroke into a very different representational space, drawing hungrily on secular imagery. This is alterity at work in a liberating revision of the imaginative space of the kitchen from a dead metaphor into a live act of homely remembrance. In the lordly kitchen of the Middle English text, flesh (which would have been an uncertain and perhaps rare part of a nun's diet) functions as an uneasy and unstable image,

---

51 The standard discussions of food imagery in such gendered religious contexts remain the essays collected in C.W. Bynum, *Holy Feast and Holy Fast: The Religious Significance of Food to Medieval Women* (Berkeley, CA, 1987) and *Fragmentation and Redemption: Essays on Gender and the Human Body in Medieval Religion* (New York, 1992). For a recent rumination on the impact of these essays, see N. Watson, 'Desire for the Paṣt', *Studies in the Age of Chaucer*, 21 (1999), 59–97.

52 References to the Latin *De doctrina cordis* are to Gerardus Leodiensis, *Speculum concionatorum ad illustrandum pectora auditorum, in septem libros distributum* (Naples, 1607), hereafter cited as *De doctrina*. This reference, p. 69, with the marginal gloss 'Claustrum est coquina' (For when you entered into the cloister you placed your heart into a kitchen. And just as a kitchen cannot exist without fire, so the Lord's cloister cannot exist without tribulation.) The *editio princeps* is Paris, 1506.

53 *Doctrine of the Hert*, p. 23, ll. 718–21.

a kind of suppressed surplus, part of the symbolic capital of a lay household which in a monastic or para-monastic environment becomes a superfluous commodity that registers, engages with and tempts towards a denied and rejected form of secular living.

In Middle English, the substantive 'mete' was routinely used to describe a range of foods, not just flesh. But it is clear from the large-scale allegories of cooking performed later in the book that fleshliness is an important part of the imaginary kitchen generated by the allegorical narrative. While the Latin text uses 'carnis' and 'cibus' variously (and often interchangeably) throughout its kitchen allegories, the Middle English is often more specific in its lexis. 'Mete' and flesh are closely bound up in the vernacular text. The Latin allegory always refers to the table as 'mensa', but the vernacular text translates this throughout as 'mete-table'. The 'mete-table' is introduced by way of the Bernardine quotation 'His mete is my penaunce.'[54] This penance invites Christ to visit the soul to attend a feast: 'He that mekly doth penaunce and hath gladnes and delite theryn, he biddith oure lorde to þe fest.'[55] As lord, he will dine regally and on the best food, in a scene that invokes precisely the kind of social performance that the audience would have turned their backs on through entering religion. The social space described in this scene can only be read symbolically by 'gostly sisters':

> The condicioun of al tho that biddyn þeire frendis to the fest; whan thei ben set and servid, because thei wold chere þeire frendes, first they begynne and tast of the same mete and than rehete þeire frendes. Right so, thi gladnes and meknes of thi penaunce, þe wiche is the duresse of religioun … is cause that he wille sitte with the and ete with the. This etyng of oure lord is the gladnes of the in thi penaunce.[56]

The status of the taboo object slithers around in this passage. Penance is 'mete' for God, but not only must the meat be prepared for him, it must first be tasted by the nun herself, which will then trigger 'This etyng of oure lord'. Syntactically this almost sounds as if the nun herself becomes the meat consumed by Christ (as in fact she will be later on). The forbidden or fetishized object is stripped of its primary signification by being turned into a representational space embodying (enfleshing) the duress of the hard regime of religious life, an explication that is not found in the Latin text. But even that needs to be further elided by the suppression of the forbidden

54 Ibid., p. 11, ll. 260–61.

55 Ibid., p. 11, ll. 261–62.

56 Ibid., p. 11, l. 262–p. 12, l. 268.

object in the next movement of this section. Here, generic and perhaps residually fleshly 'mete' becomes bread, specifically the bread that King David ate with Misiboseth as a sign of his reconciliation to him. Bread now supplants meat as the dominant (and imaginatively more manageable) image for penance: 'For brede in holy writ ofte tymes is callid penaunce, tribulaciouns and persecuciouns, be þe wiche þou shuldist be fulfillid and wex fat gostly be the meke suffraunce of hem.'[57] This is bread that the cloisterer shares with Christ himself (the Eucharistic image is now beginning to assert itself): 'This is a cloystreris bred; ete it gladly, sister. It is hard with such that etith þis brede grucchingly.'[58]

Lefebvre's sense that representational space 'serves to fragment desire and doom it to anxious frustration, to the non-satisfaction of local needs' is powerfully performed in the representational space of the meat-tasting dinner party which is transformed and reformed into the sour loaf of cloistral discipline, rather in the manner of Conscience's dinner party in passus 13 of *Piers Plowman*.[59] But a doctrinally correct interpretation of this social scene is always going to be a prerequisite for spiritual progress: it will go hard with the nun who does not eat the cloistral bread or grudges the change of imaginative and spiritual perspective it requires. Giving up the meat of the feast and settling for the bread of tribulation is part of the process of 'pulverizing the self'. Only the bread-which-is-not-meat of penance will make the nun spiritually fat. The hardships suffered by the nuns are as nothing compared to those of Christ: they are like a small morsel of bread dipped in the 'ayselle' (vinegar) of Christ's passion:

> Put it not away fro the, but tempere thi sorowis with his sorowis, and þou shalt fynde it þan a savery mete.
>
> There is also anoþer maner of sauce, the wich stont upon oure lordis owen table. That sause, yif it be usid, maketh al maner mete of penaunce swete. What is that sause, trowist þou? Trewly, mynde of endeles reward ... This is callid sause of aromatik, for what that ever is ete therwith is made swete.[60]

---

57 Ibid., p. 13, ll. 307–9.

58 Ibid., p. 13, ll. 313–14.

59 For discussion of this scene in *Piers Plowman* in the context of catechetic preparation and reform of earthly life, see V. Gillespie, 'Thy Will Be Done: *Piers Plowman* and the *Pater Noster*', in A.J. Minnis (ed.), *Middle English Religious Texts and Their Transmission: Essays in Honour of Ian Doyle* (Cambridge, 1994), pp. 95–119.

60 *Doctrine of the Hert*, p. 13, ll. 324–31.

The fetishized and suppressed 'meat' term has suddenly come charging back into the imaginative space, this time temptingly accompanied by a side order of sweet aromatic sauce.

The lexical range of 'mete' in *The Doctrine of the Hert* is problematic precisely because it is fuzzy and overlaps into various sorts of symbolic surplus and suppressed desire. It is associated with fleshly hunger:

> The fende aspieth ful sclily to what synne þou are most disposid, and þat synne he profreþ most, wenyng that þou hungrist lustes, and þerof he profreth the such mete as he hath for to sclake þin hunger. Do thou þan as a daungerous delicat womman, resceyve noon of his meete but þrow it ayen in his face! What is desire of the flesh but hunger of lustes?[61]

Even though the sense of 'mete' as a generic term for food is still dominant here, it is already becoming contaminated and extended. Hunger, desire for flesh-meat and sin are all linked together, and the representational space allows and indeed requires the performance of an act of secular petulance and courtly aloofness of a kind that no nunnery would ever have tolerated. 'Mete', hunger, lust and flesh all flow into each other.

Slightly later in the text, the nun's own heart must be readied 'as meete þat must be etyn.'[62] It is difficult to suppress the fleshly resonances of 'mete' in that image-set, especially when the passage continues: 'Oure lord Jhesu, that so tendirly and so merciably hath made himself redy to þe for to be etyn in the blessid sacrament of the aughter, axith the same of the that thou make þin hert redy for to be etyn of him.'[63] Christ is food and he is (rather worryingly) 'tendir'. Unlike the Eucharist, the image refuses to transubstantiate but remains imaginatively both bread and flesh. The fleshiness of Christ starts to permeate the text from this point on in a kind of incarnational leakage which more and more draws fleshly images into the lexical ambit of the generic term 'mete': Christ is the lamb. The Eucharist is fleshly meat: '"My flessh … is very gostly mete, and my blode is very gostly drynke."'[64] The manna eaten by the Israelites is not bread but 'Cristes flessh and his blood.' The heart of the nun must be flayed, roasted and basted in readiness for being eaten by Christ.

Heat, meat, eat: the text imaginatively loiters around the kitchen and is full of the work and smells of cooking. Isaac tells his son to 'bringe …

61 Ibid., p. 17, l. 488–p. 18, l. 493.

62 Ibid., p. 19, l. 569.

63 Ibid., p. 20, ll. 570–72.

64 Ibid., p. 21, ll. 643–44.

home summe mete bi his huntyng', and Jacob kills the young kid to 'make summe soupyng' for his father.[65] But Isaac will not eat the kid until it has been skinned and flayed. The text is suddenly awash with flesh and skin, and the allegory struggles to get the claustral space back into focus:

> Take þou þerfor, sister, þees too kedes, þi body and thi soule, and make þerof mete, able to be etyn and receyvid of hym, þin hevenly fadre … Thou must nedis flee þin hert fro þe olde skynne of his own wille, and also þi body fro þe skynne of temporal goodes, þat þou mow to þi lord be made able for to be receyvid.[66]

The messy business of readying food for the table always threatens to overwhelm the allegory of spiritual aspiration and penitential preparation. The head of any animal is the hardest part to flay, just as cloisterers who think of themselves as 'more discrete, more witty, and more kunnyng'[67] than other nuns will find it hardest to break their own will. The eel is a 'slyper fissh' to flay: likewise some nuns are slippery in always finding excuses to put off confronting their own evil wills. When the heart is finally flayed it must be roasted in the fire of tribulation. The heat of the fire is the hardness of religious life:

> the wiche a rawgh hert þat was never provyed, is rostid and made redy for to be receyvid of Cristes mouth, yif it have lardir of charite, ellis it farith in the rostyng as a lene hen: it wil raþer bren þan rost … for defaught of lardir … A lene hen is not wont to be rosted with another lene hen, but with a fatte hen.[68]

Likewise, a nun that lacks the fatness and the lard that comes from devotion and charity will be basted by the fatness of her spiritually plumper sisters. How close would this primal culinary scene – this representational space – be to the experience of most of its readers, inside and outside the cloister? Probably sufficiently close for its audacious imagery to engage with sublimated desires every bit as powerful and compelling as sex.

The physicality soon returns, with the next section describing how to tell when your heart is properly roasted 'by ensample þat kokes usyn.' A cook knows when 'flessh' is properly cooked in three ways: when it gives

65 Ibid., p. 22, ll. 656, 659.
66 Ibid., p. 22, ll. 667–69, 678–80.
67 Ibid., p. 23, ll. 691–92.
68 Ibid., p. 24, ll. 726–29, 731, 744–45.

to a fingernail pressed against it; when the blood is dried up, and when the meat falls away from the bone. These tips are to be remembered not for their culinary usefulness, of course, but because they offer another spatial representation that can be stripped of its literal sense and charged with a metaphorized and metonymized spiritual symbolism. But the Middle English text has to work hard here to invoke the higher plane of interpretation: 'Good sister, undirstonde weel þees thre þinges and kepe hem wel in þin hert.'[69] The Latin, more secure in the chilly allegory it has been unfolding, merely exhorts 'Hec tria in corde tuo considera' (Ponder these three things in your heart).[70] The assaying finger represents the testing of the 'sovereyne' or abbess of the house; the dried blood is the withdrawal of 'carnal affections' – and for once that glib phrase is re-charged with all sorts of juicy significance. The Middle English text keeps playing with the word 'carnel' for several paragraphs as if relishing a suppressed and forbidden word, rolling it round the mouth and savouring its lexical taste: 'Is it not a merveylos þing þat þine hert, þe wiche hath be so longe in Godis kechyn, is not yit dried up from al maner affeccioun of carnel frendes?'[71]

There is an unsettling attempt in this section to project the whole process of cooking back on to Christ in his passion –

> He was flayn whan his cloþis were take from hym and was put naked upon þe crosse. He was rostid upon þe spite of þe crosse be þe Jues, þe wiche were his kokis, in gret tribulacioun. But he was not brennyd because þe þrid wantid not, þe wiche was þe fatnes of charite that flowid oute be þe fyve gret holis of his body.
>
> What was ellis þe blood flowyng oute of his woundis, but þe holy anoynement of charite? Good sister, put undir þe panne of thin hert and gadre inow of þis precious oynement, and þan schalt þou lakke no lardir in tyme of tribulacioun.[72]

– unsettling because it presents the familiar Passion narrative in a strange and domestic light, with the crucifixion as a kind of macabre barbecue, whose physicality gets under the familiar defences engendered by long exposure to that brutal story. The text has drifted from a fairly abstract use of food imagery in its opening movement to an increasingly physical,

69 Ibid., p. 25, ll. 783–84.

70 *De doctrina*, p. 77.

71 *Doctrine of the Hert*, p. 26, ll. 811–13.

72 Ibid., p. 25, ll. 769–77.

dynamic and disturbing scenario of cooking. This is much more intensely the case in the Middle English version as its excisions and elisions from the Latin text remove much of the exegetical framework and argumentative *ordinatio* that serve to keep the narrative elements under the control of the interpretative decorums of religious allegory. In the Latin, each of the cooking acts described above is supported by an array of typological and other proof texts; the allegory is always the junior partner in the work of the text, and always subordinate to the orthodox exegetical framework that constrains and directs it. By virtue of the translator's artful syncopation of the sections of the Latin original, however, in the Middle English text we are brought imaginatively and directly into this powerful scene of the secular household at work over the spit before a great feast. But the food to be roasted is the heart of each nun. The household is now the self.

Once the heart has been prepared 'as mete that shuld be etyn', the nun is ready to be arrayed as the bride of Jesus, who is, in a curious hangover from the kitchen scene, described throughout the next chapter as 'the lombe'.[73] The power of this imagery is such that the text is here forced to exhort its audience: 'Good sister, undirstonde þis gostly and not flesshly.'[74] At the literal level of the metaphor, spiritual union becomes an unsettling act of mutual cannibalism: Christ eats the heart of the nun as she eats the lamb in the Eucharist. Mystical marriage is a 'maner tastyng of swetnes of joye.'[75] The nun is reminded of her 'tendre' age, of the needs of other 'tendre' novices and of 'tendre' souls. The nun should stay away from 'unclene wordis' and 'flesshly loveris', as if being asked to become a spiritual vegetarian and observe food taboos. None of the equivalent Latin terms have these adjectival enhancements. It is as if the text can't resist playing teasingly with the fleshy lexis it has finally released into the narrative.

It is really only in this cooking section of the *Doctrine* that the allegory takes fire, as it were, and it does so much more fiercely in the Middle English than in the Latin, which is much more carefully fitted up with a carapace of interpretative proof texts and exposition. Because so much of this is streamlined in the Middle English version, the allegorical spaces are allowed more powerful alterity, more imaginative purchase on the representational space, and more profound engagement with an absent household imaginary. The vernacular text, by its focus on the narrative trajectory of the allegorical vehicle, its enrichment of the lexis of the narrative and its omission of much of the clericalized apparatus of proof texts, generates what

73 Ibid., p. 27, l. 874.

74 Ibid., p. 28, l. 887.

75 Ibid., p. 31, ll. 1012–13.

Lefebvre would call an *heterotopia* (p. 163), a contradictory place, a place that contrasts with the everyday life of its target audience. By virtue of the vitality of its realisation of the allegory, the Middle English text also makes possible an engagement with the *imaginaire* of any secular readers who come into contact with it. It seeks to teach its audience how to jump out of the frying pan of secular domesticity into the fire of spiritual self-annihilation, but occasionally gets singed by the heat of its own imaginative play.

6

The Doctrine of the Hert and its Manuscript Context[1]

Catherine Innes-Parker

The Doctrine of the Hert is a fifteenth-century translation of the thirteenth-century *De doctrina cordis*, intended as an instructional text for 'symple soules, which oure lord bought with his precious blode and therto also hathe chosyn to his spouses, as ben thoo that dwellyn in religioun'[2] – in other words, nuns. The place of the Middle English *Doctrine* in the broader corpus of vernacular theology in fifteenth-century England has yet to be addressed, but its manuscript context suggests that it has much to teach us concerning both the rise of vernacular theology among female religious readers and the appropriation of devotional works by lay readers – and the concern that the spread of vernacular theology aroused among the clerical authors and adaptors of such texts.

The movement of vernacular theology from the context of the convent into the lay realm was both a response to a growing demand among lay readers for guides to private devotion and a catalyst for the rise of individual devotional practices that began to challenge (albeit quietly and without dissent) the domination of the institutional church over private

1 I would like to thank the Social Sciences and Humanities Research Council of Canada for the funding which made the initial research for this paper possible. I would also like to thank the University of Prince Edward Island Office of Research and Development and the Research Grants Committee for funding to attend the *Rhetoric of the Anchorhold/Doctrine of the Hert* Conference at Gregynog, Wales, in July 2005, where this paper was first presented.

2 C. Whitehead, D. Renevey and A. Mouron (eds), *The Doctrine of the Hert: A Critical Edition with Introduction and Commentary* (Exeter, 2010), p. 3, ll. 15–17. Hereafter abbreviated as *Doctrine of the Hert*.

thought and practice. As Nicholas Watson has shown, Archbishop Arundel's Constitutions of 1409 and the official licencing of Nicholas Love's *Mirror of the Blessed Life of Jesus Christ*[3] were an attempt to control the movement of devotional texts into the lay world.[4] However, the continuing translation of devotional works into Middle English for female religious and lay audiences and the history of the ownership of manuscripts containing vernacular theology of all kinds in the fifteenth century clearly shows that Arundel's attempt to bridle lay (and women) readers was unsuccessful. The connection between Middle English writings and Lollardy that underlay Arundel's concern was too simplistic, and the church's own encouragement of vernacular instructional texts in response to the Fourth Lateran Council had begun a process which was too far advanced to suppress.[5] Nevertheless,

---

3 Nicholas Love, *The Mirror of the Blessed Life of Jesus Christ*, ed. by M.G. Sargent (Exeter, 2005).

4 N. Watson, 'Censorship and Cultural Change in Late-Medieval England: Vernacular Theology, the Oxford Translation Debate, and Arundel's Constitutions of 1409', *Speculum*, 70 (1995), 822–64. Watson has refined (and somewhat tempered) his discussion in further articles, particularly 'Visions of Inclusion: Universal Salvation and Vernacular Theology in Pre-Reformation England', *Journal of Medieval and Early Modern Studies*, 27 (1997), 145–87 and '*Ancrene Wisse*, Religious Reform and the Late Middle Ages', in Y. Wada (ed.), *A Companion to The Ancrene Wisse* (Cambridge, 2003), pp. 197–226.

5 The anxiety created by Arundel's Constitutions and their disapprobation of translation into the vernacular is discussed by A. Sutherland, '*The Chastising of God's Children*: A Neglected Text', in H. Barr and A.M. Hutchison (eds), *Text and Controversy from Wyclif to Bale: Essays in Honour of Anne Hudson* (Turnhout, 2005), pp. 353–74, and by N. Watson, 'The Composition of Julian of Norwich's *Revelation of Love*', *Speculum*, 68 (1993), 637–83, and 'Conceptions of the Word: The Mother Tongue and the Incarnation of God', in W. Scase, R. Copeland and D. Lawton (eds), *New Medieval Literatures 1* (Oxford, 1997), pp. 85–124. The ongoing use of the vernacular in spite of such attempts to suppress it is discussed by J. Simpson, 'Saving Satire after Arundel's *Constitutions*: John Audelay's "Marcol and Solomon"', in Barr and Hutchison (eds), *Text and Controversy*, pp. 387–404. For further discussion of the challenge that vernacular theology raised to conventional, clerical authority see, among others, E. Duffy, *The Stripping of the Altars: Traditional Religion in England c. 1400–c. 1580* (New Haven, CI, 1992); S. Beckwith, *Christ's Body: Identity, Culture and Society in Late Medieval Writings* (London, 1993); E.M. Ross, *The Grief of God: Images of the Suffering Jesus in Late Medieval England* (Oxford, 1997), and especially R.N. Swanson, 'Passion and Practice: the Social and Ecclesiastical Implications of Passion Devotion in the Late Middle Ages', in A.A. MacDonald et al. (eds), *The Broken Body: Passion Devotion in Late-Medieval Culture* (Groningen, 1998), pp. 1–30.

clerical unease with the increasing availability of vernacular devotional works remained. Both in the convent and in the lay world, devotional works which encouraged private meditation and the imaginative reconstruction of the passion also encouraged individual access to the divine that was not necessarily dependent upon the mediation of church and cleric. But, when texts intended to guide the reader in the 'chamber of the heart'[6] moved into the private chamber of the manor, this meant that devotional teachings and practices also became accessible without the foundation of a conventual education or rule. Outside of the convent walls, Arundel attempted to restrict the circulation of texts which encouraged private, lay devotion and failed. Within the convent, however, there were other ways of dealing with the growth of individual devotional practices. Some, like the author of *The Chastising of God's Children*,[7] actively discouraged private prayer and devotion. Others, however, encouraged the establishment of individual devotional practices within the context of the conventual life, practices which were not only governed by rule and reclusion, but founded in reading programmes which developed individual prayer and meditation

---

6 The concept of the 'chamber of the heart' became important with the rise of affective devotion in the twelfth century. Anselm of Canterbury begins chapter 1 of his *Proslogion* thus: 'Come now, little man,/turn aside for a while from your daily employment,/escape for a moment from the tumult of your thoughts./Put aside your weighty cares,/let your burdensome distractions wait,/free yourself awhile for God/and rest awhile in him./Enter the inner chamber of your soul,/ shut out everything except God/and that which can help you in seeking him,/and when you have shut the door, seek him./Now, my whole heart, say to God,/"I seek your face,/Lord, it is your face I seek."' *The Prayers and Meditations of Saint Anselm with the Proslogion*, tr. Sister B. Ward (London, 1973), p. 239. Although the *Proslogion* was written at the request of Anselm's brethren, many of Anselm's prayers and meditations were, in fact, addressed to educated lay readers, and the concept of the 'chamber of the heart' was quickly adopted (and adapted) by others, including writers of guidance literature for women, who placed it within a firmly religious setting. For example, the author of the *Ancrene Wisse* likens the chamber of the heart to the anchorhold in which his readers are enclosed, and founds his discussion of the meditation which occurs in the chamber of the heart in the ascetic, enclosed life which they lead. *Ancrene Wisse: A Corrected Edition of the Text in Cambridge, Corpus Christi College, MS 402 with Variants from Other Manuscripts*, ed. by B. Millett, vol. 1, EETS OS 325 (2005), pp. 36–7; cp. 39, p. 133. The concept continued to be adapted in guidance literature right through to the fifteenth century, addressed to both lay and religious readers.

7 *The Chastising of God's Children and the Treatise of Perfection of the Sons of God*, ed. by J. Bazire and E. Colledge (Oxford, 1957).

through instruction rooted in the communal life of the convent. Indeed, I will argue, the fifteenth-century clerical scribes who penned two of the surviving copies of the *Doctrine* may have intended it, along with its companion texts, to lay a firm conventual groundwork for its readers before they moved on to devotional works which stressed private devotion and individual access to the divine.[8]

The Doctrine of the Hert survives in four manuscripts dating from the early to the mid fifteenth century, all of which are suitable for private reading, small enough to be held easily in the hand. The two earliest manuscripts, Oxford, Bodleian Library, MS Laud Misc. 330 and Cambridge, Trinity College, MS B.14.15, contain only the *Doctrine*. In the other two, Durham, University Library, MS Cosin V.III.24 and Cambridge, Fitzwilliam Museum, MS McClean 132, the *Doctrine* is followed by two other treatises: 'A letter of religious gouernaunce sent to a religious woman' and 'A letter sent to a religious womman of þe twelue frutes of þe Holy Gost', edited together by J.J. Vaissier as *The Tree & xii. Frutes of the Holy Goost* (and hereafter referred to as the *Tree* and the *Twelve Fruits*, respectively).[9] Both texts, like the *Doctrine*, are clearly addressed to nuns, and together the three texts form a detailed examination of the communal spirituality of the convent and the devotional progress of the individual nun.

What is known of the medieval provenance of manuscripts containing the *Doctrine* and the *Tree* and the *Twelve Fruits* bears out the internal evidence of the texts: the treatises were owned by women religious, although they also reached a wider audience, particularly among lay women. MS B.14.15 (containing the *Doctrine* alone) was owned by Christina St Nicholas, a Franciscan minoress of London, who donated the manuscript to the 'office of the abbessey' upon her death in 1455.[10] London, British Library, MS Add. 24192 (containing only the *Tree* and the *Twelve Fruits*) was annotated

8 Indeed, this may have been at least part of the purpose behind the translation of *De doctrina* into Middle English, and was certainly on the agenda of the author of *The Tree & xii. Frutes of the Holy Goost*. *A Deuout Treatyse Called the Tree & xii. Frutes of the Holy Goost*, ed. by J.J. Vaissier (Groningen, 1960).

9 These treatises also survive, on their own, in London, British Library, MS Add. 24192, and were printed by Robert Coplande in 1534 (STC 13608; see *Deuout Treatyse*, ed. Vaissier, pp. xxixff.). All citations from the *Tree* and the *Twelve Fruits* are from Vaissier's edition.

10 D.N. Bell points out that in 1455 the abbess of the London minorites at the Abbey of BVM and St Botolph without Aldgate was one 'Christina' (*What Nuns Read: Books and Libraries in Medieval English Nunneries* (Kalamazoo, 1995), p. 149).

by Dorothy Coderington, a sixteenth-century nun of Syon, which also owned at least two printed editions of the text.[11] MS Laud Misc. 330 also has a tenuous, but unproven, connection to Syon.[12] Finally, in her will of 1481, Margaret Purdans, a widow of St Giles', Norwich, left a copy of 'le Doctrine of the herte' to Bruisyard, an East Anglian Franciscan convent, 'after the death of the Lady Margaret Yaxley.' Margaret Yaxley was a nun at Bruisyard in 1480.[13]

Of the two manuscripts which combine the *Doctrine* with the *Tree* and the *Twelve Fruits*, however, little is known. MS McClean 132 is a deluxe manuscript, perhaps a presentation copy, which was copied in the south, possibly in London. MS Cosin V.III.24 is a plainer manuscript in several hands, probably copied in Norfolk.[14] Yet it is these two manuscripts which

---

11 Dorothy Coderington's signature appears in Ampleforth Abbey, MS C.v.130, and Margaret Windsor, prioress of Syon in 1518 and 1539, owned Cambridge, Trinity College, MS C.7.12. See *Deuout Treatyse*, ed. Vaissier, pp. xxv and xxxii–xxviii, and Bell, *What Nuns Read*, pp. 176 and 183.

12 At the end of the *Doctrine* the short lyric 'Syke and sorowe deeply' is written out. Sister M.P. Candon points out the existence of these lines in manuscripts of the *Mirror of Simple Souls*, 'but in very few others connected with religious and devout women', in the introduction to her earlier doctoral edition of the *Doctrine* (Sister M.P. Candon (ed.), '*The Doctrine of the Hert*, Edited from the Manuscripts with Introduction and Notes' (unpublished doctoral dissertation, Fordham University, 1963), p. ix). More recently, however, Pollard has identified nine fifteenth-century manuscripts in which this lyric occurs, in combination with the *Mirror of Simple Souls*, *The Chastising of God's Children*, the works of Rolle, Hilton, Suso, St Bridget, and Julian of Norwich. The lines also occur at the end of *The Feitis and the Passion of Oure Lord Jhesu Crist*, a prayer cycle written by an enclosed woman religious for a 'religious sister,' and the first of two texts in Oxford, Bodleian Library, MS Holkham Misc. 41. Three of these manuscripts are ascribed to Sheen Charterhouse, and Pollard has argued that the lyric may have had some special connection to Syon. W.F. Pollard, 'Bodleian MS Holkham Misc. 41: a Fifteenth-Century Bridgettine Manuscript and Prayer Cycle', *Birgittiana*, 3 (1997), 43–53 (pp. 45–46).

13 Bell, *What Nuns Read*, pp. 121–2.

14 MS Cosin V.III.24 was written by three different scribes, one of whom Vaissier tentatively identifies as, possibly, John Shirley (d. 1456). The second scribe was Robert Bailey, possibly a Carmelite from Burnham, Norfolk (d. 1503), and the third, one 'Willelmus', who copied the *Twelve Fruits* (*Deuout Treatyse*, ed. Vaissier, pp. xv–xx). Stocks and Doyle suggest that the first main scribe was a commercial copyist, with a hand similar to that of the second southern scribe of Cambridge, University Library, MS Hh.i.11 and to scribes of Bury St Edmunds. The manuscript has been carefully corrected, leading them to conjecture that it

I wish to focus on, combining as they do the three treatises. I would like to outline here some of the effects of this affiliation, and to suggest a possible reason for it. In particular, I will explore two issues that have emerged from my study of these texts: the question of how manuscripts are structured to guide readers through a programme of spiritual development, and the question of how professional religious women's devotional instruction influenced lay devotional reading and practice.

Candon quite rightly identifies the *Doctrine* as an ascetical rather than a mystical treatise, which begins with the preparation of the heart through purgation and moves the reader to the threshold of union with Christ in its final exploration of ecstatic love.[15] Yet the author clearly expects a certain amount of spiritual progress on the part of its readers following on from the text as it stands: the final book is manifestly a beginning, not an end, as the reader is instructed in the cutting of the heart from all carnal affections, that she may experience the sweetness of the love of God, which is described in some detail.

The Middle English 'compiler' indicates that the treatise is intended to be read or heard,[16] suggesting that it would be useful both for private devotion and for public reading in the convent. It is this dual purpose that makes the *Doctrine* so adaptable, as it, like other Middle English devotional works initially addressed to an audience of female professional religious, moves into the lay world. In addition, the literary and imaginative richness of both the *Doctrine* and its companion texts places it well within the tradition of vernacular devotion that appealed so readily to lay readers. The treatise abounds with metaphors, divisions, subdivisions and enumeration, but unlike Candon (who refers to 'the monotony of the constant mathematical divisions and banal repetitions'),[17] I would argue that these are helpful as an aid to the reader's memory as well as a 'way in' to a text that is not necessarily intended to be read straight through, but to be 'picked at' and meditated upon.[18]

---

was 'probably prepared as an exemplar for further and fairer copies.' There is space left for initials at the opening of the *Tree* (three-line) and the *Twelve Fruits* (four-line) but the decoration is not complete (E.V. Stocks, with revisions by A.I. Doyle, 'Draft Catalogue of Medieval Manuscripts in the University Library' (unpublished catalogue, Durham University). The manuscript belonged to 'Iohannes Waynfleet', the Dean of Chichester (d. 1481).

15 Candon, *Doctrine*, p. lvi.

16 *Doctrine of the Hert*, p. 3, l. 31.

17 Candon, *Doctrine*, p. lxxix.

18 The author of the *Ancrene Wisse* specifically recommends such reading strategies. He tells his anchoritic readers to read from his book each day when they

Indeed, the author's repeated advice to engaging in holy reading, devout prayer and meditation is reinforced by the authorial strategy of division and subdivision, as well as by the use of metaphor and enumeration. For example, in book 3 (on knowledge) readers are instructed to open their hearts as a book, equating the book of the conscience, which is to be read in this life, to the book whereby readers shall be judged. The author identifies three lessons to be read in the book of conscience: sorrow for the sin, peril and wretchedness of the world; songs of joy for everlasting bliss, and woe for everlasting damnation. He then outlines seven hindrances to opening the book, imaged as seven clasps which bind the book, and compared in some detail to the seven seals of the Apocalypse. Once the apocalyptic lamb has opened the clasps one can clearly read the book of the conscience. The reader is then ready to open her heart as a door, through which she can welcome her beloved guest, Christ. The seven hindrances, which include defending, excusing and hiding sin; the dangers of worldly communion and the love of the world; and the peril of Hell in contrast to the joy of Heaven, refer the reader specifically back to the three lessons to be read in the book of the conscience. Indeed, meditating upon and overcoming these hindrances inevitably leads to the 'reading' of the lessons themselves. The author's strategy of division and enumeration is an aid to such meditation, which, with such mnemonic aids, is no longer restricted to the actual moment of reading. The 'reader' can 'read' the book of the conscience, even when she is not reading the *Doctrine.*

From this point in the text, knowledge and its interpretation become central. In book 4 the heart is grounded in the twelve articles of faith, which stabilize understanding through spiritual strength. Book 5 focuses

---

are at leisure. He also tells them that it is meant to be read in two ways: straight through, or in bits and pieces, often referring back to what he has said earlier. He recommends an 'intertextual' approach to reading, referring the anchoresses to other books which they might own, such as an English translation of the Life of St Margaret, and a description of the joys of heaven, which might refer to *Hali Meiðhad* or *Sawles Warde* (*Ancrene Wisse*, ed. Millett, p. 93, l. 931 and p. 154, ll. 113–14). Finally, he reinforces the importance of reading by recommending that holy reading is even more important than prayer (Ibid., p. 109, ll. 1553–6). The author of the *Doctrine* frequently echoes imagery and ideas familiar to readers of the *Ancrene Wisse*. This does not necessarily imply that the author knew the *Ancrene Wisse*, but since the *Ancrene Wisse* is the earliest example of a Middle English instructional text for enclosed women, and draws upon Latin forerunners such as Aelred of Rievaulx's *De institutione inclusarum*, it is not unlikely that its imagery was drawn from (and contributed to) a familiar set of themes and metaphors that continued to influence writing for women religious.

on counsel, which enables the reader to know to whom her heart should be given and how. Book 6, on understanding, focuses on thinking with the heart through holy meditation, and book 7, the final preparation for the soul's union with God through love, speaks of wisdom as the knowledge of the sweetness of God, which can be experienced in this life as ecstatic love.

In light of the emphasis on reading in the *Doctrine*, it is interesting that in its final chapter the author describes spiritual, ecstatic love by comparing it to seven tokens of amorous, fleshly love – tokens that would be more than familiar to readers of medieval romance. Like the *Ancrene Wisse*'s metaphor of the Christ-Knight, this comparison draws upon the imagery of chivalric love: its effects on the lover and the response of the beloved. Similarly, in book 5, the text echoes a number of images also found in the *Ancrene Wisse*, as the author asks if the heart is to be sold, riven from us by force when we try to put it away, or freely given – and, if given, who better to give it to than Christ, our beloved, who has given his heart in return for ours.[19] In some feminist analyses of such imagery, the appeal to the reader of romance is regarded with a certain condescension (bordering on scorn), which proposes that readers of secular romance (i.e. women and laypersons) were considered by the authors of these texts to be too simple to cope with the complexities of the kind of religious treatise addressed to male, clerical audiences.[20] Such readings suggest that these authors 'dumb down' their texts for women whose reading before entering the convent was the medieval equivalent of a Harlequin romance.[21] Contrary to such readings, I would argue that this appeal to readers of secular romance is an appeal to a sophisticated reading strategy that they would have brought with them from the secular world. Readers are expected to be able to read the metaphors in this text with the same kind of scrutiny (and, indeed,

---

19 See *Ancrene Wisse*, ed. Millett, part 7, p. 149, l. 184–p. 150, l. 206. The *Ancrene Wisse* is the first text to introduce such imagery into vernacular devotion.

20 See, for example, E. Robertson, *Early Devotional Prose and the Female Audience* (Knoxville, Tennessee, 1990), ch. 4 *passim*, esp. pp. 70–74; and R. Bradley, 'In the Jaws of the Bear: Journeys of Transformation by Women Mystics', *Vox Benedictina*, 8 (1991), 116–75, especially pp. 132–43.

21 For a more detailed discussion of the issues involved here, and an alternate reading, see my articles 'The Lady and the King: *Ancrene Wisse*'s Parable of the Royal Wooing Re-examined', *English Studies*, 75 (1994), 509–22, and '*Ancrene Wisse* and *Þe Wohunge of Ure Lauerd*: The Thirteenth-Century Female Reader and the Lover-Knight', in J. Taylor and L. Smith (eds), *Women, the Book and the Godly* (Cambridge, 1995), pp. 137–47.

introspection) demanded of the readers of complex and multi-valent metaphors of romance, such as Gawain's pentangle and Orfeo's harp.

The *Doctrine* thus explores the spiritual world of the convent using complex literary devices that would have resonated in the minds of its readers. In a similar manner, book 1 uses familiar household imagery to represent the spiritual preparation of the heart for God, comparing the heart to a house that is to be cleaned and arrayed, meat that is to be cooked, and a bride who is to be adorned. Renevey has shown that the homely but detailed metaphors of domesticity are complex and compelling and, indeed, particularly suited to their female audience.[22]

If the *Doctrine* prepares the heart for God within the context of the virtuous conventual life, the *Tree* and the *Twelve Fruits* move to the growth of the heart in devotion. Although there is no evidence that the author of these two texts was specifically responding to the *Doctrine* (or even knew it),[23] the compilers of MS Cosin V.III.24 and MS McClean 132 chose to follow the *Doctrine* with the two letters which comprise the *Tree* and the *Twelve Fruits*, and their inclusion is not a random one. The compilers clearly saw a connection between the material contained in the *Doctrine* and the *Tree* and the *Twelve Fruits* and chose to combine the three texts in order to create a sequence that would provide a complex examination of the spiritual life of the nuns to whom they are addressed.

The *Tree* continues the use of complex metaphor, as the nun is compared to a tree planted in the garden of religion, which must be rooted in meekness, and watered by compunction. Its branches are pruned by the renunciation of worldly goods, they spread broadly through charity, and grow tall through contemplation. In addition, the *Tree* also includes metaphors drawn from

---

22 D. Renevey, 'Household Chores in *The Doctrine of the Hert*: Affective Spirituality and Subjectivity', in C. Beattie, A. Maslakovic and S. Rees Jones (eds), *The Medieval Household in Christian Europe c.850–c.1550: Managing Power, Wealth, and the Body* (Turnhout, 2003), pp. 167–85. See also Vincent Gillespie's article in this volume. Again, this is a device familiar from the *Ancrene Wisse*, which uses the anchoress's daily life and surroundings to image her spiritual development. See Savage and Watson's introduction to their translation of the *Ancrene Wisse* (A. Savage and N. Watson (eds and trans), *Anchoritic Spirituality: Ancrene Wisse and Associated Works* (New York, 1991)) and my article 'Fragmentation and Reconstruction: Images of the Female Body in *Ancrene Wisse* and the Katherine Group', *Comitatus*, 26 (1995), 27–53.

23 It is important here to remember that the *Doctrine* is a fifteenth-century translation of a thirteenth-century text. The date and authorship of the *Tree* and the *Twelve Fruits* is not known, but the treatises survive in mid- to late-fifteenth-century manuscripts.

the daily life of the nun, as does the *Twelve Fruits*, changing daily 'routine' into a means of personal and communal growth.[24]

The author's focus is always on the communal life, and much of the discussion of prayer and meditation centres around the divine service. Prayer, he tells his readers, can be both vocal (spoken and sung during the canonical hours) and mental (meditation in the soul).[25] Meditation on Christ's passion is particularly recommended, both as a means of focusing the mind during the divine service[26] and in the 'pryuy chaumbre of [the] hert.'[27] Indeed, in addition to the focus on the communal prayer of the divine service, private reading, prayer and meditation are also urged. In some cases, even private prayer has a communal focus: for example, intercessory prayer is recommended 'after none whan þou walkist in þe gardyn.'[28]

At other times, however, private prayer is centered on the individual nun's devotional relationship with Christ. The reader is particularly urged to morning meditation, for 'such mentall prayeris bi meditacioun is right swete, meritorie, and precious to a deuoute soule.'[29] However, the author advises: 'if þou wilt come to such mery mornyng of meditacioun, þou must as moche as þou mayst sequester þi self from al maner outeward noyses and distracciouns, and so entre in to þe pryuy chaumbre of þin hert and þere exclude alle þinges be nethe god.'[30] Apparently, even in the cloister distractions occur, and it is necessary to enter the chamber of the heart, which is enclosed in the nun's cell, itself enclosed in the cloister and the convent.

Private prayer is intended to be accompanied and inspired by passion meditation, the ultimate flowering of mental prayer. Contemplation is thus both intense and affective: 'Seye þerfor with þe same holy bernard, and say it inwardly and ententefolly þus: O good ihesu how myghtily þou clippidest me, and embraced me to þe with þin holy armes of þi passiun … O good

---

24 See, for example, the *Tree*'s description of the nun's spiritual clothing (*Deuout Treatyse*, ed. Vaissier, p. 7), the contrast between the nun's life before entering into religion with the daily life of the convent (ibid., p. 10), and the discussion of visitors (ibid., p. 13) and benefactors (ibid., p. 15). The *Twelve Fruits* uses images of clothing, gardening, harvest, commerce, servants, nursing mothers and others.

25 Ibid., pp. 18f., p. 22.

26 Ibid., pp. 19–22.

27 Ibid., p. 29. Passion meditation pervades this text, and is also useful for the teaching of patience, and for arming the soul against spiritual enemies.

28 Ibid., p. 27.

29 Ibid., p. 28.

30 Ibid., pp. 28–9, my punctuation.

ihesus þou lovedist me þan ful hoot.'[31] As a result, although mental prayer is intended to be silent, often, the author suggests, it 'must nedis breke oute and sende oute his flaumys and lemys of loue' and 'persith heuen'.[32] This focus on passion meditation is, in fact, implicit throughout the text, as passion meditation is linked to the metaphor of the nun as a tree being planted (in humility, modelled by Christ's nativity, 'conversations' and passion),[33] pruned (by despising temporal goods, modelled by the poverty of Christ in his birth, life and passion),[34] and finally growing to its full height or maturity (through prayer and meditation). Passion meditation thus shapes not only the nun's communal and private prayer, but also her communal life and individual virtue.

At the end of the text, the author observes that the tree must bear the twelve fruits of the Holy Ghost, but laments that he does not have leisure to speak of these. He returns to this subject in the final treatise, the *Twelve Fruits*, where he outlines the twelve fruits in twelve chapters, echoing the structural pattern of the *Doctrine*. The fruits are, in order: Charity, Joy, Peace, Patience, Sufferance (or perseverance in prayer), Goodness, Benignity (or gentleness of heart), Mildness, Faith (here defined as faithful living, not the articles of faith, which the author assumes that his readers adhere to as does he),[35] Manner of Good Living (or moderation), Continence and Chastity (specifically *not* virginity which, the author suggests, is much easier than chastity. Chastity denotes purity of life *after* falling and is therefore more difficult). Each chapter describes a single fruit, outlines how that fruit is to be achieved (often using the same technique of enumeration and classification as the *Doctrine*), and ends with its four virtues. The *Tree* and the *Twelve Fruits*, then, provide a structure which guides the nuns through the stages of their devout communal life, as well as addressing their individual spiritual growth.

Once again, the *Twelve Fruits* abounds with metaphors of battle, buildings, fire, weather, plants and fields. Again, too, the author seems to expect a complex reading which will lead to progress in spiritual growth. One example will suffice, although there are many. In chapter 2, on Joy, the author outlines twenty causes of spiritual joy which (parallelling the kind of progression already seen in the *Doctrine*) move the reader through an initial process of contrition and confession to the virtuous life within the

31 Ibid., p. 32.

32 Ibid., p. 28.

33 Ibid., p. 1.

34 Ibid., p. 17.

35 The articles of faith are clearly outlined in the *Doctrine*, book 4.

convent, climaxing with the joy of contemplation. The section is carefully structured. The first five causes outline the joy of a clean conscience, discharged from the burden of sin through contrition and freed from the bonds of the fiend by confession to a condition of rest from the torment of evil affections and remorse. The next five outline the virtue and devotion of good living, in which virtue won through grace leads to reward, the witness of the Holy Ghost to a devout life leads to the soul's security, and the counsel of the Holy Ghost leads to fellowship. The next four describe the contemplative life that the nuns, spared from the labour of active life, are called to, reminding them that their meditation lifts them above earthly things to rest in the sight of heaven, and that their spiritual occupations of reading and praying will bring them into Christ's presence, where they will have direct speech with him. The final six recount the benefits of such holy living, including the easy yoke of divine love and gladness of the soul. The twentieth cause of spiritual joy, and its climax, is contemplation leading to spiritual illumination.

Contemplation is described in a delightful metaphor as rivers of honey and butter. The honey of the godhead of Christ is gathered from the flowers and the air, as the gentle bee of cleanness brings the honey of contemplation of sweet heavenly things to the hive of the soul. Similarly, as butter is churned from milk gathered from a cow, so too the butter of the passion (representing Christ's manhood) is churned on the cross, and gathered from the bitter pains of Christ's body through contemplation; tender compunction then brings the butter of Christ's passion to the churn of the heart, in order to make it soft and supple. As the contemplative soul sucks the honey and eats the butter, it attains rest, sureness, delight, joy, love and savour in Christ. However, this grace of contemplation is given only to those whom Christ inspires to forsake the world, as he leads the soul by herself, and speaks to her heart when she is alone, giving her suck of his sweetness and love, stirring her to holy prayers, meditation and tears. The soul, Christ's spouse, experiences divine sweetness and love. Finally, as she gathers her heart together and sets it in Christ, he opens the gates of heaven to the eye of the soul and kindles the fire of love in her heart.[36] Again, the text echoes much of the imagery of the *Ancrene Wisse*, yet moves beyond it, explicitly calling the soul who achieves this state a contemplative soul, ravished in the love of God.

The *kind* of contemplation envisioned here, and the specific means of achieving it, are not explicitly described. However, the *Tree* and the *Twelve*

---

36 *Deuout Treatyse*, ed. Vaissier, pp. 59–61.

Fruits are not intended as 'stand alone' instruction; rather, these texts are envisioned as one step in a continuum, from which the nuns are intended to progress to other, more complex texts. In the *Tree*, the author stresses the importance of reading as a means of eschewing idleness and refreshing the soul in prayer and meditation.[37] In particular, he states:

> Also I wold þou were occupied, namly on haly dayes with redyng of deuoute bokes, as is Stimulus amoris or such oþer. In þe wich specialy I recomende to þi meditacioun þe holy passioun of oure lord ihesu, and namly after complyn and after matynes, and leve it wel: it shal enflawme þi soule feruently in his loue.[38]

The author of the *Tree*, then, recommends that his nuns move on from his instruction to further reading: specifically, passion meditation and the *Stimulus amoris*.[39] Indeed, the *Stimulus* explores precisely the kind of meditation which would bring this complex series of metaphors to life, as it elaborates upon many of the concepts and metaphors encountered in the *Doctrine*, the *Tree* and the *Twelve Fruits*, applying them specifically to the individual soul's meditation upon and response to the passion.[40]

The Middle English *Stimulus amoris*, a translation of James of Milan's treatise on meditation and the contemplative life, survives, in whole or in part, in sixteen manuscripts, which range from manuscripts containing the *Stimulus* alone to large collections of devotional material such as the Vernon and Simeon manuscripts. Of those whose medieval provenance is known, all were owned by or associated with laywomen or convents, suggesting that the author of the *Tree* was not inattentive to either the needs or interests of his female readers.[41]

One manuscript of the Middle English *Stimulus*, however, represents

---

37 Ibid., p. 16.

38 Ibid., p. 32, my punctuation.

39 *The Prickynge of Love*, ed. by H. Kane, Elizabethan and Renaissance Studies (Salzburg, 1983).

40 For example, the metaphors of the book, honey, and fire (among others) are found in the *Stimulus*. The *Stimulus* also incorporates the pattern of division and enumeration found in both the *Doctrine* and the *Tree* and *Twelve Fruits*, including six things necessary to know how Christ suffered (ch. 4), the four stirrings of the soul (ch. 5), and seven blessings (ch. 7), as well as more traditional lists such as the seven deeds of mercy and the ten commandments.

41 For a complete description of the manuscripts, see *Prickynge of Love*, ed. Kane.

particularly well the kind of reading envisioned by the author of the *Tree*, completing the careful instruction of his nuns by taking the reader through an introductory meditation to a more sophisticated discussion of the function of passion meditation in private devotion. Durham, University Library, MS Cosin V.III.8 contains *The Privity of the Passion*,[42] a passion meditation based on the pseudo-Bonaventuran *Meditationes vitae Christi*[43] and ordered around the canonical hours, followed by the Middle English *Stimulus* (here attributed to Hilton). The provenance of the manuscript is unknown, but it was clearly intended for private devotion. The *Privity* moves the reader through the day and through the passion, while the *Stimulus* guides the reader through his or her affective meditative *response* to the passion. If the manuscripts containing the *Doctrine*, the *Tree* and the *Twelve Fruits* are intended as a guide to the communal life which provides the opportunity and preparation for the contemplative life, then MS Cosin V.III.8 is a guide to individual contemplation within the chamber of the heart, taking the reader from the practical preparation of the heart for contemplative prayer into the prayer itself, and finally into the contemplative union with Christ and meditative life for which such prayer is designed.

That MS Cosin V.III.8 was intended to be read in a way that reflected the individual reader's progress in meditation is also suggested by the two miniatures which open the texts. The *Privity* opens with a miniature of Christ carrying a T-shaped cross on his shoulder, looking back over his shoulder, as if to invite the reader to follow him through his passion.[44] The *Stimulus* opens with an illuminated capital F, depicting the crucified Christ.[45] These miniatures, like the texts they illustrate, suggest that the compiler of the manuscript expected a complex development in the lay

---

42 D.N. Baker (ed.), 'The Privity of the Passion', in A.C. Bartlett and T.H. Bestul (eds), *Cultures of Piety: Medieval English Devotional Literature* (Ithaca, NY, 1999), pp. 194–211, with a translation on pp. 85–106. The *Privity* is also edited from the Thornton manuscript (Lincoln Cathedral, MS 91), by C. Horstmann (ed.), *The Yorkshire Writers: Richard Rolle of Hampole, an English Father of the Church, and His Followers*, 2 vols (London, 1895–96), vol. 1, pp. 198–218.

43 Johannis de Caulibus, *Meditationes vitae Christi*, ed. by M. Stallings-Taney, *CCCM* 153 (Turnhout, 1998).

44 The miniature takes the place of an initial, possibly a Q (the text would thus have read '[Q]wo so desyres …'). See Stocks and Doyle, 'Draft Catalogue'.

45 The cross is suggested, but not explicitly portrayed, by the capital F. However, in order to achieve even the suggestion of a cross, the scribe has had to alter the first line of the text, altering 'Al for-wondrid of owre-self auzt vs for to be' to 'For wondred of our self aght we to be' – an alteration that seems deliberate, given the illustrations here. See *Prickynge of Love*, ed. Kane, p. 1.

reader's response to Christ's passion as he or she moved through the book. The two illuminations evoke the compassionate Christ, who offers himself in love that others may follow, and the suffering Christ, who dies and bleeds on the cross for our salvation. Like the texts, the pictures move the reader from meditation on the passion to an affective response to the passion.

Although the manuscripts have no historical link, the author of the *Tree* clearly envisions just such a progression in his readers' instruction and living. The simple meditation in *The Privity of the Passion*, designed around the canonical hours, provides the most basic form of contemplative 'mental prayer' in such a way that it could be used both in the divine service and in private devotion, as recommended by the *Tree* author. The *Stimulus*, on the other hand, provides a more sophisticated discussion of the meditative heights to which such prayer could take the soul (and how to achieve them). The full measure of meditation on the passion is thus achieved by the combination of the two texts, rather than by either one on its own.[46] The two texts together thus complete the carefully constructed programme of

---

46 The *Privity* on its own may seem to offer only a simplified form of passion meditation for the laity, as does Love's *Mirror*. It is in its combination here with the *Stimulus amoris* that it is lifted above a simple passion text to form the foundation of a more sophisticated kind of meditation. There are, however, other texts that use apparently 'simple' passion meditation as the crowning achievement of the spiritual instruction of the convent or monastery. For example, Bonaventure's thirteenth-century meditative text *Lignum vitae* was written for Franciscan friars with the express purpose of helping the reader conform to Christ in his crucifixion (St Bonaventure, *The Soul's Journey into God. The Tree of Life. The Life of St. Francis*, tr. E. Cousins, The Classics of Western Spirituality (New York, 1978), p. 119). The *Lignum vitae* contains a total of 48 meditations, each briefly describing an event in Christ's life (or at the end, a metaphor, such as 'Jesus, Inscribed Book') followed by a model prayer. It is significant that, while the meditations are 'simple' and the language is 'unsophisticated', Bonaventure clearly sees this form of contemplation as requiring the fullness of his friars' memory, intellect and will – no simple achievement, after all. Interestingly, the *Lignum vitae* survives in a fifteenth-century Middle English translation (in Cambridge, St John's College, MS G.20 and New York, Columbia University, MS Plimpton 256). Here, the meditations are expanded and altered to be suitable for the devout lay reader, but while that reader is considered to be of 'rude understanding' (i.e. illiterate in Latin), he or she is also expected to be able to interpret a complex and sophisticated metaphor which is used not only as a structural device, but also as a means of cultivating meditative practice. Indeed, in MS G.20, the text is combined with two other extremely complex texts which require a concentrated and sophisticated reading (*Friar Sanal's Vision* and a *Tretys of Love*).

reading proposed by the author of the *Tree* and expanded by the compilers who combined the *Doctrine*, the *Tree* and the *Twelve Fruits*.

Nevertheless, there is no evidence that MS Cosin V.III.8 itself would have been read as part of such a comprehensive reading programme, grounded in the ordered routine of the convent. The medieval provenance of MS Cosin V.III.8 is unknown, but it is interesting that it fits the description of a manuscript 'of Hilton and Bonaventure' bequeathed by Cecily Neville, Duchess of York, to her granddaughter, the Prioress of Syon, in her will.[47] This suggests that, whoever owned MS Cosin V.III.8, it was suitable for both conventual and lay readership and similar to manuscripts owned by lay readers. The *Stimulus* itself was clearly considered appropriate for lay readership; in London, British Library, MS Harley 2254 (which also fits the description of Cecily Neville's bequest) the *Stimulus* follows Hilton's *Mixed Life*.[48] In contrast to the manuscripts containing the *Doctrine* and the *Tree* and the *Twelve Fruits*, MS Harley 2254 suggests a reading programme designed for and rooted in a specifically lay context. The fact that the *Mixed Life* precedes the *Stimulus* suggests that it is intended to provide a context for the meditative instruction in the *Stimulus* that is grounded in the lay world, in the same way that the author of the *Tree* and the *Twelve Fruits* presupposes a reading context firmly grounded in the conventual life.

Of course, determining the 'suitability' of a text for lay or religious readers is not so simple. In fact, MS Harley 2254 was owned by a laywoman, Joanna Newmarche, who gave it to the Dominican convent of Dartford.[49] Such manuscripts (and many others) illustrate the complex inter-relationships between devout laywomen and nuns, showing that texts which encourage a sophisticated, individual piety were read by both, yet in quite different contexts and under quite different circumstances. And, it must be stressed, the direction of manuscript transmission went both

---

47 C.M. Meale, '"oft siþis with grete deuotion I þought what I miȝt do pleysyng to god": The Early Ownership and Readership of Love's *Mirror*, with Special Reference to its Female Audience', in S. Oguro, R. Beadle and M.G. Sargent (eds), *Nicholas Love at Waseda* (Cambridge, 1997), pp. 19–46 (31).

48 Other manuscripts that combine Love/Bonaventure and Hilton include Cambridge, University Library, MS Add 6686; Yale, Beinecke Library, MS 324 and Cambridge, University Library, MS Hh.1.11.

49 See M.C. Erler, 'Exchange of Books Between Nuns and Laywomen: Three Surviving Examples', in R. Beadle and A.J. Piper (eds), *New Science Out of Old Books: Studies in Manuscripts and Early Printed Books in Honour of A.I. Doyle* (Aldershot, 1995), pp. 360–373 (361–362), and Doyle, 'Origins and Circulation of Theological Writings', n. 51.

ways, as nuns gave or bequeathed manuscripts to laywomen, and laywomen did the same for individual nuns or convents. Overall, the manuscripts of the Middle English *Stimulus* and their provenance seem to demonstrate this fluidity of exchange through their incorporation of a text, elsewhere recommended as part of a sophisticated programme of spiritual instruction designed for nuns, into manuscripts suitable for private lay devotion. As a consequence, such texts often ended up *outside* the strictly controlled conventual life to which the *Doctrine*, the *Tree* and the *Twelve Fruits* are a guide, and without the foundational material which they offer.

Although this fluidity of reading is nothing new to scholars of medieval women's devotion, the appearance of meditative texts both outside the convent and outside the kind of strict reading programme envisioned by the author of the *Tree* begs the question of the *consequences* of the increasingly broad availability of vernacular devotional material, in particular, passion meditation, in manuscripts designed for individual devotion, whether intended for nuns or laywomen.

By making religious works available in the vernacular, clerical authors attempted to guide their readers, restricting excess, reducing error and enclosing devotional practice within the carefully controlled realm of church and sacrament. Yet, as works of spiritual guidance became more widely available, the focus on the individual in works of affective devotion had the potential to undermine clerical control of theology and practice. Vernacular devotional texts empowered readers to take responsibility for their own salvation and to develop an individual, private relation with the crucified Christ which could potentially bypass the mediation of church and cleric. Passion meditation, in particular, with its stress on seeing, feeling, knowing and imagining, moves the compassionate understanding of Christ's passion and the imitation of Christ's life and suffering into the realm of ordinary human experience. The shift from communal devotion to individual devotion enabled a freedom in prayer which encouraged the focus on the individual already present in passion meditation. By relocating the 'chamber of the heart' from a body enclosed in a clerically-controlled conventual or anchoritic life into the layperson's body, moving back and forth freely between the 'privy chamber' and the secular world, these texts had the potential to subvert and undermine the very clerical instruction which they were meant to affirm.[50]

---

[50] Two examples specifically concerned with the 'chamber of the heart' can be found in the textual history of the *Disce mori* and the *Fervor amoris*. The *Disce mori* (addressed to a 'sister Alice'), and its derivative, *Ignorancia sacerdotum* (addressed to, and deploring the ignorance of, clergy whose Latin is insufficient

In short, literacy itself could be dangerous, threatening the status quo and empowering the individual. Consequently, as I suggested above, as the readership of vernacular devotional texts expanded, so too did clerical anxiety about the potential uses and abuses of these texts. This anxiety was aroused partly because of the fear of heresy; for example, Archbishop Arundel's Constitutions of 1409 were, in part, an attempt to eradicate the threat of Lollardy by controlling the spread of vernacular literature outside

---

to guide their parishioners), include a chapter on arraying a bed for Christ to rest in when the soul has been cleansed by confession (a similar theme to that in book 1 of the *Doctrine*, although handled with a different metaphor). In this text, the freedom of the reader's meditation in the chamber of the heart is confined within the boundaries of the professional religious life. The late-fourteenth/early-fifteenth-century *Fervor amoris*, or *The Contemplations of the Dread and Love of God*, is addressed to both professional religious and educated lay readers, although the author's focus is clearly on the laity (See *Contemplations of the Dread and Love of God*, ed. by M. Connolly, EETS 303 (1993), p. xv). In the *Contemplations*, after outlining the four degrees of love, the author includes a final chapter concerning how the reader may be stirred to devotion by prayer, instructing him or her to withdraw into the chamber of the heart and meditate upon the passion of Christ. Here, the chamber of the soul, which the reader is instructed to 'ymagine in þin herte', is literally moved into the private chamber of the manorhouse, as the author instructs his readers: 'Whan þou schappest þe to preie or haue eny deuocion, fond to haue a priue place from alle maner noise, and time of reste wiþoute eny letting. Sitte þer or knele as is þi moste eise' (ibid., ch. AB, p. 41, ll. 1–3). It is clear that the author does not consider his lay readers to be in any way inferior to professional religious: 'þay þou be a lord or a laidi, housbond-man or wif, þou maist haue as stable an herte and wil as some religious þat sitteþ in þe cloistre. But soþ it is þat þe moste seker wey is to fle as religious don; but for alle mowe not be men or women of religion, þerfore of eche degre in þe world God haþ ichose his seruauntis' (ibid., ch. Z, pp. 40–41, ll. 36–42).

Both of these two chapters on the 'chamber of the heart' are, however, often extracted from their contexts as the ultimate (or penultimate) instruction in a longer work of guidance and found on their own, sometimes entitled *Bonum lectum* (the chapter from the *Disce mori* concerning the arraying of the bed in the chamber of the heart) and *Bono oratio* (the excerpt from the *Contemplations*). *Bono oratio*, in particular, is sometimes found in compilations which include more sophisticated devotional texts, but it is also often included with the kinds of basic texts found in a primer (*Pater noster*, *Ave*, Creed, the ten commandments, the five wits, the seven acts of mercy, etc.) and intended to provide only the most basic instruction. Once uprooted from their original institutional context, these meditations become accessible to a wide (and, arguably, unprepared) readership. It is this process that seems to cause the kind of clerical unease of which I speak.

clerical jurisdiction. Love's *Mirror* was one attempt to reassert this control, enclosing meditation on the life and passion of Christ in a sacramental, eucharistic context.

Arundel and Love were largely concerned with lay readers. Other authors, however, were deeply concerned with the rise of individual devotional practices within the convent as well. Nowhere is this more clear than in *The Chastising of God's Children*, a late-fourteenth-century text addressed to a 'religious sister,' which translates and adapts a number of Latin texts, including a Latin version of the *Ancrene Wisse*, from which it takes its title.[51] The author is clearly uncomfortable with the idea of vernacular devotional literature, commenting that while he feels inadequately prepared to write 'opinli' of spiritual matters in either English or Latin, he is particularly concerned about writing 'in english tunge, for it passiþ fer my wit to shewe ȝou in any maner vulgare þe termes of diuinite.'[52] He urges his readers to devote themselves to the recitation of Latin verses from scripture (especially the psalms), or liturgical prayer: 'aftir þe ordynaunce of holi chirche, and in þe maner as it was ordeyned of oure hooli fadirs'[53] – i.e. in Latin – rather than private devotion. While he does not go so far as to condemn the translation of the hours, psalms and litany into English, he does discourage it:

> but uttirli to usen hem in englisshe and leue þe latin, I hold it nat commendable, ... for if a mannes confessour ȝiueþ him in penaunce to seie his sautir wiþoute any oþer wordis, and he gooþ forþ and seiþ it in englisshe and nat in latyn as it was ordeynd, þis man, I wene, dooþ nat his penaunce.[54]

Indeed, he asserts that it is better to pray in Latin without understanding the words than to indulge in private ecstasies of meditative prayer.[55]

The *Chastising* author's unease with the vernacular may, in fact, be related to the tension leading up to Arundel's Constitutions. Annie Sutherland has recently suggested that the *Chastising* ought to be viewed as a text that was written and revised over time.[56] She argues that the author's attitude towards the vernacular becomes more strained as the text progresses, and

---

51 *Chastising*, ed. Bazire and Colledge, p. 95, l. 1.

52 Ibid., p. 95, ll. 14–18.

53 Ibid., p. 221, ll. 4–6.

54 Ibid., p. 221, ll. 16–22.

55 Ibid., p. 222.

56 This is a central point throughout Sutherland's article, '*Chastising of God's Children*'.

his allegiance to Latin more adamant – that he is explicitly aware 'that he is writing at a time of fierce controversy between Latin and the vernacular', and that this controversy leads him to 'wage a battle of sorts between his own instincts and his awareness of the needs of his audience.'[57] She outlines in some detail the inconsistency with which Biblical quotations are treated in terms of the use of Latin and English, and concludes that the author's 'shifts in biblical hermeneutics' suggest that 'he composed *The Chastising* over a period of time and perhaps even that he died (or at least abandoned work on the treatise) in the midst of a process of revision.'[58] The tension revealed in the text concerning the issue of translation thus reflects the growing controversy which developed between the time the treatise was begun and the time it was finished. The author allies himself, in the end, with the repression of any translation that would make 'a solitary encounter' with the Bible possible for the laity and the illiterate.[59]

Indeed, the author of the *Chastising* actively discourages individual prayer, reminding his readers that the spiritual joy which can be compared to spiritual drunkenness and which manifests itself in joyful song or tears, skipping, running or dancing is often present in the 'first begynnyng'[60] of the spiritual life, as God pampers his young children. However, as the spiritual 'child' matures, this grace is withdrawn. The resulting interaction between spiritual joy and despair is a necessary step on the road to spiritual maturity.[61] The kind of ecstatic prayer that is the goal of spiritual growth in the *Doctrine*, the *Tree* and the *Twelve Fruits* is thus identified as spiritual immaturity in the *Chastising*.

The authors of the *Doctrine* and the *Tree* and the *Twelve Fruits* address the problem of individual devotion and the potential abuse of vernacular meditative texts in a different way. Rather than discouraging meditative and ecstatic devotion, the translator of the *Doctrine* locates the bulk of his translation as preparatory material for women religious readers, grounding the pursuit of ecstatic love in the regulated communal life. Before the reader can achieve the wisdom which is necessary to 'cut' her heart to God (the subject of the seventh and final book), she must move through the steps outlined in the first six books, learning to prepare her heart in fear of God, keep her heart through pity, open her heart through knowledge, make her heart stable through truth, give her heart through counsel and lift up her

57 Ibid., p. 364.
58 Ibid., pp. 372–3.
59 Ibid., p. 373.
60 *Chastising*, ed. Bazire and Colledge, p. 103, l. 20.
61 Ibid., pp. 102–4.

heart through understanding. Each of these books uses metaphors that are appropriate to the life of the convent, including enclosed buildings, books, doors and gates, to describe the process of how the individual heart can grow in the love of God through its enclosure within a community. The individual heart is thus prepared for meditation and individual devotional practice specifically within the context of the communal life. In a similar way, the author of the *Tree* and the *Twelve Fruits* uses the metaphor of the tree, planted in the 'garden of religion' and bearing the fruits of the Holy Spirit, to ground his texts firmly within the conventual life. Via his carefully designed reading programme, he also addresses the problem of the potential abuse of vernacular meditative texts like the *Stimulus* and the devotional practices to which it is a guide, by providing them with a carefully worked-out foundation in the religious life. Indeed, he often advises his readers to develop communal devotional practices and, even in their private devotions, to avoid being 'singular.' The scribes who combined the *Doctrine* with the *Tree* and the *Twelve Fruits* took the process one step further, constructing a complex reading programme designed to prepare readers for more sophisticated and contemplative devotion.

In this light, it is important to consider the dating of the manuscripts under consideration here. Both MS Cosin V.III.8 (the *Privity* and the *Stimulus*) and MS Harley 2254 (the *Mixed Life* and the *Stimulus*, hence probably composed for a lay readership), date to the early fifteenth century, and by the mid fifteenth century MS Harley 2254 was already in the possession of Dartford. These manuscripts thus coincide with the rise of lay ownership of vernacular theology which so alarmed Arundel and Love, and which is also reflected in the provenance of many other manuscripts of the Middle English *Stimulus* (which date largely from the fourteenth and early fifteenth centuries). MS Cosin V.III.24 and MS McClean 132 (containing the *Doctrine*, the *Tree*, and the *Twelve Fruits*), on the other hand, date from the mid fifteenth century, after the spread of vernacular theology was well under way both in the convent and the lay world. The *combination* of the three texts, in other words, post-dates the debate over translation and the concern with individual devotional practice and thought reflected in Arundel's Constitutions and in the composition of the *Chastising* and Love's *Mirror*.

The compilation of MS Cosin V.III.24 and MS McClean 132, as well as the *Tree* author's concern to ground his readers' perusal of meditative works in his own foundational text, may well have been a response to the spread of vernacular theology among readers (religious women and laypersons) who were, in the eyes of the authors and/or scribes, unprepared for such heady stuff. The structure of MS Cosin V.III.24 and MS McClean 132, as we have seen, suggests that they were intended to reinforce clerical control over the beliefs and practices of their readers. The intent is not, it must be stressed, to *discourage* private devotion (as in the case of the *Chastising*); rather, the *Doctrine*, the *Tree* and the *Twelve Fruits* encourage devotion that is rooted in the life and rule of the convent, yet moves the individual devotee into an advanced realm of meditative communion with God within the chamber of the heart. Indeed, one of the explicit aims of the author of the *Tree* is to provide his nuns with a specific reading programme where the reading of meditative texts such as the *Stimulus* remains firmly grounded in the instruction of his own texts and in the rigour of convent life.

The responses of clerical authors to the rise of vernacular theology were thus widely varied. The author of *The Chastising of God's Children* attempted to restrain individual devotion, while the translator of *The Doctrine of the Hert* and the author of *The Tree & xii. Frutes of the Holy Goost* anchored individual prayer and meditation firmly within the context of the convent. However, the spread of vernacular devotional texts also brings me to my final question, concerning the influence of professional religious women's devotional instruction on lay devotional reading and practice.

The audience for vernacular devotional texts included two groups, professional religious women and laypersons, who were conventionally considered 'illiterati' and traditionally disempowered, cut off from the textual (and conventionally Latin) dissemination of spiritual ideas and practice. Yet, as I have argued elsewhere, texts such as *The Feitis and Passion of Oure Lord Jesus Christ* (Oxford, Bodleian Library, MS Holkham Misc. 41) suggest that medieval women, even within a strictly enclosed life, were able to develop ways of reading, particularly in passion meditation, that enabled them to reconstruct and, to some extent resist, the conventional authority embedded in texts written for and about them.[62] I would suggest that the (often transgressive) reading strategies of professional religious women readers were, however unconsciously, encouraged and spread as a result of the wider dissemination of vernacular theology to an increasingly literate lay audience, meaning that a potential form of subversion and empowerment which began as a female strategy gradually became a lay practice. While many of the texts and manuscripts I have discussed seem, at least in part, intended to reinforce clerical control, they also open their readers to the exploration of religious conviction in the private sphere, creating a space where literacy could lead to an evolution of individual

62 See my article, 'Anchoritic Elements of Holkham Misc. 41', in E. Herbert MacAvoy and M. Hughes Edwards (eds), *Intersections of Gender and Enclosure in the Middle Ages* (Cardiff, 2005), pp. 172–81.

thought and practice, outside institutional control. With greater literary and devotional freedom came greater interpretative freedom – and, indeed, greater doctrinal freedom, at least in the privacy of the heart.

A literate laity was, to some extent at least, an empowered laity. Swanson has demonstrated how vernacular passion narratives and meditations can work against their authors' purpose, undermining the institutional church and empowering individuals, in particular the gentry, as vernacular works enable them to practise a private spirituality outside the church. With the increased private access to faith made possible by the flourishing of vernacular texts (and, later, the spread of printing), spirituality became more personal and individual, less institutional, and this had a significant impact not only on the religious lives of readers but also on their social and political ideas and actions.[63]

With hindsight, we can see that rising lay literacy and increased lay access to devotional works coincided with a growing clerical concern about heresy and even reform from inside the church, as well as the rise of individual devotional practices. Arundel and Nicholas Love were concerned with lay reading in the vernacular, and sought to enclose it within the control of church and sacrament. Yet, like the laity, professional religious women were exposed to texts which encouraged and promoted individual devotion within the 'chamber of the heart'. The author of the *Chastising*, like Arundel, sought to repress such individual practice, retreating behind the walls of the convent and the barriers of language, and enclosing his readers' prayers within the context of the divine service and behind the screen of Latin. The combination of the Middle English *Doctrine* and the *Tree* and the *Twelve Fruits*, with its carefully prescribed reading programme, seems a much more enlightened attempt to stem this tide. While the texts reflect a concern about individual devotional practice outside the context of the convent, they also portray a respect for their readers that is not found in the *Chastising*. The compilers assume that their readers, properly prepared, are fully capable of affective, meditative devotion. Grounding the devotional practices of religious women firmly within the context of the convent, they simultaneously open to them the depth and intensity of affective meditation within the individual heart and soul.

---

63 See Swanson, 'Passion and Practice', pp. 1–30. Ellen Ross and Eamon Duffy draw attention to the wide range of religious practices and beliefs and the sophistication of lay piety in the fifteenth century (Ross, *Grief of God*; Duffy, *Stripping of the Altars*).

Part III

European Vernacular Translations

7

The French Translations of *De doctrina cordis*[1]

Anne Elisabeth Mouron

> I counceyl you, þerfor, my loved suster, to kepe your hart and mynde diligentlye, for ther ys the good dede and evyll. Wherfor, sayth Scriptur: 'with all diligence kepe thy hert, for of it cummyth lyfe.' (Prov. 4:23)[2]

> Note qu'il sont vii estruisemens en l'Escripture entour la disposition du cuer … Le second nous aprent Salemon. C'est garder le cuer es proverbes: *Omni custodia serva cor tuum quoniam ex ipso vita procedit* (Prov. 4:23). Garde en touttes manieres ton cuer car de ce naist la vie.[3]

In the first quotation, from *The Manere of Good Lyvyng*, a fifteenth-century Middle English translation of the thirteenth-century *Liber de modo bene*

1 I would like to thank Professor Jeanette Beer for reading this paper and contributing many very helpful comments.

2 *The Manere of Good Lyvyng*, Oxford, Bodleian Library, MS Laud Misc. 517, fol. 90v. For the Latin original, see *Liber de modo bene vivendi*, *PL* 184, col. 1253D.

3 *Le traitiers de la doctrine du cuer*, Douai, Bibliothèque municipale, MS 514, fol. 2r (Note that there are seven instructions concerning the heart's disposition … Solomon teaches us the second, that is, to keep the heart, in Proverbs: *Omni custodia serva cor tuum quoniam ex ipso vita procedit*. In all cases keep your heart for from it life is born.) Note that in all transcriptions, abbreviations have been expanded silently. Modern punctuation, capitalisation and word-division have been added. V/u, i/j c/t transcriptions correspond to modern usage.

vivendi, the author advises his reader, a nun, to 'kepe [her] hart'. Sharing the same biblical quotation, this advice reflects the major concern of the second quotation, which is taken from a fifteenth-century French translation of another thirteenth-century Latin text, *De doctrina cordis*.[4]

In his survey of the surviving manuscripts and early editions of *De doctrina* in Latin and in European vernaculars, Hendrix lists two manuscripts of *De doctrina* in French: Troyes, Bibliothèque municipale, MS 1384 and Douai, Bibliothèque municipale, MS 514.[5] However, two more at least have survived – Oxford, Bodleian Library, MS Holkham Misc. 42 and Paris, Bibliothèque nationale, MS fr. 13272 – the latter of which has been changed considerably, and for this reason will not be taken into consideration here.[6]

Contrary to the Middle English *Doctrine of the Hert*, which does not translate the Latin prologue, but instead writes one of its own,[7] none of the three French manuscripts considered here provide a new prologue or any insight from the translator. Both MS Douai and MS Holkham have a standard IP-prologue.[8] In MS Troyes, however, the greater part of the prologue is missing, the translation beginning with the division of the text into seven 'ensaignemens'.[9] When one compares all three French manuscripts, it quickly becomes apparent that MS Holkham and MS Douai are two different versions of the same translation. However, the latter

---

4 Gerardus Leodiensis, *Speculum concionatorum, ad illustrandum pectora auditorum, in septem libros distributum* (Naples, 1607), Oxford, Bodleian Library, 8º L 12 Th. BS. Henceforth cited as *De doctrina*. Whenever relevant, the 1506 edition and Oxford, Bodleian Library, MS Lat. th. f. 6 have also been consulted.

5 G. Hendrix, *Hugo de Sancto Caro's traktaat De doctrina cordis. Vol. 1: Handschriften, receptie, tekstgeschiedenis en authenticiteitskritiek*, Documenta Libraria 16/1 (Louvain, 1995), pp. 149–50. For Troyes, MS 1384, see specifically, p. 91; for Douai, MS 514, p. 30. Henceforth cited as Hendrix, *Hugo I*.

6 I am very grateful to the French scholar Geneviève Hasenohr for drawing my attention to the existence of these two other manuscripts. She characterizes Paris, B.N., MS fr. 13272 as a translation 'diluée et interpolée'. There is also a translation into French of an excerpt on confession in Angers, Bibliothèque municipale, MS 403 (390). See Hendrix, *Hugo I*, p. 14. The three manuscripts discussed in this essay are henceforth referred to simply as MS Troyes, MS Douai and MS Holkham.

7 See my essay, '*The Doctrine of the Hert*: A Middle English Translation of *De doctrina cordis*', pp. 85–108, in this volume.

8 For a definition of the IP-prologue, see Hendrix, *Hugo I*, pp. 165–9.

9 MS Troyes, fol. 1r. This corresponds in the Latin to the 'Divisio sequentis operis in septem tractatus', *De doctrina*, p. 4.

does not seem to be a copy of the former. Not only do they not always share the same division of the text into sections,[10] mistakes[11] or additions,[12] both sometimes also vary in their vocabulary or the order of their words.[13] The fact that both manuscripts are independent versions of the same translation shows that there must have been other manuscripts of this French translation which have not survived. Considering the great number of Latin manuscripts of *De doctrina* still extant, this may not be surprising. Nevertheless, it is interesting to note that both in England, with four surviving Middle English manuscripts, and in France, with four surviving manuscripts (but with the knowledge that others must have circulated) there seems to have been a steady demand for vernacular translations of *De doctrina*. When compared with the fifteen or so manuscripts of the

---

10 MS Douai has a new section on fol. 48r: 'De la vesve'; MS Holkham has none at the corresponding place in the text (fol. 36vb). MS Douai has a new section on fol. 50r: 'De la folle', with no corresponding new section in MS Holkham (fol. 38rb).

11 Translating the following Latin sentence, MS Holkham mistakenly collapses the two highlighted clauses together, but MS Douai has the correct translation: '... quia pars eorum cecidit, Lucifer scilicet cum suis, et pars remansit. *Integri quidem sunt per qualitatem meriti, praerupti per qualitatem numeri*', *De doctrina*, p. 265. '... por la partie des angeres qui chaierent, Lucifer ovec les suens, e la partie qui demora qui sont entier por la qualite del conte', MS Holkham, fol. 119rb. '... pour la partie des angeles qui queirent, Lucifer avoec les siens, et la partie qui demoura qui sont entier pour la qualite de merite. Et si sont trauve ou derompus pour le quantite de conte', MS Douai, fol. 132v.

12 For example, MS Holkham has the three words 'en la croiz' where MS Douai has 'y', the former being a more accurate translation of 'crucifixus': 'Non cum Christo crucifixus, sed Iudae suspendio es suspensus', *De doctrina*, p. 269. 'Tu n'es mie afichez *en la croiz* avec nostre seingnour, ainz es verraiement penduz avec Judas', MS Holkham fol. 121ra. 'Tu n'es mie affichies avoec nostre seigneur ains y es vraieme[n]t pendus avoec Judas', MS Douai, fol. 134v.

13 In the following sentence, for example, the translation of 'vtil[is]' varies with the manuscripts: 'O quam laudabile, et *vtile* exercitium, cordis sui reuocatio', *De doctrina*, p. 259. 'E com c'est *utile* chose e com tout fait a loer li exercices de rapeler son cuer', MS Holkham, fol. 117ra. 'O que *proufitable* chose et que tout fait a loer li exercisse de rapeller son cuer', MS Douai, fol. 130r. Next, the translation of 'praemeditatus' demands two adverbs in French, but their order is different in both manuscripts: '... coram iudice summo in foro confessionis praemeditatus accede', *De doctrina*, p. 10. '... devant le jugeour de ta confession, porpense toi *bien ancois*', MS Holkham, fol. 4rb. '... devant le jugeur de ta confession, prepense toy *anchois bien*', MS Douai, fols 5r–v.

Ancrene Wisse which have survived, however, the vernacular circulation of *De doctrina* is still limited.[14]

Unfortunately, there is not much information on any of the three French manuscripts. *A Handlist of Manuscripts in the Library of the Earl of Leicester at Holkham Hall* simply and succinctly describes MS Holkham as 'Commentaires sur l'Ecriture, being Latin scriptural quotations accompanied by a commentary in French prose', and dates it from the thirteenth century.[15] The manuscript does not identify either the text or its author. *Le traitiers de la doctrine du cuer* is the only text in the manuscript, which has been copied by several scribes.[16] Its provenance is unknown, but it seems that at one time it belonged to a certain Henry Spelman.[17] This is most probably Sir Henry Spelman (1563/4–1641), 'historian and antiquary', who 'helped to found the Society of Antiquaries'.[18] He wrote several books on political, ecclesiatical and historical subjects and 'founded an Anglo-Saxon readership at Cambridge', where he had been an undergraduate.[19]

The *Catalogue général des manuscrits des bibliothèques publiques des départements* attributes MS Douai to Gerard of Liège. The provenance is unknown, and it seems that such information has been deliberately destroyed.[20] The manuscript is paper rather than parchment, but this may

---

14 This excludes the Latin and French versions of the *Ancrene Wisse*. For a list of manuscripts of the *Ancrene Wisse*, see *Ancrene Wisse, A Corrected Edition of the Text in Cambridge, Corpus Christi College, MS 402, with Variants from Other Manuscripts*, ed. by B. Millett, EETS 325 (2005), p. ix.

15 *A Handlist of the Manuscripts in the Library of the Earl of Leicester at Holkham Hall*, abstracted from the catalogue of William Roscoe and F. Madden and annotated by S. De Ricci (Oxford, 1932), p. 56, no. 661.

16 The title is taken from MS Troyes, fol. 144v; MS Holkham gives no title to the text.

17 The name 'Henrici Spelman' is found in the top margin of fol. 1r. The *Handlist* also mentions it: 'Sir Henry Spelman coll.' *Handlist of the Manuscripts*, p. 56.

18 S. Handley, 'Spelman, Sir Henry (1563/4–1641)', in H.C.C. Matthew and B. Harrison (eds), *Dictionary of National Biography*, vol. 51 (Oxford, 2004), pp. 791–3.

19 J. Venn and J.A. Venn, *Alumni Cantabrigienses. Part I: From the Earliest Times to 1751*, vol. 4 (Cambridge, 1927), p. 130.

20 'Les indications qui se trouvaient sur la garde et le premier feuillet ont été enlevées', *Catalogue général des manuscrits des bibliothèques publiques des départements publié sous les auspices du ministre de l'instruction publique*, vol. 6 (Paris, 1878), p. 306.

be explained by its fifteenth-century date.[21] It seems to have been the work of one scribe, and the French translation of *De doctrina* is again the only text in the manuscript.

As for MS Troyes, the *Catalogue* is also quite brief in its description of the manuscript.[22] It is an in–4° paper volume of 195 folios containing three different texts, all three in French and all three anonymous. The first is the translation of *De doctrina* into French, and this is by far the longest work in the manuscript. The second text is described thus: 'Cy commence ly traitiers sur *Laudate Dominum in Sanctis eius*',[23] which is a discussion of Psalm 150:1. Finally, the last text is given as: 'Cy commence ung livret de l'estat de perfection, ouquel l'acteur introduit Dieu parlant par maniere de ung pere a son filz ou fille, et aucune fois les responces du filz. Aucune fois aussy l'acteur parle de Dieu en la tierce personne.'[24] All three texts appear to be the work of the same scribe. In this case the provenance of the manuscript is known: 'Clairvaux, sans numéro'.[25] Finally, the *Catalogue* dates it from the fifteenth century.[26]

None of the three manuscripts divide the material into seven books as the Latin edition and the Middle English translation do.[27] However, all French versions have many separate sections marked by larger initials, but these do not necessarily agree with the Latin edition of 1607 or among themselves. For example, the Latin ends its section 'Diuisio sequentis operis in septem Tractatus'[28] thus:

> Praeter ista dona, ex abundanti nostrum faciemus digressum. Circa cordis praeparationem attende, quod cor praeparandum est, sicut domus praeparatur ad dignum hospitem recipiendum: sicut praeparatur cibus

---

21 Ibid., vol. 6, pp. 305–6.

22 Ibid., vol. 2 (Paris, 1855), p. 574.

23 (Here begins the treatise on 'Laudate Dominum in Sanctis eius'.)

24 (Here begins a booklet on the state of perfection in which the author introduces God speaking as a father to a son or daughter and sometimes with the answers of the son. Sometimes the author speaks of God in the third person.) The *Catalogue* does not provide folio numbers.

25 See also G. Hendrix, '*De doctrina cordis*: Manuscripts of Clairvaux and Cîteaux Provenance', *CCC*, 28 (1977), 94–100.

26 *Catalogue général des manuscrits*, vol. 2, p. 574.

27 Note that the text is not always divided into seven books in the Latin either. MS Lat. th. f. 6 divides the work into two books.

28 *De doctrina*, p. 4. (The division of the following work into seven treatises.)

> ad comedendum, et sicut sponsa praeparatur ad sponso suo placendum. Ecce triplex ratio, siue modus praeparandi.[29]

The next section, entitled 'De Praeparatione cordis ad similitudinem domus praeparandae',[30] begins: 'Praepara ergo cor tuum, tanquam domum ad magnum hospitem Christum Dominum tuum recipiendum.'[31] MS Holkham has no division here; the text simply carries on.[32] MS Douai has a new section, but it occurs a few lines earlier:

> Or te volons monstrer comment par les dons du saint esperit ainssi appropries li cuer est appareillies, gardes et aouvers et les aultres choses. Or veons doncques le premier.
>
> *Preparate corda vestra Domino.* Appareillies vos cuers a nostre Seigneur. Car on doit le cuer appareillier ainsi comme la maison que on appareille pour rechevoir un grant hoste, ainsi que on appareille la viande pour mengier, ainsi comme l'espeuse s'appareille pour son espeux. Ichi trouvons trois raisons et trois manieres d'appareillemens. [*New section in Latin*] Appareilles donc ton cuer ainsi que une maison pour rechevoir si grant hoste comme nostre Seigneur Jhesu Crist.[33]

MS Troyes appears to have its new section in the same place as the Latin, but is missing the first comparison – that is, 'sicut domus praeparatur ad

---

29 *De doctrina*, pp. 5–6 (In addition to [dividing this text into seven treatises according to] these gifts, from their overflowing, we shall make a subdivision. Take note concerning the preparation of the heart that the heart must be prepared, as a house is prepared for the receiving of a worthy guest, as food is prepared to be eaten, and as a spouse prepares herself to please her husband. Here are three reasons or ways of being prepared.)

30 Ibid., p. 6 (Concerning the preparation of the heart in the likeness of a house to be prepared.)

31 Ibid., p. 6 (Prepare then your heart, just as you would prepare your house in order to receive the great guest, Christ, your Lord.)

32 See MS Holkham, fol. 3ra–b.

33 MS Douai, fol. 3v (We wish then to show you how, by the gifts of the Holy Ghost thus appropriated, the heart is made ready, kept, and opened, and the other things. Then let us see the first. *Preparate corda vestra Domino.* Make your hearts ready for our Lord. For one must make the heart ready as the house which one makes ready in order to receive a great guest, as one prepares food to eat, as the wife made herself ready for her husband. Here we find three reasons and three types of preparations. [*New section in the Latin*] Make your heart ready then as a house in order to receive such a great guest as is our Lord Jesus Christ.)

dignum hospitem recipiendum.'[34] At times all versions agree on the text's division. The section 'Primum praeparatorium domus, est Mundare'[35] in the Latin also corresponds to new sections in all three French manuscripts.[36]

Contrary to the Middle English, whose division into seven books with no subdivisions into various sections makes the reading arduous, especially with the very long first book of the treatise, the many limited sections in the Latin and the French versions make the reading more manageable. They also make it much easier to find one's way around the text. Unlike other vernacular manuscripts, where pointed fingers and trefoils mark passages in the text, the three French manuscripts are devoid of such signs in the margins. Having different sections may be another way of drawing attention to specific parts of the text, but it is impossible to say, when the three manuscripts differ, whether this is due to the translator, the scribe or the Latin manuscript used for the translation.

Oxford, MS Holkham Misc. 42 and Douai, MS 514

As has been mentioned above, both manuscripts are copies of the same translation and can therefore at first be examined together.[37]

When one compares both translations, the Holkham–Douai translation follows the Latin text more closely than the Troyes translation. The section entitled in Latin 'Primum praeparatorium domus, est Mundare' begins thus in the Latin: 'Munda ergo hospitium cordis tui, si vis Christum hospitem habitare: quod fit per timorem, qui expellit, et eijcit peccata, tanquam immunditias hospitij cordis tui; quia sicut dicit Ecclesiasticus cap. 1. Timor Domini expellit peccatum',[38] and is translated in MS Holkham as

> Monde donques l'ostel de ton cuer, se tu vues avoir tel hoste com nostre Signour Jhesu Crist, et ce doit estre fait parmi cremor qui chace et met

---

34 See MS Troyes, fol. 1v.

35 *De doctrina*, p. 7 (The first preparation of the house is cleansing.)

36 See MS Holkham, fol. 3va; MS Douai, fol. 4v; MS Troyes, fol. 2r.

37 Note that MS Douai in its present form has an incomplete version of the text, for the seventh sign of ecstatic love is missing. The section missing is about one page long in the Latin edition.

38 *De doctrina*, p. 7 (Purify then the guesthouse of your heart, if you wish Christ to dwell therein as a guest: which is done through fear, which expels and casts out sins, just as dirt [is expelled] from the guesthouse of your heart. For, as Ecclus. ch. 1 says: 'The fear of the Lord expels sin'.)

> fors ausi com ordure les pecchiez fors de l'ostel del cuer. De ce dist Ecclesiastes: *Timor Domini expellit peccatum*. C'est a dire la cremours nostre Signour chace fors les pecchiez.[39]

But this is how MS Troyes translates the same excerpt: 'Nettoie donc l'ostel de ton cuer par vraie confession, se tu vuelz Jhesu Crist herbergier et ce te convient il faire par le don de paour qui boute hors tous pechiez ausy come les ordures de l'ostel.'[40] The briefest examination of this passage suffices to show that in its form, syntax and vocabulary, as well as in its contents, the Holkham–Douai translation is nearer the Latin.

As a matter of fact, the Holkham–Douai translation chooses Latinate vocabulary or more antiquated expressions much more regularly than MS Troyes:

> ... *rationes, et allegationes suas* ordinat, et affirmat.
> ... ordene *ses raisons et ses allegations* et les afferme.
> ... ordonne et aferme *toutes ses raisons*.[41]

> Hoc bellum necesse habes experiri in angustijs *conscientiae remordentis*.
> Ceste guerre pues tu bien esprover enz es destresces *de la remordaunte conscience*.
> Ceste guerre esprouveras tu et sentiras en angoisses *de remors de conscience*.[42]

---

39 MS Holkham, fol. 3va–b (Purify then the guesthouse of your heart, if you wish to have such a guest as is our Lord Jesus Christ, and this must be done through fear, which drives out and puts out sins as dirt [is driven] out of the guesthouse of your heart. Of this Ecclesiastes says: *Timor Domini expellit peccatum*, that is to say, the fear of our Lord puts out sins.) For the same passage, see MS Douai, fol. 4v.

40 MS Troyes, fol. 2r (Clean then the guesthouse of your heart by true confession, if you wish to receive Jesus Christ as a guest, and this you must do by the gift of fear, which throws out all sins like dirt from the guesthouse.)

41 *De doctrina*, p. 10 (... orders and confirms his reasons and allegations); MS Holkham, fol. 4rb (... orders his reasons and his allegations and confirms them) (see also, MS Douai, fol. 5r); MS Troyes, fol. 3v (... orders and confirms all his reasons). My italics.

42 *De doctrina*, p. 246 (you have to experience this war in the distresses of a fretting conscience); MS Holkham, fol. 111rb (you can truly experience this war in the distresses of a fretting conscience) (see also, MS Douai, fol. 124r); MS Troyes, fol. 122r–v (you will experience and feel this war in pangs of conscience's remorse). My italics.

> … vt *illud suspendium eligas.*
> … si que *tu elises cel pendement.*
> … pour ce que *tu desires estre pendus.*[43]

> … quae sunt duodecim fructus *ligni vitae.*
> … que aucun apelent les .xii. fruiz *de la lingne de vie.*
> … que cil maistre apellent .xii. fruis *de l'arbre de vie.*[44]

This Latinate vocabulary is all the more noticeable in MS Douai, which dates from the fifteenth century, when one could have expected the scribe to modernize it, as is the case in MS Troyes. The MS Douai scribe may have been non-interventionist, but he may also have thought that the imitation of Latin conferred 'gravitas' to the text.

A much longer analysis is required in order to discuss variants adequately, but at times the Holkham–Douai translation features changes in the text. In book 1 the text considers four kinds of women: 'vidua[e]', 'repudiata[e]', 'sordida[e]', 'meretric[es]';[45] each kind is then examined in turn. The first ends thus:

> In huius significatione filij Israel fastidientes manna in deserto, ad carnes, quas in Aegypto reliquerant, suspirabant. Numer. 11. Noli charissime, ad ea, quae reliquisti in Aegypto huius mundi suspirare: noli manna deserere, id est, lectionem, orationem, et claustrum fastidire; quin potius temporalia ista, quae retro sunt, cum Apostolo ad Philipp. 3. obliuiscens, ad spiritualia, ad aeterna, quae ante sunt, intentione, et desiderio totaliter te extendas.[46]

---

43 *De doctrina*, p. 268 (… so that you choose that hanging); MS Holkham, fol. 120rb (… so that you choose that hanging) (see also, MS Douai, fol. 134r); MS Troyes, fol. 131r (… since you desire to be hanged).

44 *De doctrina*, p. 275 (… which are the twelve fruits of the tree of life); MS Holkham, fol. 124ra (… which some call the twelve fruits of the tree of life) (see also, MS Douai, fol. 137v); MS Troyes, fol. 135v (… which these masters call twelve fruits of the tree of life). My italics. There is no way of expressing the difference between 'lingne' and 'arbre' in English.

45 *De doctrina*, p. 86 (widows, repudiated women, dirty-minded women, harlots.)

46 Ibid., p. 87 (In this meaning, the sons of Israel in the desert, feeling disgust for manna, sighed for the meat which they left behind in Egypt. Num. 11. Dearest, do not sigh for these things which you have left behind in the Egypt of this world: do not abandon manna, that is, reading and prayer, and do not feel disgust for your cloister; yea indeed, with the Apostle (Philipp. 3) forgetting all

And this is how the Holkham–Douai translation renders this passage:

> En senefiance de ce la manne anuia as fils Israel es desers quant il lor souvint des aus et des oignons et de la char que il ma[n]goient en Egypte, ausi auquant qui sont es desers del enclostre sont anuiet de la lecon de meditacions des psaumes et souspirent as deliz trespassez qui sunt senefie par les aus et les oignons. Car a larmes et a angoisse de cuer et de conscience aimme l'on les deliz de cest munde, ausi com les aus et les oignons covient mangier a larmes, si com dist Sainz Gregoires.[47]

It would be interesting to see how this passage is rendered in the other vernaculars, for remembering eating garlic and onions with regret appears to be a very French characteristic![48]

None of the French translations has major additions, but the Holkham–Douai translation sometimes has material which is absent from the Latin edition. This is how the section entitled 'De sacramento altaris'[49] ends in the Latin edition and in the Troyes manuscript: 'Attende quod appositum est ante faciem tuam; imo dixit in plurali, Quae apposita sunt, etc.'[50] 'Dist par aventure Salemon par plurel "pran te garde queis choses on te met devant".'[51] And this is the way the Holkham–Douai translation ends this section:

---

these temporal things which are now behind you, through intention and desire put all your efforts into the spiritual things, into the eternal things which are in front of you.)

47 MS Holkham, fol. 37ra–b (In this meaning, the sons of Israel were not happy with manna in the desert, when they remembered the garlic and onions and the meat which they ate in Egypt. In the same way, some people who are in the desert of religion, are not happy with the reading of meditations on psalms, and sigh for pleasures they have left behind, which are signified by the garlic and the onions. For it is in tears and in anguish of heart and of conscience that one loves the pleasures of this world, as one must eat garlic and onions in tears, as Saint Gregory says), MS Douai, fol. 48v. MS Troyes, fols 42r–v follows the Latin.

48 The Middle English also follows the Latin and does not mention garlic or onions. *Doctrine of the Hert*, p. 28, ll. 906–11.

49 *De doctrina*, p. 56 (Concerning the sacrament of the altar.)

50 *De doctrina*, p. 62 (Notice what is put in front of you; he said in the plural, 'the things which are placed', etc.) This refers to Prov. 23:1, quoted earlier in the text. See *De doctrina*, p. 57. The passage ends identically in the 1506 Edition and in MS Lat. th. f. 6, fol. 45br.

51 MS Troyes, fol. 29v (Solomon says by chance in the plural: 'take notice of what things are placed in front of you'.)

Entent quele chose on met devant toi, ains dite queles choses par le plurel. Entent donc queles choses on[52] met devant toy en la table de l'autel. C'est venisons dou ciel deliciouse. Car tes sires Jhesu Criz fist venison[53] de son propre cors por ce que il donnast a toi deliciouse refection. Car il fu fustez ausi com venisons de sengler quant il fu chaciez de Pylate a Herode et de Herode renvoiez a Pylate. Apres il fu traciez d' abais de chiens quant li Juif crierent: 'Crucifige, crucifige', si com on list en la persone de lui: *Circumdederunt me canes multi*. C'est moult de chien m'environerent. Apres il fu fichiez de saiettes quant il fu affichiez de clous a la croiz. Apres il fu perciez del espie quant uns des chevaliers li ouvri son coste a[54] sa lance et adonc fu prise ceste noble venisons. Et c'est ce que Jeremies dist ... *Venatione ceperunt animam meam*. C'est il pristrent m'ame par chacerie, c'est a dire ma vie. Ausi com nostre sires desist: Ma vie est prise ausi com venisons, par fuitement de leu en leu, par abaiz de chiens, en leu de saiettes claufichiez, de l'espie de lance tresperciez. Iceste venisons a l'ascension fu presentee a la court celestiene avec le son de la buisine. C'est avec la jubilation des angles. Ausi com on a acoustume a corner a l'eure que on presente la venison, dont li angle s'esmerveillerent de tel present et il disoient la parole que Ysaies dist: *Quis est iste qui venit de Edom et cetera*? Qui est cil qui vient de Edom, qui vaut autant comme garnisons et senefie le monde qui encontre Deu est garniz et encontre les suens de vices et de pechiez. Voies donques voies com granz choses te sunt appareillies en la table de l'autel. Voies le grant estude que nostre Sires mist a appareillier lui meismes por estre ta viande.[55]

---

52 MS reads 'ont', fol. 24vb.

53 MS reads 'venisons', with a correction dot under the second 's' of the word.

54 MS reads 'de' with correction dots under the word, and the correct reading 'a' superscript.

55 MS Holkham, fols 24va–25ra (Notice what thing is put in front of you, or rather, what things are said in the plural. Notice then what things are put in front of you on the table of the altar. This is delicious venison from heaven. For your Lord, Jesus Christ, made venison of his own body, so that he might give you delicious restorative food. For he was hunted like wild boar venison, when he was driven away from Pilate to Herod and from Herod sent back to Pilate. He was later pursued by the barking of dogs, when the Jews shouted at him: 'Crucifige, crucifige', so that one reads about him: *Circum dederunt me canes multi*, that is, many dogs surrounded me. After that he was pierced with arrows, when he was fixed to the cross by nails. Then he was stabbed with a spear, when one of the knights opened his side with his lance and thus was this noble venison caught. And this is what Jeremiah ... says: *Venatione ceperunt animam meam*, that is, they took my soul, that is my life, by hunting; as if our Lord said: My life has been

The courtly tone of this addition is unmistakable and suggests, if not necessarily a courtly audience, at least an audience familiar with courtly circles and hunting practices. In this regard it is interesting to note that Christ is compared to a boar, an animal more usually associated with the devil or sins.[56]

Despite this singular addition, it seems on the whole that vernacular versions of *De doctrina* do not add much to the Latin text. Apart from its prologue, the Middle English *Doctrine of the Hert* rarely adds anything to the Latin. However, it drastically reduces the length of the text by frequent, often sizeable omissions. There is no such reduction in the Holkham–Douai translation, although omissions occur, ranging from one line to two pages in length. In the section 'De tertio ornatu domus, scilicet Mensa',[57] the text refers to St Bernard's comparison of God's food with the reader's penance, emphasizing that he must eat this food if he wishes to please God: 'Tunc, et tecum ipse comedit, cum in eadem poenitentia ipse delectatur. Nam (sicut dicit Chrysostomus:) si tibi placet tua poenitentia, ei placet; si tibi displicet, nec ei placet. Vis tu, quod ei placeat, quod tibi conspicit displicere?'[58]

---

taken like venison chased from place to place, by the barking of dogs, crucified by arrows, pierced by a spear's blade. On Ascension day, this venison was presented to the heavenly court with the sound of trumpets, that is with the angels' jubilation, as it is customary to sound the trumpet when venison is presented. Hence the angels marvelled at such a present and said the words which Isaiah said: *Quis est iste qui venit de Edom*, etc?, that is, who is he that comes from Edom, etc.? [Edom] which is the equivalent of garrison and means the world which is manned against God and his own with vices and sins. See, then, see what great things are prepared on the table of the altar for you. See what great care our Lord put into preparing himself in order to be your food.) The same passage can be found in MS Douai, fols 33r–34r. Note that an even longer version of this passage occurs in Paris, Bibliothèque nationale, MS 13272, fols 36r–v.

56 R. Barber, *Bestiary, Being an English Version of the Bodleian Library, Oxford MS. Bodley 764 with all the Original Miniatures Reproduced in Facsimile* (Woodbridge, 1993, repr. 1999), p. 87; F. McCulloch, *Medieval Latin and French Bestiaries* (Chapel Hill, 1960), 'boar – *aper*', pp. 97–8; J. Voisenet, *Bêtes et hommes dans le monde médiéval. Le bestiaire des clercs du Ve au XIIe siècle* (Turnhout, 2000), pp. 85, 332, 340, 359.

57 *De doctrina*, p. 34 (Concerning the third ornament of the house, that is, the table.)

58 Ibid., p. 34 (Then he himself eats with you, when he himself is delighted in the same penance. For (as Chrysostom says:) if your penance pleases you, it pleases him; if it displeases you, it does not please him. Do you want that what he sees displeases you should please him?)

The Latin continues with the following passage, which the Holkham–Douai translation omits:[59]

> Hoc enim ornamentum mensae paenitentiae, est bonus vultus hospitis, item paenitentis. Non enim diligit hospitem tristem, et (vt ita dicam) grinnosum. Mensam hanc poenitentiae ornare docet Ecclesiasticus 29. dicens: Transi hospes, et orna mensam. Quod dicit, Transi, refertur ad strenuitatem, et velocitatem, vt non pigritetur, qui talem hospitem inuitauit. Quod sequitur, Orna mensam, refertur ad inuitantis hilaritatem, vt (iuxta vulgare) non ploret, quod ipse dat ad comedendum; sed, sicut dicit Ecclesiasticus 35. In omni dato hilarem fac vultum tuum.[60]

The passage, though, is duly translated in MS Troyes.[61] It is difficult to see why this passage should have been deliberately omitted. It is certainly not a case of reducing the number of biblical quotations and their gloss.[62] Besides, the Middle English version, which, as has been noted above, often omits large chunks of the Latin text, certainly considers these lines essential to the understanding of the text, for it does not omit them either.[63] There appears to be no rationale behind these omissions in the Holkham–Douai translation. The most likely explanation is that these passages were already missing in the Latin manuscript the translator used.

This brief examination of the Holkham–Douai translation seems to intimate that the translator's main objective is a faithful translation of the Latin, whether in the choice of its vocabulary or in its contents. Apart from a new medium, French, there appears to be no concession made to a different

---

59 See MS Holkham, fol. 14ra; MS Douai, fol. 18r.

60 *De doctrina*, pp. 34–5 (Truly this ornament of the table of penance is the hosts's happy face, that is the penitent's. Truly he does not like a sad host, and (as I shall say) a grumbling host. Ecclus. 29 teaches us how to adorn this table of penance, saying: Go, host, and adorn the table. When he says 'Transi' he refers to briskness and swiftness, so that he who has invited such a guest may not be slow. What follows, 'orna mensam', refers to the cheerfulness of he who is inviting, that (according to the proverb) he may not weep over what he himself gives to eat; but, as Ecclus. 35 says: Have a cheerful face in all your gifts.)

61 MS Troyes, fol. 15r.

62 In this regard note that MS Holkham differs slightly from MS Douai, for the former often has a Latin quotation where the latter only gives the translation. See, for example, MS Holkham, fols 120rb, 120va, 120vb, 121va, 122ra, 122rb, and so on.

63 'But now, yif thow wilt wel plese this gest … in the fest of penaunce, schew glad chere.' *Doctrine of the Hert*, p. 12, ll. 273–81.

and less intellectual audience. Although there is no way of knowing, this may indicate a religious rather than a lay audience.[64]

The *Catalogue général des bibliothèques des départements* states that MS Douai's provenance is unknown. The manuscript seems to contain some clues as to its possible origin, however. One of its characteristics is regular annotations in the margin, mostly in Latin but some also in French.[65] They often give references to biblical quotations,[66] but they may also repeat a point made by the text.[67] Most of them (but not all) are written in an extremely small script and very difficult to decipher. This would hint at a clerical hand and therefore seems to exclude a lay origin for the manuscript.

MS Douai's text itself, moreover, perhaps points to an Augustinian origin. There is one characteristic of the translation which it does not share with MS Holkham or MS Troyes. Indeed, MS Douai singles out St Augustine by almost systematically referring to him as 'mon sire saint Augustin':

> Pour ce dist mon sire Saint Augustins: *Fluvis bona* …
> Et mon sire Saint Augustin dist: *Bonorum ingeniorum* …
> Si comme dist mon sire Saint Augustin: *Seipsum examinabat* …
> Car messire Saint Augustin dist: *Nic[h]il infelicius* …
> Car si comme messire Saint Augustin dist: *Penitencia* …
> De quoy dist messire Saint Augustin: … *Heu quam* …[68]

---

64 Compare with Paris, B.N., MS fr. 13272 which was probably destined for a secular audience and has major changes. See A. Mouron, 'Paris, B.N., MS fr. 13272: A French Translation of *De doctrina cordis*', in D. Renevey and C. Whitehead (eds), *The Medieval Translator/ Traduire au Moyen Age 12* (Turnhout, 2010).

65 In the left-hand margin next to the section title: 'Quelles sont Les noeches', one finds the title repeated: 'quellez sont lez noeches', MS Douai, fol. 56v.

66 For example, ibid., fols 2v, 4r, 6r, 7v, and so on.

67 For example where the text reads: 'c'est Jhesu Crist qui donna la chainture a la chananee', ibid., fols 76r–76v, the following note occurs on the left-hand margin: 'Cingulum tradidit Chananeo. pro. 31', ibid., fol. 76v.

68 Ibid., fol. 1r (For this reason my lord St Augustine says: *Fluvis bona* …); ibid., fol. 2r (And my lord St Augustine says: *Bonorum ingeniorum* …); ibid., fol. 4v (As says my lord St Augustine: *Seipsum examinabat* …); ibid., fol. 12v (For my lord St Augustine says: *Nic[h]il infelicius* …); ibid., fol. 18v (For as my lord St Augustine says: *Penitencia* …); ibid., fol. 19v (Of which my lord St Augustine says: … *Heu quam* …), etc.

This way of referring to the Bishop of Hippo does not extend to the other authorities quoted in the text, such as St Gregory, St John Chrysostom, Cassiodorus, St Bernard or Seneca.[69] The only other individual who is regularly granted the same honour is God:

> Dont nostre Sire dist: *Perdam nomen* …
> Pour ce dist nostre Sire par Isaie: *Creavi fructum* …[70]

This way of differentiating between St Augustine and the other Fathers of the Church suggests perhaps that the translation was made for Augustinian canons or Dominican friars. This should not be surprising, as some Latin manuscripts of *De doctrina* are known to have been read among these orders.[71] It is perhaps more surprising that a regular audience would require a vernacular text.

Troyes, MS 1384

As has been alluded to above, MS Troyes contains three different texts, all in French and all of a religious nature. Contrary to the Middle English translation of *De doctrina*, which specifically indicates that the 'tretice' applies to a 'mynche' (a nun),[72] there is no *indication* in the manuscript as to the recipient of the French translation. In this respect, it is worth observing that MS Troyes often seems to suppress references to the female reader found in the Latin edition. For example, one reads in book 1 of the Latin: 'Noli ergo, charissima, timere iudicium mortis.'[73] At this point, MS

---

69 'Pour che dist saint Grigoire: *Cogitatio premii* …', MS Douai, fol. 20r, see also fol. 20v; 'A che meisme dist Crisostome', ibid., fol. 15v, see also fol. 16r; 'Dont y dist Cassiodorus: *Pax vera est* …', ibid., fol. 12v; 'Et che dist saint Bernart: *Lingua leta et* …', ibid., fol. 4v, see also fol. 18r; 'Dont y dist Senecque: *Oratio que veritati* …', ibid., fol. 2r, see also fol. 29v.

70 MS Douai, fol. 6v (Of which our Lord says: *Perdam nomen* …); ibid., fol. 12r (For this reason our Lord says through Isaiah: *Creavi factum* …).

71 For Dominican ownership, see Basel, Öffentl. Bibliothek der Universität, MSS A.VIII.9, A.X.57; The Hague, Koninklijke Bibliothek, MS 135 F 6 (Hendrix, *Hugo I*, pp. 15, 28), etc. For Augustinian canons or canonesses, see Einsiedeln, Stiftsbibliothek O.S.B., MS 220; Cologne, Diözesanbibliothek, MS 248 (Hendrix, *Hugo I*, pp. 32–3, 45) etc.

72 'How and in what wyse a mynche shuld make redy here hert to God be þe yifte of drede', *Doctrine of the Hert*, p. 4, ll. 41–2.

73 *De doctrina*, p. 81 (Dearest lady, do not fear the judgement of death.)

Troyes simply reads: 'Ne redoute dont pas le iugement de la mort';[74] the reference to the female reader is absent. Similarly, MS Troyes sometimes changes the gender of the addressee. Whereas the Latin reads 'caelestis esto filia', 'filia' obviously referring to a female reader, MS Troyes translates: 'soies celestien',[75] thus alluding to a male reader instead.[76] In book 2, in the translation of the first folly, the Middle English omits the reference to women as gossips,[77] but MS Troyes has no qualm about translating the passage:

> Mais il i a aucuns qui ausi comme femmes pueent mout parler et pau souffrir. Bataille de femmes est en tencier car ellez sont fortes en la langue et flebes en mains, ce dit saint Jehan Bouche d'Or. Ausi comme cis qui a asseis ensaingniet et pau fait est de la maniere a la femme.[78]

The omission of references to a feminine reader and the retention of disparaging remarks about women presumably make sense if the manuscript was destined for the monks of Clairvaux. However, as Pierre de Virey's catalogue of 1472 lists three Latin manuscripts of *De doctrina* in Clairvaux, one may wonder why a French translation was felt necessary.[79]

As far as a very brief look suggests, variants are usually only a few words long and mostly insignificant – that is, they can be largely explained by the translator using a different Latin manuscript or by the process of translation.[80]

---

74 MS Troyes, fol. 39r (Do not fear the judgement of death); or in book 7 where the Latin reads: 'Attende *charissimam* Augustinum …', *De doctrina*, p. 278. MS Troyes translates: 'Regarde Saint Augustin', fol. 137r.

75 *De doctrina*, p. 274 (Be a heavenly daughter.) MS Troyes, fol. 135r (Be heavenly.) Note that in English the adjective does not indicate the sex of the addressee.

76 'Celestien' is the masculine form of the adjective.

77 See my essay on *The Doctrine of the Hert* in this volume, p. 91.

78 MS Troyes, fol. 81r (But there are some who like women can talk a lot and suffer little. Fights amongst women are quarrels and disputes, for they are strong in their tongue but weak in their hands, as St John Chrysostom says. Similarly, he who has taught a lot and has done little is like a woman.) For the same passage, see also MS Douai, fol. 91v.

79 A. Vernet, *La bibliothèque de l'abbaye de Clairvaux du XIIe au XVIIIe siècles* (Paris, 1979), V 1261–1263, p. 224.

80 For example: 'quando *claustrum intrasti*' (*De doctrina*, p. 36) is translated as 'quant *tu prins abit de religion*' (MS Troyes, fol. 16r); or 'sunt iusti *in regno vitae aeternae*' (*De doctrina*, p. 48) as 'sont les justes *en sainte esglise*' (MS Troyes, fol. 22r), my italics.

Occasionally, one encounters a more meaningful variant. For example, in book 1, one reads:

> Sicut enim *magnis viris* sedes praeparatur, ita praeparanda est sedes tribunalis Domino per iudicium examinationis, et iustitiam executionis: vt scilicet te ipsum examines per iudicium, et per iustitiam punias, et castiges.[81]

this is translated as:

> Ausi comme *a ces maistres de juges de court de plait* on appareille ung siege pour seoir, ausi a nostre Sire dois tu apparillier ung siege en toy par jugement de confession ou tu te dois jugier. Et par justice de penance donc tu dois ton corps punir et chastier.[82]

This differs from the Holkham–Douai translation:

> Car autresi com on apparelle *as granz signors* sieges pour jugier, ausi doit on apparellier a nostre Signour siege par jugement d'examination et la justice d'execucion, en tel maniere que tu examines toi meismes par jugement et toi meismes chasties par justice.[83]

Whereas the Latin remains vague, MS Troyes is quite specific, which may indicate that the translator had some legal knowledge.

There is at least one interesting variant, moreover, which one encounters repeatedly throughout the manuscript, and which is probably the translator's choice. When the Latin quotes from St John Chrysostom, the translator actually translates his name. For instance, 'Contra tales dicit *Chrysostomus*'[84]

---

81 *De doctrina*, p. 26 (For as a seat is prepared for great men, a judgment seat must be prepared for our Lord by the judgement of examination and by the justice of the execution of the sentence: namely that you examine yourself by judgment, and punish and chastise yourself by justice), my italics.

82 MS Troyes, fol. 10r (As one prepares a seat for these master judges of courts of common pleas for them to sit, in the same way you must prepare a seat for our Lord in yourself by judgement of confession, in which you must judge yourself, and by justice of penance you must punish and chastise your body), my italics.

83 MS Holkham, fols 10rb–va (For, as one prepares a seat for judging for great lords, one must also prepare a seat for our Lord by judgement of examination and justice of execution, in such a way that you examine yourself by judgement and chastise yourself by justice.) For the same passage, see MS Douai, fol. 13r.

84 *De doctrina*, p. 289 (Against such people Chrysostom says), my italics.

is translated in MS Troyes as 'De telz dit *saint Jehan Bouche d'Or*',[85] thus enhancing the value of his words.

Additions, too, seem to be kept to a minimum in frequency and quantity, and are not worth mentioning. By far the most interesting aspect of the translation lies with its very frequent omissions. These range from a few lines to lengthy passages (up to one or two pages from the Latin edition), and they appear to be the work of the translator.[86] For instance, in book 5 it is said that the reader should give her heart to Christ who gave his to the reader when soldiers pierced his side, thus opening a way for the reader's heart to enter into his through faith and meditation.[87] At this point the Latin continues:

> … et ibidem charissima cor tuum per fidem, et meditationem, quoad intellectum, per amorem, et compassionem quantum ad [a]ffectum studeas collocare. In cuius positionis, seu locationis figura praeceptum fuit in lege, Deutero. 31. Quod in latere arcae foederis liber legis poneretur. Quid enim per librum legis, nisi cor humanum intelligitur? qui liber legis appellatur, eo quod in eo lex naturalis scripta est, vt dicit Augustinus. Quid per Arcam foederis, nisi caro Christi figuratur, cuius passione confoederati sumus Deo? Quid per latus Arcae, nisi plaga lateris Christi designatur; in quo ponendus est liber, id est; cor humanum, secundum quod monet Psalmista, dicens, Psal. 47. Ponite corda vestra in virtute eius? Virtus Christi propria amor est, in quo tanquam in loco suo cor est ponendum. Attende autem, quod corda dicit, non ora: multi enim ora ponunt in virtute, qui corda habent posita in infirmitate; vt illi, qui grandia docent, et nulla, vel minima faciunt.[88]

---

85 MS Troyes, fol. 142r (of such people says St John Chrysostom), my italics. MS Holkham translates: 'contre celes dist Cristosomos', fol. 130rb; and MS Douai: 'Contre che dist Crisostomez', fol. 144r.

86 Omissions of a few words are not considered here, as they could all too easily result from the Latin manuscript used by the translator.

87 See *De doctrina*, pp. 246–7; MS Troyes, fol. 122v; MS Douai, fol. 124r; MS Holkham, fol. 111va.

88 *De doctrina*, p. 247 (… and so, my dearest, endeavour to establish your heart in that same place, through faith and meditation so far as your mind is concerned, and through love and compassion so far as your feelings are concerned. In the figure of this position or of this placing, it was ordered in the law, Deut. 31, that the book of the law be put in the side of the Ark of the Covenant. Truly, what is understood by the book of the law, if not the heart of man, which is called the book of the law in that in it is written natural law, as St Augustine says. What is represented by the Ark of the Covenant, if not Christ's flesh, by whose passion we

The text then goes on – 'Ingrediatur ergo cor tuum, charissima, ad cor Domini Dei tui'[89] – and this is where the translator resumes his translation – 'Entre donc tes cuers ou cuer Dieu'[90] – having omitted the whole passage. There is no such omission in the other manuscripts. The text continues uninterrupted in the Holkham–Douai translation, which fully translates the Latin.[91]

What the translator has left out in MS Troyes is not any part of the argument (i.e., your heart must enter God's heart by faith and meditation), but part of the exegesis which examines the meaning of this 'positionis'. Indeed, it seems that passages omitted by the translator are often further explanations or developments of a given point, the omission of which does not detract from the argument, but reduces the exegesis offered by the Latin text. Thus it is not unusual for such passages to begin with 'sicut'/'sic'/ 'ita'/'unde'. Typically, therefore, where the Middle English translation in book 2 reduces the ten follies of the Latin text to the first five,[92] MS Troyes retains the ten follies but does not translate them in their entirety. The sixth folly, for example, ends in Latin thus:

> Si ergo proprium sensum contra contradictiones, propriam voluntatem, et persecutiones vis defendere pro inimicis, contra amicos, et adiutores tuos pugnas. E contra, fauores, et applausus secularium, hostes nostri sunt, qui nos decipiunt. Sed vir insipiens non cognoscet, *et stultus non intelliget haec: Psal. 91. Iuxta quod dicitur Prouerb. 14. Vade contra virum stultum, et nescit labia prudentiae. Quasi diceret: Stultus non cognoscet aduersarium suum.*[93]

---

are joined to God? What is indicated by the side of the Ark, if not the wound in Christ's side, in which the book must be put, that is, the heart of man, according to what the Psalmist advises, saying, in Ps. 47: Put your hearts in his strength. Christ's proper strength is love, in which the heart must be put as in its own place. Notice, moreover, that he says 'hearts' not 'mouths': indeed many put their mouth in his strength who have put their heart in weakness; as do those who teach great things, and do nothing or little.) I would like to thank Professor K. Cathcart for help in translating the beginning of this excerpt.

89 Ibid., p. 247 (Let your heart, then, dearest, enter in the heart of the Lord, your God.)

90 MS Troyes, fol. 122v (Let then your heart enter God's heart.)

91 MS Holkham, fol. 111va–b; MS Douai, fols 124r–v.

92 See my essay on *The Doctrine of the Hert* in this volume, pp. 88–94.

93 *De doctrina*, p. 171 (If then you want to defend your proper sense against contradictions and your proper will against persecutions, you are fighting for your enemies and against your friends and helpers. On the contrary, the favours and

The translator here omits from the Latin the passage in italics, in this case two biblical quotations and their interpretation.[94] Unsurprisingly, the Holkham–Douai translation does not follow suit, and renders the same passage in its entirety.[95]

Omissions of authorities from a translation are not unique to this translation. Nicholas Love, for instance, acknowledges doing the same in his translation of *The Mirror of the Blessed Life of Jesus Christ*:

> þe forseid Bonauenture in þis boke of cristes life makeþ a longe processe aleggyng many auctoritees of seynt *Bernard*, þe whiche processe þouh it so be þat it is ful gude & fructuouse as to many gostly lyueres; neuerles for it semeþ as inpertynent in gret party to many comune persones & symple soules, þat þis boke in english is writen to … þerefore we passen ouere shortly takyng þereof þat semeþ profitable & edificatife to oure purpose at þis tyme.[96]

What is perhaps unexpected in MS Troyes, however, is that there is no suggestion that the translation was done for 'comune persones & symple soules'. On the contrary, MS Troyes is a Clairvaux manuscript, hence the translation was probably intended for Cistercian monks. Could it be, then, that the French translation was a kind of basic rendering, an aid to help with the reading of the Latin text?

The way patristic and biblical quotations are handled in MS Troyes points in this direction. In MS Troyes, these quotations are regularly first given in Latin, and then translated into French. For example: '*Hospes fui et non colegistis me.* Je fus hostes et vous ne me herberjastes pas.'[97] As is the case here, more often than not MS Troyes does not indicate that it translates the biblical quotation. In this it differs from the other manuscripts, which usually precede the translation of their biblical quotations with formulas

applause of secular men are our enemies who deceive us. But the senseless man does not recognise them, and the fool does not understand these things: Ps. 91, according to what is said in Prov. 14: Go against the foolish man, and he does not know the lips of prudence. As if he said, the fool does not recognise his adversary), my italics.

94 See MS Troyes, fol. 83v.

95 MS Holkham, fol. 77va; MS Douai, fol. 93v.

96 Nicholas Love, *The Mirror of the Blessed Life of Jesus Christ*, ed. by M.G. Sargent (Exeter, 2004), p. 118, ll. 11–18.

97 MS Troyes, fol. 2r (*Hospes fui et non colegistis me* [Matt. 25:43]. I was a guest and you did not receive me.)

such as 'c'est a dire' (that is to say). The same quotation is rendered thus in MS Holkham: '*Hospes fui et non collegistis me. C'est a dire*, Je fui hostes, vous ne me herbergastes mie.'[98] It may not be a coincidence that the same occurs in the Middle English translation, where the translator almost always clearly indicates his translation of the biblical verse by adding: 'he seith', or other words to the same effect, at the beginning or in the middle of it. The same quotation in the Middle English reads, '*Hospes fui, et non collegistis me.* "I come to yow as a gest" *he wil sey*, "and ye wold not receyve me."'[99] In MS Troyes, this absence of a clear indication between quotation and text may suggest that the intended audience had the necessary skills to understand (at least) some of the Latin and thus to recognize what was a translation of the verse.

Interestingly, if paraph signs are used throughout MS Troyes, they are not there to mark new paragraphs, but are placed at the beginning of Latin quotations, which are further highlighted from the vernacular text by being underlined. This emphasis on the Latin quotations could be seen as a way to read the French side by side with a Latin text, for it greatly helps the reader finds his way through the text. This would not be a unique phenomenon. Roger Ellis comments about Richard Rolle's translation of the Psalter: 'Rolle's translation is not a substitute for the original, which, in any case, he copies out in full, but a means of familiarizing the reader with the original Latin.'[100]

In a catalogue of the abbey of Clairvaux of *c.*1520, one finds a reference to 'De la preparation et doctrine du cueur. Et deux autres traictez', which has been identified as Troyes, MS 1384.[101] In the same 1520 catalogue, N 187 is believed to refer to one of the three Latin manuscripts of *De doctrina* listed in Pierre de Virey's earlier catalogue.[102] One can be confident, then, that the abbey had, at the same time, at least one Latin manuscript and a translation into French. When one browses through the 1520 catalogue, one encounters, perhaps surprisingly, many titles in French, including, for instance, *L'Ordinaire de l'ordre de Cisteaux*, the *Regle de sainct Augustin*, the *Homelies sainct Gregoire*, and *De vita Christi de Ludolphe en*

---

98 MS Holkham, fol. 3va, my italics. For the same line in MS Douai, see fol. 4r.

99 *Doctrine of the Hert*, p. 7, ll. 69–70, my italics.

100 R. Ellis, 'The Choices of the Translator in the Late Middle English Period', in M. Glasscoe (ed.), *The Medieval Mystical Tradition in England* (Exeter, 1982), pp. 18–46 (29).

101 Vernet, *Bibliothèque de l'abbaye de Clairvaux*, N 181, p. 596 (Of the preparation and of the doctrine of the heart and two other treatises.)

102 Ibid., N 187, p. 597.

françois.[103] It would seem, therefore, that by the late fifteenth century the monks of Clairvaux were finding translations into the vernacular increasingly useful. It may be that by then not all monks were proficient in Latin, or not proficient enough to decipher heavily abbreviated Latin texts. Indeed, a hundred years earlier, John Trevisa had already alluded to clerics' imperfect grasp of Latin:

> CLERICUS Ye kunneth speke and rede and understonde Latyn; than it nedeth not to have siche an Englisshe translacioun.
>
> DOMINUS I denye this argument; for though I can speke and rede and understonde Latyn, ther is myche Latin in thes bokes of cronicles that I can nought understonde, *neither thou, without studiyng and avisement and loking of other bokes.*[104]

But it may also be that the vernacular offered a different approach to the text, as Luther intimated: 'I thank God that I can hear and find my God in the German tongue, the way I do here [i.e. in *Theologica Germanica*], in a manner in which I and the German theologians with me so far did not find Him even in Latin, Greek, or Hebrew.'[105]

Conclusion

The Holkham–Douai and the Troyes translations are primary translations of *De doctrina cordis*; in other words, they do not aim at 'discover[ing] the text anew in [their] own language.'[106] The examples cited above also show that they are faithful translations; MS Troyes is a much freer translation than Holkham–Douai, but, unlike the Middle English version, they are all translations, not adaptations.

A much more in-depth analysis of the French *Doctrine du cuer* is needed, but one thing this brief assessment has confirmed is that this text, whether

---

[103] Ibid., respectively, N 1606, p. 570; N 1619, p. 572; N 1567, p. 565; N 1563, p. 565. There are many more examples in the catalogue.

[104] John Trevisa, 'Dialogue between the Lord and the Clerk on Translation', in J. Wogan-Browne et al. (eds), *The Idea of the Vernacular* (Exeter, 1999), pp. 130–4 (132).

[105] *The Theologia Germanica of Martin Luther*, tr. B. Hoffman (New York, 1980), p. 54.

[106] R. Copeland, *Rhetoric, Hermeneutics, and Translation in the Middle Ages* (Cambridge, 1991), p. 93.

in Latin or in the vernacular, is very much a text 'en mouvance'. Like the Middle English *Doctrine of the Hert*, none of the French manuscripts considered here acknowledge that their text is a translation from the Latin, and, like the Middle English *Doctrine*, none of these three manuscripts refer to the text's author. This lack of a single 'auctoritas' repeatedly linked with the text may go some way to explain its 'mouvance'.

None of the versions of *De doctrina cordis* considered here, in Latin, medieval French or Middle English, has an epilogue or conclusion. But one translator could very well have added words such as those found at the end of *La compileison de la vie de gent de religion*, a French translation of part of the *Ancrene Wisse*:

> Ore vus pri ieo ducement ke vus regardez cest escrit isci au comencement souent, e deske a la fin ententivement. E atret le lisez ou devant vus lire facez. E metez i vostre quer; e vus i poez[107] veer e oir verraiment, se vus vivet religiousement. e amez Deu leaument … Ore donc metez ci vostre quer, e entiuement escutez, e devotement oez.[108]

[107] The text reads 'iuostre' and 'ipo-ez'.

[108] *The French Text of the Ancrene Riwle, Edited from Trinity College Cambridge MS R.14.7*, ed. by W.H. Trethewey, EETS 240 (1958, repr. 1971), p. 160 (I pray you gently, then, that you look at this text here at the beginning often and carefully until the end, and that you read it or have it read in front of you slowly. And put your heart therein, and you can see and truly hear, whether you live religiously and love God faithfully. Put then your heart therein, and listen carefully, and hear devoutly), punctuation has been modernised.

8

A Middle Dutch Translation of *De doctrina cordis*: *De bouc van der leeringhe van der herten* in Vienna, Österreichischen Nationalbibliothek, MS 15231

Marleen Cré

> Hier hent de bouc van der leeringhe van der herten die ghescreuen was int iaer ons Heeren als men screef .m.cccc. ende xlvi up de xxii. dach van wedemaent.[1]

Of all the vernaculars into which the mid-thirteenth-century Latin treatise *De doctrina cordis* was translated, Middle Dutch is the only vernacular to offer translations of both the long (IP) and short (HV) versions of the text, whereas the translations into English, German, French and Spanish are all made from the short version (HV) of the Latin original, and the translation

---

[1] G. Hendrix, *Hugo De Sancto Caro's traktaat De doctrina cordis. Vol. 2: Pragmatische editie van De bouc van der leeringhe van der herten naar handschrift Wenen, ÖNB, 15231*, Documenta Libraria 16/2 (Louvain, 1995), 'Scissio', ll. 500–502 (Here ends the book of the doctrine of the heart that was written in the year of our Lord when one wrote 1446 on the 22nd day of June.) All references to *De bouc van der leeringhe van der herten*, the Middle Dutch version of *De doctrina cordis*, are to this edition, hereafter cited as Hendrix, *Hugo II*. References to the Dutch text are to section title and line numbers. All translations into English are mine.

into Italian may well have been made from the IP-version.[2] The Middle Dutch HV-translation survives in two fifteenth-century manuscripts[3] and a rewriting of the translation into the Cologne dialect in a manuscript dated 1465.[4] As it is intriguing that it was deemed useful to translate the long version of *De doctrina*, a complex text full of biblical, classical and patristic allusion, for an audience of fifteenth-century nuns, this essay will – unlike the accompanying discussions of the vernacular translations of *De doctrina* – focus on the most important textual witness of the Middle Dutch IP-translation, Vienna, Österreichischen Nationalbibliothek, MS 15231. This manuscript was used and copied in a community of Augustinian canonesses within the sphere of influence of the Windesheim Chapter, and was very probably translated for them. The Augustinian canonesses of the Odegem Abbey of St Trudo were eager for reform, and the Windesheim Chapter with which they came to be associated sought to control the spiritual lives of the female religious whose pastoral care was entrusted to them. These seemingly conflicting desires and needs were met to perfection in *De doctrina*, and they seem to have been intrumental in the decision to translate the Latin text into the vernacular of Western Flanders for the St Trudo sisters.

I

The Middle Dutch translation of the IP-version of *De doctrina cordis*, variously attributed to Hugh of St Cher or Gerard of Liège,[5] occurs in two manuscripts: Vienna, ÖNB, MS 15231 and Vienna, ÖNB, MS Ser. nov. 12805. The latter originated around 1500, and is a copy of MS 15231, which,

---

2 For the English, French, German and Spanish translations, see the essays of Anne Mouron, Karl-Heinz Steinmetz and Anthony Lappin in this volume. The Italian translation survives in Florence, Bibliotheca Medicea Laurenziana, MS Ashb. 253 (333–265). See G. Hendrix, *Hugo De Sancto Caro's traktaat De doctrina cordis. Vol. 1: Handschriften, receptie, tekstgeschiedenis en authenticiteitskritiek*, Documenta Libraria 16/1 (Louvain, 1995), p. 149. Hereafter cited as Hendrix, *Hugo I*.

3 The Hague, Koninklijke Bibliotheek, MS 135 F 6, which was owned by the Dominicans of Huissen, and Cologne, Diözesanbibliothek, MS 248, owned by the Augustinian canonesses of the convent Jerusalem in Venraai.

4 This Ripuaric 'umschrift' can be found in Berlin, Staatsbibliothek zu Berlin – Preußischer Kulturbesitz, MS Germ. qu. 1077. For a stemma of these manuscripts, see Hendrix, *Hugo I*, p. 151.

5 For a detailed discussion of *De doctrina*'s authorship, see Nigel Palmer's essay in this volume.

as we learn from the colophon, was finished on 22 June 1446.[6] That the Middle Dutch text is a translation of the so-called IP-version means that the text includes in its prologue the translation of a line that includes a reference to 'ignaros predicatores': 'Hoc dicitur contra *ignaros predicatores* qui, uim uerborum sacrorum ignorantes et per hoc eadem frangere et exponere nescientes, ipsa uerba usque ad corda audientium non transmittunt.'[7] This is translated into Middle Dutch as: 'Eerst mueghenze ghezeit ziin ieghen *de predicaers die ongheleert* ziin, die de cracht van de heilighen woorden niet en weten noch de scrifturen niet en verstaen. Ende aldus zo en zendese niet de woorden toter herten van hemlieden diese horen.'[8]

The IP-version of *De doctrina* can be distinguished from the HV–version of the text, so-called because, where the IP-prologue has the reference to the unlearned preachers, the HV-prologue has a different sentence, in which the words 'in hoc verbo' occur: 'In *hoc verbo* ammonetur predicator ut uerbum salutis diligenti et familiari expositione studeat eliquare ut sic ipsum uerbum facilius ad cor audientium transfundatur.'[9] In Middle Dutch, this sentence reads: 'In dit woert wort die predikaer vermaent dat hi dat woert der salicheit mit vlitigher ende dienstachtiger bedudinge ontbinde opdat also dat woert overgestort werde toter harten der geenre diet horen.'[10]

To distinguish versions of texts by their prologue is one way in which *De doctrina* scholar Guido Hendrix orders the large number of manuscripts in which versions of the Latin and translated *De doctrina* occur.[11] Another way in which Hendrix distinguishes between types of *De doctrina* texts is

---

6 Hendrix, *Hugo II*, pp. ix–xi.

7 Hendrix, *Hugo I*, pp. 165–6, my italics.

8 Hendrix, *Hugo II*, 'Proloog', ll. 7–10, my italics (First these words may be said to unlearned preachers, who are ignorant of the power of holy words and do not understand the Scriptures. And because of this they do not send the words into the hearts of those who hear them.) 'These words' refer to 1 Sam. 7:3: 'Preparate corda vestra domino' (Prepare your hearts unto the Lord.)

9 Hendrix, *Hugo I*, pp. 165–6, my italics.

10 M. De Cock and G. Hendrix (eds), *Dat boec vander bereydinge des harten. Middelnederlandse vertaling van De praeparatione cordis (Hugo van Saint-Cher, pseudo-Gerard van Luik),* De doctrina sive praeparatione cordis 2 (Ghent, 1986), 'Proloog', ll. 4–7 (In this word the preacher is admonished to disclose the word of blessedness with diligent and helpful meaning so that the word will be shed into the hearts of those who hear it.) 'In this word …', the reference here is to Isa. 40:2: 'Loquimini ad cor Ierusalem' (Speak ye to the heart of Jerusalem.)

11 Hendrix lists 208 manuscripts which contain full, partial, or fragmentary texts of the Latin and translated *De doctrina*. *Hugo I*, pp. 7–12, and pp. 13–105 for a description of the manuscripts.

to see whether they include certain passages he terms 'macrovariants' (as opposed to microvariants: deleted words, etc.). He distinguishes at least five different manuscript groups on the basis of which macrovariant they include, testifying to the complex textual tradition of *De doctrina*.[12]

What is interesting about the Middle Dutch translation of *De doctrina* in Vienna, ÖNB, MS 15231, is that Hendrix believes it was translated from Leiden, Bibliotheek der Rijksuniversiteit, MS BPL 2579, a pivotal manuscript in the transmission of *De doctrina*.[13] Not only does the Leiden manuscript contain the long version of the text (fols 1–109v), it also contains passages to be inserted in the text (fols 135r–147v; including all of the macrovariants absent in fols 1–109v), as well as indications by means of 'vacat'-inscriptions and insertion signs showing where the IP-prologue could be transformed into the HV-prologue, and more 'vacat'-inscriptions showing where the text could be abbreviated. The Leiden manuscript, then, could serve as the copy text for both the IP- and the HV-versions of the text.[14] As it is a mid-thirteenth-century manuscript Hendrix argues that, if the author of *De doctrina* himself edited his text – that is, if he added to it and designed a shorter version of the text (possibly to be used for different purposes) – the Leiden manuscript may have autograph elements.[15]

In his introduction to his pragmatic edition of *De bouc van der leeringhe van der herten*, Hendrix argues that the Middle Dutch translation in Vienna, ÖNB, MS 15231 must have been translated from the Leiden manuscript (or a faithful copy or a text version similar to it) because it has a feature that occurs only in this particular Latin text. The first of the

---

12 Ibid., pp. 170–73. The complex tradition is also the direct result of the length of the original text, which meant that summaries were frequently made. In view of this complex tradition, too, it is perhaps more correct to talk about the Middle Dutch text as the translation of *an* IP-version, rather than of *the* IP-version.

13 Hendrix, *Hugo II*, pp. xvii–xviii, referring back to *Hugo I*, pp. 165–92. See also *Le manuscrit Leyde Bibliothèque de l'Université, BPL 2579, témoin principal des phases de rédaction du traité De doctrina cordis*, facsimile edn with intro. by G. Hendrix, De doctrina sive praeparatione cordis 1 (Gent, 1980). In what follows I will refer to this manuscript as the Leiden manuscript. In the absence of an accessible transcription of the Leiden manuscript or a critical edition of the IP-version of *De doctrina*, the subsequent discussion has been taken from Hendrix, *Hugo I*.

14 Hendrix, *Hugo I*, pp. 177–89.

15 Fols 65–80 and 81–92 got lost, and the missing text was copied from Basel, Öffentl. Bibliothek der Universität, MS B.X.22. Hendrix argues that the replacement of the missing text, copied from a good manuscript, proves that the Leiden manuscript was considered a valuable textual witness. Ibid., pp. 177, 188–9.

macrovariants Hendrix distinguishes is a passage discussing four signs of virginity (rather than three).[16] In addition to the four signs of virginity the *Bouc* mentions, it also signals a fifth sign of virginity. This can derive only from the Leiden manuscript, the only manuscript that has both the three signs of virginity found in some manuscripts and the four signs of virginity found in another group.[17]

On fol. 28v, the Leiden manuscript lists three signs of virginity:

1. verecondia in vultu
2. paupertas in rebus
3. simplicitas in sermone

On fol. 145v, four signs of virginity are listed:

1. duritas mamillarum
2. paupertas in rebus
3. simplicitas in sermone
4. faciei reuelatione et capitis nuditas

The Middle Dutch text first lists these four signs of virginity:

1. de hartheit van haren barsten ende ghemeenlike de cleenheit[18]
2. aermoede van tideliken goede[19]
3. de gracelicheit ende de zoeticheit ende de simpleheit van den voyze[20]
4. maechden pleghen metten bloten hoofde te gane[21]

To these signs, the Middle Dutch text adds a fifth, which it selects from the three signs of virginity listed earlier in the Latin text:

---

16 Ibid., p. 170. This passage occurs in the 'Praeparatio' section of the *Bouc*, at the point at which it defines what the true bride of Christ should be like. This is followed by a list and discussion of the four kinds of 'wives', i.e. sinners, who cannot marry Christ (Hendrix, *Hugo II*, 'Praeparatio', ll. 2552–883).

17 Hendrix, *Hugo II*, pp. xvii–xviii.

18 Ibid., 'Praeparatio', ll. 2892–3 (the hardness of their breasts and generally their smallness.)

19 Ibid., 'Praeparatio', ll. 2963–4 (poverty of temporal goods.)

20 Ibid., 'Praeparatio', ll. 3008–9 (the gracefulness and the sweetness and the simplicity of the voice.)

21 Ibid., 'Praeparatio', ll. 3070–71 (virgins usually walk with their heads uncovered.)

5. ten desen vier tekenen van den maechdomme mochtme een viifste nomen, twelke es scamelheit int aenschiin[22]

Thus, Hendrix argues, the Middle Dutch translation in Vienna, ÖNB, MS 15231 is special, because it derives from the manuscript that seems to be the key to the dissemination of *De doctrina* in two versions, an editorial decision he feels might have been made by the author of *De doctrina* himself.[23] In addition, he argues that Vienna, ÖNB, MS 15231 not only presents the translator's autograph, but also records the translator's work in progress.[24] The Middle Dutch translation found in Vienna, ÖNB, MS 15231, then, gives the long variant of the text, the longest extant variant perhaps, and was translated from the Leiden manuscript, which Hendrix considers to be the most important witness of the Latin text of *De doctrina cordis*.

II

The Leiden manuscript came to be owned by the Augustinian Priory of Groenendaal, the monastery which was co-founded by the Brabant mystic Jan van Ruusbroec in 1343. The manuscript has damaged ownership marks on fol. 1r and fol. 147v, in either case under the last line of text: 'Liber monasterii beate marie uiridiualli in zonia'.[25] Vienna, ÖNB, MS 15231 was owned by the abbey of St Trudo, a community of Augustinian canonesses since 1248, which, in 1446, the date mentioned in the colophon, was situated in Odegem, not far from Bruges:[26] 'Desen bouc behoort toe den clooster van sint Truudt buten Brugghe .xix.'[27]

After 1456, St Trudo Abbey, originally a member of the congregation of Arrouaise (1146–1248) and later of the congregation of St Victor (1248–1456), associated itself with the Windesheim Chapter, a grouping of priories inspired by the spirituality of the Modern Devotion and the writings of Jan van Ruusbroec,[28] when Abbess Pieternelle van Aertrike (1456–76) brought

---

22 Ibid., 'Praeparatio', ll. 3094–5 (to these four signs of virginity one may add a fifth, which is timidity in their faces.)

23 Hendrix, *Hugo I*, p. 189.

24 Hendrix, *Hugo II*, pp. xi–xiv.

25 Hendrix, *Hugo I*, p. 190.

26 From now on I will refer to Vienna, ÖNB, MS 15231 as the St Trudo manuscript.

27 Hendrix, *Hugo II*, 'Scissio', ll. 503–4 (This book belongs to the convent of St Trudo outside Bruges .xix.)

28 The Windesheim Chapter was formed in 1395, when three Augustinian priories

Adriaen de Moye, an Augustinian canon professed in the Windesheim Priory of Elsegem near Oudenaarde, as rector to the abbey.[29] On Adriaen's return to Elsegem in 1478, Abbess Jacomine Terdelans (1476–1513) entreated the prior of Windesheim to ensure pastoral guidance for St Trudo from within the Windesheim Chapter, and he asked the prior of Groenendaal, the Augustinian priory co-founded by Jan van Ruusbroec, which had become part of the Windesheim Chapter in 1412, to appoint one of his monks, Jan van Mueninck, as rector to the Abbey and another, Jacob de Dinther, as his assistant ('mee-pater').[30]

Where and when exactly the Leiden manuscript was translated, and

---

that grew from Modern Devotion brother-houses (Windesheim, Mariënborn and Nieuwlicht) teamed up with the Augustinian priory of Eemstein, a monastery influenced by Groenendaal. Its agenda of reform, along the lines of Geert Grote's and Ruusbroec's examples and spirituality, proved successful, and about 125 years after it was formed it incorporated more than a hundred priories. In addition, other, much smaller but similar, chapters were formed in the image of the Windesheim Chapter, such as the Chapter of Sion (or Holland) in 1418 and the Chapter of Venlo in 1455. The most complete account of the history of the Windesheim Chapter remains J.A.R. Acquoy, *Het klooster te Windesheim en zijn invloed* (Utrecht, 1875–1880). Also see R.Th.M. Van Dijk, 'Het Kapittel van Windesheim 1395–1995: Terugblik en Vooruitzicht', in A.J. Hendrikman, P. Bange, R.Th.M. Van Dijk, A.J. Jelsma and G.E.P. Vrielink (eds), *Windesheim 1395–1995: Kloosters, Teksten, Invloeden* (Nijmegen, 1996), pp. 3–4.

29 There were only thirteen houses of female religious who were direct members of the Windesheim Chapter: Engelendaal at Bonn, Barberendaal at Tienen, Bethanië at Mechelen, Facons or Mariëndaal at Antwerp, Galilea at Ghent, St Agnes in Dordrecht, Bethanië in Arnhem, Bronope near Kampen, St Maria and St Agnes at Diepenveen, Jeruzalem in Utrecht, Mariënburg in Nijmegen, Mariënveld or Oude Nonnen in Amsterdam, Onze Lieve Vrouw in Arnhem. See W. Scheepsma, *Medieval Religious Women in the Low Countries: The Modern Devotion, The Canonesses of Windesheim and Their Writings*, tr. D.F. Johnson (Woodbridge, 2004), p. 12. As the Chapter had limited the number of female houses that could be members of the Chapter itself, many communities of women religious associated themselves with the Chapter by placing themselves under the authority of a prior of a convent that was incorporated into the Chapter. See K. Van Wonterghem, 'De Geschiedenis van de Sint-Trudoabdij te Odegem, te Brugge en te Male', in *Male: Burcht en Abdij* (Brugge, 1981), pp. 27–108 (52–4). Elseghem Priory was incorporated into the Windesheim congregation in 1420. Adriaan de Moye arrived at Odegem in 1462. He had previously been rector at the Priory Mariënveld in Amsterdam. See U. Berlière, E. Brouette and N. Huyghebaert (eds), *Monasticon Belge* (Maredsous, 1890–1993), vol. 7, pp. 689, 699.

30 Van Wonterghem, 'De Geschiedenis', p. 58.

who exactly instigated the translation, is difficult to reconstruct because of lack of evidence. The St Trudo manuscript is dated 1446, and the Western Flanders dialect in which the text is written suggests that it was translated in the Bruges region, possibly within St Trudo's.[31] It seems likely that there were informal contacts between St Trudo and Windesheim Chapter priories before 1456, which could explain how the Latin model of the *Bouc* ended up in St Trudo's in the early 1440s.[32] Kristina Van Wonterghem suggests that Modern Devotion influence began to make itself felt in the abbey around 1440: the Abbey Chronicle records that at this time the canonesses desired to reform the abbey and 'te zijn wat ze behoorden te zijn',[33] and that the desire for reform, supported by most of the canonesses, led to the affiliation with Windesheim.[34]

Even though the exact story of the translation of *De bouc van der leeringhe van der herten* cannot be reconstructed, and the actual translation of the text and ownership of the St Trudo manuscript pre-dates the documented relations between the sisters and the Windesheim movement, it is remarkable how well the Middle Dutch translation of *De doctrina* fits into the spiritual environment of both St Trudo Abbey and the Windesheim Chapter in the second half of the fifteenth century. The choice of a text that centres on the theme of the heart, and the way it needs to be prepared, kept, opened, made stable, given, lifted up and cut (off), marries St Trudo's traditions and pre-Windesheim history to the spirituality of the

31 Hendrix, *Hugo II*, p. xiv. Further research is needed to establish whether the translation could indeed have been made at St Trudo's, or whether Elseghem Priory could have been the place where it originated.

32 In the absence of a critical edition of the Latin *De doctrina* and a more fully annotated edition of *De bouc van der leeringhe van der herten*, the exact relations of the Middle Dutch text with the Latin source cannot be satisfactorily discussed.

33 Van Wonterghem, 'De Geschiedenis', pp. 50–51 (to become what they ought to be.) Van Wonterghem quotes and translates from the *Cronijck der Abdie van S. Truden*, kept at the present-day abbey, which covers the history of the abbey from its origins to 1916. The first hand in this chronicle, who would have copied or recorded the abbey's mid-fifteenth-century history, stops writing in 1679.

34 For four canonesses, the need for change was so urgent that they left St Trudo when Mevrouw van der Schueren was abbess (1445–56) and went to the convent of St Mary Magdalene 'op het Spui' in Amsterdam, a member of the Sion Chapter that was also influenced by Modern Devotion spirituality. As they did not return to Odegem, the zeal for reform must have been present in their fellow sisters too. At any rate, the formal decision to leave the congregation of St Victor was taken only in 1456, when Elisabeth Van der Schueren resigned as abbess of St Trudo. Ibid., pp. 50–51. Also see *Monasticon Belge*, vol. 4, pp. 1040–44.

Modern Devotion institutionalized in the Windesheim Chapter. Ever since its beginnings as the female half of a double monastery of the Arrouaise congregation in 1149, the St Trudo 'conversae' and later canonesses followed the rule of St Augustine, and one of the saint's symbols, the flaming heart, can be found in the abbey's pictorial sources throughout its history.[35] One of the main themes in the spirituality of the Modern Devotion (and hence of the communities of the Windesheim Chapter) was purity of heart.[36]

De bouc van der leeringhe van der herten also fits the spiritual emphases in the Modern Devotion and the Windesheim movement from the mid-fifteenth century onwards.[37] Although, initially, the spirituality of the movement had a mystical undercurrent inspired by Jan van Ruusbroec, Modern Devotion and Windesheim spirituality developed different emphases from that of Ruusbroec in that it became more affective, strongly underlining suffering and poverty of spirit, and the human being as an instrument in God's hand.[38] Mysticism caused tensions in the Windesheim movement, especially where women were concerned, and these tensions erupted in the Chapter's reaction to the spiritual leadership of the mystic, Alijt Bake, prioress of the convent Galilea in Ghent from 1445 until her deposition and banishment in 1455.[39]

In 1455, the Windesheim Chapter passed a resolution that forbade Windesheim canonesses to write, copy or translate texts containing 'philosophical teachings or revelations' (i.e. speculative texts, under which mystical texts would have been subsumed):

> Nulla monialis aut soror ciuiscunque status fuerit conscribat aliquos libros, doctrinas philosophicas aut revelationes continentes per se impositamve personam ex sua propria mente vel aliarum sororum compositas sub poena carceris si qui imposterum reperti fuerint praecipitur omnibus quod statim illi ad quorum conspectum vel aures pervenerint eos igni tradere curent, similiter nec aliquem transferre praesumant de latino in theutonicum.[40]

---

35 Van Wonterghem, 'De Geschiedenis', pp. 42–3 and p. 133.

36 Scheepsma, *Medieval Religious Women*, p. 86.

37 See T. Mertens, 'Mystieke cultuur en literatuur in de late Middeleeuwen', in F.P. Van Oostrom and W. Van Anrooij (eds), *Grote Lijnen: Syntheses over Middelnederlandse Letterkunde* (Amsterdam, 1995), pp. 117–35.

38 Ibid., p. 120.

39 Ibid., pp. 124–6.

40 Quoted in Mertens, 'Mystieke cultuur', p. 208, n. 39 (No nun or sister, no matter what her status, may, either personally or through an intermediary,

An additional resolution passed by the Chapter in 1466 stipulated that women were not allowed to translate texts from Latin into Dutch without permission from the General Chapter.[41]

The resolution shows how the Chapter controlled (or tried to control) the canonesses' spiritual lives. It also shows that the canonesses *did* translate Latin texts into Dutch, and that these translations were seen as a threat, particularly to 'the well-ordered community life',[42] which needed to be safeguarded and guaranteed. Thus, all the evidence suggests that Modern Devotion spirituality became a spirituality of the cloister, with a strong emphasis on the life of the community. Mystical texts and ideas were welcomed, as long as they supported conventual reform.[43]

III

In mid- to late-fifteenth-century Windesheim circles, the *Bouc* would have been considered excellent reading for female religious, exactly because, overall, it is not a mystical text. That is not to say that it disregards any contemplative experience, any striving towards union between the soul and God. In the ascending pattern of *De doctrina*'s spiritual teaching,[44] there are many passages that do express the close relationship between the soul (i.e. the reading or listening sister) and God, yet they are all deflected towards moral or monastic themes, as if to prevent the recipient of the text from reaching for higher experiences, instead taking them back down to the everyday requirements of the community: to the 'down-to-earth'. These passages describe contemplation as a fact of life, a 'given' within the monastic life at the centre of the text, but advise that this experience remains tied to the needs of the community. Potentially mystical passages are deflected into advice about the sisters' spiritual lives in their monastic setting. In the 'Apertio' section, a passage with a mystical undercurrent turns into a moral exhortation:

---

copy books which contain philosophical teachings or revelations, whether these originate in her own mind or the minds of her sisters, on penalty of imprisonment; henceforth should any such books be discovered, it is the responsibility of all to ensure that they are immediately burned as soon as they are found or heard tell of; nor should any presume to translate such texts from the Latin into Dutch.) Translated in Scheepsma, *Medieval Religious Women*, p. 25. This resolution was repeated in the Acts of the General Chapter in 1456 and 1457.

41 Scheepsma, *Medieval Religious Women*, p. 25, n. 93.

42 Mertens, 'Mystieke cultuur', p. 126.

43 Ibid., pp. 129–30.

44 As described in Karl-Heinz Steinmetz's essay in this volume, pp. 224–27.

> De duere dan van diner herte doeste hiement opene, alstene inde begheerte van diner herten ontfancs met minnen … Dese wet,[45] daer in dat wi ons herte zijn sculdich open te doene, es de wet van onzen Heere, die ombesmet es, die anders niet en es dan de minne. Therte dan open doen in de wet van onzen Heere, en es anders niet dan onzen Heere inganc te gheuene in ons herte met minnen ende caritaten van Gode ende van onzen heuenmensche.[46]

Later the opening of the heart is interpreted morally as the admission of sin in confession: 'De mensche dan die doet zijn herte opene, alse hem zeluen bereet ten duechden ende doet dat in hem es openbaerende zijn zonde inde biechte. Maer dan zo doet ons Heere therte van de mensche opene, alse den mensche verleent zijn gracie.'[47]

In the 'Stabilitas' section, the reader is told: 'datse alle naar hem zullen moeten clemmen, die metten gheloue Christus an cleuen ende met minnen bi bliuen. Ende hier omme zo ist goet, datste Christum ancleefs.'[48] The text then goes on to say that rest in Christ is the reward in heaven for labour in this life, and applies this to the reader's task in the community, rather than to mystical work and rest: 'Du en zuls den aerbeit van diner oordene niet scuwen, daerste mede muechs bereeden zulke een stede van rusten.'[49] The contemplative, then, is a member of a community, and more specifically an Order, a *monastic* community; as such, she is a member of the body of the Church. The 'ancleeuen' (clinging) to Christ is always a communal activity,

---

45 Referred to in 1 Macc. 1:4: 'et congregavit virtutem exercituum fortem nimis et exaltatum est et elevatum cordis' (and he gathered a power, and a very strong army, and his heart was exalted and lifted up.)

46 Hendrix, *Hugo II*, 'Apertio', ll. 358–9, 362–7 (You open the door of your heart to someone, when you receive him into the desire of your heart with love … This law, in which we are indebted to open our hearts, is the law of our Lord, who is spotless, and who is nothing else but love. To open the heart in the law of our Lord, then, is nothing else than to give our Lord access to our heart with love and charity towards God and towards our fellow human beings.)

47 Ibid., 'Apertio', ll. 373–6 (Human beings, then, open their hearts, when they prepare themselves for virtues and do what is in them, revealing their sins in confession. And in this way our Lord opens the hearts of human beings, when he gives them his grace.)

48 Ibid., 'Stabilitas', ll. 254–7 (that they will all have to climb to him, who cling to Christ in faith and stay with him in love. And this is why it is good that you cling to Christ.)

49 Ibid., 'Stabilitas', ll. 266–8 (You will not avoid the [manual] labour of your order, with which you can help prepare such a place of rest.)

not an individual one.[50] In the same vein, the 'Eleuatio' section defines the climbing up to God as the ascent of 'tcruce van den cloosterliken leuene',[51] and it is implied that the lifting up of the heart toward God can only reach its perfect fulfilment in the afterlife.[52]

In other words, the *Bouc*'s stance with regard to contemplation and mystical experience is the same as the Windesheim attitude toward mysticism in the second half of the fifteenth century. Contemplation is not denied, but the readers' spiritual desires are guided towards the safe and manageable domains of the sacramental and communal.[53]

The *Bouc* contains further intense passages that skirt the purely mystical, but, again, these passages do not elaborate the theme further, and direct the focus back to more everyday devotional realities and themes. This is true even in a long passage in the 'Praeparatio' section entitled 'De trappen vander goddeliker minnen' (The steps of divine love). The fourth and highest step of divine love is that Christ has given himself to us as food and drink in the sacrament of the altar. The text describes how the person eating and the thing eaten become one without difference, an extremely loaded concept in mystical writing.

> Ende aldus als de mensche tsacrament ontfanct, zo wort tsacrament ende de mensche een. Ende hier omme gheliic dat twee ghelieven, die deen den anderen liefhebben ende minnen, alse de minne van hen beeden openbaren willen, zii en openbaren se niet ghenoech met dat deen toten anderen zeecht: Ic zoude dit of dat om huwen wille gheuen of ic zoude dit om huwen wille doen. Maer als deen toten anderen zeecht: Ic zoude hu gheuen te hetene van minen vleesche of te drinkene van minen bloede, in dit zo openbarense de upperste begheerte van minnen. Ende aldus heeft Christus ghedaen, die ons heeft ghegheuen ziin vleesch te hetene en ziin bloet te drinkene om datte de aller upperste ende de allermeeste minne openbaren ende toghen zouden, die hi te ons waert hadde.[54]

---

50 Thus, too, a fellow sister's fat of charity can baste the reader's heart she is cooking for Christ, if she herself does not have enough fat/charity. See ibid., 'Praeparatio', ll. 2074–93.

51 Ibid., 'Eleuatio', ll. 359–60 (the cross of the monastic life.)

52 Ibid., 'Eleuatio', ll. 400–559.

53 See Mertens, 'Mystieke cultuur', p. 127, for similar examples of the 'thematic lowering' of mystical content.

54 Hendrix, *Hugo II*, 'Praeparatio', ll. 1902–14 (As a human being receives the Sacrament, the Sacrament and the human being become one. Two lovers who love

Rather than continuing the theme of the mutual eating, the text goes on to teach how, when the priest, as the head of the community (the body of the Church), takes communion, the members of the community (the body of the Church) also receive communion even when they do not eat physically, and they receive God's grace within them even when the priest is in mortal sin. In addition, while the text does make reference to Christ's eating of the sister's cooked heart, his actual act of eating is never described, with the exception of one passage specifying the moral requirements of the person Christ will eat: '[Christus] en heet gheenen cloostrier noch religieus bi gracien incorporerende tenzi datte ghevleghen zi van aller tideliceit ende van aller heeghinheit van wille.'[55]

Similarly, the 'Eleuatio' section briefly describes the 'person in contemplation' via a comment on Job 39:27–9:

> Bi den haerne, die hoge ende alleene vliecht, die subtilike ende scaerp van ghezichte es, zo mueghen wi uerstaen een mensche, die in contemplacien es, die haer heeft of ghetrocken ende es of ghescheeden van der minnen van desen weerelt.[56]

However, again, the text does not sustain this view of contemplation, but reverts to a devotional lifting-up of the soul:

> Ziiste ontsteken of berrenste van den cortsen, hi es een fonteyne; ziiste ghewont, hi es medicine; duchste de doot, hi es tleuen; hebste ghebrec van hulpen, hi es de cracht; zoucste spize, hi es dat voetsele. Van hem zulste in allen dighen diin ghevouch maken, die di omme alle dinc ghegheuen es. Du zuls dan diin ongherighe ziele upheffen na dese spize,

---

each other, and want to reveal the extent of their love, do not reveal enough when the one says to the other 'I would give this or that for your sake', or 'I would do this for your sake.' But when the one says to the other 'I would give you my flesh to eat and my blood to drink', in these words they reveal the highest desire of love. And this is what Christ did, who gave us his flesh to eat and his blood to drink in order to reveal and show the very highest and the very greatest love he bore us.)

55 Ibid., 'Praeparatio', ll. 2003–4 (Christ does not eat a cloistered or religious person, incorporating him by grace, unless he is stripped of all temporariness and of all individuality of will.)

56 Ibid., 'Eleuatio', ll. 255–9 (By the eagle, which flies high and alone, and which is subtle and sharp of vision, we may understand a human being who is in contemplation, who has withdrawn and has been cut off from the love of this world.)

> diemen niement gheuen en zal dan der ziele, die haer upheffen zal … De spize … ziin goddelike troosten, die alleene ghegheuen ziin der upgheheuenen ziele.[57]

Unable to linger on these tantalizingly undeveloped mystical passages, the reader is returned firmly to an affective devotional context that acknowledges contemplative union but does not allow it a central position. It is interesting, in this respect, that the translator does not seem to have been inspired by extant mystical texts in Middle Dutch, and does not use mystical terminology where one would expect it. In the 'Scissio' section, the term 'ouerzwinghende minne' (abundant, boundless, ineffable love) repeatedly occurs.[58] This term occurs neither in Ruusbroec ('ouerwesenlijke minne' (superessential love)) nor in Hadewijch ('buten den geeste zijn' (to be outside of the spirit)), which might indicate that the translator did not know their texts, or did not associate *De doctrina* with them.[59]

The *Bouc*'s transmission beyond St Trudo Abbey reveals, if only modestly, that the text was considered useful enough to be passed on. The St Trudo manuscript served as the base text for another extant copy of the *Bouc*, Vienna, ÖNB, MS Ser. nov. 12805, dated to around 1500. The copy was probably made for the Carmelite convent of Sion (also known as St Mary's) in Bruges, who owned the manuscript.[60] A further copy of the *Bouc*, made in 1548, is no longer extant.[61] The St Trudo manuscript itself was donated to the convent Galilea in Ghent (one of the thirteen female houses within the Windesheim Chapter) by Adriane De Vos, as an inscription on fol. 176r of the manuscript tells us: 'Suster adriane de vos Religieuse van het clooster

57 Ibid., 'Eleuatio', ll. 309–19 (Are you on fire or burning with fever, he is a fountain [of cool water]; are you hurt, he is medicine; do you fear death, he is life; do you lack help, he is strength; do you seek food, he is nourishment. From him you will receive what you need in all things, who has been given to you for all things. So you will lift up your hungry soul to this food, which will be given to no one but the soul who will lift herself up … The food … is divine consolations, which are given solely to the soul who has been lifted up.)

58 See, for instance, ibid., 'Scissio', ll. 75–6, 136.

59 I am indebted to Guido De Baere for this observation.

60 There is some evidence of contacts between St Trudo Abbey and the Carmelite sisters. St Trudo Abbess Johanna Plas was buried in the Carmelite convent in 1584 because the abbey no longer had its own cemetery after they had moved into Bruges in 1566. Van Wonterghem, 'De Geschiedenis', p. 69.

61 Ibid., p. 63.

van sent Trud heft dese bouck ons clooster van galyleen ghegheuen int Jaer XV neghentich.'[62]

Though the redirecting of contemplative desire towards the sacramental and the communal seems to define *De bouc van der leeringhe van der herten* as an instrument of control, the text's richness and ensuing multifunctionality[63] may mean that the control the text exerted on the sisters' spiritual experiences was not felt as too brutal a truncation; it may also have made the *Bouc* a text that enabled its readers to select from its abundance those lessons that helped them 'te zijn wat ze behoorden te zijn',[64] in the community as well as in their personal contemplative practice.

---

62 (Sister Adriane de Vos, religious of the convent of St Trudo gave this book to our convent of Galilea in the year 1590.) Adriane de Vos (1537–1592) 'van Gent' was a wealthy canoness who helped the convent more than once. See P. Huismans and K. Van Wonterghem (eds), *Het obituarium van de Sint-Trudoabdij de Odegem, te Brugge en te Male, 1149–2002* (Brugge, 2002), p. 77. It seems likely that this gift was possible because St Trudo owned a copy of the *Bouc* at this time, possibly the one made in 1548. The exact circumstances of an individual sister's being able to present a book to another convent remain to be investigated.

63 See Karl-Heinz Steinmetz's discussion of *De doctrina*'s multifunctionality in this volume, pp. 223–37.

64 Van Wonterghem, 'De Geschiedenis', p. 51 (to become what they ought to be.)

9

De doctrina cordis and Fifteenth-Century Ecclesial Reform: Reflections on the Context of German Vernacular Versions

Karl-Heinz Steinmetz

Introduction

De doctrina cordis was composed, either by Gerard of Liège or Hugh of St Cher, in the first half of the thirteenth century.[1] The continuous tradition of this text of spiritual instruction testifies to its enduring success; in addition, a closer look at the provenance of extant manuscripts substantiates our understanding of the impact that *De doctrina* had in Germany, particularly after the Councils of Constance and Basel, which supported monastic reform programmes. Many of the Latin manuscripts were produced in prominent monastic, mendicant or canonical houses in mid- or late-fifteenth-century Germany and Austria.[2] Furthermore, most

---

1 Guido Hendrix argues for Hugh of St Cher's authorship in an extensive series of articles and editions listed in Nigel Palmer's essay in this volume and in the bibliography. Nigel Palmer takes issue with his conclusions and constructs a powerful argument in favour of Gerard of Liège's authorship in the same essay.

2 For the provenance of manuscripts, see the reliable details given in G. Hendrix, *Hugo de Sancto Caro's traktaat De doctrina cordis. Vol. 1: Handschriften, receptie, tekstgeschiedenis en authenticiteitskritiek*, Documenta Libraria 16/1 (Louvain, 1995), pp. 3–146. Henceforth cited as Hendrix, *Hugo I.* For the intersection of reform Councils and the reform movement in general, see D. Mertens, 'Reformkonzilien und Ordensreform im 15. Jahrhundert', in K. Elm (ed.), *Reformbemühungen und Observanzbestrebungen im spätmittelalterlichen Ordenswesen* (Berlin, 1989),

manuscripts with an abbreviated version of the Latin text – that is to say, a *summarium* or *capitula selecta* of *De doctrina* – and all six vernacular translations into Middle High German can be dated post-Constance.[3] In the first instance, this plethora of manuscripts has to be ascribed to the immense rise of book production in general during the second half of the fourteenth and early part of the fifteenth centuries. Yet the variety of forms into which the mid-thirteenth-century *De doctrina* was adapted is also worth closer investigation, as complete Latin text on the one hand, in the form of Latin *summarium* or *capitula selecta* on the other, and, especially, in vernacular versions. This essay will reflect on *De doctrina* as embedded in the ecclesial reform and devotional theology of fifteenth-century Germany, particularly with regard to the six extant Middle High German versions, in order to specify the function of this text in popularizing spiritual knowledge.

The components of *De doctrina cordis* and multifunctionality

De doctrina cordis[4] is a complex piece of religious instruction; the text as a whole, however, is composed according to a lucid pattern. In order to structure spiritual knowledge about how to reach mystical union with God, the text's author combines the traditional doctrine of the seven gifts of the Holy Ghost with those key sentences from the Bible that refer to the 'organ' of spirituality: the heart.[5] Constraints of space in this essay preclude a theological elaboration on each of the consecutive steps; however, a cursory examination of some doctrinal components will suffice in order to contextualize how this text supported the dissemination of devotional theology in fifteenth-century Germany.

The first book – on how to prepare one's heart ('praeparatio cordis')[6] – can be summarized as implementing sacramental theology from the Fourth

---

pp. 431–58. On the role of mendicant orders at the Councils, see also A. Zumkeller, 'Die Beteiligung der Mendikanten an der Arbeit der Reformkonzilien von Konstanz und Basel', in Elm (ed.), *Reformbemühungen*, pp. 459–68.

3 Hendrix, *Hugo I*, pp. 13–110, especially pp. 107–10.

4 Owing to the lack of a critical Latin edition, all quotations from *De doctrina cordis* in this chapter will be taken from Gerardus Leodiensis, *Speculum concionatorum ad illustrandum pectora auditorum, in septem libros distributum* (Naples, 1607), Oxford, Bodleian Library, 8° L 12 Th. BS. Henceforth cited as *De doctrina*, with page numbers.

5 *De doctrina*, pp. 1–155.

6 Hendrix, *Hugo I*, pp. 341–57, offers helpful information on this section.

Lateran Council (1215). The Council outlined the minimal requirements for a religious life: basic knowledge of – and at least annual reception of – the sacraments of confession and the Eucharist, as well as a basic insight into the sacrament of marriage. Since *De doctrina*'s author was less concerned with the visible aspect of sacramental theology than with the spiritual dimension behind it, he designed his catechesis around the metaphor of the heart, inviting the reader to visualize the heart in three images so as to facilitate a deeper understanding of the sacraments.

For confession, firstly, the heart has to be visualized as a house. The instructive household allegory can be summarized only briefly here: house cleaning corresponds to the sacrament of confession; a bed, to the peace resulting from true confession; a chair, to the examination of conscience; a table, to penance; and a candlestick, to self-knowledge.[7] Secondly, for a deeper understanding of the Eucharist it is necessary to imagine a 'spiritual kitchen' in which one's heart must be prepared for the Lord. To post-Enlightenment ears, a cooking allegory with images of skinning, roasting and larding one's heart might sound tasteless if not pathological; to medieval ears, however, this was easily digestible spiritual nourishment: did not Christ himself constitute a sacramental Eucharistic meal? Furthermore, in one Easter episode, did not Christ appear while the disciples were roasting fish on a grill? Supported by the belief that God can reveal himself even between saucepans, there exists a tradition of interpreting this passage of Luke 24:41–43 as an allegory of the passion: 'piscis assus Christus passus', the roasted fish symbolizing the suffering Christ.[8] Thirdly, for the sacrament of marriage, the author unfolds an impressive allegory of bridal mysticism, presenting the mystical virgin in a wedding dress comprised of virtues and pieces of spiritual jewellery.[9]

---

7 *De doctrina*, pp. 6–56. For background details see C. Batt, D. Renevey and C. Whitehead, 'Domesticity and Medieval Devotional Literature', *Leeds Studies in English*, 36 (2005), 195–250, especially the section by Renevey, 'Figuring Household space in *Ancrene Wisse* and *The Doctrine of the Hert*', 198–214, with interpretations and secondary literature footnoted.

8 Ibid., pp. 56–84. A helpful summary is offered by Sister M.P. Candon (ed.), '*The Doctrine of the Hert*, Edited from the Manuscripts with Introduction and Notes' (unpublished doctoral dissertation, Fordham University, 1963), pp. xxxiii–iv. Hereafter cited as Candon, *Doctrine*. The motto 'Piscis assus Christus passus' is part of the traditional exegesis of Luke 24:42 that can be found in Augustine, Bede, Bernard, Bonaventure, Aquinas etc.

9 Ibid., pp. 85–155. Candon reflects upon this passage in Candon, *Doctrine*, pp. xxxiv–v.

In evaluating this first book of *De doctrina* we can say that it functions in a number of ways. The first book presents a general catechetical instruction suitable both for an 'elite' audience of mendicants and monastics and also for simple lay people, dealing with confession as entrance door, the eucharist as centre, and ghostly marriage as the goal of spirituality. The first book constitutes the first half of *De doctrina*, the second half consisting of the six remaining books. Therefore the text of *De doctrina* exhibits predetermined breaking points: such an 'unbalanced' text can easily be partitioned, as we will see when turning to different *capitula selecta* versions.

The second book – on how to guard one's heart ('custodia cordis') – necessitates another spatial visualization of the heart: as castle and container. In a first section the author clarifies the spiritual war ('bellum spirituale') that rages during prayer and informs the reader about mistakes in and remedies for the struggle against temptation.[10] In the following section he offers comprehensive advice about 'guarding one's tongue' ('custodia linguae'). In order to shape one's communication according to the commandment of love, a careful examination of speech is needed: what is said ('quid'), to whom ('cui'), in which context ('ubi'), when ('quando') and in which way ('qualiter').[11] Subsequent to this 'school of speech', the text's author presents the classical doctrine of correcting one's neighbour ('correptio proximi') in order to revitalize and reform a social community.[12]

Here, again, a short evaluation is needed. In his second book the author of *De doctrina* offers a tripartite instruction on the topic of communication. In the first instance, he discusses how to shape the transcendental communication of prayer. Secondly, he addresses verbal communication with one's fellow human beings. Finally, he turns to the matter of social communication within a convent. The relevance of these sections is obvious. 'Custodia linguae' functions as a 'primary education' for integrating novices and newcomers into spiritual community life, whereas 'correptio proximi' is an outline of how to constantly reform social communication in order to keep other forms of community alive. These were challenging subjects for a mid-thirteenth-century theologian to tackle in his own period of monastic and mendicant expansion and reform, and also problematic for his later audience during the fifteenth-century ecclesial reform.

The third book – on how to open one's heart ('aperitio cordis') – visualizes the heart as a book and tries again to facilitate communication

---

10 Ibid., pp. 155–75.

11 Ibid., pp. 175–85; Hendrix offers a helpful overview in *Hugo I*, pp. 357–9.

12 Ibid., pp. 185–90; for the structure of 'correptio proximi', see Hendrix, *Hugo I*, pp. 359–60; for more information, also pp. 213–28.

and confession. When treating confession, and in marked contrast to the metaphorical catechesis of the first book, this section provides psychological and pastoral instruction upon how to overcome the insistent obstacles ('impedimenta') which oppose fruitful contrition and true confession. This passage aims in two different but mutually reinforcing directions: it advocates confession for a lay audience, while also raising the standards of confession for a monastic or mendicant convent.[13]

Books 4 to 7 can be read as a coherent 'mystical instruction' on how to ascend from prayer and meditation to contemplation and mystic love. Here again a cursory examination must suffice. The fourth book – on how to stabilize one's heart ('stabilitas cordis') – starts with a diligent explanation of the twelve articles of the Creed in order to equip the human heart with a firm foundation of faith.[14] The fifth book – on how to give one's heart ('datio cordis') – elaborates on how a person can imitate the kenotic (that is to say, the self-giving and self-emptying) love of Christ via true commitment, dedication and obedience, illustrated through a spiritual exegesis of shaving the monastic tonsure.[15] The sixth book – on how to lift one's heart ('levatio cordis') – offers comprehensive teaching on how to meditate and contemplate. *De doctrina*'s author focuses on hope, desire and right intention ('recta intentio') as motivating principles, the 'feet', so to speak, by which the praying person can draw nearer to God and finally reach mystical union.[16] The concluding seventh book – on how to cut off one's heart ('scissio cordis') – addresses the liberation of the heart from all 'attachments to the world', that is to say from the enslaving gravity that could easily override the spiritual dynamics of the human person reaching toward mystical union with God. In the final passage of this book, the author elaborates on seven signs of 'being in love', discussing to what extent symptoms of bodily love-sickness can also offer important insights into ecstatic mystical love.[17]

Having given a cursory exposition of the basic components of *De doctrina*, we can easily specify the multifunctionality of this text.[18] In the

---

13 Ibid., pp. 191–212. On this passage, see also Hendrix, *Hugo I*, pp. 366–8.

14 Ibid., pp. 212–44. For reflections on this passage, see Hendrix, *Hugo I*, pp. 371–405.

15 Ibid., pp. 244–55; see also Hendrix, *Hugo I*, pp. 407–12.

16 Ibid., pp. 255–75; see Hendrix, *Hugo I*, pp. 412–14.

17 Ibid., pp. 276–94. Hendrix offers further reflection on this passage, *Hugo I*, pp. 414–33.

18 For the multifunctionality of *De doctrina*, see Hendrix, *Hugo I*, pp. 241–3. On the multifunctionality of devotional texts in general, see W. Williams-Krapp,

first instance, *De doctrina* has to be read as a handbook of sacramental theology and catechetical instruction, as seen especially in passages from the first and fourth books. Secondly, the multiple references to mendicant, monastic or canonical life throughout *De doctrina* (especially 'custodia cordis', 'custodia linguae' and 'correptio proximi') demonstrate that parts of this text should be understood as a commentary on the basic rules of religious community life, offering both an introduction for novices and instruction for reforming religious superiors. Thirdly, *De doctrina* includes basic mystical theology on how to prepare the heart to experience God – especially in the bride-allegory of the first book and in Books 4 to 7.[19] We will now turn to the different text versions in order to see how this tripartite functionality of the original text operated in its subsequent reception history.

Monastic-canonical reform and German partial manuscripts

As mentioned above, the provenance of extant manuscripts both in Latin and the vernacular witnesses to a certain accumulation of copies of *De doctrina cordis* in prominent houses of the monastic and canonical reforms following the Councils of Constance and Basel, which supported not only church reform in general but also monastic reform in particular. Owing to constraints of space there can be no detailed depiction of this late medieval reform movement; some highlights must suffice.

From the perspective of the Lutheran reformation, the fifteenth century seemed to be a time of decline in the Church. Recent interdenominational historical research, however, has portrayed the fifteenth century as a time of multi-dimensional social, cultural and religious transformations that cannot be interpreted solely as a deterioration.[20]

Most leaders of monastic and canonical houses saw clearly the challenges of their times and the apparent defects of religious life, as can be concluded

---

'Ordensreform und Literatur im 15. Jahrhundert', in *Jahrbuch der Oswald von Wolkenstein Gesellschaft*, 4 (Goeppingen, 1986–87), pp. 41–51.

19 Candon, *Doctrine*, p. lvi, is correct in her interpretation of *De doctrina* as 'decidedly an ascetical … treatise', however, this does not exclude a mystical dimension.

20 For a Protestant evaluation of monastic reform see, for example, I. Mager, 'Bemühungen um die Reform der Klosterkonvente im fünfzehnten Jahrhundert. Grundzüge der Windesheimer und Bursfelder Reform', in J. Reller and M. Tamcke (eds), *Trinitäts- und Christusdogma: ihre Bedeutung für Beten und Handeln der Kirche. Festschrift für Jouko Martikainen* (Münster, 2001), pp. 223–43.

from impulses of reform during the fourteenth century that were further developed during the fifteenth century into a kind of reform-network.[21] Examples include the Benedictine reform of Kastl, promoted by Czech monasteries and the University of Prague, which was adopted by more than twenty abbeys in the Bavarian and Swabian area after 1400; the Benedictine reform of Melk, supported by the University of Vienna, which influenced prominent Benedictine houses in Austria and southern Germany around 1450; the Benedictine reform of Bursfeld, which transferred the congregation-system of Santa Giustina in Padua to Germany and reached more than thirty-six monasteries all over Middle and North Germany; and the Augustinian Raudnitz reform that spread from Czech convents to Austrian and Bavarian houses.[22] Another outstanding contribution to the work of renewal was made by the well-known Augustinian Windesheim reform.[23]

The encounter of reform-theologians at the councils of Constance and Basel was helpful for connecting and intensifying reform projects. Here, Benedictines and Augustinians could share experiences or discuss pressing questions and their relevance for monastic and canonical life: topics such as the changeover to urban culture, new territorial forms of government and their impact on religion, the differentiation of society and its influence upon the internal structure of convents, the necessity of developing a lay-centred pastoral theology and catechesis, the specific challenges of rising lay literacy and, finally, new individualistic forms of devotion and piety.

An appreciation of monastic and canonical reform is necessary for a better understanding of the adaptation of *De doctrina* in the fifteenth century. One of the aims of ecclesial reform was the improvement of theological and spiritual education. Hence there existed interdependence between the reform movement, book production, and the equipping of libraries. The reform movement, however, influenced not only the quantity of manuscripts and circulation, but also the style in which earlier works

---

21 For an excellent overview, see K. Elm, 'Reform- und Observanzbestrebungen im spätmittelalterlichen Ordenswesen. Ein Überblick', in Elm (ed.), *Reformbemühungen*, pp. 3–22. For detailed portrayals of late medieval reform see the multifaceted articles in the same volume.

22 For Benedictine reform, see P. Becker, 'Erstrebte und erreichte Ziele benediktinischer Reformen im Spätmittelalter', in ibid., pp. 23–34; on Augustinian reform, L. Milis, 'Reformatory Attempts within the Ordo Canonicus in the Late Middle Ages', in ibid., pp. 61–70.

23 On the Windesheim reform, see W. Kohl, 'Die Windesheimer Kongregation', in ibid., pp. 83–108; with further literature.

were adapted. Besides complete versions of the Latin text, some Benedictine and Cistercian abbeys, charterhouses and Augustinian convents produced and/or owned summary versions of *De doctrina*.[24] 'Summary version' here means an abbreviated text that condenses the content by displaying only its essential structure while omitting explanatory and illustrative material. Another type of abbreviated adaptation manipulates the original even more: texts that could be named *capitula selecta* versions comprise carefully isolated passages, in contrast to summary versions, which tend to retain the structure of the treatise in its original form. Various Latin examples that were owned by Benedictine and Cistercian libraries as well as by some charterhouses are extant.[25] A closer look at *capitula selecta* redactions reveals the main interests of copyists and readers: under the perspective of how to reform community life and improve standards of confession, a first group of works focuses on 'custodia cordis', 'aperitio cordis', 'custodia linguae' and 'impedimenta'.[26] With a pronounced mystical perspective on how to facilitate the experiential encounter with God, another group presents material from 'praeparatio cordis', 'scissio cordis' and 'signa amoris'.[27]

All these short versions of *De doctrina* fulfil an important demand of the reform movement: theological knowledge has to comply with 'utilitas'; that is to say, it must give useful instruction for the practical dimensions of the Christian life, rather than presenting mere theory. This is definitely the case with the above-mentioned versions: a maximum amount of relevant theological material can be retrieved from reader-friendly abbreviated texts in a minimum amount of time.

Another step in making *De doctrina* accessible to 'conversi', 'familiares' and other lay people, many of whom could not understand Latin properly, was translation into the German vernacular, as can be seen from the following examples.

The imperial Charterhouse of Buxheim owned a manuscript comprising

---

24 Examples of summary versions include MSS G^{2}, G^{7}, L^{14}, M^{15}, M^{2}, M^{18}, O^{4}, P^{12}, following the manuscript abbreviations assigned by Hendrix, *Hugo I*, pp. 7–110.

25 For examples of *capitula selecta* versions, see again Hendrix, *Hugo I*, pp. 7–110.

26 On these components of *De doctrina*, see G. Hendrix, '*De apercione cordis, De impedimentis* and *De custodia linguae*. Three pseudo-Bernardine texts restored to their true author, Hugh of St. Cher', *RTAM*, 48 (1981), 172–97. For 'reform' examples, see M^{16}, M^{17}, K^{13}, K^{15}, B^{10}, B^{19}, S^{8-10}, W^{13}, W^{10}, listed by Hendrix.

27 The two 'mystical' examples of M^{20} and B^{20} are both of Carthusian provenance.

a Middle High German summary version fragment of 'praeparatio cordis' (now preserved as Berlin, Staatsbibliothek zu Berlin – Preußischer Kulturbesitz, Ms. germ. qu. 1130, fols 71v–77r). The 1474 manuscript offers, apart from 'praeparatio cordis', elaborate Dominican material for spiritual instruction in the Alemannic dialect, such as two epistles by the reform theologian Johannes Nider, Meister Eckhart's *Rede der Unterscheidunge* and Henry Suso's sermon *Lectulus noster floridus*, alongside miscellaneous excerpts from other works of devotional theology.[28]

Another, rather short, fragment of unknown Swabian provenance dating from the same period can be found in Augsburg, Universitätsbibliothek, cod. III 1.2°14, fol. 33ra–vb, where an excerpt from 'custodia cordis' and 'custodia linguae' is integrated into a patchwork of disparate materials.[29]

A less fragmentary and more rounded mid-fifteenth-century vernacular version of 'aperitio cordis', 'custodia linguae' and 'impedimenta' is extant in Klosterneuburg, Augustinerchorherren-Stift, MS 363, fols 132r–159r,[30] a book from the imperial Augustinian house of Klosterneuburg, near Vienna, that includes further confessional material such as *Erchantnuzz der Sund* (knowledge of sin) attributed to Henricus de Hassia, as well as devotional theology by Marquart de Lindau.[31]

Detailed insight into the circulation of *De doctrina* within the reform movement can be gained from two interdependent vernacular examples extant in Bavaria: one from the Augustinian House of Rebdorf and another from the nearby Benedictine Abbey of St Walburg of Eichstätt.

---

28 A manuscript description is offered by H. Degering, *Kurzes Verzeichnis der germanischen Handschriften der Preußischen Staatsbibliothek II. Die Handschriften in Quartformat*, Mitteilungen aus der Preußischen Staatsbibliothek 8 (Leipzig, 1926; repr. Graz, 1970), pp. 191–2.

29 Manuscript description by K. Schneider, *Deutsche mittelalterliche Handschriften der Universitätsbibliothek Augsburg: die Signaturengruppen Cod.I.3 und Cod.III.1* (Wiesbaden, 1988), pp. 171–5 (174). The anonymous translator used the Latin text from Munich, Bayerische Staatsbibliothek, Clm 9648, described by B. Hernad, *Die gotischen Handschriften deutscher Herkunft in der Bayerischen Staatsbibliothek. Teil 1: Vom späten 13. bis zur Mitte des 14. Jahrhunderts* (Wiesbaden, 2000), p. 38.

30 For a manuscript description, see H.J. Zeibig, 'Die deutschen Handschriften der Stiftsbibliothek zu Klosterneuburg', *Serapeum*, 11 (1850), 102–3 (no. 8).

31 On the text of this 'knowledge of sin' treatise, see *Heinrich von Langenstein. Erchantnuzz der Sund Nach österreichen Handschriften*, ed. by R. Rudolf, Texte des späten Mittelalters und der frühen Neuzeit 22 (Berlin, 1969); for details about its origin and author, see P. Wiesinger, 'Zur Autorschaft und Entstehung des Heinrich von Langenstein zugeschriebenen Traktats "Erkenntnis der Sünde"', *Zeitschrift für deutsche Philologie*, 97 (1978), 42–60.

A late-fifteenth-century manuscript, Munich, Bayerische Staatsbibliothek, Cgm 447, written in a North Bavarian dialect in the Augustinian House of Rebdorf, presents a *De doctrina* section consisting of 'aperitio cordis', 'custodia linguae' and 'impedimenta' (fols 122r–144r), here attributed to Bernard of Clairvaux.[32] This codex enjoyed an eventful history both before and after the period of our consideration. In the year 1458, the Augustinian Windesheim reform was transferred from Kirschgarten in Worms to the North Bavarian House of Rebdorf. When 'conversus' Peter of Zutphen was travelling to Rebdorf from the convent of Boeddeken near Paderborn via Kirschgarten in Worms to support the reform, he had an interesting bundle of treatises by Jan van Leeuwen in his luggage. When Brother Peter produced a manuscript in 1459 (now preserved as Pommersfelden, Schoenbornsche Bibliothek, MS 280/2881) he translated the original Dutch text of van Leeuwen's treatises into an Upper German idiom. Cgm 447 represents a further stage of vernacular adaptation in Rebdorf by presenting the van Leeuwen passages in a very plain North Bavarian dialect along with the *De doctrina* section (in addition to pieces by Johannes Tauler, Johannes Nider, Ludolf of Saxony, Silvester of Rebdorf and so on).[33]

Cgm 447, with its collection of theological reform texts and *De doctrina* material, additionally supported the reform of another religious house. When papal visitor Cardinal Nicholas of Cues arrived at the Benedictine convent of St Walburg in Eichstätt in the 1450s, he came to realize that the nuns there maintained a rather comfortable lifestyle. Alarmed by Nicholas's report, the local bishop, John III of Eych, quickly initiated a reform campaign. Despite the protest of some aristocratic nuns, he dismissed abbess Elisabeth of Rechberg in 1456, installed in her place Sophia (from the reformed convent of Marienberg near Boppard-upon-Rhine), and introduced the reform spirit of Constance and Basel in his diocese.[34] In order to raise the levels of literacy in St Walburg, however, the support of the nearby Rebdorf convent was urgently needed, and the Augustinians lent several manuscripts to the sisters. The late-fifteenth-century codex Eichstätt,

---

32 Manuscript description by K. Schneider, *Die deutschen Handschriften der Bayerischen Staatsbibliothek München. Cgm 351–500*, Catalogus codicum manu scriptorum Bibliothecae Monacensis 5.3 (Wiesbaden, 1973), pp. 284–96.

33 On the codex, see J. Lechner, 'Der vlaemische Mystiker Johannes von Loewen in deutschen Handschriften', *Zeitschrift für Askese und Mystik*, 11 (1936), 192–209, with additional material.

34 For the history of St Walburg, see A. Fink, 'St Walburg', *Dictionnaire d'histoire et de géographie ecclésiastique*, vol. 15 (Paris, 1925), pp. 84–6, and M.M. Zunker, *Kloster- und Pfarrkirche St. Walburg Eichstätt* (Regensburg, 2001).

Kloster St Walburg, Cod. Germ. 7 is a good example of how the Benedictine nuns aggrandized their library.[35] They copied from borrowed manuscripts what was relevant for their reformed community life – in this instance a section of *De doctrina* (fols 65r–78v), the Jan van Leeuwen passages, and parts of various reform treatises from Cgm 447.[36]

After this cursory investigation, a brief evaluation is needed of the versions of *De doctrina* which were abbreviated in the vernacular. The monastic-canonical reform not only supported book production in general, but also influenced the form of textual adaptation in particular. *De doctrina* was re-read through the lens of monastic-canonical reform and adapted in several cases as an abbreviated version. Summary versions condensed the content by omitting illustrative material in order to facilitate user-friendly reading. *Capitula selecta* versions isolated relevant passages from the original in order to sharpen rhetorical power and persuasiveness. Since there existed within the Windesheim reform and within the Austrian and Bavarian reform network relevant experience of translating Latin texts into German, it was only a natural consequence that *De doctrina* was finally vernacularized.[37] At the same time, the reform perspective facilitated a specific way of understanding the doctrine of *De doctrina*: 'custodia linguae' and 'poenitentia' were viewed as the induction into spirituality, mystic love was shown as the goal, and reformed community life became its touchstone. This reform programme, however, was not limited only to monastic and canonical community life, but was also perceived as suitable (at least to a certain extent) for the urban community life of laypeople.

---

35 A manuscript description is offered by A. Friedel, *Die Bibliothek der Abtei St. Walburg zu Eichstätt*, Schriften der Universitätsbibliothek Eichstätt 45 (Wiesbaden, 2000), and J. Lechner, *Die spätmittelalterliche Handschriftengeschichte der Benedikterinnenabtei St. Walburg/Eichstätt*, Eichstätter Studien 2 (Münster, 1937).

36 For the relationship between Rebdorf and St Walburg, see again Lechner, 'Der vlaemische Mystiker Johannes von Loewen', p. 193; for details about the copied 'folia', see Schneider, *Deutsche Handschriften Cgm 351–500*, pp. 284–96.

37 For vernacularizing Latin texts in general, see N. Henkel, *Deutsche Übersetzungen lateinischer Schultexte: ihre Verbreitung und Funktion im Mittelalter und in der frühen Neuzeit* (Munich, 1988). For vernacularization in Vienna, see T. Hohmann, 'Die recht gelerten maister. Bemerkungen zur Übersetzungsliteratur der Wiener Schule des Spätmittelalters', in H. Zeman (ed.), *Die Österreichische Literatur: ihr Profil von den Anfängen im Mittelalter bis ins 18. Jahrhundert*, 2 vols (Graz, 1986), vol. 1, pp. 349–65. Within the Windesheim reform, see V. Honemann, 'Der Laie als Leser', in K. Schreiner (ed.), *Laienfrömmigkeit im späten Mittelalter*, Schriften des Historischen Kollegs. Kolloquien 20 (Munich, 1992), pp. 241–52.

Dominican reform and complete vernacular translations

Abbreviated versions of *De doctrina cordis* might have been user-friendly, but they simultaneously suffered a massive deficit: they destroyed the complex composition of the original treatise. It is for this reason that complete versions of *De doctrina* were also translated into the German vernacular. Solothurn, Zentralbibliothek, MS S 353 offers a careful translation of *De doctrina* into a Swiss dialect (fols 1r–108v) from the 1470s.[38] This manuscript was owned by the Dominican convent of St Maria Magdalena an den Steinen in Basel and includes (in addition to *De doctrina*) the *Sermones* of the Dominican reform-theologian Johannes Nider, the *Leben der hl. Elisabeth* (alongside prayers to Elisabeth) written by Dietrich de Apolda, a prose-legend of St Cecilia and so on.

At this point, some details about the house of St Maria Magdalena are illuminating. Steinenkloster was founded around 1230 as a convent for former prostitutes who wanted to do penance and live a religious life. Bishop Reich of Reichenstein, however, mandated the convent to the Dominicans of Basel in 1291 in order to guarantee a regularized lifestyle. Pope Benedict XI fully incorporated the convent into the Dominican family in the year 1304. In 1423 the Dominican reform movement finally reached Steinenkloster.[39] Thirteen nuns (symbolizing the perfect 'vita apostolica' of Christ and his twelve disciples) from the prominent reform convent of Unterlinden near Colmar arrived in Basel in order to put strict apostolic life into practice.[40] The reform was crowned with success, as can be seen from the fact that the reform movement was successfully transferred from Steinenkloster to 'St. Michael on the Island' of Bern in 1439, and (although less triumphantly) to Klingental in 1480.[41]

---

38 For a description of this manuscript see A. Schönherr, *Die mittelalterlichen Handschriften der Zentralbibliothek Solothurn* (Solothurn, 1964), pp. 27–32.

39 Basic information about the Dominican reform in Germany is given by E. Hillenbrand, 'Die Observanzbewegung in der deutschen Ordensprovinz der Dominikaner', in Elm (ed.), *Reformbemühungen*, pp. 219–72. On the reform of the male convent of Basel, see F. Egger, *Beiträge zur Geschichte des Predigerordens. Die Reform des Basler Konvents 1429 und die Stellung des Ordens am Basler Konzil 1431–1448* (Basel, 1991).

40 For details on Steinenkloster see P. Zimmer, 'Dominikanerinnen Basel. St. Maria Magdalena an den Steinen (Steinenkloster)', *Helvetia Sacra*, 4/5 (Basel, 1999), pp. 584–609. E.A. Erdin gives a comprehensive picture of its history in *Das Kloster der Reuerinnen Sancta Maria Magdalena an den Steinen zu Basel* (Basel, 1956).

41 For the Klingental reform, see R. Weis-Mueller, *Die Reform des Klosters*

What did the reform in Basel and elsewhere involve, and how could manuscripts such as MS S 353 (which included a vernacular version of *De doctrina*) support reform ideals? Prominent urban Dominican convents (Basel, Bern, Nuremberg, Augsburg, Trier, Colmar, Constance, Freiburg, St Gallen, Strasburg etc.) attracted many women from patrician families, the lower aristocracy and the rich merchantile class. When joining the order, such aristocratic or bourgeois women introduced massive problems into the convent: in many cases they maintained their status and elaborate lifestyle, thus causing a certain social stratification and tension within the community.[42] Furthermore, in many houses, the observance of the rule became a rather delicate subject. Hence the reform aimed especially at the observance of 'clausura' (enclosure) in order to ban frequent encounters with external guests, since such entertainment easily overrode monastic discipline; the elimination of private apartments in favour of simple cells and communal meals in the refectory; and spiritual education, through devotional literature in particular.[43]

The role in such a reform project for manuscripts comprising devotional theology is obvious: *De doctrina*, for example, offers a model of reformed community life. It propagates reform ideals such as 'vivere secundum regulam', 'conversatio religiosa' and 'vita apostolica'; it facilitates a life of penance ('vita paenitentiae'); it supports the interiorization of outward observance and the exteriorization of inward piety. *De doctrina* functioned (together with other devotional key texts) as a catalyst for establishing a homogenous reform network in fifteenth-century Germany. Hence it would

---

Klingental und ihr Personenkreis, Baseler Beiträge zur Geschichtswissenschaft 59 (Basel, 1956).

[42] Johannes Nider, *Tractatus de vera et falsa nobilitate*, elaborates in detail on the subject of aristocracy in the convent and on a 'spiritual solution'. A helpful scheme and discussion of this treatise has been provided by K. Schreiner, *Sozial- und standesgeschichtliche Untersuchungen zu den Benediktinerkonventen im östlichen Schwarzwald*, Veröffentlichungen der Kommission für Geschichtliche Landeskunde in Baden-Württemberg. Reihe B, Forschungen 15 (Stuttgart, 1964), pp. 98–102.

[43] On Johannes Nider's reform of convents in Austria, Switzerland and Germany, see M. Brand, *Studien zu Johannes Niders deutschen Schriften*, Dissertationes historicae 23 (Rome, 1998), pp. 19–25 with further material and literature. For the reform of Nuremberg, see also J. Kist, 'Klosterreform im spätmittelalterlichen Nürnberg', *Zeitschrift für bayerische Kirchengeschichte*, 32 (1963), 31–45. The growing level of literacy and education among German Dominican nuns is demonstrated in detail by M.-L. Ehrenschwendtner, *Die Bildung der Dominikanerinnen in Süddeutschland vom 13. bis 15. Jahrhundert*, Contubernium 60 (Stuttgart, 2004).

be misleading to draw a sharp distinction between the reform projects of different orders. Augustinian, Benedictine, Dominican and Franciscan reforms differed in many of their details depending on local and temporal circumstances. In the end, however, all the reforms propagated similar ideals and disseminated similar works of devotional theology. They worked, so to speak, on the same 'devotional market' and offered more or less similar products, only under different labels.

From the perspective of such a homogenous 'international field', the last manuscript we have to examine briefly –Berlin, Staatsbibliothek zu Berlin – Preußischer Kulturbesitz, Ms. germ. qu. 1077, dating from the year 1465 – offers few surprises. It contains a vernacular copy of *De doctrina* derived from another vernacular copy: a Ripuaric transposition of a Dutch *De doctrina* version (fols 1r–192v).[44] Such a Ripuaric adaptation of a Dutch piece made the text accessible for readers in the Cologne area,[45] and witnesses once again to how easily the circulation of *De doctrina* transcended boundaries of language and territory.

Conclusion

The early thirteenth-century *De doctrina cordis*, from either a Cistercian or Dominican milieu, offers reform ideals – such as 'vivere secundum regulam', 'conversatio religiosa' and 'vita apostolica' – that were of great relevance to the monastic and canonical reform that followed the Councils of Constance and Basel. Hence it was only a natural consequence that *De doctrina* was disseminated in fifteenth-century Germany, both in great numbers and in a variety of forms: as a complete or abbreviated Latin text, and as a complete or abbreviated vernacular version. Along with other treatises of devotional theology, *De doctrina* versions functioned as an important catalyst for ecclesial reform. The frequent companionship of *De doctrina* with writings by the Dominican reform theologian, Johannes Nider (*c.*1380–1438), who was the head of the Dominican reform movement in south Germany and the driving force behind the reform of nuns, is especially noteworthy. In relation to this, future scrupulous work on Solothurn, Zentralbibliothek,

---

44 A short manuscript description is given by Degering, *Kurzes Verzeichnis der germanischen Handschriften der Preussischen Staatsbibliothek II*, p. 180. Ripuaric is the North-Middle-Franconian dialect of the Rhineland.

45 For details about the language family of Low German, on the differences between Dutch and Ripuaric dialect, and their relevance for vernacular devotion, see K. Ruh, 'Altniederländische Mystik in deutschsprachiger Überlieferung', in A. Ampe (ed.), *Dr. L. Reypens-album* (Antwerp, 1964), pp. 357–82.

MS S 353 is urgently needed in order to ascertain to what degree this translation was gendered to cater for the specific needs of female religious, and how far it is compatible with Nider's reform theology.

10

The Spanish Translation: *Del enseñamiento del coraçon* (Salamanca, 1498)

Anthony John Lappin

The small, anonymous book *Del enseñamiento del coraçon*, published in Salamanca in 1498, has attracted a certain amount of critical attention, but not for its text, which has remained unanalysed, and, for all I know, unread during the twentieth century. Three copies survive of that printing, all in the Iberian peninsula: El Escorial, 31-V–49 (2º), and Lisbon, Biblioteca Nacional, Res. Inc. 502 and 503. The work was subsequently reprinted in a revised edition with modernized text and attributed to St Bonaventure, by Juan Varela de Salamanca, as *Doctrina cordis de sant buena ventura en romance: nueuamente corregido y enmendado* (Toledo, 1510); this exists as London, British Library, C 63 c 16; Madrid, Biblioteca Nacional, R–31600; Zaragoza, Biblioteca Universitaria, A.30.25[1], and New York, Hispanic Society. The work's popularity was not exhausted by these two editions, and a further Toledo edition was produced in 1525, which would seem to have been printed from the previous Toledo edition (one exemplar, Barcelona, Biblioteca de Catalunya, Esp. 68–8º); finally, there is a printing from the southern town of Baeza in 1551, *Doctrina cordis del serafico dotor sant buena ventura en romance: muy util y provechoso para todos los fieles christianos: nuevamente corregido y emendado* (last seen nearly a quarter of a century ago and now in private hands). The translation adheres very closely to its Latin model, and the second edition merely modernizes the language and corrects some readings of the first.[1]

[1] Although my establishment of the critical text is only partially advanced, and a full statement must wait for the publication of the critical edition, the Toledo

The subject matter of ascetical prose has few devotees in post-Francoist Spain, and those who occupy themselves with the late medieval/early Renaissance period of the reign of the Catholic monarchs are, unsurprisingly, more interested in the reception of classical, and the diffusion of secular, literature. Critical interest has centred exclusively on the endpapers, fols 118v and 119r, since they may show by whom the book was printed, or even who may have been involved in its printing and translation. I will come to these in due course, as well as to later printings of the work, after considering the nature and purpose of the translation.

Readership, real

The Escorial exemplar of the first printing of the translation does not offer many clues to the attitude of its readers to the text. It is signed, on fol. 118r, as having been checked by an inquisitor: 'expurgado./fr. A. â S. J.' Yet, since there are neither blottings nor crossings out, one may presume that he found nothing offensive, whether or not he actually read the text. One reader underlined the chapter headings; another (or at least a different pen) drew a line beside an early passage on pacific humility (fol. 9r, beginning 'ca alguna cosa ha en si mas la mansedumbre que la paz. porque mas es estar assossegado que apaziguado'). The copy of the 1510 Toledo edition in the British Library, furthermore, has no marks other than the library's own. But the Madrid exemplar shows a vibrant reading culture surrounding the book. The copy was read enough for one reader to think it worth writing the following, at the bottom of fols kiv–kiir and upside-down in relation to the text:

> fray Rodrigo de burgos tom oelabbito
> a 17 defebrero de 1572 años (fol. kiir)
> por tanto Ruegen adios porel porque
> dios depare quien Ruege por
> ellos (fol. kiv)[2]

1510 (*T*) edition generally suppresses the definite article before possessive adjectives (although this may only be due to the typesetter in parts of Salamanca 1498 (*S*)), often but not consistently represents *e* or ⁊ as *y*, renders the termination to second person present plural of verbs as *–ays* or *–eys* rather than *–ades* or *–edes*, and varies some words (e.g., *S* apostura/apostamiento, *T* compostura; *S* escusança, *T* escusacion; *S* remasajas, *T* reliquias; *S* aberturas, *T* puertas).

2 (Fray Rodrigo de Burgos took the habit on 17 February 1572 / therefore may they pray to God for him so that God may provide someone who may pray for them.)

Although Burgos is in northern Spain, and there are numerous monasteries in the vicinity, it is not possible to locate the copy as having been in a religious house thereabouts. The title page of the Madrid copy is missing, but two short poems have been written on the flyleaf, each in a different ink and hand. The first offers an expression of the battle between the mind and desires (quite suitable for the subjects covered in *De doctrina cordis*); the second praises the act of 'memento mori', perhaps as an answer to the syntactically challenged tortured soul of the first poem, who wonders how he may be freed.

> la ley de mi carne siento
> En mis mienbros que repugna
> la ley del entendimiento
> no obstante cognoscimiento
> que de fonderse propugna
> o yo hombre desdichado
> a mi quien me librara
> dela muerte del peccado
> Con que mi sen es cercado
> antes fue, y despues sera.
>
> Es tan buena la memoria
> dela muerte bien temida
> que es freno para la vida
> ⁊ espuelas para la gloria.[3]

The interest in resistance to temptation is found in the annotations to the text itself. Thus a passage on the necessity of keeping the belt of chastity tightly bound around oneself is noted in the margin, with particular emphasis upon 'no solamente nos refrenemos dela torpedad dela obra.'[4]

Other annotations emphasize elements in the text which speak of the necessity for the gentle correction of subordinates: noted in the margin at fol. kijr, ll. 2–3, 'el castigo se haze alas vezes malamente por la grandeza dela

---

3 (I feel that the law of the flesh in my limbs repels the law of understanding despite recognition that proposes to sink deeper. O, unhappy man, I! Who will free me from the death of sin with which my mind is beseiged. It was once and after will [also] be.// The memory of the well-feared death is so good that it is reins for life and spurs for heaven.)

4 fol. g[v]r, ll. 30–31 (not only should we hold ourselves back from the obscenity of the deed.)

aspereza', an opinion elucidated by the following example, again highlighted in the margin: 'Ca los que quieren castigar alos otros con señoria ⁊ autoridad son semejables alos que adoban las sartenes viejas ⁊ quieren atapar vn agujero ⁊ hazen otros muchos agujeros conel golpe del martillo ⁊ quebrantan la sarten.'[5] The final annotations regarding the text are found on fol. ciiiiv, and concern the sin of gluttony, in particular the lure of food for the lustful, and the rejection of the temptations and wiles of the devil ('el luxurioso dessea hinchir ſuvientre dela vianda delos puercos conel fijo dessgastador', ll. 3–4; '⁊ fazer lo has partir de ti confondido porque se atreuio a poner delante ti vianda tan desconuenible', ll. 9–11).[6] A bookmark was left between fols i[vii]v and i[viii]r long enough for an impression of it to be taken by the page; the book was also placed open upon another text, receiving an impression of now illegible words from that other text, at fols e[viii]v–fir. Pencil annotations to the bottom corner of the margin to fol. miiir have been erased; indeed, the only visible letters are Y^{O}.

From these annotations and other marks, it is clear that the Spanish *De doctrina* was a relatively well-thumbed work from a monastic or conventual library; perhaps, as in the case of the mid- to late-sixteenth-century Fray Rodrigo de Burgos, it was given to novices or younger monks. From the poems inscribed at the beginning of the work, it would seem that *De doctrina* was found to be useful in such an ascetic setting, particularly in its encouragement to resist temptation. Rodrigo de Burgos, and the reprintings of the work (Toledo, 1525; Baeza, 1551) show that the text was still in demand for monastic and conventual library shelves many years after its first printing, and the spiritual reading it offered continued to be appreciated beyond the early Renaissance circles in which the translation was composed, into the very different atmosphere of the Tridentine Catholic Revival. A classic of western spirituality, then, whose solid good sense married to the systematic structure given by the author's scholasticism allowed it to be appreciated for centuries after it was written. Appreciation of the literary value of the treatise is scant, although this has been more due to lack both of sympathy with the scholastic style of division and of appreciation for the very different style of reading required by a text

---

5 (Correction is sometimes carried out badly through the excess of harshness ... For those who wish to correct others with haughtiness and authority are like those who fix old pans and wish to close up a hole and they make many more holes with the hammer blow and they break the pan.)

6 (The lustful man desires to swell his belly with the food of the swine [along] with the prodigal son ... and you are to make him leave you defeated since he dared to place before you such unfitting food.)

such as this, than to any deeper judgement.[7] The author's Latin is clear while being complex and well articulated. The divisions and explanations are constantly enlivened by striking metaphors, similitudes and allegories drawn from daily life. Even though the text is ostensibly destined for the reading of a woman religious, the author does not shirk from including military and masculine comparisons, not so much to gender the text as both male and female as to provide incidentally yet another example of the general medieval unfussedness about the application of gendered metaphors and allegories to and for the opposite sex. The academic learning is impressive, but worn lightly: the wisdom of the Church Fathers (Augustine, Gregory, Cassiodorus, Chrysostom) rubs shoulders with the insights of Boethius, Seneca, Plato, and with up-to-the-minute citations of Aristotle. The structure heads resolutely but by careful increment towards a goal of union with God – one very similar, in fact, to that of works of the so-called Spanish 'mystics' of the sixteenth century, Juan de la Cruz and Teresa de Ávila – ending with a remarkable comparision between melancholic sexual love and union with the divine through spiritual love. *De doctrina* was not conceived of as a 'good read', nor should it be unfairly compared *a pari passu* with works composed in the vernacular from later centuries, but, in its uniting of that remarkably fecund scholastic means of understanding the world, the developing medieval tradition of affective piety, and the at times rather recherché world of allegorical biblical exegesis, it does bring together spiritual profit with 'divertissement' – indeed, even 'jouissance'.

The second, third and fourth printings of the Spanish translation ascribe the work to St Bonaventure. This is quite different from the *Del enseñamiento*, which is anonymous in all senses: no names are given for printer, translator or original author. Indeed, the translator's one statement about the work simply links the identity of the author of the prologue with that of the treatise as a whole.

Aqui comiença el libro que es llamado enseñamiento del coraçon. 7

---

7 The lead in this negative evaluation was given by Sister M.P. Candon (ed.), '*The Doctrine of the Hert*, Edited from the Manuscripts with Introduction and Notes' (unpublished doctoral dissertation, Fordham University, 1963), p. lxxix: 'After spending considerable time on a particular work there is something dissatisfying about classifying it as mediocre and if some future student of literary style should find in it hidden beauty and artistry, no one would rejoice more than I at the inaccuracy of the first judgment. Its [*scil. De doctrina*'s] weakness stems mainly from the monotony of the constant mathematical [*sic*] divisions and banal repetitions.'

> primeramente es puesto el prologo del que fizo el libro enel qual enseña tres cosas que deue guardar el predicador enla su amonestacion.[8]

Unlike the self-professedly clerical translator (or perhaps abridger) of the Middle English translation, the Spanish translator claims no particular authority; the work was probably anonymous already when it reached him. Subsequent attribution to St Bonaventure may simply have been a marketing ploy by Juan Varela, the work's second printer. The attribution may, however, have come about through Varela's (or someone else's) discovery of the text in a miscellany volume that also contained works by (pseudo-) Bonaventure, possibly in the library of the Dominican convent of St Peter Martyr, whose friars had brought Juan Varela only recently to Toledo from Seville. The adoption of the Latin title, *De doctrina cordis*, does support the supposition that the attribution to Bonaventure was through a now-lost manuscript.[9] The Latinate title and the attribution to the thirteenth-century Franciscan master also invested the text with an authority it was previously lacking, and signalled it as particularly suitable for those buying for mendicant libraries. Nevertheless, Bonaventure, or rather pseudo-Bonaventure, was a popular writer during this period, and numerous texts bore his name.[10] The attribution to St Bonaventure was not reversed by subsequent printers of the Spanish *De doctrina*, although the Baeza printer sought to widen the appeal of the book, claiming that it was 'muy util y provechoso para todos los fieles christianos' (very useful and profitable for all faithful Christians) on his title-page, indicating that the resolutely monastic slant of the text was no barrier to its marketing for laypeople. The fifteenth-century evidence for the circulation of the Middle English translation among laywomen and

---

8 (Here begins the book which is called Teaching of the Heart, and first of all is placed the prologue [written] by he who wrote the book in which he teaches three things that the preacher should observe in his admonitions.)

9 See G. Hendrix, 'Deux textes d'attribution incertaine à saint Bonaventure, restitués à Gérard de Liège', *RTAM*, 45 (1978), 237–8.

10 After 1500, the *Psalterium in honore Virginis Matris* attributed to Bonaventure saw two editions (Burgos: Fradrique de Basilea?, 1511?; Valencia: Juan Joffre, 1515); as did *La vida de nuestro Redentor* (Valladolid: Diego de Gumiel, 1512; and see J.M. Abad, *Post-incunables ibéricos* (Madrid, 2001), p. 151, no. 244). In addition, devotional texts attributed to the saint abounded: *El regimiento de la conciencia que se llama fuente de la vida* (Seville: Juan Pegnitzer & Magno Herbst, 5 Sept. 1502); *Soliloquio de sant Buenaventura* (Burgos: Fadrique de Basilea, 1517); *Espejo de disciplina, o libro de las cosas pequeñas para los novicios* (Seville: Estanislao Polono, 1502); *Estimulo de amor de sant buena ventura* (Toledo: Sucesor de Pedro Hagembach, c. 1505; repr. Burgos: Fradrique de Basilea, 1517).

women religious, then, is not to be wondered at, nor need we assume that laywomen were unlikely to read the text.[11]

Readership, implied

What can be reconstructed of the printing history and actual readership of *Del enseñamiento* is mirrored by the translator's idea of his future readers, who are envisioned as male religious. Thus the oft-appearing 'charissima' of *De doctrina*[12] is rendered as 'hermano' in *Del enseñamiento*,[13] if it is not simply omitted.

Possible criticism of religious superiors is toned down or omitted completely. Criticism of abbots and superiors for observing none or few of the obligations they lay upon their subordinates is reduced. Thus, from *De doctrina*: 'Ita *multi* Abbates constitutiones, et statuta ordinis, et caetera onera claustri, sic super claustrales, et alios subditos distribuunt, quod sibi *nullam, vel* modicam partem retinent',[14] *nullam* is not translated, so that it might not be thought that abbots were completely off the leash: *Del enseñamiento*: 'E ansi fazen algunos abades ⁊ priores que ordenan sobre sus subidtos muchas constituciones: ⁊ ellos retienen para si muy pequeña parte dellas.'[15] The insulting comparison of such superiors to gaolers, checking on the state of the inmates of their prisons only to ascertain the condition of their restraining devices, is registered much more simply, with a biblical echo: '⁊ no decienden a las carceles *a los visitar* sino por ver si tienen sanas

---

11 See D. Renevey, 'Household Chores in *The Doctrine of the Hert*: Affective Spirituality and Subjectivity', in C. Beattie, A. Maslakovic and S. Rees Jones (eds), *The Medieval Household in Christian Europe, c.800–c.1550* (Turnhout, 2003), pp. 167–85 (170); M.C. Erler, *Women, Reading and Piety in Late Medieval England*, Cambridge Studies in Medieval Literature 46 (Cambridge, 2002), pp. 76–7.

12 References to the Latin text of *De doctrina cordis* are to Gerardus Leodiensis, *Speculum concionatorum ad illustrandum pectora auditorum, in septem libros distributum* (Naples, 1607). Oxford, Bodleian Library, 8º L 12 Th. BS, pp. 114, 286, for example. Henceforth cited as *De doctrina*.

13 Fols 44v, 113v. Folio references to the Spanish translation are to the Escorial copy of *Del enseñamiento*.

14 *De doctrina*, p. 198 (And so *many* Abbots give out constitutions and statutes of the Order, and other demands of the cloister on monks and others beneath them, of which they keep little *or nothing* themselves.) My italics.

15 *Del enseñamiento*, fol. 77r (And so *some* abbots and priors act who establish for their subjects many constitutions and they themselves keep a very small part of them.)

las prisiones en que estan.'[16] The despective use of a proverb to describe such abbots' and priors' lack of solidarity in the manner of the lavishness of the table they keep is avoided, and reference is rather made to the common dress of the habit: 'ca aun que sean hermanos en la manera del habito: no son pero hermanos enel mantenimiento.'[17] Later in the treatise, prelates who judge harshly are compared to tyrants: this comparison is silenced by *Del enseñamiento* (*De doctrina*: 'Tales Praelatos, *imo certe tyrannos* reprehendit Dominus'; *Del enseñamiento*: 'Onde alos tales reprehende el señor'[18]). Furthermore, the possibility that the subordinates should rebel (and rebel with reason) is equally silenced. *De doctrina*: 'Noli asinum Domini tui, curae tuae commendatum sine sella agere, *ne contra te recalcitrans refiat, et dicat Dominus tuus: hoc est ad bonum ius*',[19] becomes a longer but much less incisive passage in *Del enseñamiento*:

> E por semejable manera si tu has demandar atu subdito algun officio trabajoso no ayas en desden de gelo encargar con algunas palabras mansas 7 de humildad: 7 avn con allegacion del amor diuinal porque el subdito pueda leuar mas ligeramente la carga que le pusieres. 7 no quieras cargar la bestia sin enxalmos o albarda.[20]

---

16 *Del enseñamiento*, fol. 77r (and they do not come down to the prison to visit them but rather to see if the manacles that hold them are firm.) My italics. Cp. *De doctrina*, p. 199: 'nec descendunt ad carcerem, nisi ad videndum si prisiones sui bene teneantur, ne scilicet compedes laxentur, aut vincula' (they do not come down to the prison, apart from to see if their bonds are holding them properly, lest namely the shackles or chains should become loose.)

17 *Del enseñamiento*, fols 77r–v (although they may be brothers in the style of the habit, they are not however brothers in their style of life.) Cf. *De doctrina*, p. 199: 'Vnde, licet vocent se omnes fratres, non tamen omnes scutellae sunt sorores' (So, although they all might call themselves *brothers*, not all are sisters when it comes to eating from the same dish.)

18 *De doctrina*, p. 252, my italics; *Del enseñamiento*, fol. 99r (So the Lord criticises such as these *who are without doubt tyrants*.)

19 *De doctrina*, p. 252, my italics (Do not use your Lord's ass commended into your care without a saddle [i.e., mercifully], lest it should be disobedient to you, and your Lord may say: That is right and good.)

20 *Del enseñamiento*, fols 99r–v (And in a similar way if you have to order one of those under you to undertake some hard task, do not distain to load him with it accompanied by some gentle and humble words, and even with the addition of divine love, so that he may carry the load you put upon him more lightly, and do not try to load the beast without padding or cushioning.)

The most that can be said of those that do not follow their superiors' instructions, is that, in an addition, 'se van por mal cabo'.[21] The avoidance of criticism of superiors provides a distinct parallel with the attitude of the Middle English translator: 'in which the authority of the ecclesiastical hierarchy is carefully shored up'[22] – both products no doubt of a wider European conservatism (which was only encouraged by the débâcle of the Great Schism), rather than of simply local anxieties.

Despite holding off on religious superiors, criticism is introduced specifically against the (wrong kind of) monks or friars. Thus, the waste of time in futile entertainment, 'a *fatuis* recreationes appellantur' (are called 'recreations' by the foolish), but these 'fatui' become, specifically, '*religiosos* locos' (foolish religious) in the Spanish.[23]

However, given that the evident target audience for the translation was resolutely situated within the cloister, numerous decisions made by the translator show a concern with basic scriptural education, and perhaps an anxiety that biblical texts would not be as familiar as is assumed in the Latin *De doctrina*. A particularly revealing example concerns the story of the Good Thief on the cross, which is used as an allegory for the gifts of grace within the soul:

> Horum quinque fructus collegit ille latro poenitens, qui iuxta Iesum pendens in Cruce socio ex altero latere pendenti dicebat, Lucae .23. Neque tu times Deum: Ecce correctio. Quod in eadem damnatione es: Ecce instructio. Et nos quidem iuste, nam digna factis recipimus: Ecce sui ipsius accusatio. Hic vero nihil mali gessit: Ecce boni commendatio. Memento mei Domine cum veneris in regnum tuum: Ecce oratio. Potes ergo concludere ex omnibus supradictis illud verbum Salomonis Prouerb. 19. Mors, et vita in manu linguae.[24]

---

21 *Del enseñamiento*, fol. 99v (they end up badly.) On the subject of the abandonment of vows, see F.D. Logan, *The Runaway Religious in England c. 1240–1540*, Cambridge Studies in Medieval Life and Thought, 4th series, 32 (Cambridge, 1996).

22 D. Renevey and C. Whitehead, '"Opyn þin hert as a boke": Translation Practice and Manuscript Circulation in *The Doctrine of the Hert*', in J. Jenkins and O. Bertrand (eds), *The Medieval Translator 10* (Turnhout, 2007), pp. 125–48 (134).

23 *De doctrina*, p. 13; *Del enseñamiento*, fol. 15v.

24 *De Doctrina*, p. 115 (The penitent thief picked those five fruits, he who hanging next to Jesus on the cross said to his fellow hanging on the other side, 'And you do not fear God – here is correction, – for you suffer the same punishment – here is instruction, – and we receive this punishment justly for what we have done – here is

Rather than following this structure of allusion to an element in the biblical text followed by its immediate interpretation, the translation first expounds the story, and then revisits the elements in turn, producing, in effect, a passage twice as long as the original. Here, perhaps, we see an anxiety over the readers' knowledge of the biblical text; the vernacular translation serves as a means of presenting this information, which is maintained as uncluttered by immediate allegory or interpretation as possible. The method was not an accident, and can be seen repeatedly throughout the text.

More help is provided for the reader in making sense of the allegories and metaphors used than in *De doctrina*. Thus the image of Christ on the cross as the grape being crushed to provide the wine of his blood – 'Christus in cruce fuit quasi vua pressa in torculari, vt vinum sui sanguinis nobis propinaret'[25] – is reinforced: 'Ca jhesu christo *fue estrujado* enla cruz ansi como es estrujado ⁊ *pisado* el razimo enel lagar porque diesse a nos el vino dela su sangre, *en beuer de redempcion*.'[26] The parallel between Christ's crucifixion and the winepress is made clear by the insertion of 'fue estrujado' (was crushed), the process of crushing the grape is emphasised by the expansion, 'estrujado ⁊ pisado' (crushed and trodden), and the wine of the most holy blood is given a theological gloss, absent from the Latin, which makes clear the assocation with the Eucharist: 'en beuer de redempcion' (to drink for [our] redemption.)

A similar effort to ensure that all parts of the allegory are clear is found in a related area of sustained metaphorical enology within the prologue. Here, the words of God are like grapes 'multa faecunditate repletae',[27] expanded by *Del enseñamiento*: 'que estan llenas de gran abastança *de vino*';[28] these grapes, too, must be pressed, 'vnde oportet vuam exprimere, quod est, verbum diligenter exponere vt vinum spiritualis intelligentiae vsque in cellarium cordias fluat',[29] which is expanded again to produce a

---

self-accusation; he, however, has done nothing wrong – here is the commendation of the good. Remember me, Lord, when you come into your kingdom – here is prayer.' You can therefore conclude from all of what has been said above that phrase of Solomon: 'Life and death are in the hands of the tongue' [Prov. 18:21].)

25 *De doctrina*, p. 57 (Christ on the cross was like the grape in the vine press, so that he might offer us the wine of his blood.)

26 *Del enseñamiento*, fol. 32v, my italics.

27 *De doctrina*, p. 1 (full of much fecundity.)

28 *Del enseñamiento*, fol. 1r (full of great sufficiency of wine.)

29 *De doctrina*, pp. 1–2 (thus it is necessary to press the grape, that is, to diligently expound the word so that the spiritual wine of understanding should flow unto the wine cellar of the heart.)

completely parallel structure. The grapes have to be crushed *and well trodden* and the wine must flow from them, *just as* the divine words are declaimed and the wine of understanding will flow from them into the wine cellar of the heart:

> E ansi como es menester que sean *bien pisadas* ⁊ espremidas las vuas *para que salga el vino dellas*: ansi es menester de declarar con diligencia la palabra diuinal: porque el vino del entendimiento spiritual pueda entrar ala bodega del coraçon.[30]

These are small, almost finickety, changes, but designed consistently to tighten the allegory and articulate all of its parts. A particularly fine example of this method is found when a hunting metaphor is used to distinguish different types of prayer. To emphasise the necessity of *ascent* in prayer (rather than descent), the translator reinforces the message by manipulating the vocabulary used and slightly altering the comparison. The Latin in question reads 'Vae illis, qui ad modum milui post macellum volitantis in istis inferioribus, tripas, et viscera capiunt.'[31] The Spanish reads 'Guay de aquellos que descienden a manera de bueytres ⁊ de milanos alas carnes mortezinas ⁊ alos cuerpos delas animalias que yazen muertas enel campo.'[32] The most significant change in order to strengthen the allegory by the avoidance of any contradiction is the alteration of the verb, 'capiunt' (seize), to 'descienden' (come down), since the idea of descending is picked up within the allegorical reading of the scene; moreover, *De doctrina*'s use of 'capiunt' is rejected as, according to the Latin, the scavengers do not *seize* their prey but are drawn down to lifeless corpses, as we learn as the allegory is played out: 'Isti ad praedam non ascendunt, sed descendunt, *nec praedam capiunt*, sed a praeda capiuntur; dum carnis, vel mundi delectationibus illaqueantur.'[33] The Latin is translated as 'Ca estos tales no suben ala prea mas ellos son tomados della inclinandose alas delectaciones del mundo ⁊ del

---

30 *Del enseñamiento*, fol. 1r, my italics.

31 *De doctrina*, p. 264 (Woe unto those who, like kites hovering over these lower things, seize tripe and entrails after the butchering of animals.)

32 *Del enseñamiento*, fol. 104v (Woe to those who come down like vultures and kites to butchered meat and to the bodies of animals that lie dead in the countryside.)

33 *De doctrina*, p. 264, my italics (These do not rise up to the prey, but go down; *nor do they seize the prey*, but are captured by the prey, while they are ensnared by the flesh and the delights of the world.)

[*sic*] carne.'[34] Repetition of the idea of descent would be otiose. Furthermore, the scavenging kites are placed in the unattractive company of the even less respectable vultures; the description of the pickings of the shambles are evoked, but without the detail of body parts, and the picture is widened to make the inclusion of vultures rather more believable, with the addition of the corpses of wild beasts and those which have died from disease.

Much of the expansion of similes is designed to emphasise doctrinal or moral points. The gloss on the names for the beloved in the *Cantica canticorum* is subtly expanded to emphasise the moral and doctrinal meanings of the terms:

1	Ecce quatuor nominibus eam appellat, Sororem, Amicam, Columbam, et Immaculatam;	nombra la por quatro nombres. Conuiene saber hermana ⁊ amiga paloma ⁊ sin manzilla.
2	*quasi diceret: Aperi mihi* soror in incarnatione propter naturae humane humanal communionem,	porque es hermana por la participacion dela natura que *por nos recibio el saluador* enla su encarnacion.
3	Amica mea, in passione,	E llama la amiga por la passion *que por ella recibio.*
4	Columba *mea*, in Spiritus sancti *missione.*	E paloma por *la gracia del* espiritu sancto *con que la alimpio.*
5	Immaculata, in glorificatione.	E sin manzilla por *la pureza dela* gloria con que la glorificara *enla vida que siempre ha de durar.*
6	Aperi mihi cor tuum ad orationem, os ad confessionem, spiritum ad amorem, brachia ad amplexus, manus ad operationem bonam, et eleemosynarum largitionem.	*E dize* abre *conuiene saber* el coraçon al oracion. ⁊ la boca ala confession. ⁊ la voluntad al amor ⁊ los braços para *me* abraçar. ⁊ las manos para dar largamente limosnas *alos menguadaos.*[35]

[34] *Del enseñamiento*, fol. 104v (For such as these do not rise to the prey but are taken by it, inclining themselves to the pleasures of the world and of the flesh.)

[35] *De doctrina*, p. 206; *Del enseñamiento*, fol. 80v. In the quotations and following translations, italics display the differences between the two versions, while

Moral specification is also found in the expansion given to the meaning of the 'cingulum castitatis' (belt of chastity); this 'cintura de la castidad' is bound tightly, not only 'vt ab operibus incontinentiae, sed etiam ab appenditiis abstineamus, et a delectionibus immundis nosmetipsos restringamus.'[36] In *Del enseñamiento*, the 'works of incontinence' are concretized as doing and touching and looking, and the belt is tied 'en manera que non solamente nos referenemos *dela torpedad dela obra* ⁊ de *todo tañimiento* ⁊ acatamiento no casto: mas aun delas delectationes delos pensamientos malos.'[37] Similarly, the 'delectiones immunde' are clarified as sins of thought: 'pensamientos malos'.

The style may also be simplified. Rhetorical questions are occasionally avoided, as in the following citation of St Augustine – 'Eligis tibi cibos, quos comedis, et cur similiter non eligis verba, quae dicis?'[38] – which is rendered in reported speech and in a more digestably sententious phrasing: 'E segun dize san agustin Ansi como el hombre escoge las viandas que dessea gostar ansi conuiene que escoja las palabras que quiere fablar.'[39] The desire to clarify the allegorical structure of the section being translated and an avoidance of distracting rhetorical colours come together in the following sentences: 'Nonne ad turres, et munitiones tempore hostilis vastationis hominum multitudo fugere consueuit? Aperuit [Christus] igitur tibi latus suum, tanquam fortalitiam suam, vt ibi, tanquam in loco securo

---

untranslated elements in the Latin are also provided with square brackets. (1. He names her by four names, *that is* sister and lover, dove and without stain. 2. [*as if he said, 'Open to me*] *because she is* sister through participation of human nature *that the saviour received for us* in his incarnation. 3. *And he calls her* lover through the passion that *he received for her*. 4. And [*my*] dove for [*the sending*] *the grace* of the Holy Spirit *with which he cleansed her*. 5. And spotless for the *purity of the* glory with which he will glorify her *in the life which will never end*. 6. *And he says* Open, *that is*, open your heart to prayer, and your mouth to confession, and your will to love and your arms to embrace *me* and your hands to give alms generously *to the poor*.)

[36] *De doctrina*, p. 133 (that we hold ourselves back from the deeds of incontinence, but also from the appurtenances, and from unclean enticements.)

[37] *Del enseñamiento*, fols 52r–v, my italics (such that not only it holds us back *from the shamefulness of the deed and from all unchaste touching and looking*, but even from the pleasures of evil thoughts.)

[38] *De doctrina*, p. 176 (You choose the foods you eat, and why similarly do you not choose the words which you say?)

[39] *Del enseñamiento*, fol. 68r (and as St Augustine says, just as a man chooses the foods that he desires to taste so does it behove him to choose the words that he wants to speak.)

valeas latitare.'[40] *Del enseñamiento* removes the erotema ('Nonne' being substituted by 'Onde' [wherefore]), and collapses the 'turres et munitiones' (of the real world) and the 'fortalitium Christi' (of the spiritual world) into the one concept: the 'fortaleza' ('turres' and 'munitiones' could have been literally translated as 'torres' and 'defensiones'). The allegorical articulation of the metaphor is further aided by the reminiscence of Job 7:1, 'militia est vita hominis super terram.' One should also note the care in rendering 'tempore hostilis vastationis' as 'los tiempos ⁊ *lugares* delos guerras': the translator makes changes not through incompetence but through a clear conception of the essential nature of the translator's task.

> Onde los hombres acostumbran alos tiempos ⁊ lugares de las guerras a coger se alas fortalezas. E como toda esta vida sea ansi como vna continua pelea abrio te ihesu christo el su costado ansi como vna fortaleza porque ansi como en lugar seguro te puedas asconder ⁊ amparar enella.[41]

Some insertions further imply that the reader is expected to have a low standard of ecclesiastical education. The 'aureola', the crown offered to virgins in heaven ('Nam Virginibus illa Corona decoris promitteitur, quae aureola *consueuit* appellari'),[42] is translated almost directly: 'ca a los virgines es prometida aquella corona de fermosura', apart from the second half of the sentence, in which 'learned men' or 'doctors [of the Church]' are invoked to give currency to the term: 'que es llamada *delos doctores* aureola.'[43] Later, on the same page, the Latin's 'aureola' is repeated, but with a explicatory gloss: 'aureola *e guirnalda*' – a crown of flowers, as *De doctrina* had previously described it. In a parallel motion, but perhaps surprising given Salamanca's prowess in the field of education, the explicit phrasing that evokes university teaching is removed: the 'cathedra' becomes the school ('Haec est facilis lectio. Dilectio lectio saepius recitanda est,

---

40 *De doctrina*, pp. 247–8 (Are not a crowd of men wont to flee to the towers and fortification in the time of enemy invasion? [Christ] therefore opened his side to you, like his stronghold, so that there, as in a safe place, you may hide.)

41 *Del enseñamiento*, fol. 97v (Whence men are accustomed at times and places of warfare to take refuge in fortresses. And as all of this life is like a continual struggle, Jesus Christ opened for you his side just like a fortress so that in this way, as in a safe place, you can hide and shelter there.)

42 *De doctrina*, p. 150, my italics (Now that crown of beauty is promised to Virgins, which is usually called 'aureola'.)

43 *Del enseñamiento*, fol. 58v, my italics.

de qua sponsus tuus *in cathedra Crucis* scholas tenuit, vbi mortuus est prae amore'; 'El amar por cierto es vna lecion ligera 7 mucho de repetir: porque avn enla *escuela dela cruz* a do el nuestro esposo murio por amor: touo escuelas de aquesta lecion.')[44] However, these are but touches, minor inflexions that pale into insignificance before, for example, the Middle English translator's excision of all classical authors from *The Doctrine of the Hert*.[45]

The translator's linguistic and cultural preferences

De doctrina cordis offers a depth of linguistic reference, where medieval Latin, translation and direct citation of the vernacular and awareness of etymology all have a role in the unfolding of the text. The translator's attitude to this depth in his translation is marked by a desire to both domesticate and modernize, as we shall see, first considering the reproduction of linguistic levels in the translation, and secondly the preservation or alteration of cultural references.

The etymological meaning of a word is glossed as coming from Latin: 'porque mes *es dicho en latin* de menos que quiere dezir mengua enla nuestra lengua.'[46] More importantly, ecstatic love is glossed in *De doctrina* by reference to vernacular phrasing: 'Iste autem affectus multus, et inusitatus comparatur amori ecstatico, *qui amare per amores vulgariter appellatur*. Ecstaticus enim ab ecstasi: vnde amor ecstaticus dicitur, qui mentem alienat, qui non sinit cor aliud cogitare, nisi circa rem dilectam.'[47] However, in *Del*

---

44 *De doctrina*, p. 106 (This is easy reading. Love is a reading to be repeated often, regarding which your spouse held lessons in the chair [of learning] of the Cross); *Del enseñamiento*, fol. 41v (Loving is certainly an easy lesson and one to be repeated many times; because even in the school of the cross where our spouse died for love, he taught on this lesson.) Very possibly linked to this downplaying of eduction is the omission of the learned adjectives applied to Christ as advocate for the soul: 'Considera Christum *peritum, et eloquentem* aduocatum tuum'; 'E piensa en como ihesu xpo el qual es tu abogado' (Consider the *learned and eloquent* Christ your advocate), *De doctrina*, p. 22; *Del enseñamiento*, fol. 9r.

45 Candon, *Doctrine*, pp. lx–lxi.

46 *Del enseñamiento*, fol. 42r, my italics (since 'mes' (month) is formed in Latin from 'menos' which means 'diminution' in our language); cp. *De doctrina*, p. 107: 'eo quod mensis a mene dicitur, quod defectum sonat.'

47 *De doctrina*, p. 278, my italics (This intense and uncommon emotion is to be compared to ecstatic love, called 'amer pour amours' in the vernacular. Ecstatic is from ecstasis, and so it is called ecstatic love, which numbs the mind, which suffers the heart to think on naught else other than the beloved object.)

enseñamiento this description is limited solely to the Latin, and no idiomatic vernacular phrase is provided:

> E este talante *no nombrado* es comparado al amor *que es llamado en latin* extatico de extasi, *que quiere dezir sobrepujamiento porque sobrepuja a todos los otros amores* ⁊ alça ⁊ enajena el *coraçon de si mesmo por vn sobrepujamiento marauilloso*: ⁊ no lo dexa pensar sino en aquella cosa que ama ⁊ dessea la su voluntad.[48]

The reference to Greek as the origin of the term for ecstatic love made by *De doctrina* is completely reworked. The Latin work then moves on to place the etymological origins of 'heroic love' with Cupid, 'scilicet amor apud Graecos 'ερωζ appellatur',[49] and provides a description of love's dreadful and fearsome effects – 'Est autem amor, 'ερωζ, magnum desiderium, cum magna concupiscentia, et afflictione cogitationum'[50] – before suggesting that the Greek word for 'noble' is also descended from Eros: 'Heri dicuntur viri nobiles, qui semper mollitiem, et delitias vitae quaerunt, et subiecti sunt huiusmodi passioni.'[51] In what can only be a correction, *Del enseñamiento* places 'heroic love' within medical discourse, explaining its etymological origin via the Greek word for 'noble', while adding a play on words between the 'nobility' of the sufferer and the humiliation that the disease implies ('passion *mezquina*'). All mention of Eros is suppressed:

> ⁊ a este tal amor llaman *los fisicos* erreos: porque engendra enel coraçon grandes cobdicias ⁊ desseos con tormento de pensamientos diuersos. Ca los varones nobles son llamados *en griego* erces [sic] porque por las blanduras ⁊ deleytes de aquesta vida son subiectos a aquesta passion *mezquina*.[52]

---

48 *Del enseñamiento*, fol. 110v, italics indicate changes from the Latin (And this *unnamed* emotion is compared to the love *that is called in Latin* extatic, from extasis, which means excess because *it exceeds all other loves and raises* and alienates *the heart from itself*, and allows it to think only on that thing which it loves *and which its will desires*.) Note further, the collapse of mind and heart: '*mentem* alienat … non sinit *cor* aliud cogitare nisi …' into the simplified concentration upon the heart: 'enajena *el coraçon* de si mesmo … ⁊ no *lo* dexa pensar sino …'

49 *De doctrina*, p. 279 (namely love among the Greeks was called 'Eros'.)

50 Ibid., p. 279 (And love, 'Eros', is a great desire, with great longing, and affliction of the thought.)

51 Ibid., p. 279 (Noble men are called 'Heri', who ever search for softness and the pleasures of life, and are subject to this type of suffering.)

52 *Del enseñamiento*, fol. 114v, my italics (and *physicians* call this type of love

The Aramaic cited in a Gospel passage is also not taken over into the translation: 'dixit: *Ephpheta, quod est,* Adaperire';[53] 'diziendo. Sed abiertas.'[54]

Nevertheless, it is the frequent citation in *De doctrina* of vernacular phrasing which receives most reinterpretation. Mostly the invocation of the 'vulgo' in the Latin work is parallelled by the citation of a 'refrán' (proverb) in *Del enseñamiento,* which sometimes does have the stylistic form of a vernacular proverb. I give but one example: '(sicut vulgo dicitur) ad modum serui sibi teneri pedem super guttur; alioquin nunquam faciet bonam dietam';[55] 'porque segun se dizen communmente nunca fara buena jornada *nin buena lauor* el sieruo si no le fuere puesto el pie enel pescueço'[56] (assonance on *–é-o*: 'sieruo', 'puesto', 'pescueço'). However, 'refran' is at times used for non-proverbial expressions: 'illud vulgare canticum' (that vernacular song) becomes 'el refran'.[57] The 'refran' in question does not have any assonance and is an literal translation of the exemplar: 'El tu acatamiento sea simple ⁊ amoroso ⁊ tal que faga amoroso al tu amigo.'[58] Similarly, 'iuxta vulgare, ostede eis ostium oris tui in confessione'[59] becomes the citation of another proverb: 'E segun dize el *refran*: muestra les la puerta. *conuiene saber la manifestacion dela* confession.'[60]

Direct citation of French in *De doctrina* is most often omitted; examples include the omission of any translation of 'Et vulgariter dicitur: Qui vit

---

'erreos', because it engenders great longings in the heart and desires with the torment of diverse thoughts. For noble men are called *in Greek* 'erces' [*sic*], because, through the comforts and pleasures of this life, they are subject to this ignoble suffering.)

53 *De doctrina*, p. 149 (he said, *'Ephpheta', which means* 'Be opened' [Mark 7:34].)

54 *Del enseñamiento*, fol. 58r.

55 *De doctrina*, p. 18 (as the people say, [the flesh] must be kept like a servant with a foot on its throat, otherwise it never does a good day's work.)

56 *Del enseñamiento*, fol. 8r (because, as is commonly said, the servant will never do work for a whole day or do good work if a foot is not placed upon his neck.)

57 *De doctrina*, p. 267; *Del enseñamiento*, fol. 106r.

58 *Del enseñamiento*, fol. 106r (Let your look be simple and loving and such that it should make your lover love you.)

59 *De doctrina*, p. 116 (as the common folk say, show them [sins] the door of your mouth in confession.)

60 *Del enseñamiento*, fol. 45v, my italics (And as the proverb has it: show them the door – *that is to say, by making* confession.)

á conte, ne vit à honte',[61] or of the French found in this later passage: 'Bonus vultus huius amici est consolatio spiritualis: et multum perdit, qui bonum vultum, *Gallice bonne chiere* amici sui perdit';[62] 'E el acatamiento alegre de nuestro amigo ihesu christo es la consolacion spiritual que te el da. E porende no pierde poco el que pierde el acatamiento claro de aqueste amado.'[63] Here, the 'bonus vultus' has been reinterpreted as 'acatamiento alegre' or 'cheerful look/gaze').

The avoidance of French phrases is of one cloth with other elements of domestication in the translation. In a citation of Augustine, the complaint of monks frequenting 'theatra et spectacula' is rendered as the same wandering around the squares ('plaças'),[64] as it would be some time before public theatres were once again a feature of Spanish life and a draw for Spanish religious.[65] Another citation of Augustine, this time a condemnation of sporting pastimes, is modernized via reference to contemporary Spanish ballgames, although the references to bloodsports are maintained: 'Heu quam dolendum, quam pudendum delectat, *vt cuppa impleatur, vt pila iaciatur*, vt fera capiatur, et non delectat, vt Deus acquiratur!';[66] 'O quanto es digno de confusion ⁊ verguença deleytarse el hombre *en pecar* ⁊ en *jugar a la pelota* ⁊ en andar acaça ⁊ a monte ⁊ no delaytarse en buscar ⁊ seruir al señor.'[67] A further pastime was, for the nobility, the tourney, which is described on the same page of *De doctrina*: 'Nonne bachelarij, torneatores ad sibilos fistularum, et sonitus tympanorum, clamores histrionum, exhortationes hiraldorum inter gladios constituti sufferunt, et inferunt

---

61 *De doctrina*, p. 9 (and it is said in the vernacular, 'He who lives in within their means will not live in shame'.)

62 Ibid., p. 286 (the good face of this friend is spiritual consolation; and she loses much who loses the good face, *in French 'bonne chiere'*, of her friend.)

63 *Del enseñamiento*, fol. 113v.

64 *De doctrina*, p. 25; *Del enseñamiento*, fol. 10v.

65 'Plaça' is elsewhere used as a synonym for the outside: 'Cor vagatur *foris*, et corpus per se remanet in choro', *De doctrina*, p. 258 (The heart wanders outside and the body remains by itself in the choir); 'esta el cuerpo enla claustra: ⁊ el coraçon enla *plaça*', *Del enseñamiento*, fol. 102r (the body is in the cloister and the heart in the square.)

66 *De doctrina*, p. 37, my italics (Alas, how much to sorrow, how much to be ashamed that one delights that a barrel is filled, that a ball is thrown, that a wild beast is taken, and does not delight that God is to be acquired!)

67 *Del enseñamiento*, fol. 15v, my italics (Oh, how much is it not worthy of shame and abashment that man should delight in *sinning* and *playing pelota* and in riding out hunting and into the wilderness and should not delight in searching for and serving the Lord.)

duros ictus?'[68] The 'fistulae', 'timpani', 'histriones' and 'hiraldi' are reduced to 'ministriles', 'albardanes' and, damningly, 'ribaldos', which renders *Del enseñamiento*'s view of this form of entertainment more hostile: 'Muchas vezes aceasce que al tañer delos ministriles. ⁊ alos bozes delos albardanes ⁊ alas amonestaciones delos ribaldos entran los caualleros mancebos en armas ⁊ torneos ⁊ dan ⁊ sufren grandes golpes.'[69]

Nevertheless, imagery of fighting is shifted up a register when it is applied to Christ. Thus, Jesus as the 'pugile' or boxer becomes a 'caballero' or knight: 'Quis pugilem suum de victoria redeuntem gloriosum, aspersum sanguine, liuidum, *confossum, vulneratum* in domo sua gratanter non reciperet? item, cum honore non reciperet?'[70] 'E quien no recibira alegremente en su posada al cauallero que peleo por el ⁊ vencio gloriosamente enla batalla. ⁊ viene todo cubierto de sangre ⁊ magullado?'[71] In another passage, 'strenuitas' (martial vigour) becomes 'nobleza' (nobility).[72] The 'stomachosus epulator' (short-tempered gourmand), who throws sub-standard food in his servants' faces, becomes an 'ombre de gran linaje' (man of high birth).[73]

Yet, on the other hand, and moving in the opposite direction with regard to the register, the classical-sounding 'quadriga', pulled by horses, becomes a cart pulled by oxen.[74] This is perhaps to make the passage fit more closely to the previous simile, which linked the prelates' subordinates to asses (although the animal is rather decorously unnamed in the Spanish): 'Qui vult asinum suum onerare, mollia suppondere consueuit, ne summa superposita laedat asinum, et eius dorsum excoriet';[75] 'el que quiere cargar alguna bestia primero le echa *buen albarda bien adobada:* ⁊ avn algunos

---

68 *De doctrina*, p. 37 (Do not the young men at a tourney, to the whistling of the pipes and the sound of drums, and the shouts of the performers and the encouragement of the heralds, bearing swords, receive and give fierce blows?)

69 *Del enseñamiento*, fol. 15v (Many times it befalls that, at the playing of the minstrels and the shouts of the fools and the encouragement of the ruffians, young knights put on arms and enter tourneys and give and receive great blows.)

70 *De doctrina*, p. 3 (Who would not thankfully receive into his home his fighter, returning gloriously victorious, covered with blood, bruised, pierced and wounded?)

71 *Del enseñamiento*, fol. 3r (And who would not receive cheefully into his home the *knight* who fought for him and conquered gloriously in the battle, and comes all covered with blood and bruised?), omitting 'confossem', 'vulneratum'.

72 *De doctrina*, p. 35; *Del enseñamiento*, fol. 14v.

73 *De doctrina*, p. 47; *Del enseñamiento*, fol. 19v.

74 *De doctrina*, p. 252; *Del enseñamiento*, fol. 99r.

75 *De doctrina*, p. 252 (He who wants to burden their ass usually put soft things under the load, lest it injure the ass and strip off its skin.)

cabeçaleros si la carga es pesada por que no sea la bestia *matada* ⁊ desollada.'[76] As can be seen, *Del enseñamiento* increases notably the information on the padding required by the beast of burden, as well as the dangers of not providing the cushioning, in that the beast may die – but does not suggest, as indicated above, that the beast of burden (i.e., the overburdened monk) might justifiably complain, which comprises an important part of *De doctrina*'s balance of responsibility between superior and simple monk. We are best to conclude that the intended audience is most probably more composed of monks than their abbots. Indeed, the simple food of monks becomes not just 'piso et olere' (peas and cabbage), but 'ortaliza ⁊ legumbres ⁊ *passas*' (greens and vegetables *and sultanas*).[77]

Looking to his description of women, we find the translator toning down the actions of virtuous women when faced with an improper suitor: *De doctrina* suggests that they are rather violent, and advises its readers to deal with the devil in the same way: 'Fac ergo sicut casta mulier, quae non solum solicitatorem suum non audit, imo cum indignatione eijcit, et verberibus, et conuicijs eijcit, et expellit.'[78] Yet the 'muger casta' would seem to leave both rolling pin and 'pandero' to one side: 'Pues ansi como la muger casta no solamente no oye al que la affinca ⁊ demanda: mas aun lo desecha con desden ⁊ impaciencia';[79] the 'verberibus' and the 'conuiciis' have been omitted from the translation. In a related fashion, for *De doctrina*, all illegitimate children born of adultery are to be rejected: 'Tolle ergo opera peccatorum, tanquam filios de adulterio natos';[80] for *Del enseñamiento*, it is only the bad products of such illicit unions that require rejection: 'Pues echa de ti las obras delos pecados ansi como vnos fijos *malos* engendrados en adulterio.'[81] However, an allusion to cuckoldry in *De doctrina* – 'Et in quibusdam speculis vultus prospicientium *cornuti*

---

76 *Del enseñamiento*, fol. 99r, my italics (he who wishes to load a beast first throws over a well worn-in packsaddle, and even some cushions if the load is heavy so that the beast may not be killed and skinned.)

77 *De doctrina*, p. 199; *Del enseñamiento*, fol. 77r.

78 *De doctrina*, p. 90 (Do, then, as does the chaste woman, who not only does not give ear to her would-be seducer, but rather throws him out with an angry outburst and with blows and with noisy reproaches, and utterly rejects him.)

79 *Del enseñamiento*, fol. 36r (So just as the chaste woman not only does not give ear to he who encourages her and requests her [compliance], but furthermore rejects him with disdain and impatience.)

80 *De doctrina*, p. 116 (reject the works of sinners, like sons born of adultery.)

81 *Del enseñamiento*, fol. 45v (So throw from yourself the works of the sins just like some *bad* children conceived in adultery.)

videntur'[82] – is bowlderized, and the faces become merely ugly: 'E ansi como parescen muy *feos* en algunos espejos los gestos delos que se acatan enello.'[83]

Horses, however, caused a certain amount of difficulty. As noted above, the four 'equi' drawing the 'quadriga' are turned into oxen. A mistranslation also occurs relating to horses. 'Equi *umbratici*', which are described as being 'qui ad auis volatum, aut motum folij terretur, aut resilit, trepidant, vbi non est timor',[84] are translated as 'cauallos *sombrios* que se espantan e saltan al bolar delas aues o al mouimiento delas fojas delos arboles' and again as 'cauallos sombrios e harones'.[85] Now, 'sombrío' is not otherwise found with this meaning in Spanish; its post-medieval use is to indicate the dark pigmentation of a horse's coat. 'Harón' does exist, and is taken from the Arabic 'harūn' (حرون), which specifically means a horse (or mule or donkey) which stops short and cannot be moved. 'Umbratici' has cognates in Italian and French ('ombroso', 'ombrageux'), but the similar word in Spanish, 'asombradizo', is not witnessed in any medieval text. However, 'sombrío' is given in Nebrija's *Vocabulario hispano-latino* as being the equivalent of 'umbraticus'.[86]

The translator rendered the criticism of excessive eloquence in preachers from the very start of *De doctrina* ('Veritatis enim praedicatorem non decet huiusmodi verborum compositio per rhythmos consonantium')[87] as 'Ca no conuiene al predicador dela verdad delas escripturas diuinales fablar rimado ⁊ por consonantes.'[88] Nevertheless, there is a stylistic concern shown

---

82 *De doctrina*, p. 30 (and in some mirrors the face of one looking into them is seen to have horns.)

83 *Del enseñamiento*, fol. 12r (and just as the faces of those who look in some mirrors seem very *ugly*.)

84 *De doctrina*, p. 238 (who, at the flight of a bird, or the movement of leaves, are terrified, or shrink back; they fear where this is no [cause for] fear.)

85 *Del enseñamiento*, fol. 93v (shadowy horses that are frightened and jump at the flying of birds or at the movement of the leaves on the trees.)

86 Antonio Nebrija, *Vocabulario hispano-latino* (Salamanca, 1495), fol. 94va.

87 *De doctrina*, p. 3 (composition of these [divine] words through rhythmical eloquence is not fitting for the preacher of truth.)

88 *Del enseñamiento*, fol. 1v (For it is unfitting for the preacher of the truth of the divine scriptures to speak in rhythmic *cursus* and through *homoioteleuton*.) The phrasing of *Del enseñamiento* cannot but recall the famous verses of the thirteenth-century *Libro de Alexandre*, ed. by J.C. Rigall (Madrid, 2007), p. 130, ll. 2cd: 'fablar curso rimado | por la quaderna vía,/a sílavas contadas, | que es grant maestría' (to speak in rhythmical cursus through the four-fold way, with counted syllables, for it is a great show of skill); regarding the meaning of these

within the translation. This may in part be 'rimado 7 por consonantes', presumably from mnemnonic motives. Thus, in a citation of Gregory the Great – 'Cogitatio praemij minuit vim flagelli'[89] – the loose translation is marked by a rhythmical assonance in *–ó*: 'El pensamiento del galardon / amengua el *dolor* / del açote *dela tribulacion*.'[90] Another example may be found from the addition to *De doctrina*, 'inimicus lucis Diabolus expellatur, et lucis amator Christus introducatur?'[91] (an example of antistrophe itself): 'el diablo enemigo dela luz sea desechado: / 7 sea hospedado / ihesu christo amador / de toda luz 7 *resplandor*.'[92]

The insertion of words derived from 'bastar' produces a *traductio* (the repetition of a key word or syllabic sequence) which draws the following passage in *Del enseñamiento* together:

> Mas los moros 7 los judios sienten cosas no dignas de dios 7 del su poderio: por que los judios esperan de dios riquezas 7 abastança temporal creyendo que aqui avran avn la cipdad de iherusalem *doblada* 7 abastada de toda gloria mundanal. E los moros esperan rescebir en galardon *abastança* de deleytes carnales. 7 esta tal *abastança* es de ombres bestiales que resiciberon en vano sus animas. como el anima que es substancia no veyble 7 assi ha de ser galardonada de bienes no veybles.[93]

One also finds a concern with the balancing of phrases. Thus, in a

---

lines (where 'rimado' is used to evoke both rhyme and rhythm) see idem, pp. 45–6; A. Arizaleta, *La translation d'Alexandre. Recherches sur les structures et les significations du 'Libro de Alexandre'* (Pais, 1999), pp. 152–79, and I.U. Maqua, *Panorama crítico del mester de clerecía* (Madrid, 2000), pp. 36–51. I am of course merely guessing as to the translation of the relevant part of *Del enseñamiento*.

89 *De doctrina*, p. 38 (thought of the reward lessens the force of the whip.)

90 *Del enseñamiento*, fol. 16r. Italics and divisions mine.

91 *De doctrina*, p. 40 (is the enemy of light, the Devil, to be thrown out, and the lover of light, Christ, brought in?)

92 *Del enseñamiento*, fol. 16v (the devil, enemy of the light is to be thrown out, and Jesus Christ is to be welcomed, lover of all light and brightness.)

93 *Del enseñamiento*, fol. 91v, italics indicate additions or changes to the Latin, as usual; underlining, the *traductiones* (But the Moors and the Jews accept unworthy things of God and his power, since the Jews expect riches and temporal wealth from God, believing that here they will yet have the city of Jerusalem *double* and wealthy with all worldy glory. And the Moors expect to receive as reward a *wealth* of carnal delights, and *wealth* like this is for beastial men who received their souls in vain, since the soul is an invisible substance, and so is to be rewarded with what is both good and invisible.)

description of the sick who have lost their taste for food – 'quibus cibus quantumcunque sapidus sit, eis videtur insipidus, et amarus'[94] – *Del enseñamiento* describes 'los enfermos *que han perdido el apetito.* ⁊ fallan desabrida la vianda ⁊ amarga quantoquier que sea sabrosa ⁊ bien guisada.'[95] The order of the phrase is inverted, and 'bien guisada' is added to provide a binary phrase ('sabrosa': 'bien guisada') which balances their antonyms 'desabrida': 'amarga' (>'insipidus et amarus').

To conclude, we may summarise our knowledge of the translator. Skillful, with a clear programme and motive for his translation and a consistent view of his target audience, with a knowledge of enough Greek and medical sources to correct the text he was translating, but a rather more questionable knowledge of horses which displays, nevertheless, an important link with Antonio Nebrija, the leading Spanish humanist of his day, professor at Salamanca when the *princeps* was published, author of the first grammar of a modern vernacular language and numerous other works, and who, as we shall see, has been identified as the publisher of *Del enseñamiento.*

The *princeps*

Del enseñamiento del coraçon forms part of a small group of incunabula of ascetico-mystical interest produced in Salamanca. It is a small group in comparison to other genres of books printed in Salamanca, and in comparison to the book market as it developed during the sixteenth century, where such devotional treatises made up roughly a third of all titles produced. In Salamanca, the middle-aged private lay individual in need of spiritual guidance, and wishing to read about it, had not been identified as a potential buyer, and production of ascetic works was destined primarily for the monastic market. As has been outlined above, it was most definitely for this wealthy, discerning and ascetically minded client that *Del enseñamiento* was prepared.[96]

---

94 *De doctrina*, p. 29 (howsoever tasty their food might be, it seems to them tasteless and bitter.)

95 *Del enseñamiento*, fol. 12v (the sick *who have lost their appetite* and find their food tasteless and bitter however tasty and cooked with herbs and spices it may be.)

96 There is no space here for a full study of *Del enseñamiento*'s place within Salamancan book production, but a comparison of percentages for types or genres of titles published in Salamanca up to 1500 gives 13% for devotional treatises, compared to 37% for booksellers' stock in Toledo and between 31 and 38% for the contents of private libraries in Cuenca during the sixteenth century (for

The endpapers display a woodcut of St Gregory's Mass, which had previously been used on Sebastián de Horta's *Tractatus de confessione* (1497).[97] The final leaf is adorned with a printer's shield, which was a relatively common device at the time. Between the years 1500 and 1510 Pedro Hagenbach, for example, used a shield with a representation of St Ildefonsus, archbishop of Toledo, receiving a heavenly alb from the Blessed Virgin; in itself unsurprising, since he was publishing in Toledo.[98] Guillén de Brocar identified himself with the interlaced letters *AG* underneath a boar in his editions of Fernán Pérez de Guzman, *Cronica del Rey d. Juan II* (Logroño, 1517), Pedro Ciruelo, *Dexameron theologal sobre el regimiento medicinal contra la pestilencia* (Alcalá de Henares, 1519) and *Epistola Ferdinandi de Enzinas* (Alcalá, 1524).[99]

The shield of *Del enseñamiento* is divided into two; the left field bears the five wounds of Christ; the right, a haloed eagle. The shield is further topped by a crown and surrounded by the belt of St Francis. In the point of the shield is a gothic miniscule *y*. Haebler thought that the shield was the emblem of the printer, and, when he wrote, the main printing press of Salamanca was completely anonymous.[100] Now we have rather more details concerning the development of printing in Salamanca.

The right-side eagle of *Del enseñamiento*'s shield is a representation of St John the Evangelist. If this is a printer's shield, then we may assume that the printer's name was Juan. And so springs to mind the name of Juan Porras, who had inherited the Salamancan printing business from his father in 1487 and who continued publishing until 1520.[101] Yet the other elements of the shield may point in another direction. There was another

---

these figures, see S.T. Nalle, 'Literacy and Culture in Early Modern Castile', *Past and Present*, 125 (1989), 65–96 (p. 84). The incunabula from Salamanca are listed in F. Vindel, *El arte tipográfico en España durante el siglo XV*, 10 vols (Madrid, 1945–51), II: *Salamanca, Zamora, Coria y Reino de Galicia* (1946), pp. 3–220; and VIII: *Dudosos de lugar de impresión. Adiciones y correcciones a toda la obra* (1951), pp. 135–88.

97 Vindel, *El arte*, II, pp. 133–4.

98 F. Vindel, *Escudos y marcas de impresores y libreros en España durante los siglos XV a XIX (1485–1850)* (Barcelona, 1942), pp. 46–8, nos 51–3.

99 Vindel, *Escudos*, pp. 27, 30, nos 27, 30.

100 C. Haebler, *Bibliografía ibérica del siglo XV*. I: *Enumeración de todos los libros impresos en España y Portugal hasta el año 1500 con notas críticas* (La Haya & Leipzig, 1903); II: *Segunda parte* (La Haya & Leipzig, 1917) [Facsimile reprint: Madrid, 1992], I, p. 113.

101 M.A.V. García, 'Identificación de la primera imprenta anónima salmantina', *Investigaciones históricas*, 14 (1997), 25–33; J.M. Abad, *Los primeros tiempos de la imprenta en España (c. 1471–1520)*, Arcadia de la letras 19 (Madrid, 2003), pp. 67–8.

John working in Salamanca during this period, the German Juan Giesser, first witnessed as sole printer of a book in 1500.[102] In his printing of the *Vita y procesus Sancti Thome Cantuarensis* (Salamanca, 1506), there is an almost identical reproduction of Hagenbach's alb within a shield (mentioned above). The difference in Giesser's printing is the presence, in the upper part of the page above the shield, of St Francis in his habit receiving the stigmata from a crucifix.[103] The presence of St Francis would explain both the belt of St Francis around the shield of *Del enseñamiento* and the wounds of Christ in the shield itself. The predeliction for Franciscan imagery thus inclines the identification of the printer of *Del enseñamiento* towards Giesser, a German printer, born in Silgenstadt, Hassia.[104] It also places *Del enseñamiento* within a Franciscan sphere of influence, as in late medieval England and Italy, and in the attribution of the later printing of the work to St Bonaventure. The *y* at the point of the shield may be understood as another allusion to Giesser's name: *y* for Yohannes.

However, Vindel, on the basis of the use nearly forty years later of a *Y* in various anonymously printed publications in Granada, one of which, while still silent over the name of the printer, claims to have been published 'Apud inclitam Granatam, in aedibus Antonii Nebrissensis',[105] linked *Del*

---

102 Vindel, *El arte*, II, pp. 190–91.

103 Vindel, *Escudos*, p. 79, no. 76.

104 When might Giesser have started working in Salamanca? Vindel, *El arte*, II, pp. xvi–xvii, supposes that a foreign printer used the second roman type, first seen in Nebrija's *Introductiones latinae* in 1495 (see pp. 73–5, no. 48) and continuing to be used until 1499 (in Petrus Pentarcus, *Ars constructionis*; see pp. 157–8, no. 103).

105 (In noble Granada, in the house of Antonio Nebrija.) According to the reproductions in Vindel, *Escudos*, the *Y* (a distinctly humanist form of the letter, different to the Gothic miniscule *y* of *Del enseñamiento*) was initially used twice in the frontispiece to Tomás Torquemada, *Copilacion de las instrucciones del Officio de la Santa Inquisicion* (1537), reused in Nebrija's *Habes in hoc volumine … rerum a Fernando et Elisabe Hispaniorum* (1545), and later in *Cédulas provisiones y ordenanzas de los Señores Reyes de Castilla …* (1551) (Vindel, *Escudos*, p. 105, nos 129–30). Another style of inclusion of the *Y* in the printing design is found in Nebrija, *Habes in hoc volumine* (1545) (ibid., p. 104, nos 127–8), together with an end page possessing a much more complicated design that also contains the *Y*, similar to that in Nebrija's glossed edition of Virgil, *Opera cun A. Nebrissensis familiaribus phrasibus* (1546); both designs contain the same motto (ibid., p. 106, nos 131–2). Another style is found in Sancho de Salaya, *Repertorio de los tiempos* (1542) and *Aesopi fabulae* (1545) (ibid., p. 103, no. 124). Pedro Mercado, *De febricum differentiis* (1583) offers yet another version (ibid., p. 103, no. 126). It is the latter which is claimed to have been published in Nebrija's own house. The *Aesopi fabulae*

enseñamiento to Nebrija: as professor of the university, he would have found it convenient to hide his direct involvement in the production of books, although his phrasing in his prologue to his *Dictionarium latino-hispanicum* ('como mas copiosamente dispute en el primero libro de aquella obra que *publicamos* de la castellana gramatica'[106]) would indicate direct involvement in the business of publication, and a late-sixteenth-century author described Nebrija's printworks, presumably in Salamanca, as something of common knowledge.[107]

Further linguistic work on the text will be necessary before any judgement over Nebrija's direct involvement in the translation can be offered. However, one may note that the translation appeared the year after Nebrija was relieved of his teaching duties to concentrate upon his researches (in essence, a five-year sabbatical funded by the archbishop of Toledo). It is probably impossible to prove that the translation was carried out by him, although in its accuracy and fidelity to the text, its sober vernacular style which shuns the Latinate syntax and diction previously so favoured for the Spanishing of texts, and the possible use of his dictionary for the translation (in the matter of 'umbraticus'/'sombrío', discussed above), *Del enseñamiento* would seem to come from his circle. This deduction does not exclude Haebler's view of the authorship (which is not very much more than an uninspired guess), 'Este curioso libro con ninguna palabra acusa el nombre del autor que debió ser un religioso de Salamanca.'[108] The significance of the *Y* in Juan Giesser's shield, then, remains to be unravelled. The answer to that may well be the same as that supplied by my Wexford-born grandmother, who would reply to a four-year old's incessant (and anaphoric) questioning with the unyielding response '*Y* is a crooked letter and ye can't straighten it.'

---

may have been a reprint of the Salamanca edition of a work with the title of *Fabelle Esopi* (1491), for this latter work, see Vindel, *El arte*, II, pp. 39–40, no. 26.

106 fol. ivb, my italics (as I discoursed more fully in the first book of that work that *we published* about Castilian grammar.)

107 Vindel, *El arte*, II, p. xxi. The work in question, as cited by Vindel, is Agustino Gerónimo Román, *Repúblicas del mundo* (Medina del Campo, 1575), fol. 214v: 'Esto se puede decir lícitamente porque en la oficina del maestro Antonio de Lebrixa parecen ciertas paginas de metal con todas necesarias y se imprimieron antes con ellas.' (This we can correctly claim because in the workshop of *maestro* Antonio de Lebrixa [i.e. Nebrija], there are certain metal forms with all their appurtenances and in earlier days they printed with them.)

108 Haebler, *Bibliografía ibérica*, I, p. 112 (This unusual book gives no indication at all of the name of its author, who must have been a religious from Salamanca.)

Bibliography

Manuscripts

De doctrina cordis:

Basel, Öffentl. Bibliothek der Universität, MS A.VIII.9
Basel, Öffentl. Bibliothek der Universität, MS A.X.57
Basel, Öffentl. Bibliothek der Universität, MS B.X.4
Basel, Öffentl. Bibliothek der Universität, MS B.X.6
Basel, Öffentl. Bibliothek der Universität, MS B.X.22
Berlin, Staatsbibliothek zu Berlin – Preußischer Kulturbesitz, Ms. lat. oct. 272
Berlin, Staatsbibliothek zu Berlin – Preußischer Kulturbesitz, Ms. theol. fol. 327
Berlin, Staatsbibliothek zu Berlin – Preußischer Kulturbesitz, Ms. theol. lat. qu. 172
Cambrai, Bibliothèque municipale, MS 838
Cambridge, Peterhouse College, MS 203
Cambridge, University Library, MS Ff. 3.24
Charleville-Mézières, Bibliothèque municipale, MS 87
Cologne, Historisches Archiv der Stadt Köln, MS W* 151
Durham, The Dean and Chapter Library, MS B.III.18
Durham, The Dean and Chapter Library, MS B.III.19
Einsiedeln, Stiftsbibliothek O.S.B., MS 220
Frankfurt, Stadt- und Universitätsbibliothek, MS Carm. 10
Frankfurt, Stadt- und Universitätsbibliothek, MS Lat. qu. 6
Freiburg im Breisgau, Universitätsbibliothek, MS 111
Fritzlar, Dombibliothek, MS 38
Graz, Universitätsbibliothek, MS 577
Kraków, Uniw. Jag., Bibl. Jagiellońska, MS 1382
Leiden, Bibliotheek der Rijksuniversiteit, MS BPL 2579
Liège, Bibl. Grand Séminaire, MS 6 N 20
Lilienfeld, Stiftsbibliothek O.C.S.O., MS 136
Mainz, Stadtbibliothek, MS I 48
Mainz, Stadtbibliothek, MS I 311
Mainz, Stadtbibliothek, MS I 317
Mainz, Stadtbibliothek, MS II 27
Munich, Bayerische Staatsbibliothek, Clm 7984

Munich, Bayerische Staatsbibliothek, Clm 9648
Munich, Bayerische Staatsbibliothek, Clm 18647
Munich, Bayerische Staatsbibliothek, Clm 21232
Oxford, Bodleian Library, MS Lat. th. f. 6
Oxford, Bodleian Library, MS Laud Misc. 208
Oxford, Bodleian Library, MS Laud Misc. 479
Oxford, Bodleian Library, MS Laud Misc. 530
Oxford, University College, MS D62–63
Paris, Bibliothèque nationale de France, MS lat. 15958
Prague, Národní knihovna České republiky, MS XI–I.A.14
Salzburg, Bibliothek Erzabtei St. Peter, MS a.III.30
Salzburg, Bibliothek Erzabtei St. Peter, MS a.VII.18
Salzburg, Bibliothek Erzabtei St. Peter, MS b.III.10
Trier, Stadtbibliothek, MS 745
Uppsala, Universitetsbibliothek, MS C 631
Vienna, Österr. Nationalbibliothek, MS 1052
Vienna, Österr. Nationalbibliothek, MS 4316
Wiesbaden, Hessische Landesbibliothek, MS 17
Wrocław, Biblioteka Uniwersytecka, MS I.Q.108
Würzburg, Universitätsbibliothek, M.ch.f.219
Würzburg, Universitätsbibliothek, M.ch.f.229

The English translation: *The Doctrine of the Hert:*
Cambridge, Fitzwilliam Museum, MS McClean 132
Cambridge, Trinity College, MS B.14.15
Durham, University Library, MS Cosin V.III.24
Oxford, Bodleian Library, MS Laud Misc. 330

French translations: *Le traitiers de la doctrine du cuer*:
Douai, Bibliothèque municipale, MS 514
Paris, Bibliothèque nationale de France, MS fr. 13272
Oxford, Bodleian Library, MS Holkham Misc. 42
Troyes, Bibliothèque municipale, MS 1384

Dutch translations: *De bouc van der leeringhe van der herten*:
Cologne, Diözesanbibliothek, MS 248
The Hague, Koninklijke Bibliotheek, MS 135 F 6
Vienna, Österr. Nationalbibliothek, MS 15231
Vienna, Österr. Nationalbibliothek, MS Ser. nov. 12805

German translations:
Augsburg, Universitätsbibliothek, cod. III 1.2°14
Berlin, Staatsbibliothek zu Berlin – Preußischer Kulturbesitz, Ms. germ. qu. 1077
Berlin, Staatsbibliothek zu Berlin – Preußischer Kulturbesitz, Ms. germ. qu. 1130

Eichstätt, Kloster St. Walburg, Cod. Germ. 7
Klosterneuburg, Augustinerchorherren-Stift, MS 363
Munich, Bayerische Staatsbibliothek, Cgm 447
Solothurn, Zentralbibliothek, MS S 353

The Italian translation:
Florence, Bibliotheca Medicea Laurenziana, MS Ashb. 253 (333–265)

Gerard of Liège, attrib., *De duodecim utilitatibus tribulationum*:
Paris, Bibliothèque nationale de France, MS lat. 14955
Munich, Bayerische Staatsbibliothek, Clm 6977
Vienna, Österr. Nationalbibliothek, MS 4316

—, *Paris sermons*:
Paris, Bibliothèque nationale de France, MS lat. 16483

—, *Septem remedia contra amorem illictum* and *Quinque incitamenta ad Deum amandum ardenter*:
Troyes, Bibliothèque municipale, MS 1890

Deuout Treatyse Called the Tree & xii. Frutes of the Holy Goost, A:
Cambridge, Fitzwilliam Museum, MS McClean 132
Durham, University Library, MS Cosin V.III.24
London, British Library, MS Add. 24192

Feitis and the Passion of Oure Lord Jhesu Crist, The:
Oxford, Bodleian Library, MS Holkham Misc. 41

James of Milan, *Stimulus amoris* (in Middle English translation):
London, British Library, MS Harley 2254
Durham, University Library, MS Cosin V.III.8

Privity of the Passion, The:
Durham, University Library, MS Cosin V.III.8

Pseudo-Bernard, *The Manere of Good Lyvyng*:
Oxford, Bodleian Library, MS Laud Misc. 517

Early printed editions

De doctrina cordis, editio princeps (Paris, 1506):
Oxford, Bodleian Library, Vet. E1.f.1

De doctrina cordis, Gerardus Leodiensis, Speculum concionatorum ad illustrandum pectora auditorum, in septem libros distributum [...] (Naples, 1607):
Oxford, Bodleian Library, 8º L 12 Th. BS

Spanish Translations: *Del enseñamiento del coraçon* (Salamanca, 1498):
El Escorial, 31-V–49 (2º)
Lisbon, Biblioteca Nacional, Divisão de Reservados e Manuscritos, Inc. 502 and 503

—: *Doctrina cordis de sant buena ventura en romance: nueuamente corregido y enmendado* (Toledo, 1510):
London, British Library, C 63 c 16
Madrid, Biblioteca Nacional, R–31600
New York, Hispanic Society
Zaragoza, Biblioteca Universitaria, A.30.25[1]

—: *Doctrina cordis de sant buena ventura en romance: nueuamente corregido y enmendado* (Toledo, 1525):
Barcelona, Biblioteca de Catalunya, Esp. 68–8º

—: *Doctrina cordis del serafico dotor sant buena ventura en romance: muy util y provechoso para todos los fieles christianos: nuevamente corregido y emendado* (Baeza, 1551): in private hands

Andreas, Valerius, *Bibliotheca Belgica* (Louvain, 1623)

Deuout Treatyse Called the Tree & xii. Frutes of the Holy Goost, A (London, 1534):
Ampleforth Abbey, MS C.v.130
Cambridge, Trinity College, MS C.7.12

Fabricius, Johann Albert, *Bibliotheca latinae media et infirmae aetatis* (Hamburg, 1735)

Foppens, Jean François, *Bibliotheca Belgica* (Brussels, 1737)

Miraeus, Aubertus, *Bibliotheca ecclesiastica* (Antwerp, 1639)

Nebrija, Antonio, *Vocabulario hispano-latino* (Salamanca, 1495)

Quétif, Jacques, and Jacques Échard, *Scriptores ordinis Praedicatorum recensiti*, 2 vols in 4 (Paris, 1719–23)

Trithemius, Johannes, *Liber de scriptoribus ecclesiasticis* (Basel, 1494)

—, *Cathalogus illustrium virorum Germaniam suis ingenijs et lucubrationibus omnifariam exornantium* (s.l. et a. [Mainz, 1495])

Modern editions and secondary sources

Abad, J.M., *Post-incunables ibéricos* (Madrid, 2001).

—, *Los primeros tiempos de la imprenta en España (c. 1471–1520)*, Arcadia de la letras 19 (Madrid, 2003).

Acquoy, J.A.R., *Het klooster te Windesheim en zijn invloed* (Utrecht, 1875–1880).

Aelred of Rievaulx's De institutione inclusarum: Two English Versions, ed. by J. Ayto and A. Barratt, EETS 287 (1984).

Ahlers, G., *Weibliches Zisterziensertum im Mittelalter und seine Klöster in Niedersachsen*, Studien zur Geschichte, Kunst und Kultur der Zisterzienser 13 (Berlin, 2002).

Alan of Lille, *Elucidatio in Cantica*, *PL* 210.

Ampe, A., 'Een oud Florilegium Eucharisticum in een veertiende-eeuws handschrift', *OGE*, 31 (1957), 301–24; 32 (1958), 56–90; 38 (1964), 23–55.

Ancrene Wisse, The English Text of the Ancrene Riwle: Ancrene Wisse, Edited from MS. Corpus Christi College, Cambridge, 402, ed. by J.R.R. Tolkien, EETS 249 (1962).

—, *The French Text of the Ancrene Riwle, Edited from Trinity College Cambridge MS R.14.7*, ed. by W.H. Trethewey, EETS 240 (1958, repr. 1971).

—, *Ancrene Wisse, A Corrected Edition of the Text in Cambridge, Corpus Christi College, MS 402, with Variants from Other Manuscripts*, ed. by B. Millett, 2 vols, EETS 325 (2005) and 326 (2006).

Ancrene Wisse: Guide for Anchoresses, tr. H. White (Harmondsworth, 1993).

Anselm, St, *The Prayers and Meditations of Saint Anselm with the Proslogion*, tr. Sister B. Ward (London, 1973).

Arizaleta, A., *La translation d'Alexandre. Recherches sur les structures et les significations du 'Libro de Alexandre'* (Pais, 1999).

Armstrong, C.A.J., 'The Piety of Cicely, Duchess of York: A Study in Late Mediaeval Culture', in C.A.J. Armstrong, *England, France and Burgundy in the Fifteenth Century* (London, 1983), pp. 135–56.

Arnold, K., *Johannes Trithemius (1462–1516)*, Quellen und Forschungen zur Geschichte des Bistums und Hochstifts Würzburg 23, 2nd revised edn (Würzburg, 1991).

Aubert, R., 'Gérard de Liège, cistercien'; 'Gérard de Liège, dominicain', in A. Baudrillart et al. (eds), *Dictionnaire d'histoire et de géographie ecclésiastique*, vol. 20 (Paris, 1984), cols 776f.

—, 'Hugues de Saint-Cher', in A. Baudrillart et al. (eds), *Dictionnaire d'histoire et de géographie ecclésiastique*, vol. 25 (Paris, 1995), col. 287.

Auer, A., *Ein neu aufgefundener Katalog der Dominikaner Schriftsteller*, Dissertationes historicae 2 (Paris, 1933).

—, *Leidenstheologie im Spätmittelalter*, Kirchengeschichtliche Quellen und Studien 2 (St. Ottilien, 1952).

Axters, S.G., 'Nederlandse mystiek in het buitenland. Van Rupert van Deutz tot

Ruusbroec', *Verslagen en mededelingen van de Koninklijke Vlaamse Academie voor Taal- en Letterkunde* (nieuwe reeks) (1965), 163–325.

Bachelard, G., *The Poetics of Space*, tr. M. Jolas (Boston, 1994).

Baker, D.N. (ed.), 'The Privity of the Passion', in A.C. Bartlett and T.H. Bestul (eds), *Cultures of Piety: Medieval English Devotional Literature* (Ithaca, NY, 1999), pp. 85–106.

Barber, R., *Bestiary, Being an English Version of the Bodleian Library, Oxford MS. Bodley 764 with all the Original Miniatures Reproduced in Facsimile* (Woodbridge, 1993, repr. 1999).

Barratt, A., *The Book of Tribulation ed. from MS Bodley 423*, Middle English Texts 15 (Heidelberg, 1983).

Bataillon, L.-J. and N. Bériou, '"G. de Mailly" de l'ordre des Frères prècheurs', *Archivum fratrum Praedicatorum*, 61 (1991), 5–88.

—, G. Dahan and P.-M. Gy (eds), *Hugues de Saint-Cher († 1263), bibliste et théologien*, Bibliothèque d'histoire culturelle du moyen âge 1 (Turnhout, 2004).

Batt, C., D. Renevey and C. Whitehead, 'Domesticity and Medieval Devotional Literature', *Leeds Studies in English*, 36 (2005), 195–250.

Becker, P., 'Erstrebte und erreichte Ziele benediktinischer Reformen im Spätmittelalter', in Elm (ed.), *Reformbemühungen*, pp. 23–34.

Beckwith, S., *Christ's Body: Identity, Culture and Society in Late Medieval Writings* (London, 1993).

Bell, D.H. (ed.), *The Libraries of the Cistercians, Gilbertines and Premonstratensians*, Corpus of British Medieval Library Catalogues 3 (London, 1992).

—, *What Nuns Read: Books and Libraries in Medieval English Nunneries*, Cistercian Studies Series 158 (Kalamazoo, 1995).

Berlière, U., E. Brouette and N. Huyghebaert (eds), *Monasticon Belge* (Maredsous, 1890–1993).

Bernard, St, *A Rule of Good Life*, tr. A. Batt (Doway, 1633; repr. Menston, 1971).

Bloomfield, M.W. et al., *Incipits of Latin Works on the Virtues and Vices, 1100–1500 A.D.* (Cambridge, MA, 1979).

Boeren, P.C., *La vie et les oeuvres de Guiard de Laon 1170 env. – 1248* (The Hague, 1956).

Boethius, *Philosophiae consolatio*, ed. by L. Bieler, *CCSL* 94 (Turnhout, 1984).

Bonaventure, St, *The Soul's Journey into God. The Tree of Life. The Life of St Francis*, tr. E. Cousins, The Classics of Western Spirituality (New York, 1978).

Book of Common Prayer, The (Cambridge, 1922).

Boyle, L.E., 'The Fourth Lateran Council and Manuals of Popular Theology', in T.J. Heffernan (ed.), *The Popular Literature of Medieval England* (Knoxville, 1985), pp. 30–60.

Brand, M., *Studien zu Johannes Niders deutschen Schriften*, Dissertationes historicae 23 (Rome, 1998).

Brouette, É. et al., *Dictionnaire des auteurs cisterciens*, vol. 1 (Rochefort, 1975).

Bynum, C.W., *Jesus as Mother: Studies in the Spirituality of the High Middle Ages* (Berkeley, CA, 1982).

—, *Holy Feast and Holy Fast: The Religious Significance of Food to Medieval Women* (Berkeley, CA, 1987).

—, *Fragmentation and Redemption: Essays on Gender and the Human Body in Medieval Religion* (New York, 1992).

Cannon, C., 'Enclosure', in C. Dinshaw and D. Wallace (eds), *The Cambridge Companion to Medieval Women's Writing* (Cambridge, 2003), pp. 109–23.

—, *The Grounds of English Literature* (Oxford, 2004).

Carruthers, L., 'In Pursuit of Holiness Outside the Cloister: Religion of the Heart in *The Abbey of the Holy Ghost*', in B.M. Kienzle (ed.), *Models of Holiness in Medieval Sermons*, Textes et Études du Moyen Âge 5 (Louvain-La-Neuve, 1996), pp. 211–27.

Carruthers, M., 'The Poet as Master Builder: Composition and Locational Memory in the Middle Ages', *New Literary History*, 24 (1993), 881–904.

Catalogue général des manuscrits des bibliothèques publiques des départements publié sous les auspices du ministre de l'instruction publique, vol. 2 (Paris, 1855); vol. 6 (Paris, 1878).

Chartularium Universitatis Parisiensis, vol. 1, ed. by H.S. Denifle and A. Chatelain (Paris, 1889).

Chastising of God's Children and the Treatise of Perfection of the Sons of God, The, ed. by E. Colledge and J. Bazire (Oxford, 1957).

Cloud of Unknowing and the Book of Privy Counselling, The, ed. by P. Hodgson, EETS OS 218 (1944).

Coleman, J., *Medieval Readers and Writers, 1350–1400* (New York, 1981).

Conlee, J.W. (ed.), '*The Abbey of the Holy Ghost* and *The Eight Ghostly Dwelling Places* of Huntington Library HM 744', *Medium Aevum*, 44 (1975), 137–44.

Connolly, M. (ed.), *Contemplations of the Dread and Love of God*, EETS OS 303 (1993).

Copeland, R., *Rhetoric, Hermeneutics, and Translation in the Middle Ages* (Cambridge, 1991).

Cornelius, R.D., *The Figurative Castle: A Study of the Medieval Allegory of the Edifice* (Bryn Mawr, 1930).

Cottiaux, J., 'L'office liégeois de la Fête-Dieu. Sa valeur et son destin', *Revue d'histoire ecclésiastique*, 58 (1963), 5–81, 405–59.

Coxe, H.O. (ed.), *Catalogus codicum MSS qui in collegiis aulisque Oxoniensibus hodie adservantur*, Pars. 1 (Oxford, 1852).

— (ed.), *Bodleian Library, Quarto Catalogues II. Laudian Manuscripts* (Oxford, repr. 1973).

Dailey, P., 'Questions of Dwelling in Anglo-Saxon Poetry and Medieval Mysticism: Inhabiting Landscape, Body and Mind', in R. Copeland, D. Lawton and W. Scase (eds), *New Medieval Literatures* 8 (Turnhout, 2006), pp. 175–214.

Davies, R.T. (ed.), *Medieval English Lyrics* (London, 1963).

D'Avray, D.L., *The Preaching of the Friars* (Oxford, 1985).

Dean, J.M. (ed.), *Six Ecclesiastical Satires*, TEAMS (Kalamazoo, MI, 1991).

de Certeau, M., *The Practice of Everyday Life*, tr. S. Rendall (London, 1984).

de Cock, M. and G. Hendrix (eds), *Dat boec vander bereydinge des harten. Middelnederlandse vertaling van De praeparatione cordis (Hugo van Saint-Cher, pseudo-Gerard van Luik)*, De doctrina sive praeparatione cordis 2 (Ghent, 1986).

De duodecim utilitatibus tribulationum, *PL* 207, cols 989–1006.

Degering, H., *Kurzes Verzeichnis der germanischen Handschriften der Preußischen Staatsbibliothek II. Die Handschriften in Quartformat*, Mitteilungen aus der Preußischen Staatsbibliothek 8 (Leipzig, 1926; repr. Graz, 1970).

de Lubac, H., *Medieval Exegesis. Volume 1: The Four Senses of Scripture*, tr. M. Sebank (Edinburgh, 1998).

Deuout Treatyse Called the Tree & xii. Frutes of the Holy Goost, A, ed. by J.J. Vaissier (Groningen, 1960).

Doctrine of the Hert, The, Sister M.P. Candon (ed.), '*The Doctrine of the Hert*, Edited from the Manuscripts with Introduction and Notes' (unpublished doctoral dissertation, Fordham University, 1963).

Doyle, A.I., 'A Survey of the Origins and Circulation of Theological Writings in English in the Fourteenth, Fifteenth and early Sixteenth Centuries with Special Consideration of the Part of the Clergy Therein' (unpublished doctoral dissertation, Cambridge University, 1954).

—, 'The Shaping of the Vernon and Simeon Manuscripts', in B. Rowland (ed.), *Chaucer and Middle English Studies in Honour of Rossell Hope Robbins* (London, 1974), pp. 328–41.

Duffy, E., *The Stripping of the Altars: Traditional Religion in England c. 1400-c. 1580* (New Haven, 1992).

Edwards, A.S.G., 'The Middle English Manuscripts and Early Readers of *Ancrene Wisse*', in Wada (ed.), *Companion*, pp. 103–12.

Egger, F., *Beiträge zur Geschichte des Predigerordens. Die Reform des Basler Konvents 1429 und die Stellung des Ordens am Basler Konzil 1431–1448* (Basel, 1991).

Ehrenschwendtner, M.-L., *Die Bildung der Dominikanerinnen in Süddeutschland vom 13. bis 15. Jahrhundert*, Contubernium 60 (Stuttgart, 2004).

Ellis, R., 'The Choices of the Translator in the Late Middle English Period', in M. Glasscoe (ed.), *The Medieval Mystical Tradition in England* (Exeter, 1982), pp. 18–46.

Elm, K. (ed.), *Reformbemühungen und Observanzbestrebungen im spätmittelalterlichen Ordenswesen* (Berlin, 1989).

—, 'Reform- und Observanzbestrebungen im spätmittelalterlichen Ordenswesen. Ein Überblick', in Elm (ed.), *Reformbemühungen*, pp. 3–22.

Erdin, E.A., *Das Kloster der Reuerinnen Sancta Maria Magdalena an den Steinen zu Basel* (Basel, 1956).

Erler, M.C., 'Exchange of Books Between Nuns and Laywomen: Three Surviving Examples', in R. Beadle and A.J. Piper (eds), *New Science Out of Old Books:*

Studies in Manuscripts and Early Printed Books in Honour of A.I. Doyle (Aldershot, 1995), pp. 360–73.

—, *Women, Reading and Piety in Late Medieval England*, Cambridge Studies in Medieval Literature 46 (Cambridge, 2002).

Falmagne, T., *Un texte en contexte. Les* Flores paradisi *et le milieu culturel de Villers-en-Brabant dans la première moitié du 13ᵉ siècle*, Instrumenta patristica et mediaevalia 39 (Turnhout, 2001).

Felten, F.J., 'Zisterzienserinnen in Deutschland. Beobachtungen und Überlegungen zu Ausbreitung und Ordenszugehörigkeit', in *Unanimité et diversité cisterciennes. Filiations – réseaux – relectures du XIIe au XVIIe siècle. Actes du quatrième colloque international du CERCOR* (Saint-Étienne, 2000), pp. 345–400.

—, 'Der Zisterzienserorden und die Frauen', in H. Schwillus and A. Hölscher (eds), *Weltverachtung und Dynamik*, Studien zur Geschichte, Kunst und Kultur der Zisterzienser 10 (Berlin, 2000), pp. 34–135.

Fink, A., 'St Walburg', in A. Baudillart et al. (eds), *Dictionnaire d'histoire et de géographie ecclésiastique*, vol. 15 (Paris, 1925).

Friedel, A., *Die Bibliothek der Abtei St. Walburg zu Eichstätt*, Schriften der Universitätsbibliothek Eichstätt 45 (Wiesbaden, 2000).

García, M.A.V., 'Identificación de la primera imprenta anónima salmantina', *Investigaciones históricas*, 14 (1997), 25–33.

Gibbs, M. and J. Lang, *Bishops and Reform 1215–1272, with Special Reference to the Lateran Council of 1215* (London, 1934).

Gilchrist, R., *Gender and Material Culture: The Archaeology of Religious Women* (London, 1994).

—, *Gender and Archaeology: Contesting the Past* (London, 1999).

Gillespie, V., 'Strange Images of Death: The Passion in Later Medieval English Devotional and Mystical Writing', *Analecta Cartusiana*, 117 (1987), 110–59.

—, 'Vernacular Books of Religion,' in J. Griffiths and D. Pearsall (eds), *Book Production and Publishing in Britain 1375–1475*, Cambridge Studies in Publishing and Printing History (Cambridge, 1989), pp. 317–44.

— and M. Ross, 'The Apophatic Image: The Poetics of Effacement in Julian of Norwich', in M. Glasscoe (ed.), *The Medieval Mystical Tradition in England*, V (Cambridge, 1992), pp. 53–77.

—, 'Thy Will Be Done: *Piers Plowman* and the *Pater Noster*', in A.J. Minnis (ed.), *Middle English Religious Texts and Their Transmission: Essays in Honour of Ian Doyle* (Cambridge, 1994), pp. 95–119.

— (ed.), *Syon Abbey, with the Libraries of the Carthusians*, ed. A.I. Doyle, Corpus of British Medieval Library Catalogues 9 (London, 2001).

—, 'Anonymous Devotional Writings', in A.S.G. Edwards (ed.), *A Companion to Middle English Prose* (Cambridge, 2004), pp. 127–49.

—, 'Vernacular Theology', in P. Strohm (ed.), *Middle English: Oxford Twenty-First Century Approaches to Literature* (Oxford, 2007), pp. 401–20.

—, 'Religious Writing', in R. Ellis (ed.), *The Oxford History of Literary Translation in English, vol. 1: 700–1550* (Oxford, 2008), pp. 234–83.

Goering, J., *William de Montibus (c. 1140–1213): The Schools and the Literature of Pastoral Care* (Toronto, 1992).

Goswin of Bossut, *Send me God. The Lives of Ida the Compassionate of Nivelles, Nun of La Ramée, Arnulf, Lay Brother of Villers, and Abundus, Monks of Villers*, tr. and intro. M. Cawley and with a preface by B. Newman, Medieval Women: Texts and Contexts 6 (Turnhout, 2003).

Gunn, C., *Ancrene Wisse: From Pastoral Literature to Vernacular Spirituality* (Cardiff, 2008).

Haebler, C., *Bibliografía ibérica del siglo XV.* I: *Enumeración de todos los libros impresos en España y Portugal hasta el año 1500 con notas críticas* (La Haya & Leipzig, 1903); II: *Segunda parte* (La Haya & Leipzig, 1917) [Facsimile reprint: Madrid, 1992].

Hamburger, J., *Nuns as Artists: The Visual Culture of a Medieval Convent* (Berkeley, CA, 1997).

Handley, S., 'Spelman, Sir Henry (1563/4–1641)', in H.C.C. Matthew and B. Harrison (eds), *Dictionary of National Biography*, vol. 51 (Oxford, 2004), pp. 791–3.

Handlist of the Manuscripts in the Library of the Earl of Leicester at Holkham Hall, A, abstracted from the catalogue of William Roscoe and F. Madden and annotated by S. De Ricci (Oxford, 1932).

Häring, N., 'Der Literaturkatalog von Affligem', *Revue bénédictine*, 80 (1970), 64–96.

Harrod, H., 'Extracts from Early Wills in the Norwich Registries', *Norfolk and Norwich Archeological Society*, 4 (1855), 335–6.

Hauréau, [J.]B., *Notices et extraits de quelques manuscrits latins de la Bibliothèque nationale*, vol. 4 (Paris, 1892).

Heinrich von Langenstein. Erchantnuzz der Sund Nach österreichen Handschriften, ed. by R. Rudolf, Texte des späten Mittelalters und der frühen Neuzeit 22 (Berlin, 1969).

Hendrix, G., 'Gerardus Leodiensis — *De doctrina cordis*', *CCC*, 27 (1976), 135–8.

—, 'Cistercian Sympathies in the 14th-century *Catalogus virorum illustrium*', *CCC*, 27 (1976), 267–78

—, '*De doctrina cordis*: Manuscripts of Clairvaux and Cîteaux Provenance', *CCC*, 28 (1977), 94–100.

—, 'Handschriften en in handschrift bewaarde vertalingen van het aan Gerard van Luik toegeschreven traktaat *De doctrina cordis*. Een overzicht', *OGE*, 51 (1977), 146–68.

—, 'Deux textes d'attribution incertaine à saint Bonaventure, restitués à Gérard de Liège', *RTAM*, 45 (1978), 237–8.

—, 'Drukgeschiedenis van het traktaat *De doctrina cordis*', *Archives et bibliothèques de Belgique/Archief- en bibliotheekwezen van België*, 49 (1978), 224–39.

—, 'À la recherche de "frater Thomas de ordine fratrum heremitarum sancti Augustini"', *RTAM*, 46 (1979), 214–15.

—, 'Handschriften van het traktaat *De doctrina cordis*. Aanvullende opsomming', *OGE*, 54 (1980), 39–42.

—, 'Het Leidse handschrift BPL 2579 en de tekstoverlevering van het traktaat *De doctrina cordis*', *OGE*, 54 (1980), 158–81.

—, 'Hugh of St. Cher O.P., Author of two texts attributed to the 13th-century Cistercian Gerard of Liège', *CCC*, 31 (1980), 343–56.

—, 'Les *Postillae* de Hugues de Saint-Cher et le traité *De doctrina cordis*', *RTAM*, 47 (1980), 114–30.

—, *Le manuscrit Leyde Bibliothèque de l'Université, BPL 2579, témoin principal des phases de rédaction du traité De doctrina cordis à attribuer au dominicain français Hugues de Saint-Cher (pseudo-Gérard de Liège)*, facsimile edn with an intro. by G. Hendrix, De doctrina sive praeparatione cordis 1 (Gent, 1980).

—, '*De apercione cordis*, *De impedimentis* and *De custodia linguae*. Three pseudo-Bernardine Texts restored to their true author, Hugh of St. Cher', *RTAM*, 48 (1981), 172–97.

—, 'Kleine queste naar de auteur van *De duodecim utilitatibus tribulationum*', *OGE*, 56 (1982), 109–24.

—, 'Onderzoek naar het œuvre van "Gerardus Leodiensis"', *OGE*, 56 (1982), 300–341.

—, 'Le *De doctrina cordis*, source directe du *Chastel perilleux*', *RTAM*, 50 (1983), 252–66.

—, 'Onderzoek naar het œuvre van "Gerardus Leodiensis". Tweede deel', *OGE*, 58 (1984), 281–99.

—, 'Luik, Gerard van, geestelijk schrijver', in *Nationaal Biografisch Woordenboek*, vol. 12 (Brussels, 1987), cols 437–42.

—, *De lange redactie van De doctrina cordis (Hugo van Saint-Cher, pseudo-Gerard van Luik) in Middelnederlandse vertaling uitgegeven naar de handschriften Wenen, O.N.B., 15231 en Ser. nov. 12805*, De doctrina sive praeparatione cordis 3–4 (Ghent, 1987).

—, 'Note relative aux manuscrits des traités *De doctrina cordis* et *De praeparatione cordis*', *RTAM*, 54 (1987), 255–6.

—, 'De vertalingen van *De doctrina cordis* en *De praeparatione cordis* (Hugo van Saint-Cher, Pseudo-Gerardus Leodiensis)', in *Miscellanea Neerlandica. Opstellen voor Dr. Jan Deschamps ter gelegenheid van zijn zeventigste verjaardag* (Louvain, 1987), part 2, pp. 19–29.

—, '"Der Literaturkatalog von Affligem". Some notes on a *Catalogus virorum illustrium*', in A. Raman and E. Manning (eds), *Miscellanea Martin Wittek. Album de codicologie et de paléographie offert Martin Wittek* (Louvain/Paris, 1993), pp. 181–8.

—, *Hugo De Sancto Caro's traktaat De doctrina cordis. Vol. 1: Handschriften, receptie, tekstgeschiedenis en authenticiteitskritiek*, Documenta Libraria 16/1 (Louvain, 1995).

—, *Hugo De Sancto Caro's traktaat De doctrina cordis. Vol. 2: Pragmatische editie van De bouc van der leeringhe van der herten naar handschrift Wenen, ÖNB, 15231, autograaf van de Middelnederlandse vertaler*, Documenta Libraria 16/2 (Louvain, 1995).

—, *Hugo de Sancto Caro's traktaat De doctrina cordis. vol. 3. Pragmatische editie van Dat Boec van der bereydinge des harten naar handschrift Den Haag, Koninklijke Bibliotheek, 135 F 6*, Documenta libraria 16/3 (Louvain, 2000).

— (ed.), *Hugo de Sancto Caro's traktaat De doctrina cordis. vol. 4. De sermoenen in handschrift Parijs Bibliothèque Nationale, 16483*, ed. by G. Hendrix, Documenta libraria 16/4 (Louvain, 2000).

Henkel, N., *Deutsche Übersetzungen lateinischer Schultexte: ihre Verbreitung und Funktion im Mittelalter und in der frühen Neuzeit* (Munich, 1988).

Hernad, B., *Die gotischen Handschriften deutscher Herkunft in der Bayerischen Staatsbibliothek. Teil 1: Vom späten 13. bis zur Mitte des 14. Jahrhunderts* (Wiesbaden, 2000).

Hillenbrand, E., 'Die Observanzbewegung in der deutschen Ordensprovinz der Dominikaner', in Elm (ed.), *Reformbemühungen*, pp. 219–72.

Hohmann, T., 'Die recht gelerten maister. Bemerkungen zur Übersetzungsliteratur der Wiener Schule des Spätmittelalters', in H. Zeman (ed.), *Die Österreichische Literatur: ihr Profil von den Anfängen im Mittelalter bis ins 18. Jahrhundert* (Graz, 1986), vol. 1, pp. 349–65.

Holdsworth, C., 'Hermits and the Power of the Frontier', in K. Bates et al. (eds), *Saints and Saints' Lives: Essays in Honour of D.H. Farmer, Reading Medieval Studies*, 16 (1990), 55–76.

Holy Bible, The: Douay Version Translated from the Latin Vulgate.

Honemann, V., 'Gerhard von Lüttich', in K. Ruh et al. (eds), *Die deutsche Literatur des Mittelalters. Verfasserlexikon*, 2nd edn, vol. 2 (Berlin/New York, 1980), cols 1233–5.

—, 'Der Laie als Leser', in K. Schreiner (ed.), *Laienfrömmigkeit im späten Mittelalter*, Schriften des Historischen Kollegs. Kolloquien 20 (Munich, 1992), pp. 241–52.

Horstmann, C. (ed.), *Yorkshire Writers: Richard Rolle of Hampole, an English Father of the Church, and His Followers*, 2 vols (London, 1895–6).

Huismans, P. and K. Van Wonterghem (eds), *Het obituarium van de Sint-Trudoabdij de Odegem, te Brugge en te Male, 1149–2002* (Brugge, 2002).

Hussey, S.S., 'Implications of Choice and Arrangement of Texts in Part 4', in D. Pearsall (ed.), *Studies in the Vernon Manuscript* (Cambridge, 1990), pp. 61–74.

Innes-Parker, C., 'The Lady and the King: *Ancrene Wisse*'s Parable of the Royal Wooing Re-examined', *English Studies*, 75 (1994), 509–22.

—, 'Fragmentation and Reconstruction: Images of the Female Body in *Ancrene Wisse* and the Katherine Group', *Comitatus*, 26 (1995), 27–53.

—, '*Ancrene Wisse* and *Þe Wohunge of Ure Lauerd*: The Thirteenth-Century Female

Reader and the Lover-Knight', in J. Taylor and L. Smith (eds), *Women, the Book and the Godly* (Cambridge, 1995), pp. 137–47.

—, 'Anchoritic Elements of Holkham Misc. 41', in E. Herbert MacAvoy and M. Hughes Edwards (eds), *Intersections of Gender and Enclosure in the Middle Ages* (Cardiff, 2005), pp. 172–81.

Jager, E., *The Book of the Heart* (Chicago, 2000).

James, M.R., *A Descriptive Catalogue of the Manuscripts in the Library of Peterhouse* (Cambridge, 1899).

Johannis de Caulibus, *Meditationes vitae Christi*, ed. by M. Stallings-Taney, *CCCM* 153 (Turnhout, 1998).

Julian of Norwich, *A Book of Showings to the Anchoress Julian of Norwich*, ed. by E. Colledge and J. Walsh, Studies and Texts 35 (Toronto 1978).

Kaeppeli, T. and [E. Panella], *Scriptores ordinis Praedicatorum medii aevi*, 4 vols (Rome, 1970–93).

Kemper, T.A., *Die Kreuzigung Christi. Motivgeschichtliche Studien zu lateinischen und deutschen Passionstraktaten des Spätmittelalters*, Münchener Texte und Untersuchungen zur deutschen Literatur des Mittelalters 131 (Tübingen, 2006).

Kist, J., 'Klosterreform im spätmittelalterlichen Nürnberg', *Zeitschrift für bayerische Kirchengeschichte*, 32 (1963), 31–45.

Kohl, W., 'Die Windesheimer Kongregation', in Elm (ed.), *Reformbemühungen*, pp. 83–108.

Lechner, J., 'Der vlaemische Mystiker Johannes von Loewen in deutschen Handschriften', *Zeitschrift für Askese und Mystik*, 11 (1936), 192–209.

—, *Die spätmittelalterliche Handschriftengeschichte der Benedikterinnenabtei St. Walburg/Eichstätt*, Eichstätter Studien 2 (Münster, 1937).

Lecoy de la Marche, A., *La chaire française au moyen âge spécialement au XIII*[e] *siècle d'après les manuscrits contemporains* (Paris, 3rd edn, 1886).

Lefebvre, H., *The Production of Space*, tr. D. Nicholson-Smith (Oxford, 1991).

Lerner, R.E., 'Poverty, Preaching and Eschatology in the Revelation Commentaries of Hugh of St Cher', in K. Walsh and D. Wood (eds), *The Bible in the Medieval World* (Oxford, 1985), pp. 157–91.

—, 'The vocation of the Friars Preacher: Hugh of St. Cher between Peter the Chanter and Albert the Great', in Bataillon et al. (eds), *Hugues de Saint-Cher*, pp. 216–31.

Libro de Alexandre, ed. by J.C. Rigall (Madrid, 2007).

Logan, F.D., *The Runaway Religious in England c. 1240–1540*, Cambridge Studies in Medieval Life and Thought, 4th series, 32 (Cambridge, 1996).

—, *A History of the Church in the Middle Ages* (London, 2002).

Love, Nicholas, *The Mirror of the Blessed Life of Jesus Christ*, ed. by M.G. Sargent (Exeter, 2005).

Luther, M., *The Theologia Germanica of Martin Luther*, tr. B. Hoffman (New York, 1980).

McCulloch, F., *Medieval Latin and French Bestiaries* (Chapel Hill, 1960).

Mager, I., 'Bemühungen um die Reform der Klosterkonvente im fünfzehnten Jahrhundert. Grundzüge der Windesheimer und Bursfelder Reform', in J. Reller and M. Tamcke (eds), *Trinitäts- und Christusdogma: ihre Bedeutung für Beten und Handeln der Kirche. Festschrift für Jouko Martikainen* (Münster, 2001), pp. 223–43.

Mangenot, É., 'Hugues de Saint-Cher', *Dictionnaire de théologie catholique*, vol. 7 (Paris, 1921), cols 221–39.

Mantingh, E., *Een monnik met een rol. Willem van Affligem, het Kopenhaagse 'Leven van Lutgart' en de fictie van een meerdaagse voorlezing*, Diss. Utrecht (Hilversum, 2000).

Maqua, I.U., *Panorama crítico del mester de clerecía* (Madrid, 2000).

Meale, C.M. (ed.), *Women and Literature in Britain 1150–1500* (Cambridge, 2nd edn, 1996).

—, '"oft siþis with grete deuotion I þought what I miȝt do pleysyng to god": The Early Ownership and Readership of Love's *Mirror*, with Special Reference to its Female Audience', in S. Oguro, R. Beadle and M.G. Sargent (eds), *Nicholas Love at Waseda* (Cambridge, 1997), pp. 19–46.

— and J. Boffey, 'Gentlewomen's reading', in L. Hellinga and J.B. Trapp (eds), *The Cambridge History of the Book in Britain, vol. III. 1400–1557* (Cambridge, 1999), pp. 526–40.

Mertens, D., 'Reformkonzilien und Ordensreform im 15. Jahrhundert', in Elm (ed.), *Reformbemühungen*, pp. 431–58.

Mertens, T., 'Mystieke cultuur en literatuur in de late Middeleeuwen', in F.P. Van Oostrom and W. Van Anrooij (eds), *Grote Lijnen: Syntheses over Middelnederlandse Letterkunde* (Amsterdam, 1995), pp. 117–35.

Michaud-Quantin, P., 'Guy de l'Aumône, premier maître cistercien de l'université de Paris', *Analecta sacri ordinis Cisterciensis*, 15 (1959), 149–219.

Mikkers, E. (ed.), 'Le traité de Gérard de Liège sur les Sept Paroles de Notre Seigneur en Croix', *Collectanea ordinis Cisterciensium reformatorum*, 12 (1950), 176–94; 13 (1951), 18–29.

—, 'Robert de Molesmes (saint), fondateur de Cîteaux, vers 1028–1111. II. La spiritualité cistercienne', in *Dictionnaire de spiritualité*, vol. 13 (Paris, 1988), cols 738–814.

Milis, L., 'Reformatory Attempts within the Ordo Canonicus in the Late Middle Ages', in Elm (ed.), *Reformbemühungen*, pp. 61–70.

Millett, B., 'The Genre of *Ancrene Wisse*', in Wada (ed.), *Companion*, pp. 29–44.

Minnis, A.J., *Medieval Theory of Authorship: Scholastic Literary Attitudes in the Later Middle Ages* (Aldershot, 1984).

Morton, V. with J. Wogan-Browne (tr.), *Guidance for Women in Twelfth-Century Convents*, The Library of Medieval Women (Cambridge, 2003).

Mouron, A., 'The *Manere of Good Lyvyng*: the Manner of a Good Translator?', *Medium Aevum*, 78 (2009), 300–22.

—, 'Paris, B.N., MS fr. 13272: a French translation of *De doctrina cordis*', in D. Renevey and C. Whitehead (eds), *The Medieval Translator 13* (Turnhout, 2010).

Mulder-Bakker, A.B., *Lives of the Anchoresses. The Rise of the Urban Recluse in Medieval Europe*, tr. M. Heerspink Scholz (Philadelphia, PA, 2005).

—, and J. Wogan-Browne (eds), *Household, Women and Christianities in Late Antiquity and the Middle Ages*, Medieval Women: Text and Contexts 14 (Turnhout, 2005).

Nalle, S.T., 'Literacy and Culture in Early Modern Castile', *Past and Present*, 125 (1989), 65–96.

Pantin, W.A., *The English Church in the Fourteenth Century* (Cambridge, 1955).

—, 'Instructions for a Devout and Literate Layman', in J.J.G. Alexander and M.T. Gibson (eds), *Medieval Learning and Literature: Essays Presented to Richard William Hunt* (Oxford, 1976), pp. 398–422.

Parkes, M.B., 'Stephen Batman's Manuscripts', in M. Kanno et al. (eds), *Medieval Heritage: Essays in Honour of Tadahiro Ikegami* (Tokyo, 1997), pp. 125–56.

Pelster, F., 'Der Heinrich von Gent zugeschriebene *Catalogus virorum illustrium* und sein wirklicher Verfasser', *Historisches Jahrbuch*, 29 (1918), 253–68.

Pollard, W.F., 'Bodleian MS Holkham Misc. 41: a Fifteenth-Century Bridgettine Manuscript and Prayer Cycle', *Birgittiana*, 3 (1997), 43–53.

Prickynge of Love, The, ed. by H. Kane, Salzburg Studies in English Literature, Elizabethan and Renaissance Studies 92:10 (Salzburg, 1983).

Pseudo-Bernard, *Liber de modo bene vivendi ad sororem*, *PL* 184.

Raciti, G., 'Jean de Limoges', *Dictionnaire de spiritualité*, vol. 8 (Paris, 1974), cols 614–18.

Renardy, C., *Le monde des maîtres universitaires du diocèse de Liège, 1140–1350. Recherches sur sa composition et ses activités*, Bibliothèque de la Faculté de Philosophie et Lettres de l'Université de Liège 227 (Paris, 1979).

Renevey, D., *Language, Self and Love: Hermeneutics in the Writings of Richard Rolle and the Commentaries on the Song of Songs* (Cardiff, 2001).

—, 'Household Chores in *The Doctrine of the Hert*: Affective Spirituality and Subjectivity', in C. Beattie, A. Maslakovic and S. Rees Jones (eds), *The Medieval Household in Christian Europe c.850–c.1550: Managing Power, Wealth, and the Body* (Turnhout, 2003), pp. 167–87.

—, 'Figuring Household Space in *Ancrene Wisse* and *The Doctrine of the Hert*', in D. Spurr and C. Tschichold (eds), SPELL 17 (Tübingen, 2005), pp. 69–84.

—, and C. Whitehead, '"Opyn þin hert as a boke": Translation Practice and Manuscript Circulation in *The Doctrine of the Hert*', in J. Jenkins and O. Bertrand (eds), *The Medieval Translator 10* (Turnhout, 2007), pp. 125–48.

Reynaert, J., 'Hadewijch: mystic poetry and courtly love', in E. Kooper (ed.), *Medieval Dutch Literature in its European Context*, Cambridge Studies in Medieval Literature 21 (Cambridge, 1994), pp. 208–25.

Rice, N., 'Spiritual Ambition and the Translation of the Cloister: *The Abbey and Charter of the Holy Ghost*', *Viator*, 33 (2002), 222–60.

Richard Rolle and þe Holy Boke Gratia Dei: An Edition with Commentary, ed. by M.L. Arntz, Elizabethan and Renaissance Studies 92:2 (Salzburg, 1981).

Riddy, F., '"Women talking about the things of God": A Late Medieval Sub-Culture', in Meale (ed.), *Women and Literature*, pp. 104–27.

Robertson, E., *Early English Devotional Prose and the Female Audience* (Knoxville, TE, 1990).

—, '"This Living Hand": Thirteenth-Century Female Literacy, Materialist Immanence, and the Reader of the *Ancrene Wisse*', *Speculum*, 78 (2003), 1–36.

Ross, E.M., *The Grief of God: Images of the Suffering Jesus in Late Medieval England* (Oxford, 1997).

Ruh, K., 'Altniederländische Mystik in deutschsprachiger Überlieferung', in A. Ampe (ed.), *Dr. L. Reypens-album* (Antwerpen, 1964), pp. 357–82.

—, 'Guiard von Laon', in K. Ruh et al. (eds), *Die deutsche Literatur des Mittelalters. Verfasserlexikon*, 2nd edn, vol. 3 (Berlin/New York, 1981), cols 295–9.

Salih, S., 'At Home; out of the House', in C. Dinshaw and D. Wallace (eds), *The Cambridge Companion to Medieval Women's Writing* (Cambridge, 2003), pp. 124–40.

Savage, A. and N. Watson (eds and trs), *Anchoritic Spirituality: Ancrene Wisse and Associated Works*, Classics of Western Spirituality (New York, 1991).

Scheepsma, W., *Medieval Religious Women in the Low Countries: The Modern Devotion, The Canonesses of Windesheim and Their Writings*, tr. D.F. Johnson (Woodbridge, 2004).

—, *De Limburgse sermoenen (ca. 1300). De oudste preken in het Nederlands*, Nederlandse literatuur en cultuur in de Middeleeuwen 26 (Amsterdam, 2006).

Schneider, K., *Die deutschen Handschriften der Bayerischen Staatsbibliothek München. Cgm 351–500*, Catalogus codicum manu scriptorum Bibliothecae Monacensis 5.3 (Wiesbaden, 1973).

—, *Deutsche mittelalterliche Handschriften der Universitätsbibliothek Augsburg: die Signaturengruppen Cod.I.3 und Cod.III.1* (Wiesbaden, 1988).

Schneyer, J.B., *Repertorium der lateinischen Sermones des Mittelalters für die Zeit von 1150–1350 (Autoren: E–H)*, [vol. 2], Beiträge zur Geschichte der Philosophie und Theologie des Mittelalters: Texte und Untersuchungen 43/2 (Münster i.W., 1970).

Schönherr, A., *Die mittelalterlichen Handschriften der Zentralbibliothek Solothurn* (Solothurn, 1964).

Schreiner, K., *Sozial- und standesgeschichtliche Untersuchungen zu den Benediktinerkonventen im östlichen Schwarzwald*, Veröffentlichungen der Kommission für Geschichtliche Landeskunde in Baden-Württemberg. Reihe B, Forschungen 15 (Stuttgart, 1964).

Seneca, *Ad Lucilium epistulae morales*, ed. and tr. by R.M. Gummere, Loeb Library, 3 vols (London, 1953).

Sharpe, R., *Titulus: Identifying Medieval Latin Texts. An Evidence-Based Approach* (Turnhout, 2003).

Simpson, J., 'Saving Satire after Arundel's Constitutions: John Audelay's "Marcol and Solomon"', in H. Barr and A.M. Hutchison (eds), *Text and Controversy from Wyclif to Bale: Essays in Honour of Anne Hudson* (Turnhout, 2005), pp. 387–404.

Smalley, B., *The Study of the Bible in the Middle Ages* (Oxford, 3rd edn, 1983).

—, *The Gospels in the Schools c.1100–c.1280* (London, 1985).

Standaert, M., 'Gérard de Liège, cistercien, 13e siècle', in *Dictionnaire de spiritualité*, vol. 6 (Paris, 1967), cols 276–9.

Steele, F.J., *Towards a Spirituality for Lay-Folk: The Active Life in Middle English Religious Literature from the Thirteenth Century to the Fifteenth* (Salzburg, 1995).

Stirnemann, P., 'Les manuscrits de la *Postille*', in Bataillon et al. (eds), *Hugues de Saint-Cher*, pp. 31–42.

Stocker, M., *Judith: Sexual Warrior* (New Haven, 1998).

Stocks, E.V. and A.I. Doyle, 'Draft of Catalogue of Medieval Manuscripts in the University Library', Durham University Library.

Summa Virtutum de Remediis Anime, ed. by S. Wenzel, The Chaucer Library (Athens, GA, 1984).

Supplementary Lives in Some Manuscripts of the Gilte Legende, ed. by R. Hamer and V. Russell, EETS OS 315 (2000).

Sutherland, A., '*The Chastising of God's Children*: A Neglected Text', in H. Barr and A.M. Hutchison (eds), *Text and Controversy from Wyclif to Bale: Essays in Honour of Anne Hudson* (Turnhout, 2005), pp. 353–74.

Swanson, R.N., 'Passion and Practice: the Social and Ecclesiastical Implications of Passion Devotion in the Late Middle Ages', in A.A. MacDonald et al. (eds), *The Broken Body: Passion Devotion in Late-Medieval Culture* (Groningen, 1998), pp. 1–30.

Tarvers, J.K., '"Thys ys my mystrys boke": English Women as Readers and Writers in Late Medieval England', in C.C. Morse, P.R. Doob and M. Curry Woods (eds), *The Uses of Manuscripts in Literary Studies: Essays in Memory of Judson Boyce Allen* (Kalamazoo, 1992), pp. 305–27.

Thompson, S., *Women Religious: The Founding of English Nunneries after the Norman Conquest* (Oxford, 1991).

Thomson, S.H., *The Writings of Robert Grosseteste, Bishop of Lincoln, 1235–1253* (Cambridge, 1940).

Tugwell, S., 'Were the Magdalen nuns really turned into Dominicans in 1287?', *Archivum fratrum Praedicatorum*, 76 (2006), 39–77.

Turner, D., *Eros and Allegory*, CSS 156 (Kalamazoo, 1995).

Vance Smith, D., *Arts of Possession: The Middle English Household Imaginary*, Medieval Cultures 33 (Minneapolis, 2003).

Van den Boogaard, N., 'Les insertions en français dans un traité de Gérard de Liège', in *Marche romane. Mélanges de philologie et de littératures romanes offers Jeanne Wathelet-Willem* (Liège 1978), pp. 679–97.

Van Dijk, R.Th.M., 'Het Kapittel van Windesheim 1395–1995: Terugblik en Vooruitzicht', in A.J. Hendrikman, P. Bange, R.Th.M. Van Dijk, A.J. Jelsma and G.E.P. Vrielink (eds), *Windesheim 1395–1995: Kloosters, Teksten, Invloeden* (Nijmegen, 1996), pp. 3–4.

Van Mierlo, J., 'Wanneer leefde Geraard van Luik?', *OGE*, 23 (1949), 409–12.

Van Wonterghem, K., 'De Geschiedenis van de Sint-Trudoabdij te Odegem, te Brugge en te Male', in *Male: Burcht en Abdij* (Brugge, 1981), pp. 27–108.

Venn, J. and J.A. Venn, *Alumni Cantabrigienses. Part I: From the Earliest Times to 1751*, vol. 4 (Cambridge, 1927).

Verger, J., 'Hugues de Saint-Cher dans le contexte universitaire parisien', in Bataillon et al. (eds), *Hugues de Saint-Cher*, pp. 13–28.

Vernet, A., *La bibliothèque de l'abbaye de Clairvaux du XIIe au XVIIIe siecles* (Paris, 1979).

Vindel, F., *Escudos y marcas de impresores y libreros en España durante los siglos XV a XIX (1485–1850)* (Barcelona, 1942).

—, *El arte tipográfico en España durante el siglo XV*, 10 vols (Madrid, 1945–51), II: *Salamanca, Zamora, Coria y Reino de Galicia* (1946); VIII: *Dudosos de lugar de impresión. Adiciones y correcciones a toda la obra* (1951).

Vita venerabilis virginis Christi Juliane de Corelion, ed. by J.-P. Delville, in *Fête-Dieu (1246–1996). 2. Vie de Sainte Julienne de Cornillon*, Université Catholique de Louvain. Publications de l'Institut d'Études Médiévales: textes, études, congrès 19/2 (Louvain-la-Neuve, 1999).

Voisenet, J., *Bêtes et hommes dans le monde médiéval. Le bestiaire des clercs du Ve au XIIe siècle* (Turnhout, 2000).

Wada, Y. (ed.), *A Companion to the Ancrene Wisse* (Cambridge, 2003).

Watson, N., 'Desire for the Past', *Studies in the Age of Chaucer*, 21 (1999), 59–97.

—, '*Ancrene Wisse*, Religious Reform and the Late Middle Ages', in Wada (ed.), *Companion to the Ancrene Wisse*, pp. 197–226.

—, 'Visions of Inclusion: Universal Salvation and Vernacular Theology in Pre-Reformation England', *Journal of Medieval and Early Modern Studies*, 27 (1997), 145–87.

—, 'Censorship and Cultural Change in Late-Medieval England: Vernacular Theology, the Oxford Translation Debate, and Arundel's Constitutions of 1409', *Speculum*, 70 (1995), 822–64.

—, 'The Composition of Julian of Norwich's *Revelation of Love*', *Speculum*, 68 (1993), 637–83.

—, 'Conceptions of the Word: The Mother Tongue and the Incarnation of God', in W. Scase, R. Copeland and D. Lawton (eds), *New Medieval Literatures* 1 (Oxford, 1997), pp. 85–124.

Webb, D., *Solitude: The Medieval Discovery of Personal Space* (London, 2007).

Weis-Mueller, R., *Die Reform des Klosters Klingental und ihr Personenkreis*, Baseler Beiträge zur Geschichtswissenschaft 59 (Basel, 1956).

Welkenhuysen, A., 'Een harts-tochtelijke queeste. Guido Hendrix en zijn *De doctrina cordis*', in L. Kenis and F. Gistelinck (eds), *Illi qui vitae lustra tredecim valens explevit. Bij de vijfenzestigste verjaardag van Guido Hendrix* (Louvain, 2003), pp. 7–13.

—, 'Bibliografie van Guido Hendrix', in Kenis and Gistelinck (eds), *Illi qui vitae lustra tredecim valens explevit*, pp. 33–55.

Whitehead, C., *Castles of the Mind: A Study of Medieval Architectural Allegory* (Cardiff, 2003).

—, D. Renevey and A. Mouron (eds), *The Doctrine of the Hert: A Critical Edition with Introduction and Commentary* (Exeter, 2010).

Wiesinger, P., 'Zur Autorschaft und Entstehung des Heinrich von Langenstein zugeschriebenen Traktats "Erkenntnis der Sünde" ', *Zeitschrift für deutsche Philologie*, 97 (1978), 42–60.

Williams-Krapp, W., 'Ordensreform und Literatur im 15. Jahrhundert', in *Jahrbuch der Oswald von Wolkenstein Gesellschaft*, 4 (Goeppingen, 1986–87), pp. 41–51.

Wilmart, A., 'Gérard de Liège. Un traité inédit de l'amour de Dieu', *Revue d'ascétique et de mystique*, 12 (1931), 349–430.

—, 'Reg. lat. 71 (fol. 34–62). Les traités de Gérard de Liège sur l'amour illicite et sur l'amour de Dieu', in A. Wilmart, *Analecta Reginensia. Extraits des manuscrits de la Reine Christine conservés au Vatican*, Studi e Testi 59 (Vatican City, 1933), pp. 181–247.

Wogan-Browne, J. et al. (eds), *The Idea of the Vernacular. An Anthology of Middle English Literary Theory 1280–1520* (Exeter, 1999).

—, *Saints' Lives and Women's Literary Culture: Virginity and its Authorizations* (Oxford, 2001).

Zeibig, H.J., 'Die deutschen Handschriften der Stiftsbibliothek zu Klosterneuburg', *Serapeum*, 11 (1850), 102–3.

Zimmer, P., 'Dominikanerinnen Basel. St. Maria Magdalena an den Steinen (Steinenkloster)', *Helvetia Sacra*, 4/5 (Basel, 1999), pp. 584–609.

Zink, M., *La prédication en langue romane avant 1300*, Nouvelle bibliothèque du moyen âge 4 (Paris, 1976).

Zumkeller, A., 'Die Beteiligung der Mendikanten an der Arbeit der Reformkonzilien von Konstanz und Basel', in Elm (ed.), *Reformbemühungen*, pp. 459–68.

Zunker, M.M., *Kloster- und Pfarrkirche St. Walburg Eichstätt* (Regensburg, 2001).

Index